This pioneering book opens up for us the great but largely unnoticed world of Christian writing in the Hindi language, India's majority language. Meticulous in its detailed attention to hitherto unnoticed literature, *Hindi Christian Literature in Contemporary India* maps subtly the interplay of language, politics, and culture today, while yet mindful of the long history of interactions between Hindus and Christians, India and the West. In this way, Peter-Dass uncovers for us a vital and enduring form of Christianity in India that will surprise those who know only Indian Christian theology in English, while shedding light too on Hindi culture more widely, and even Hinduism in the 21st century.

Francis X. Clooney, *SJ, Parkman Professor of Divinity, Professor of Comparative Theology, Harvard University, USA*

This ground-breaking and wide-ranging scholarly work on Hindi Christian literature provides a greatly overdue and much needed investigation into the articulation of Christian faith in North India, where over half a billion people speak Hindi. In a study that will have significant implications for the study of religion in general, Rakesh Peter-Dass deftly probes the complicated interconnections between language, social context, history and audience to provide an account of regional Christianity that is both innovative and persuasive.

Arun W. Jones, *Dan and Lillian Hankey Associate Professor of World Evangelism, Emory University, USA*

In the context of Hindu nationalists' longstanding proclivity to conflate Hindi, Hindu, and Hindustan (or India), and in an environment where the "Indianness" of Christianity is regularly contested, Christians' linguistic choices are always political. With lively and accessible prose that moves compellingly from one intriguing topic to another, Peter-Dass explores the political influences on and ramifications of literature produced intentionally and self-consciously in Hindi by India's Christians. Both a survey of this understudied genre and a critical analysis of its most salient obsessions, the volume introduces readers to authors like John Henry Anand, Benjamin Khan, Din Dayal, and Richard Howell, who, because of the inaccessibility of Hindi to many western (and even other Indian) scholars, have not received the attention they deserve. Pleasurably disorienting in its multilingual presentation, *Hindi Christian Literature in Contemporary India* offers a novel and important way of thinking about the relationship of Christianity and Indian culture.

Chad M. Bauman, *Professor of Religion and Chair, Butler University, USA*

Hindi Christian Literature in Contemporary India

This is the first academic study of Christian literature in Hindi and its role in the politics of language and religion in contemporary India. In public portrayals, Hindi has been the language of Hindus and Urdu the language of Muslims, but Christians have usually been associated with the English of the foreign 'West.' However, this book shows how Christian writers in India have adopted Hindi in order to promote a form of Christianity that can be seen as Indian, *desī*, and rooted in the religio-linguistic world of the Hindi belt.

Using different studies, the book demonstrates how Hindi Christian writing strategically presents Christianity as linguistically Hindi, culturally Indian, and theologically informed by other faiths. These works are written to sway public perceptions by promoting particular forms of citizenship in the context of fostering the use of Hindi. Examining the content and context of Christian attention to Hindi, it is shown to have been deployed as a political and cultural tool by Christians in India.

This book gives an important insight into the link between language and religion in India. As such, it will be of great interest to scholars of religion in India, world Christianity, religion, politics, and language, interreligious dialogue, religious studies and South Asian studies.

Rakesh Peter-Dass is Assistant Professor of Religion at Hope College, USA. His research and teaching focus on the intersections of religion with business, language, law, and politics.

Routledge Studies in Religion

American Catholic Bishops and the Politics of Scandal
Rhetoric of Authority
Meaghan O'Keefe

Celebrity Morals and the Loss of Religious Authority
John Portmann

Reimagining God and Resacralisation
Alexa Blonner

Said Nursi and Science in Islam
Character Building through Nursi's Mana-i harfi
Necati Aydin

The Diversity of Nonreligion
Normativities and Contested Relations
Johannes Quack, Cora Schuh, and Susanne Kind

The Role of Religion in Gender-Based Violence, Immigration, and Human Rights
Edited by Mary Nyangweso and Jacob K. Olupona

Italian American Pentecostalism and the Struggle for Religious Identity
Paul J. Palma

The Cultural Fusion of Sufi Islam
Alternative Paths to Mystical Faith
Sarwar Alam

Hindi Christian Literature in Contemporary India
Rakesh Peter-Dass

For more information about this series, please visit: www.routledge.com/religion/series/SE0669

Hindi Christian Literature in Contemporary India

Rakesh Peter-Dass

Routledge
Taylor & Francis Group
LONDON AND NEW YORK

First published 2019
by Routledge
2 Park Square, Milton Park, Abingdon, Oxon OX14 4RN

and by Routledge
52 Vanderbilt Avenue, New York, NY 10017

Routledge is an imprint of the Taylor & Francis Group, an informa business

British Library Cataloguing-in-Publication Data
A catalogue record for this book is available from the British Library

Library of Congress Cataloging-in-Publication Data
A catalog record for this book has been requested

ISBN: 978-0-367-32223-6 (hbk)
ISBN: 978-0-367-33063-7 (ebk)

Typeset in Sabon
by Apex CoVantage, LLC

For Sharon

Contents

Acknowledgments x

1 Politics of religion 1

2 The making of a genre 47

3 Linguistic choices 79

4 Shaping identity 105

5 Christians in India 147

6 Message matters 190

Index 221

Acknowledgments

Many people and groups helped this book. Their support has been invaluable, and though I bear sole responsibility for the final manuscript, their encouragement runs deep and wide.

Insightful conversations with advisors and colleagues have enriched this study. In this regard, Professor Francis X. Clooney, S.J., deserves a particular word of thanks. This book would be impossible without his early and consistent support, thoughtful critique, and pastoral advice. Frank mentored a voyage into the study of new and unused sources. I am also grateful to key advisors who read the manuscript in full or part and guided this project with constructive insights: Professors Susan Abraham, Ali S. Asani, Arun W. Jones, Charles M. Stang, and Ronald F. Thiemann. This study was collaborative and the following people deserve special recognition for their substantial contributions: Rev. Dr. John H. Anand (my primary collaborator in India), Emily Burgoyne (my primary advisor at Angus Library, Oxford), Rev. Dr. Ashis Amos, Daniel Manorath (who travelled to Lucknow to gather sources on my behalf), and Ram Ikbal Rai (who made research trips across central and north India possible). John H. Anand, the long-serving editor of Hindi Theological Literature Committee, deserves special credit. He spent countless hours educating me on Hindi Christian history, endured endless rounds of questions, sent me hundreds of Hindi Christian materials on request, and introduced me to Hindi Christian writers.

The ideas in this book were presented at various venues. I am grateful for the feedback I received from participants of academic gatherings at Harvard University, Harvard Divinity School, St. Mary's Church at the University of Oxford, Asian Theological Summer Institute at the Lutheran Theological Seminary in Philadelphia, New England and Maritime Region of the American Academy of Religion, Boston College, Wabash Center for Teaching and Learning in Theology and Religion, American Academy Religion, Thirteenth Assembly of the World Council of Churches, and Hindi Theological Literature Committee.

My research required considerable support from institutions. I am grateful for their generosity. The South Asia Institute at Harvard supported two long research trips to India. Harvard Divinity School's Dissertation Fellowship and Travel Grant supported a third research trip. The Selva J. Raj Endowed International Dissertation Research Fellowship of the American Academy of Religion and the Educational Grant Program of the Evangelical Lutheran Church in America offered the time to complete the project and use the missionary archives of Angus Library at the University of Oxford. In India, two institutions deserve special recognition. The Hindi Theological Literature Committee, based in Jabalpur, served as the primary source of Hindi Christian texts and history. The Indian Society for Promoting Christian Knowledge partnered in Delhi. In concert, these publishers provided research personnel and timely guidance. Other publishers also supported this study, and I am thankful to the *International Journal of Hindu Studies* and *Nidan: International Journal for Indian Studies* for their permission to republish parts of their works in chapters 1 and 3. Finally, I am thankful to my editors and anonymous reviewers at Taylor & Francis-Routledge. Their feedback has sharpened the book.

Rakesh Peter-Dass
May 2019
Holland, Michigan

1 Politics of religion

Hindi Christian politics

On a Sunday morning 225 years ago, William Carey walked into a local market in Bengal and started speaking to a congregation of Muslims.[1] It was the winter of 1794 and Manicktullo *Bāzār* was busy. Carey had just arrived in India – in November 1793, to be precise. At the market that day, the Baptist missionary was accompanied by his local assistant (*muṃśī*). Local clerks played an important role in the work of missionaries in India. Carey's *Journal* is replete with references to his 'Munshi.' The munshi helped him learn the vernacular, translate scripture, preach to locals, teach in school, and run the press. Carey could not speak proper Bengali and was unable to preach for months after he reached Bengal. The munshi translated and spoke for him most days. As it turned out, Carey would be glad his 'Munshi' was with him.[2]

Carey was happy with the turnout that day. "Our Congregation," he wrote, "consisted principally of Mahometans, and has increased every Lord's Day; they are very inquisitive; and we have addressed them upon the subject of the Gospel with the greatest freedom."[3] It is unclear whether "congregation" referred to a group of Christian converts or interested Muslims or some combination thereof. At the very least, the *Journal* makes it clear that Carey had found an eager audience that was growing every Sunday in the *bāzār*. Various topics were discussed but none generated more interest than two: Which was better, the Quran or the Gospels? Who was greater: Mohammed or Jesus? The debate on the first topic was vigorous. Each side spoke freely. Carey argued most Muslims could not read Arabic. If you could not read Arabic, he asked, how could you follow the Quran? Also, if you could not read it, how could you know if it was true? The 'Mahomedans' countered by claiming they had learned Quranic instructions and one of them had even read it in Arabic. Then, in their turn, the Muslims pressed. "The Quran was sent to confirm the Words of Scripture" because "Jews, and Christians had corrupted the Bible, which was the reason why God made the revelation by Mahomet." The Quran was clearly an improvement on the Bible. So why settle for second best?

The conversation on who was better was equally lively. Carey posed the question: Who was better, Mohammed or Jesus? The Muslims replied, Carey notes, "Mahomet was the Friend of God, but Esau, by whom they mean Jesus, was the Spirit of God." A friend was more important than a spirit. One could relate to a friend, spend time with a friend, have a personal relationship with a friend. What could the spirit do? Carey fell silent, it seems, for his clerk piped up. But who is higher, Munshi countered, your friend or your soul or spirit? Carey thought Munshi was clever – "shrewd," he writes – but the Muslims were not impressed. Carey does not record the Muslims' response to Munshi but Carey's notes suggest the Muslims left unconvinced of the superiority of Christianity. "All this [back and forth] they bore with good temper; but What effect it may have time must determine." The interplay between listeners and preachers was complicated. Christians preached and the Muslims talked back. The Muslims countered and the Christians talked back. Carey records numerous such encounters in his journals. The encounters were open-ended – at least, Carey logs them that way. Discourses on religious conversions in contemporary India portray a different interplay of voices. The next story from 1993 illustrates the difference. Two centuries after Carey's encounter, Indian Christians find themselves in a situation where states and governments have found it necessary to curb the perceived threat of Christian evangelism to social order in India. Carey's encounter with Muslims does not represent the standard encounter between missionaries and others. In some cases, the encounter was fruitful – in others, hostile. I have employed the Muslims-Carey chat-in-the-market (*bāzār bātcīt*) to contrast it with public perceptions of Christian evangelism in contemporary India.

On March 12, 1993, two hundred years after the *bāzār bātcīt*, a group of Christian leaders walked into a meeting with the governor of Andhra Pradesh. Governor Krishan Kant had called the meeting. Bishop Franklin Jonathan was in attendance and recorded the exchange. The Christians met Kant for more than an hour, and Jonathan was impressed. Kant was "a good scholar, top-class politician and a political leader desirous of national unity and communal harmony."[4] Kant had something specific on his mind. He wanted to talk about evangelism. He wanted to and proceeded to criticize Christian mission. He doubted Christian motives and questioned their actions. Kant praised Christians as learned and enlightened but was adamant in alleging that evangelism was a social problem. For Kant, propagating religion was not an invitation to a conversation but a slippery slope to discord. It needed to stop. The Christian community and Christian leaders are "most enlightened," Kant felt, but it was the governor's "request" (*āgrah*) that all forms of evangelization "be voluntarily stopped for at least fifty years."[5]

Kant made a request. It was not a demand. Jonathan took pains to note this. Kant was a state official in secular India and could hardly demand that Christians in India voluntarily self-curtail their constitutional right to profess and propagate religion. Kant did not say his ask was a request. Jonathan described it as such. One wonders whether Jonathan was being diplomatic in print. Noticeably, Jonathan does not print the Christians' response. Did they talk back? Did they refuse the 'request'? Did they agree to consider it? Did they offer any response, then or later, to the governor? It is clear that Kant's request did generate some reflection on Jonathan's part. "What is the meaning," Jonathan wrote, "of evangelism? Is it to share the love of God with others?"[6] "Have we," Jonathan wondered, "sent the wrong signal to those who are outside the church?"[7] Jonathan was sympathetic to Kant. Yet his response to Kant is absent from his public report. It is unclear whether the Christian leaders did much after the meeting or whether Christian communities paid any heed to Kant's ask.

Comparing the encounters is revelatory. Contemporary perceptions of Christian activities have focused on evangelistic practices by Christians. While the social footprint of Christian churches in India – through their many hospitals, schools, colleges, orphanages, and charities – garners little public attention, conversions and evangelistic practices have come to occupy a primary place in public perceptions of Indian Christians. State governments and lawmakers have felt increasingly motivated to intervene in such practices in order to 'protect' easily-swayed 'Hindus' from converting. Studies have traced the relevance of caste context behind such motivations.[8] Nevertheless, in contemporary narratives of Christian evangelism the agency to refuse Christian claims seems to have disappeared. According to accounts of Hindu nationalists, 'naïve and easily-swayed Hindus' need to be protected from the aggression of Christian evangelists. Underlining the opposition to Christian conversions in India is the perception that one cannot be both a loyal Christian and an Indian. This perception is being fostered by a pair of complementary forces in contemporary India: Hindu nationalism and Hindi nationalism.

Hindu nationalism and Hindi nationalism are complementary ideas. A Hindu is original to India and India is Hindu. A Christian or Muslim is a foreigner and not Indian. Allegiance to one group (India) cannot overlap with allegiance to another group (Christianity, Islam). Aligning with both identities can only divide an Indian's loyalty. Hindu nationalism argues that pitting one identity against the other is the outcome of confusion on what it means to be 'Indian.' A central feature of Hindutva has been portrayals of Muslims as a "community outside the 'national mainstream' " and intent on undermining "Indian/Hindu culture and civilization."[9] A 'true Indian' is anyone who recognizes India, the land of Hindus, as her geographic fatherland and cultural motherland. 'Indian' and 'Hindu' are synonymous, and for Hindu nationalists, as Richard G. Fox puts it, a *bharatiya* ('of India') is a 'Hindian.' As such, attributes like Hindu, Christian, Muslim, Sikh, Tamil, and Dravidian are sectarian identities that should never be confused with and empowered over an Indian's essential identity, which is Hindian.[10] The third attribute of an Indian is loyalty to Hindi. This is the central claim of

Hindi nationalists. Hence, advocates for the national primacy of Hindi in India made claims regarding the foreignness of Urdu and Muslims that echoed the claims made by Hindu nationalists.

Both movements – Hindu nationalism and Hindi nationalism – matured around the same time, the quarter century preceding 1947. Both movements had similar demographic attributes. Hindu nationalism drew support from Hindu, urban, young, lower-middle class, and 'forward caste' groups like Brahmans, Kayasths, Khatris and Baniyas (medium- and small-scale merchants).[11] Hindi nationalists drew support from Hindus, urban, middle class, educated, forward castes like Brahmans, Kayasths, Bhumihars (land-holders), Rajputs, and Baniya groups like Agarwals and Vaishyas.[12] Both movements complemented each other. "Hindi, Hindu, Hindustan," or "Hindi, Hindu, India," the slogan went.[13] The movement to Hinduize India had a willing and enthusiastic partner in the movement to Hinduize Hindi and Hindi-ize India.[14] Finally, both movements had their geographic center in north India, further cementing the fusion of language and religion as a central attribute of the national identity under construction by the religious group dominant in the corridors of political power in independent India.

In contemporary India, religions have languages. This idea has been expressed in certain ways. Hindi is the language of Hindus, Urdu is the language of Muslims, and Christians have associated most frequently with English, the language of the 'West.' In public imaginations, English remains the language of India's colonizers (more on this later). In contemporary India, English is ascendant due to its status as the primary language of global advantage.[15] Yet English remains a 'foreign' language. As Christopher King has noted, Hindi has become synonymous with Hindu, and Urdu has become synonymous with Islam (more on this later). However, to the fusion of language and religion another type of claim is linked. These arguments are related to autochthonicity. And the lingo-religious argument described earlier morphs into a linguistic-religious-geographic moniker. Hindi is not merely the language of Hindus in India but rather is the language of the autochthonous Hindus of India. Urdu is the language not merely of Muslims of India but rather of Islamic invaders of India. Similarly, the argument goes, English is the language Christians in India have received and adopted from their Western and colonizing predecessors. When Urdu and English are portrayed as foreign and intruders, the religions linked with them are portrayed as foreign and intruders as well. Hindi and Hindu nationalists are not the only agents of such conflations. The linguistic organization of pre- and post-independence India strengthened the connection of ethnicity and religion with language and political power. The movement for Indian independence promoted Hindustani as the national language and from the process Hindi in the Devanagari script emerged as the national language. The emergence of Hindi in the nation's story, though controversial, continues to shape ideas regarding nationality and Indianness in terms of Hindi idioms.

Shaped by a sense of the Hindu-Hindi-ness of the nation, Christian writers in India have promoted Hindi as the proper language of Indian Christians in order to promote Christians as Indian, *deśī*, and rooted in the linguistic world of Hindi. Hindi Christian works counter the politics of religion and language prevalent in independent India. In light of the widespread perception of Christians as aggressive evangelists, followers of a foreign faith, and culturally not Indian, Hindi Christian works present a religion that is linguistically Hindi, culturally Indian, and theologically open to Hindu and Muslim ideas. Works of Hindi Christian prose and poetry convey a certain type of religious identity that is intentionally Hindi, Indian, and political. In this book, I explain why and how this identity has taken shape and manifests itself today. Hindi Christian works are political in nature, aim to sway public perceptions, promote particular forms of citizenship, and do all this in the context of fostering the use of Hindi. This attention to language takes different forms. It is shaped by the foundational idea that religion and language are intertwined in India. It is essential to recognize the place of languages in India's story and the relation of languages to ethno-religious identities in India in order to grasp the impulses surging through Hindi Christian arguments. As the book proceeds, I add details to the story of languages and religions in India.

India's religious history is a story of languages. English, Hindi, Sanskrit, Tamil, and Urdu have influenced the politics of religion in India. Dravidians used Tamil and other languages to develop distinct religious ideas. Sanskrit was deployed to manage the political power of certain social groups. Hindi and Urdu were shaped by relations between Muslims and Hindus in classical India and continue to do so in India today. Linguistic cultures influenced each other too. Tamil influenced Sanskrit and Sanskrit influenced Tamil. Urdu influenced Hindi and Hindi influenced Urdu. English influenced Hindi, and English has been influenced by many other Indian languages. Further, India's religious history is a story of multilingualism. In Vedic horse sacrifices, for instance, different groups speak different languages and the four priests are supposed to call the sacrificial horse with four different names.[16] Emperor Ashoka had the empire's values inscribed in Pali and other languages spoken throughout the empire. Sanskrit and Urdu encountered each other in Mughal courts.[17] Hindi and Urdu were co-languages of Muslim and Hindu literature till the politics of the nineteenth century intervened.[18]

The politics of religion and of language have shaped each other. Christian deployments of Hindi fit this pattern. But a lacuna haunts our understanding of religion and language in contemporary India. Hindi Christian sources are not the subject of the academic study of religion. A few scholars study these sources.[19] Hindi sources are part of literary history.[20] Hindi literature is part of scholarship beyond South Asia in studies of devotionals, poems, and novels.[21] Indian Christians use many languages in addition to Hindi. Recently published sources of Indian Christian literature would reveal sources mostly from southern India (for instance, in Malayalam and

Tamil) and in English. Recent research has examined vernacular Christianity in Marathi.[22] However, Hindi Christian sources are not the subject of current studies of language and religion in India. I correct this lacuna and present a study of Christian materials in 'modern standard Hindi.' These materials cover hymns, poems, guidebooks, theology-ethics, stories, and translation choices. Or, in the vocabulary of Hindi Christian materials, I examine *gīt-sangīt* (songs), *bhajan* (hymns), *kathā* (stories, or narratives), *kavitā* (poetry), *dharmavijñān* (theology), *nītiśāstr* (ethics), *ārādhănā* (worship), *gāiḍ* or *sandarśikā* (guidebooks), *ṭīkā-ṭippaṇī* (scriptural commentary), *darśan* (philosophy), and *itihās* (history).[23] Hindi Christian sources are attuned to the politics of language and religion in India. I show why this is the case, describe the forms in which this attention is manifested, examine the nature of Christian attention to Hindi, and explain the political claims embedded in Hindi Christian ideas.

Attention to the politics of language and religion is evident in three distinct, overlapping, and ongoing debates in Hindi Christian works. These debates are the subjects of chapters 3–5. Should Christians in India use Hindi, and if they should, how should they use Hindi in ways distinct from Hindu ideas and Western ideas? This debate, which is the focus of chapter 3, has played out in discussions on translation choices when trying to express Christian ideas in Hindi. A parallel debate has played out over media representations of Indian Christians. This is the focus of chapter 4. The question of representation emerged as a topic of discussion particularly after state television (Doordarshan) started airing religious programs in the 1980s. The third debate, which is the focus of chapter 5, is concerned with the ways in which Christians must act in a multifaith society such as is found in India. Commentaries on the subject of national participation explore proper Christian notions on citizenship, relation with people of other faiths, discipleship, and identity in India. By 'Hindi Christian sources' I mean a corpus of materials in post-1940 central and north India written and published in modern standard Hindi. As a language of religious communities, Hindi is not exclusively Christian in purpose. However, the book studies Protestant Hindi Christian materials available in India through both 'mainline' and independent publishers.

What is Hindi Christian?

I deal with Hindi Christian works. Such a claim raises certain questions. First, what is 'Hindi,' as I use the term? Second, is 'Hindi Christian' a justifiable descriptor? Finally, what does it mean to call a Christian work a Hindi Christian work? What makes a Christian work particularly Hindi? The rest of this section answers the first question. The next section answers the second question. The second chapter answers the third question, but I can preview the second chapter here with brief comments. It is the essential attribute of a Hindi Christian work that it does not use Hindi merely because that happens to be the local language or the popular language in the region. Rather, a Hindi Christian work includes reflections on why Hindi should be used. It comments on the effect of using Hindi on the content of the work. It chooses to use Hindi specifically to serve an unserved audience and draws discriminatingly from the world of Hindi idioms. In each aspect of its work, it asks how Hindi influences the Christian idea under examination. In doing so, it grounds Christian ideas in Hindi rather than simply expressing Christian ideas in Hindi. As such, theology, ethics, poetry, liturgy, and other aspects of Christian life are given new terms and a network of ideas at home in the religious worldviews of Hindi-speaking India. I will say more on this in the second and third chapters. But for now, I return to the first question. What do I mean by 'Hindi' in the term 'Hindi Christian'?

By 'Hindi,' I mean 'modern, standard Hindi.' The emergence of modern, standard Hindi can be traced to Middle Indo-Aryan language forms.[24] What is 'standard' about 'modern, standard Hindi' is its geographic use and standardized form (at least its written form, though variations in pronunciation exist). It has a geographic reach. It is spoken by the people in particular regions and has the loyalty of its speakers. It is easy to use and is a popular medium in which local people communicate. In this sense, Hindi is a regional language of India. As a matter of practice, all Indian languages are regional since no language is the primary language used by all Indians. Uday Narayan Tiwari, an influential biographer of Hindi, has explained the historic status of Hindi: a ' "regional language' is the name for peoples' language" and "the language that occupied this position in a particular time and place was known by this designation."[25] From 600–1200 CE, developed forms of Middle Indo-Aryan language occupied this position. By the thirteenth and fourteenth centuries, Modern Aryan languages had become the local or regional languages. Among Indian languages, Hindi was the language of the middle part of the country, and modern forms of literary Hindi and Urdu can be traced to the Khaṛī Bolī ("standing speech" or "stand[ard] speech") form of western Hindi spoken near Meerat and Bijnor in modern-day Uttar Pradesh.[26] Spoken together, Hindi-Urdu was called Hindustani. As a descriptive term, 'Hindustani' itself was the invention of John Gilchrist, a colonial linguist, who coined the term in eighteenth century to 'unify' distinct languages spoken in north India. Hindustani, in Gilchrist's construction, was a single language with three dialects differentiated by the extent to which they used Sanskrit, Persian, and Arabic. This 'Hindustani' was eventually conflated with Urdu and given status as the language of official business during the Raj in large parts of northern India.[27]

Hindi-Urdu share a "virtually identical" grammar and core vocabulary with differences in usage and terminology so minor that it is not possible to clearly tell whether someone is speaking 'Hindi' or 'Urdu.'[28] Suniti Chatterji's influential history of Indo-Aryan languages divides the development of Indian languages into three periods: Old Indo-Aryan (or Vedic Sanskrit) from 1500 BCE to 500 BCE; Middle Indo-Aryan (or Prākrit) from 500 BCE to 1000 CE; and New Indo-Aryan from 1000 CE onward.[29] Colin Masica adapts Chatterji's history and proposes slightly different time-periods: 1500 BCE–600 BCE for Old Indo-Aryan; 600 BCE–1000 CE for Middle Indo-Aryan; and 1000 CE onward for New Indo-Aryan.[30] Hindi-Urdu belong to the New Indo-Aryan family of languages.

Hindi or Hindustani appeared at the tail end of a long history and it took 11 centuries, roughly from 1100 CE to 1800 CE, to develop. For the linguistic genealogy of Hindi, Chatterji's *Indo-Aryan and Hindi*, published 76 years ago, is still the standard account.[31] The story of Hindi begins "somewhere in Europe" where a Primitive Indo-European language was spoken in its undivided state by a group of people philologists have called *Wiros*, the Primitive Indo-European word for 'man.' The *Wiros* did not develop a material culture of any high order. What they did leave behind was a language and a well-organized society. Their society was patriarchal and made up of a collection of clan groups. They showed respect for women and developed a religion where the unseen forces of nature (viewed as God or Gods) were characterized as beneficial rather than harmful. God or Gods lived in heaven above, as distinct from humans, who lived on earth. Gods were not anthropomorphic beings. Conjectures about this people and their society have, as a result, been the province of linguistic paleontology rather than of archeology. Half-nomadic and half-settled, the *Wiros* travelled and took their language and social organization with them. One group of *Wiros* left the homeland to travel south. These Indo-Iranians or Aryans reached northern Mesopotamia by 2000 BCE.

Indo-Iranian or Aryan culture and religion were the predecessors of both Vedic Indians and pre-Zoroastrian Iranians. Once they arrived in India after 1500 BCE, the Aryans encountered non-Aryan cultures in the Indus Valley and Dravidian peoples. The Aryans were not indigenous to India. Indus Valley artifacts do not include Aryan motifs. As an instance, horses, popular in Aryan culture, are absent in Valley seals, pottery, and other leftovers. Aryans slowly migrated from Eastern Iran into Punjab in Western India. Archeological and linguistic evidence suggests the arrival of the Aryans was not in the form of a sudden invasion but rather in the form of a slow migration, which eventually led to the development of culture that mixed Aryan and Dravidian elements. There is evidence that the Indus Valley script was not a proto-Aryan script but belongs to the Dravidian group of languages.[32] The encounter between the Aryans and non-Aryan people profoundly changed the Aryans and their language. Aryan or Indo-Iranian language changed into Indo-Aryan, represented in its developed form in the *Rig Veda*. The Indian Aryans laid the foundation of the Vedic culture. The language of the Indo-Aryans took two forms: a spoken form, Prākrit, and a cultured, written form, Sanskrit.

From 1000 BCE onward, Sanskrit became the language of religion and higher intellectual life in upper India and the forebearer of Hindu culture. By 600 BCE, Prākrit and Sanskrit had begun to spread south into the Deccan and mingled with well-established groups of Dravidian speakers, whose native speech was too fixed to adopt Aryan elements. Yet, by this point the Aryan language had superseded India's non-Aryan languages and was dominant from Afghan to Bengal. The grammar of Sanskrit was fixed by Pāṇini around the fifth century BCE. By 500 BCE, Vedic culture and Sanskrit had fully incorporated (upper) Indian culture. Prākrit developed unimpeded along with Sanskrit, and where Sanskrit was standardized more or less from the fifth century BCE, Prākrit (the spoken dialects of Aryan India) differed considerably. One such Prākrit to gain prominence in northern India was Western Apabhraṁśa, which had established itself as the lingua franca in upper India by the tenth century CE.

Western Apabhraṁśa is the immediate predecessor of both Braj-bhāṣā (a modified form of Western Apabhraṁśa) and Hindustani. When the Turks and Iranians (with their Persian language) conquered north India in the tenth and eleventh centuries CE, Western Apabhraṁśa and its local dialects were dominant in the region. It is in the history of Turkish and Iranian rulers of India that the first reference to 'Hindi' appears as a language distinct from Prākrit and Sanskrit. The *Tabaqāt-i-Akbarī* of 1022 CE reports a poem by the Rajput king of Kalanjar "in the Hindū tongue." This tongue's first name was simply *Hindī* or *Hindwī* (*Hindawī*), which meant the language of Hind or India or 'of the Hindus' (the 'Hindus' being a geographic designation, and not a religious one, for the people who lived beyond the Indus river). As Chatterji notes, however, this early 'Hindī' was most likely not Braj-bhāṣā or later Hindustani. We have no Hindi or Hindustani before the thirteenth and fourteenth centuries CE. However, after the Muslim ruling house had been established at Delhi in the sixteenth century, the common language of the masses in northern India at the time, Braj-bhāṣā, started to gain prominence. Braj-bhāṣā was written in the Devanagari script. Even as the language became the medium of courts and of culture and poetry, it remained a specialized literary dialect rather than a popular, colloquial one. That role was assumed by the language popular in the markets of Delhi, a dialect of Western Hindi. This vernacular was called Hindi. Its other name – that arose later in the seventeenth century – was *Zabān-e-Urdū*, or 'language of the camp.' 'Urdu' is a Persianized spelling of a Turkish word that means tent, dwelling, or encampment and identified the spoken language popular in the Delhi camps of the Muslim rulers. Urdu developed a Perso-Arabic vocabulary and an Arabic script. This form of Hindi – with its Perso-Arabic vocabulary and Arabic script – had become the language of Muslim nobility and religious men in the seventeenth and eighteenth centuries.

Two forms of Hindi or Hindustani were developing in the seventeenth and eighteenth centuries: the Hindustani of Delhi, and a Deccan dialect of Hindustani popular among north Indian Muslims settled in the Deccan. It was the north Indian Muslims in the Deccan who set the stage for the literary separation between Hindustani or proper Hindi and Braj-bhāṣā. Trying to assimilate among their Hindu neighbors, Deccan North Indian

Muslims adopted the Delhi language they brought with them and started writing it in the Persian script, which was still the language of the Muslim power centers in Delhi. North Indian Hindi speakers adopted this Deccan practice and started using Delhi Hindi in its Persianized form. By the beginning of the eighteenth century, this Persianized Delhi Hindi acquired a new name: *Hindōstānī*. By 1970, the name was accepted by north Indians and Indianized by the Hindus as *Hindūsthānī*. However, north Indian Hindus of the Eastern Provinces continued their attention to Delhi Hindi in its Braj-bhāṣā form.

Toward the end of the eighteenth century, Braj-bhāṣā Hindi came to acquire the name *Khaṛī Bolī* (or "standing language") as distinct from dialects like Braj-bhāṣā and Awadhī proper, which were designated 'fallen languages' or *Paṛī Bolī*. Hindustani or Hindi therefore emerged in the eighteenth century in two forms: High Hindi (Khaṛī Bolī Hindi in the Devanagari script) and Urdu (Persianized Hindi in the Arabic script). This modern Hindi was common to both Hindus and Muslims. Two forms of the same language, Nagarai Hindi and Persianized Hindi (Urdu) had identical grammar, shared common words and roots, and employed different scripts. This common Hindi became the lingua franca of upper India after the eighteenth century. In the course of the nineteenth century, Hindi, written in the Devanagari script, developed a more standard style in competition with better-established languages like Urdu and growing languages like English. Hindi prose literature and novels in nineteenth century are partly responsible for the development of modern standard Hindi.[33]

Chatterji has identified five forms of Hindi or Hindustani.[34] (1) The Urdu language, as spoken with a combination of Persian, Arabic, and Hindi words. It is written in Perso-Arabic, which is the Arabic script for the Persian language. Its vocabulary is highly Persianized and its literary use did not emerge before the end of the seventeenth century. In its highly Persianized form, High Urdu is a language of Muslim culture and poetry in India. (2) High Hindi or Devanagari Hindi, which has a grammar identical to Urdu but employs the Devanagari script. It uses many words from the regional Hindi (Prākrit) and dips deep into Sanskrit for words of higher culture. Perso-Arabic Urdu and Sanskritized Hindi share a common element or form; this common element is Khaṛī Bolī. 'Sanskritized Hindi' was not invented during the nineteenth-century. It can be traced not to debates on Hindi-Urdu or to the Hindi movement of the nineteenth and twentieth centuries but to the older 'literary tradition of Hindi.' A fifteenth-century poet in Gwalior may have been the first to incorporate Sanskritic themes (from the Mahabharat and the Ramayan) into Braj-bhāṣā poetry. Awadhi in the Devanagari script and Sanskritic lexical style can be found in Sufi poems from the middle of the twelfth century. Sanskrit loan words appear in Hindi spoken around Delhi in the sixteenth century and seventeenth-century dictionaries of Hindustani vocabulary record Sanskritic loan words.[35] It was a Brahman anthropologist who coined the term 'Sanskritization' to refer to the spread of Brahmans over India and the influence of their ideas and practices on the other groups of people they encountered on the subcontinent; for the most part, Sanskritization was a form of Hinduization, to the extent that Brahman communities tried to convert the people they encountered to Hinduism.[36] (3) Hindustani, which is the name for the common Khaṛī Bolī that maintains in its vocabulary a balance between Perso-Arabic Urdu and Sanskritized Hindi. Chatterji has described it as "just Hindi not highly Sanskritised." It is the combination of and median between Urdu and High Hindi and as such was promoted strongly by the Indian National Congress as the only national language of post-independence India (more on this in later sections). (4) Then there is 'vernacular Hindustani,' a collective reference to regional dialects and forms of Hindi. These vernacular forms provided the grammar and vocabulary for Hindustani. As such, High Urdu and High Hindi can be considered refinements of vernacular Hindustani. (5) Finally, Bāzār Hindi or 'market Hindi' is a simplified form of types (1) and (2) and the language of the masses in India. It is the most used language in India and the language that is mentioned as the mother tongue by nearly 500 million speakers today. In this book, I use Hindi to mean High Hindi and quotidian, 'market' Hindi spoken with a preponderance of Sanskrit words, and written in the Devanagari script.

While the spoken history of modern Hindi can be traced to the New Indo-Aryan period, written forms of Hindi are more recent. Tiwari has argued that the use of Khaṛī Bolī for literary construction is not older than the seventeenth or eighteenth centuries.[37] However, the use of a 'Nagari' or 'Devanagari' script dates from the seventh-eighth centuries. The meaning of 'nagari' remains unclear. However, since the script used to write Khaṛī Bolī was the script used to write Sanskrit, which is considered a heavenly language,[38] the script came to be known as 'Devanagari.' 'Dev' means 'heavenly' or 'god' while 'nagari' means 'belonging to a city or town' or 'civil.' Devanagari, or literally 'divine city writing,' acquired its name from the belief that it probably originated in a city.[39] By the eleventh century, the Devanagari script was fully developed and quite popular in middle and north India. Palm-leaf inscriptions in Devanagari from Gujarat, Rajasthan, and Maharashtra are available.[40] The Hindi script has developed differently from the Urdu script. These differences loom larger in formal and literary levels, where Hindi borrows its lexicon more from Sanskrit while Urdu borrows its lexicon more from Arabic and Persian.[41]

At least three applications of the term 'Hindi' are possible. 'Hindi' refers to a spoken language of recent provenance that in the modern era is distinguished from spoken Urdu. 'Standard Hindi' denotes a language written in the Devanagari script in a relatively standardized form. Its pronunciation and spoken forms are less standardized. Standard Hindi is in general use in most of central and north India. It gained currency in the period leading up to the 1860s as a "medium of education and instruction" and by the 1900s Hindi had become a "well established vehicle for journalism and *belles letters*" in central and north India.[42] Hindi is probably the third-most used language in the world. Due to its growing popularity in the Indian subcontinent and beyond, "Hindi in the Devanagari script" was recognized as an official language of India in 1947. Hindi's popularity must be understood in the context of the nineteenth-century movement to promote Hindi as the language of Hindus and Indians (more on this later).[43] Hindi and Urdu were together for most of Hindi's history. Hindi's forerunner, Hindustani, was an amalgam of Hindu and Urdu, both languages spoken similarly but written with different scripts.[44] Nationalism is partly responsible for their split.[45] So is Indian politics.[46]

As a macroterm, 'Hindi' can also refer to an assembly of cognates. In this sense, Hindi is a collection of 49 cognates like Awadhī, Banjārī, Bhojpurī, Bundelī/Bundelkhandī, Chhattisgarhī, Haryānvī, Kharī Bolī, Lodhī, Magadhī/Magahī, Mārwārī, Nāgpuriā, Pahārī, Rājasthānī, and Sargujiā. Historically, languages like Awadhī and Braj-bhāṣā should be correctly understood as cognates of Hindi. Stuart McGregor notes, "[i]t is historically and linguistically inappropriate to speak of early Braj-bhasha and Avadhi as dialects of Hindi, which they long preceded as literary languages." From the perspective of literary studies in the twenty-first century, however, they can be considered "as falling within a composite 'literary tradition of Hindi'."[47] The languages listed along with Hindi in India's census can be understood as part of the 'Hindi family.'

According to the 2001 census reports, 422 million Indians named Hindi as their mother tongue. Around 258 million Indians, or 25.09 percent of Indians named standard Hindi as their mother tongue.[48] In this book, 'Hindi' always refers to modern, standard Hindi.[49] Recently released data from India's decennial census of 2011 adds depth to our understanding of Hindi's position in India. In 2011, there were 528 million speakers of Hindi in India.[50] Uttar Pradesh (U.P.) had the most Hindi speakers (188 million), followed by Bihar (81 million), Madhya Pradesh (64 million), and Rajasthan (61 million).[51] The number of people who listed Hindi as their mother tongue has grown at a steady pace over the past 40 years, from 203 million in 1971 to 528 million in 2011. Decade over decade, Hindi users grew by 27 percent over 1971–1981, 28 percent over 1981–1991, 28 percent over 1991–2001, and 25 percent over 2001–2011. Hindi was not the fastest growing language during the last 40 years. That distinction belongs to Sanskrit, which grew by 176 percent over 1971–1981, a whopping 715 percent over 1981–1991, lost 72 percent users over 1991–2001, yet rebounded and gained 76 percent over 2001–2011! In real terms, however, the number of persons who listed Sanskrit as their mother tongue peaked at 49,736 in 1991 and stood at a meagre 24,821 in 2011 – well, meagre in Indian terms.[52]

Hindi is by far the largest language in India. Over the past 40 years, the strength of Hindi users as a proportion of the total population has steadily increased. In 1971, Hindi users accounted for 37 percent of the total population, 38 percent of the population in 1981, 39 percent in 1991, 41 percent in 2001, and 44 percent in 2011.[53] Analysis of data on internet language trends adds further depth to our understanding of Hindi's reach in the modern world. According to a 2017 report by KPMG, the consulting firm, there are 521 million speakers of Hindi in India. Of them, 254 million are Indian language literates who use Hindi (over English) as their primary language to read, write, and converse.[54] Hindi users will soon surpass English users in the digital age. Hindi Internet users are expected to surpass English Internet users by 2021.[55]

Finally, 'Hindi' also marks a cultural state of affairs, referring to a geographic area – India's 'Hindi area,' so to speak – that is shaped by Hindi's history and its widespread use. While Hindi is used throughout India and around the world, the sources studied in this book are part and parcel of the life in India's Hindi area.[56] The borders of Madhya Pradesh, Chhattisgarh, and Jharkhand constitute the southern and south-eastern boundaries of this area. The eastern border of Rajasthan and the northern border of Gujarat makes up its western limit. Bihar and Uttar Pradesh respectively mark the eastern and north-eastern limits of this Hindi area. Haryana, the Union Territory of Delhi, Himachal Pradesh, and Uttarakhand make up its northern limit.[57] Users of modern standard Hindi in its spoken and written forms can certainly be found outside this territorial map and beyond India, but the 'Hindi area' denotes the limits of the linguistic geography of this book. A few more notes on the scope of this book are helpful at this point.

The book deals primarily with mainline Protestant materials in the Hindi area. The Hindi Christian sources I have studied are the handiwork of Anglican, Baptist, Congregationalist, Lutheran, and Methodist groups and institutions in the region. These materials are mostly from the Hindi Theological Literature Committee, Lucknow Publishing House, and the Indian Society for the Promotion of Christian Knowledge. Based, respectively, in Jabalpur (Madhya Pradesh), Lucknow (Uttar Pradesh), and Delhi, these publishers produce most of the Hindi-language Christian materials in the Hindi area.[58] Among these publishers, the Hindi Theological Literature Committee deserves special mention. Founded in 1954, the Committee has been the most prominent producer and promoter of Christian works in Hindi.[59] Publications by Roman Catholic institutions enrich the body of works published by mainline Protestant Christians in the Hindi area. The same can be said of the social footprint of Roman Catholic institutions in areas like health care, education, and charity. There is a rich history of Roman Catholic Hindi literature in the region. The Hindi area is home also to Syrian Catholic, St. Thomas, Orthodox, evangelical, and Pentecostal Christians.[60] I pay limited attention to this diversity when examining Hindi Christian claims regarding the politics of language and religion in India. My sources are limited to mainline, Protestant Christian sources in Hindi.

In this book, I examine Hindi Christian works in independent India. The output of the Hindi Theological Literature Committee has been instrumental to this study. Yet the Committee's work must be understood in the context of the much-longer history of Hindi Christian publications in India. An early example of Hindi Christian literature comes from 1877 in the form of a published account of a person's conversion. In pamphlet form, such accounts were quite in line with the type of publications popular at the time among missionaries who were trying to promote conversions. "Bhayaharṇ Dās," the convert, seems to have been illiterate. His conversion account is, as a result, written by one Rāmsiṁh, who attested to the account's veracity by "signing" the pamphlet.[61] The slim pamphlet was titled *Kaise Pāyā Muktidātā, arthāt Bhayaharṇadās kā Itihās* subtitled "How I Found the Saviour, or The Shepherd Convert of Monghyr" in English, and widely circulated. It was published by The Rev. Thomas Evans, a Baptist missionary at Monghyr (or Munger) on the banks of the Ganges river in Bihar, and printed at the Medical Hall Press in Benaras. The Welsh Baptists were also known for such publications as *Rām Parīkṣā* ("A Character Examination of Ram," in two editions), *Shiv Parīkṣā* ("A Character Examination of Shiva," in two editions), and *Sat Gurū kī Bulāhat* ("The Teacher's Call," in two editions).[62]

Many features of the pamphlet reflect strategic choices by its publisher. It was written in Kaithi, a popular local dialect of Hindi, for widespread appeal. The decision to use Kaithi over Hindustani suggests an interest in local and mass appeal rather than an appeal to the Hindu elite, the officers of the Raj, or an upper-caste audience. The account is polemic in nature and spends a considerable number of pages on the protagonist's first-person account of why he wanted to leave Hinduism, the religion of his birth. For Bhayaharṇ Dās, Hinduism was corrupt, dominated by greedy learned men who shamed people into guilt and therefore into supporting them, and was spreading its corruption from town to town. Dās does not dismiss Hinduism as polytheist or erroneous. Rather, the argument is aimed at the irreversible corruption of an admirable religion. The message to Hindus seems to be as follows: even if you think Hinduism is intrinsically acceptable, it is beyond redemption these days. This should motivate you to look elsewhere and you will see that Christianity provides a great alternative. It offers salvation and *mukti* without ritualism and priests. The Protestant tinge of the argument is evident. So is the strategic nature of the choice of location where the pamphlet was published. Benaras is one of Hinduism's holiest sites, the city of Shiva and the Ganges, and as Diana Eck has described it, the city of all India, good life, and of death and liberation.[63]

Banaras remains a site of Hindu pride.[64] The city has long been venerated as one of the seven cities of pilgrimage in Hinduism and is said to contain within itself all seven cities. The earliest Purāṇas (c. fourth-sixth cen. CE) speak of Siva's arrival in the city. The city's rulers promoted the Hindu tradition, supported schools of Sanskrit, and sponsored the education of Brahmans. Its rulers, merchants, Brahmans, and pilgrims jointly fostered the story of Kāśi (Banaras) as the sacred space with its divine links, ancient heritage, and power to heal and liberate. Colonial Christians reached Banaras at the tail end of the eighteenth century. Never more than a few hundred in number at a time, the Britishers regarded their time in Banaras as a "kind of moral exile" and Indians an "inferior race."[65] Europeans lived on the outskirts of the city, following the colonial practice of segregation. They built a school and a Christian Missionary Society in Banaras. After the First War of Independence or Mutiny of 1857, the Raj emerged when the Government of India Act of 1858 transferred India's governance from the East India Company to the British Crown through the Secretary of State.

Indo-British relations in Banaras did not change under the Raj. Despite some debate, the link between missionaries and the government continued unabated. Pamphleteering was part of empire-endorsed Christian activity.[66] In the nineteenth century, Banaras would become the site from which Hindi was promoted as the language of the Hindus – Sanskrit remained a language of the Brahmans. Given the place of Banaras in the Hindu imagination, the place of Sanskrit and schools of Hindu learning, and the Christo-colonial history in the city, the publication of the conversion account in Banaras in the local vernacular sought to achieve multiple aims through a single medium. It criticized Hinduism without denigrating the city, it took a swipe at holy and learned Hindus (Brahmans), it offered Christianity as a better religious alternative, and it spoke with the voice of an insider to a Hindu-heavy audience. The pamphlet's impact remains unknown. It was well-circulated but it did not lead to any mass conversions. Some may have converted after being influenced by this pamphlet or others of its ilk, but most probably the pamphlet suffered the same failure as the Christian enterprise in Banaras – which was largely unsuccessful when it came to conversions.[67]

Banaras was not the only site of Hindi Christian literary activity. Hindi translations of the gospels and Hindi Christian materials were a large part of the output of the Baptist missionaries in Serampore, with the first translation of Hindi gospels around 1818. An 1875 account of (Protestant) Christian vernacular publications mentions Benjamin Schultze's 1743 *Summa Doctrinae Christianae* as the "first Christian book printed in Hindustani."[68] The book was published by the Orphan House in Halle. By 1917, a comprehensive list of Christian literature prepared by the missionary council in central and north India catalogued 490 books in Hindi (this list is discussed later). For the purpose of this book, I commissioned an update of the 1917 list with materials published up till 2010. This updated 2010 catalogue of Hindi Christian works is the main source of published works for this book. The 1917 list is available online for public access.[69] The 2010 catalogue is also available online for public access.[70] The 1917 and 2010 catalogues of Hindi Christian works are discussed in chapter 2. The neglect of Hindi Christian works recurs in publications on Christianity in India. The India section of *Asian Christian Theologies* is a case in point.

Asian Christian Theologies, published in 2002, is an unparalleled collection of Christian sources in Asia. It catalogues works by 103 writers in

17 languages: Bengali, Danish, English, French, German, Hindi, Kannada, Khasi, Malayalam, Marathi, Mizo, Naga, Oriya, Punjabi, Sanskrit, Tamil, and Telugu.[71] Despite its scope, it omits the vast majority of Hindi Christian authors and publications. Two Hindi Christian texts are cited among the nearly 1130 books in the India section of *Asian Christian Theologies*. James Massey's *Masīhī Dalit: Ik Itihāsik Parīkshā* ("Christian Dalits: A Historical Analysis"), published in 1993,[72] and Vandana Mataji's 2-volume *Śabd, Śaktī, Sangam* ("Word, Power, Union"), published in 1995, make an appearance.[73] The collection includes indirect references to other Hindi Christian works: Vandana Mataji, whose English-language works are referenced in *Asian Christian Theologies*,[74] wrote hymns in Hindi; Viman Tilak's poetry crossed over Marathi and Hindi;[75] and James Massey does much work in Hindi. The absence of most works in Hindi can be partly explained by the book's focus on English-language sources. *Asian Christian Theologies*, the editors explain, offers "a survey of the writings in English." Yet the editors also tip their hand toward a broader goal when they write that they will survey English writings while "drawing on the writings in many languages of the region."[76] Given this appeal to other languages, the severe paucity of Hindi entries is conspicuous. The paucity is even more glaring in a multi-volume compendium that makes the claim that "[e]xtensive research has been undertaken to ensure that a wide range of vernacular materials are included and outlined."[77]

Language and religion

In *Constructing Indian Christianities*, Bauman and Young raise an important question: Who is an Indian Christian? The query is complicated. What is the defining marker? Is it religion – *Christianity*? Is it a nation – *India*? Or, is it culture – a certain *Indian-ness*? Is it all these things, none of which can be packed into a neat definitional box? Is it none of them? They question whether a term like 'Indian Christian' "impose[s]" an "alien taxonomy on phenomena that in the final analysis remain fluid and stubbornly unreifiable."[78] Similar questions can be raised of a book that studies Hindi Christians. What is 'Hindi Christian'? What is a 'Hindi Christian' source or material or publication? Is it defined by its 'Hindi-ness'? Or, by its 'Christian-ness'? The danger of reification remains, but taxonomy is problematic, more so when it makes exclusive and permanent claims. The titular plural in *Constructing Indian Christianities* responds to the danger in naming through a counterclaim to conventional studies of Christianity in India. It hints at the state of permanent diversity that characterizes Christianity in India. Further, it claims that Christianity in India is a process, maybe not uniquely so but a process, nevertheless. Indian Christianities are always under construction.

'Hindi Christian' is a useful, if relatively unknown, descriptor. As a descriptive term, 'Hindi Christian' has a history. It has been in use at least since 1970. The term appears in a preface by C. W. David to a popular book on Christian discipleship. David was the editor of the Hindi Theological Literature Committee at the time and was trying to use his influential perch to promote Hindi Christian works. He writes: "[i]t is the misfortune of Hindi Christian literature that it has very few readers. . . . Hindi speakers are requested to awaken and, by reading good books, to remove their shame and be enlightened."[79] David's appeal did not fall on deaf ears. By the middle part of the twentieth century, Hindi was a Christian language and had mass appeal through the many hymns and devotional songs (*bhajan*) in Hindi.

Congregations in central and northern India share Hindi. This shared heritage has fostered many of the Hindi Christian works still in widespread use. The movement in the twentieth century toward ecumenical relations catalyzed joint efforts among Hindi-using congregations and institutions. One such prominent collaboration is the production of *Ārādhǎnā ke Gīt*. It is the primary hymnbook of mainline Hindi-speaking churches in central India. The Madhya Pradesh Christian Council and the Methodist Church in India have been publishing *Ārādhǎnā ke Gīt* together for the last 45 years. Regular updates to *Ārādhǎnā ke Gīt* have kept the hymnbook up to date and have made it popular in Hindi-speaking congregations in Madhya Pradesh, Uttar Pradesh, and Bihar.

Ārādhǎnā ke Gīt was commissioned by the Madhya Pradesh Christian Council as a revision of the Hindi hymnal, *Masīhī Gīt Sangrah*, in which "the paucity of contemporary Indian compositions, the dominance of difficult Western compositions, and the absence of easy, clear, and currently popular language was starting to be painfully felt."[80] It was produced "so that one book might be printed which would be suitable for both Hindi and Urdu speaking areas in M.P., U.P. and Bihar."[81] A Hymn Book Revision Committee began its work in the first week of March 1967 after conducting a survey of Hindi-speaking congregations to solicit views on which hymns and *bhajans* to include or exclude. The Methodist hymnbook was also undergoing a revision at the time, and in 1970, the Methodist Revision Committee joined the Christian Council's committee. *Ārādhǎnā ke Gīt* includes traditional and contemporary *bhajans* (devotionals). It includes well-known songs and anonymous compositions. Provenance, however, was not a major concern of the publishers. "We have made every effort," they explain, "to discover and acknowledge the authors and composers of the Indian songs and bhajans but still [we] are uncertain about many."[82] The main criteria for inclusions in the book has been a song's popularity. Most of the songs included in the book enjoy mass appeal and are in regular use. As such, the songs are recognizable and bridge the liturgies of congregations across a swath of India's Hindi area.

In addition to worship, theological education also unites Hindi-speaking congregations. Mainline denominations run joint seminaries dedicated to instruction in Hindi. Hindi, along with English, is the language of instruction in many seminaries in north India, some of which, like Leonard

Theological College in Jabalpur, Madhya Pradesh, focus on preparing pastors and church leaders for Hindi-speaking congregations. Joint publication houses have also enriched shared theological education in Hindi. The Hindi Theological Literature Committee was set up as one such joint venture by a variety of denominations that use Hindi. The Committee has served as the primary patron of Hindi Christian publications in India. It distributes its output in India through a partnership with the Indian Society for Promoting Christian Knowledge. The Society has book shops across the country and promotes Hindi Christian literature beyond the Hindi area.

Hindi-speaking churches have established joint ventures in literature, liturgy, and theological education. Their use of Hindi has brought them together. This collective focus on Hindi has gained depth and patronage over the years. "The Principals of theological colleges, church bishops, pastors, publication houses, distributors of our books, boards, and missionary organizations from the Hindi regions are giving [us] their full support" to Hindi Christian ventures.[83] This support represents a sea change in denominational attitudes toward Hindi Christian literature. Across a span of geographies, denominations, and contexts, Christians in India's Hindi-speaking region belie uniformity. Yet they have fostered ecumenical collaborations, common institutions of learning, standardized hymnbooks, common liturgies, and shared literature.

The intellectual history of religious studies in South Asia helps shed more light on the intelligibility, function, and usefulness of lingo-religious descriptors like 'Hindi Christian' in studying Christianity in India. Such descriptors allude to the role of language and religion in the formation of faith and identity. They point to a family of influences. The late Selva J. Raj wrote an ethnography of the ritual life of 'Santal Catholics' that shed light on the ways in which Santali tribal and Roman Catholic elements are combined in religious life. In its attention to the role of language, this book goes beyond Raj's work on Santal Catholics. The interface of multiple strands, Raj explains, enabled this community to "construct a distinct identity for itself that is *authentically tribal*, *fully Indian*, and *genuinely Christian*."[84] Kerry P.C. San Chirico writes of the *Khrist Bhaktas* of the Hindi belt who worship Christ in personal and communal devotion, yet remain unbaptized and Hindu according to the religious taxonomy of the Constitution of India and its Census Bureau. They have adapted Catholic beliefs and Hindu temple practices to a *bhakti* mode of religious life.[85]

Like Raj and San Chirico, Vasudha Narayanan draws attention to Hindus and Christians who are "multiritual" and "polytheological" in their religious expressions. Practices based on the view that religious lines are blurry permeate the religious landscape of India. As an instance, *khrist bhaktas* are part of the north Indian religious landscape. Rajasthan has pilgrimage sites shared by Muslims and Hindus. Hindus and Christians worship at The Church of the Infant Jesus in Bangalore.[86] Hindu, Muslim, and Christian venerate Sister Alphonsa in Kottayam as a healer.[87] Satya Sai Baba claims that he does not speak for any sect or doctrine but preaches respect, unity, and the glory of God. In similar vein, Hindus argue that that multiple paths lead to God.[88] Forms of God are prolific, and gods can exist as partial and particular manifestation of the 'one' God.[89] Angelika Malinar argues that the theology of the Bhagavad Gita, one of Hinduism's most sacred and influential scripture, can be called 'cosmological monotheism' because the Gita presents Krishna as the "highest and only god of liberation and creation" while acknowledging other gods as "partial manifestations" of Krishna.[90]

Similarly, Islam teaches that God sends different prophets to different peoples. Chapter 16, verse 36 of the Koran is an ideal example of this sentiment: "We indeed sent a messenger unto every community, 'Worship God, and shun false deities!' Then among them were those whom God guided; and among them were those who were deserving of error." Other verses affirm the idea that every community has its own messenger (10:47), its own book (45:28), and is called to worship God (21:25).[91] God has revealed many ways and many religions and many creeds and many rites and many legal codes.[92] As such, "variegated religious forms do not contravene the validity and efficacy of one another" but are part of the repeated calling back of humans to God.[93] Raj and Dempsey say of Christianity in India that it is "neither homogenous nor uniform but essentially plural and diverse."[94] "Christianity" in India is a congeries of beliefs and practices inspired by faith traditions and social histories whose constituents are never too far from change.[95]

David Mosse has critiqued "short-time-frame ethnographies" that unearth cultural adaptations with a bias toward disjunctions between culture and Christianity and that pay inadequate attention to the stability in beliefs and practices embedded in centuries-long traditions like Orthodox and Catholic Christianity in India. As a "source of distinctive forms of thought, action, and modes of signification" he writes, studies of "profoundly localized" Christianity that eschew presenting the relation between "culture" and "Christianity" as continuity or rupture offer a necessary corrective to studies of Indian Christianity. The Tamil Catholicism of the pseudonymous Alapuram in his work charts a rich terrain with features that have gradually emerged from the "complex intercultural space" between Catholicism and Tamil cultural forms.[96]

Drawing on Mosse's corrective in *The Saint in the Banyan Tree*, I explore the space created by Hindi Christian materials between Hindi "culture," Hindu-Christian relations, and the politicization of language and religion in India. I interrogate the many ways in which Hindi Christians have created credible and recognizable linguistic features that seek to function in a religious milieu that is affected by Hindu practices and Hindi cultural forms. I study the particular ways in which Hindi and Christianity continue to function in India. This is partly in response to Mosse's critique that most scholarship on Indian Christianity has sought to either find a gap between 'local' culture and Christian claims or to suggest they are undistinguishable.

Mosse's research on Tamil Catholics did not support this division; and, he therefore invites scholars of Indian Christianity to take a deeper look at these relations. This book accepts Mosse's invitation. It looks at the relation between a language and certain religious ideas. In line with Mosse's findings, Hindi Christian materials reveal neither a continuity with existing claims nor a complete rejection of available resources. Rather, a middle ground emerges that is clearly marked to insist Christianity is culturally Indian, idiomatically Hindi, and home grown.

The milieu

In *Religions in Practice*, John R. Bowen describes a private *pūjā* (worship) in a village in Madhya Pradesh. A father gathers his family, lights a cow-dung cake, sprinkles water around the fire, and offers portions of prepared food to the fire. The fire purifies the food. The food is now blessed. Portions of food are offered because purified parts can cleanse the whole. Blessing all the food by sacrificing parts of it also allows the blessed food to be shared. The remaining food – now blessed food (*prasād*) – is then shared in a family meal.[97] Family rites and public festivals permeate the religious landscape of India. Accompanied by chants and prayers, *bhajans* and *pujā* resound through the many villages, towns, and cities in the region. Growing up in a small town in Madhya Pradesh, I woke up most days to sound of temple-bells and *bhajans* coming from the Hindu temple down the road. Once in a while an *azān* would break through from the mosque across town. Festival plays, street theaters, religious holidays color the landscape with a religious hue. *Bhakti* shapes north India. Hawley's observation 30 years ago is apt even today: "north India [is] a place where *bhakti* is spoken."[98] Ganesh, Hanuman, Krishna, Lakshman, Lakshmi, Ram, Saraswati, and Sita adorn temples, books, factory floors, shops, schools, hospitals, government offices, calendars, posters, clothes, and bodies. The image of God, in Diana Eck's apt phrase, is "visible everywhere in India."[99] *Bhakti* (devotion), *śraddhā* (veneration), and *pūjā* are the means of reaching out to God.

Bhakti is a religious language and a way of being. One is a devotee of, and in relationship with, God. These relations are complementary, and in most cases reciprocal. Devotees worship, bring gifts, and go on pilgrimages. The deities protect, grant wishes, and help manage the ups and downs of life. I use *bhakti* in this broader sense to refer to the general relationship formed between a devotee and the divine. The relationship between a *bhakt* and her god(s) is personal, reciprocal, continual, and special. A devotee may have a special relationship with one main god while engaging other minor gods as needed. Hindu devotees shift among different main gods at different occasions or elevate more than one god above other gods or may assign different religious meaning to one god elevated above others. Within *bhakti* traditions, however, the tendency is to elevate one god above others and to foster life-long loyalty to one god over other gods.

The word '*bhakti*' emerged around 2500 years ago. It appears in the *Svetasvatara Upanishad* and the Bhagavad Gītā, by far the most influential Hindu scripture on *bhakti*. *Bhakti* denotes love or devotion directed to a deity or God.[100] At the root of the word '*bhakti*' is the Sanskrit verb *bhaj*. In the *Rig Veda* (c. 1700–1500 BCE), *bhaj* meant to divide, distribute, allot, or apportion. The verb later developed to mean to obtain as one's share, to partake, to receive, or to enjoy. It has a noun form, *bhakta*, which denotes a worshipper or votary. By the time the Mahabharata was composed during 300 BCE to 300 CE, *bhaj* acquired a vassalic form; it meant to declare for, prefer, choose (e.g., as a servant) or to serve, honor, revere, love, or adore. *Bhakta* acquired commensurate connotations in the Mahabharat, where it meant to be engaged in, occupied with, attached to or devoted to, loyal, faithful, honoring, worshipping, and serving.[101]

Since its origin, *bhakti* has existed as one path to liberation among other paths – like those of *jñānā* (knowledge), *karma* (action), and other types of disciplines. In the Bhagavad Gītā, as an instance, the *bhakti* path to liberation is mentioned in conjunction with the path of knowledge and that of proper action. Around 1200 year ago in Tamil Nadu, however, a new form of *bhakti* emerged that understood loving devotion to God as the only path to liberation. The great eleventh-century teacher, Rāmānuja, exemplified one interpretation of this type of devotion-based liberation. Rāmānuja draws a distinction between two types of *bhakti*, a lower *bhakti* and a higher *bhakti*.[102] Lower *bhakti* is a discipline of knowledge in which a devotee seeks a better understanding of *Brahman* (God). This discipline of knowledge is a form of indirect knowledge of God and is based on the scriptures. Through *jñāna-yoga*, which is the systematic exploration of scripture under the guidance of a teacher, a devotee comes to know God. The discipline of knowledge complements a discipline or proper actions (*karma-yoga*), which consists of doing what is obligatory and permissible without attachment to the fruits of those actions. The discipline of indirect knowledge is then a discipline of knowledge-and-work. When done with the intention of the love of God, this combination discipline constitutes a discipline of devotion (*bhakti-yoga*). Rāmānuja suggests that too much of one's ego still survives in love for God. Hence, this form of *bhakti* constitutes a lower form of *bhakti*. While lower, this type of discipline helps a devotee walk on the path toward the higher form of *bhakti*.

Higher *bhakti* is a form of direct knowledge of God. It occurs in the form of an epiphany of the divine, an "ever-deepening relationship of intimacy," with the divine. It is still cognitive in nature and a form of knowledge, even if an ineffable intimate knowledge of God. Even as Rāmānuja locates knowledge of God in devotion of God, *bhakti* for him is still grounded in "the context of necessary social and religious obligations."[103] *Bhakti* did not remain in Tamil Nadu but spread outward, reaching the west, then the north and eventually reaching the eastern parts of India. As the personal-devotional form of *bhakti* spread from southern India, many of the main features set during its time in Tamil Nadu spread with it. As *bhakti* spread throughout India, it acquired certain features. Some features separated it from the 'intellectual' *bhakti* of Rāmānuja. Yet, as Schelling notes, many of its main features were set in its Tamil Nadu days. These features include a devotion that is substantially personal, expressively emotional, scornful of doctrines, suspicious of religious authorities, defiant of orthodoxy, physically immersive, intentionally disruptive, grounded in communities, egalitarian in outlook and distinctively open in its symbols and songs. Further, *bhakti* is mostly in the form of oral poetry and songs and not in the form of literature.[104]

Bhakti in north India is characterized by a few features. It constitutes a deep and personal relationship between a devotee and her God. Further, it is reciprocal: the devotee offers praise, worship, and gifts and receives blessings. It is also continual: a devotee may not visit a temple or pray ritually every day, but the relationship is a constant presence in the thoughts and acts of the devotee. She expects that the divine sees the devotee whenever the divine is called upon. Finally, *bhakti* tends to be broadly exclusive. A devotee may pray to different saints or holy people at different times, but *bhakti* is usually layered, with one supreme deity the focus of devotion and a range of secondary 'saints' available as needed. While a *bhakt* can be in relationship with multiple divinities for particular purposes – as an instance, Sister Alphonsa for health, Ganesh for good luck, Lakshmi for wealth, Saraswati for wisdom, and Hanuman for protection – a specific divinity primarily occupies the devotee's devotion. It is in the context of this larger, four-fold sense that Hindi Christian sources express *bhakti*. *Bhakti* as found in Hindi Christian sources reflects a combination of 'southern' *bhakti* – with its fusion of personal devotion and proper actions – and pan-Indian *bhakti*, with its passionate, unorthodox, egalitarian form. Hindi Christian notions of devotion and love of God do not scoff at rituals or doctrines. Yet at their core lies a commitment to the liberation of the body and soul in this world and the world to come.

Bhakti and Christianity share motifs and vocabulary in India. A comparison by Sabapathy Kulandran in 1957 listed the following shared features.[105] In their essence, both modes of religious expressions describe the human response to the divine. Both religious traditions embody a whole-hearted trust and commitment to another. They characterize God as the 'other' in whom one places complete trust. The power of trust can be found in the love poems of Mirabai, the seventeenth-century *bhakti* saint. Mirabai sings:

> He's bound my heart with the powers he owns, Mother –
>   He with the lotus eyes.
>
> Arrows like spears: this body is pierced,
>   And Mother, he's gone away.
> When did it happen, Mother? I don't know

> But now it's too much to bear.
> Talismans, spells, medicines –
> I've tried, but the pain won't go.
> Is there someone who can bring relief?
> Mother, the hurt is cruel.
> Here I am, near, and you're not far:
> Hurry to me, to meet.
> Mira's Mountain-Lifter Lord, have mercy,
> Cool this body's fire!
> Lotus-Eyes, with the powers you own, Mother,
> With those powers you've bound.[106]

One moment Krishna is far. The other moment he is near and ready to meet. God may be the 'other' to whom a bhakt relates, but God/Krishna is not completely removed from the devotee. *Bhakti*, Kulandran continues, rises above legalism and ritualism. As such, *bhakti* traditions undermine caste claims and caste-based distinctions. Important differences remain. The most important difference, Kulandran argues, concerns the nature of God and the sources of salvation. Unlike Christianity, which posits a God distinct from creation and Jesus Christ as the only source of salvation, *bhakti* tends toward monism and offers itself to Hindus as one among many paths to liberation.

David Scott has also characterized Christianity and *bhakti* as responses to the sacred. He goes as far as to conflate the two phenomenon and jointly call it "Hindu and Christian *Bhakti*." In Scott's construction, Christianity and Hindu have a "common" human response to the divine in the "personalist tradition of religious devotion of *bhakti*" that both Christianity and Hinduism share.[107] Given the overlaps between Christianity and Hinduism, Scott proposes that *bhakti* can be used as the gateway to a fuller Indian understanding of Christianity. *Bhakti* is the bridge that links the Christian faith to the Hindu faith. Hindu and Christian *bhakti*, Scott explains, is characterized by love of God, personal devotion to God, the experience of grace, utter self-surrender to God, and the power of God's love. In Scott's construction of religion, *bhakti* provides the proper orientation for "outward" religious acts like worship and devotion and "inward" religious acts like faith and love.[108]

Bhakti and Christianity further share a concern for social relations. Poems of the *bhakti* tradition, Schelling writes, started to take shape during the eighth and ninth centuries, drew inspiration from excluded sections of society, challenged social hierarchies, and spread revolutions across kingdoms. *Bhakti* has led to uncontainable movements for spiritual freedom and fostered persistent demands for social and economic equality. It has nurtured the human yearning to connect with something greater and served as a way to experience the transcendent. "At the root of bhakti," Schelling observes, "coils the formidable old hunger for human freedom, a sense of the world's inexplicable mystery, and the conviction that each of us forms some personal relationship to that mystery."[109]

Not all comparisons between Christian devotion and *bhakti* were appreciative or positive. Some comparisons sought to present *bhakti* as the antidote to Christian colonialism in India. As Dipesh Chakrabarty and Tapan Raychauduri have noted, *bhakti* as loving devotion became a source of political unity among nationalist authors in the nineteenth and early twentieth centuries.[110] Comparativist scholars during the British Raj were wary of certain forms of *bhakti*. George Abraham Grierson (1851–1941), the leading ethno-linguist, found much to admire about the *bhakti*-focused writings of Indian religious leaders like Sitaramsharan Bhagvan Prasad (1840–1932). Grierson would go so far as to trace the origin of Hindu *bhakti* to early Nestorian Christianity via the theology of the great eleventh-century Hindu theologian, Rāmānuja. He retreated from that claim later.[111] Despite his retreat, Grierson found many parallels with Christian motifs in Hindu *bhakti*: God's unwavering love for humanity, God's grace, self-surrender, abandoning the world for God, cleaving away from sin, being 'reborn' as a bhakta. Yet not every form of *bhakti* earned a positive review. Grierson was critical of Krishna-*bhakti*, which he considered was based on the love of a man for a woman and corrupted by an extreme form of *bhakti* veering on the edge of lust. Contrary to Krishna-*bhakti* was Ram-*bhakti*, which was based on the love between a father and a son, lacked any hint of sensual licentiousness, and was a good approximation of the Christian motif of God's love for humans.[112]

Arun Jones draws a distinction between certain versions of Christianity and *bhakti* traditions, which he designates 'local religion.' He argues that nineteenth-century evangelical Christianity found its place in the religious milieu shaped and nourished by *bhakti*.[113] In the motifs and practices of *bhakti* groups, evangelical Christianity unwittingly found substantial echoes. Jones identifies five areas of resemblance.[114] In theology, both religious groups looked to a divine savior for liberation. Devotees sought a personal, intimate relationship with their savior. Both groups further shared a form of religious expression that emphasized personal experience of the divine rather than rituals and doctrines. This form of religious expression fostered vernacular expressions. In terms of social outlook, *bhakti* and evangelical Christianity shared a reformist impulse that provided counterpoints to formal religion, orthodoxies, and religious hierarchies. Both religious traditions further stressed on communal formation as the main means to religious devotion. Worshipping communities were the primary locus of *bhaktas* and evangelical Christians in North India. (Jones writes of evangelical Christians in Hindi North India but has very little to say about the *Hindi*-ness of Christianity in North India.) Finally, both groups shared a demography, drawing members primarily from groups on the periphery of society.

Despite the sharing of motifs and practices, Jones notes, *bhakti* and Christianity could not be (con)fused in nineteenth-century north India.

Important differences remained. As an instance, where *bhakti* was henotheistic in outlook, evangelical Christianity had a different sense of divine self-expression. Similarly, where *bhakti* groups challenged social hierarchies in their motifs and form of organization, evangelical Christianity emphasized the development of personal holiness, though Jones seems to suggest that evangelical Christianity had high(er) degree of social activism than *bhakti* traditions in North India. Jones's general thesis is on point: nineteenth-century evangelical Christianity in India found hospitable spaces in the religious milieu shaped by north Indian *bhakti* traditions. His observation that this hospitality was "coincidental" and "unwitting," however, needs to be qualified.[115] On the matter of the relationship between motifs in *bhakti* traditions and motifs in the evangelical Christianity of Hindi north India in the nineteenth-century, Jones may be right. But as I discuss in following sections, the devotional hymns of mainline, Protestant Hindi Christians in the twentieth-century show an affinity with and explicit adoption of the motifs and language of *bhakti*. In the Hindi area, connections between Hindi Christianity and *bhakti* appear weak at first glance. While the practice of *bhakti* populates the Hindi area, I have not found direct references in Hindi Christian sources to the works of the *bhakti* saints like Ravidas, Kabir, Nanak, Surdas, Mirabai, and Tulsidas. Yet Hindi Christian books and hymns demonstrate a robust affinity to the ideas and terms of *bhakti*. While a Hindi Christian may not describe Christianity as a *bhakti* religion, thematic analogies between the world of *bhakti* and Hindi Christian expressions are evident. Hindi Christian devotionals provide the most fertile ground to examine this evidence.[116]

Hindi Christian hymns include direct references to *bhakti* and *bhakts*. Noticeably, 'official' collections of Hindi Christian hymns present Christian *ārādhănā* as *bhakti*. *Ārādhănā ke Gīt* has a special place in Hindi Christian liturgy given its role as a primary source of devotional songs and other *bhajans*. It has also led to standardization of Hindi Christian devotionals. *Ārādhănā ke Gīt* has wide acceptance among mainline Protestant Christian congregations that use Hindi. The hymnbook is also noteworthy for its reliance on the motifs and vocabulary of *bhakti*. The topical index of *Ārādhănā ke Gīt* lists songs for 'Worship and Adoration' under the category '*Ārādhănā*.' In this popular hymnbook, *ārādhănā* is synonymous with *bhakti*. The publishers of the hymnbook categorize all songs related to the adoration and worship of God as "*Ārādhănā (Bhakti)*."[117] In their construction, Christian worship is *bhakti*. A few examples follow (emphases mine). The first hymn in the hymnbook describes Christian devotion as *bhakti*. In a Hindi rendering of 'How Great Thou Art,' its fourth verse reads:

Āegā khrist sāth baḍī mahimā ke,	Christ will come in great glory,
Sāth usăke hogā ek ānand mahān,	With him shall be great joy,
*Tab **bhakti-bhāv** aur dīnătā se maiṁ jhukkar,*	Then bowing with humble devotion,

Gāuṃgā yah, "prabhu, kaisā mahān."	I shall sing, "Lord, How Great Thou Art."

(Number 1; translated by R. M. Clark)

The third hymn uses *bhakti* for devotion:

Ab āe tere pās	Now we come close to you,
Ārādhănā karne ko,	So that we may worship you,
Praśaṃsā ***bhakti*** *se kareṁ,*	May our praise be devoted to you,
Aur prārthănā saccī ho.	And our prayers be true.

(Number 3; anonymous composer)

So does Hymn 29:

Duniyāṁ kā racne vālā vahī,	He is the one who creates the world,
Bhaktoṁ *ke dil kā ujālā vahī,*	He enlightens the heart of devotees,
Pāpin kāraṇ janmā vahī,	He is the one born to fix sin,
Sūlī par caṛhne vālā vahī.	He is the one to climb the cross.

(Number 29; composed by Ahsan)

And Hymn 403:

Bhakti *se, stuti se,*	With devotion, with praise,
Is din ko pavitr māneṁ.	Consider this day holy.
Khrist yīśu ke dvārā mere,	Through Christ Jesus,
Pāpoṁ ko kṣamā kar tu de,	You forgive my sins.
Bhakti *se, stuti se,*	With devotion, with praise,
Is din ko pavitr māneṁ.	Consider this day holy.
Ānand se āeṁ tere ghar,	May we enter your house with joy,
Ārādhănā ho saccāī se;	May our worship be true;
Hamārī ***bhakti*** *aesī ho*	May our devotion be such
Ki bhāe vah svarg meṁ tujhe.	That it pleases you in heaven.

(Number 403; "O Happy Day," translated by Phillip Doddridge)

Evangelical Christians in north India in the twentieth century have also described their devotion as *bhakti*. *Jīvan Saṅgīt* ("Life Music") was published in 1994 and is a popular publication among evangelical Christians in Madhya Pradesh. It is the primary hymnbook of churches affiliated with Mid-India Christian Services, a well-established evangelical Christian organization based in Damoh, Madhya Pradesh. Hymn 2 of *Jīvan Saṅgīt* is the popular Hindi Christian hymn "*Terī Ārādhănā Karūṁ.*" Its second verse reads:

Sṛṣṭī ke har ek kaṇ kaṇ meṁ	In every kernel of the universe
Chāyā hai terī hī mahimā kā rāj	Your glory reigns
Pakṣī bhī karte haiṁ terī praśaṃsā	Even the birds sing your praise

Har pal sunāte haiṁ ānand kā rāg	Sounding your joy always
Merī bhī ***bhakti*** *tujhe grahaṇ ho*	May my worship be acceptable to you
Hṛday se prārthănā karūṁ.	This is my heartfelt prayer.

(Number 2; anonymous composer)

Then there is "*Śaraṇ meṁ āe haiṁ hum*," Hymn 329 in *Jīvan Saṅgīt*, which has a counterpart in a Hindu devotional song of the same name. Between the two songs, only some words are different. Among these slight changes, *yīśu* (Jesus) in the Christian version is *bhagvan* (Lord) in the Hindu version. The third and fifth verses of the hymn respectively read:

Na hum meṁ bal hai	We lack strength,
Na hum meṁ shakti,	We lack power,
Na hum meṁ sādhan	We lack the means
Na hum meṁ ***bhakti***.	We lack devotion.
Tumhāre dar ke hum haiṁ bhikāri,	We are beggars at your doorstep,
Dayā karo he dayālu yīśu.	Show us mercy, merciful Jesus.
Pradhān kar do mahān ***bhakti***,	Grant us great devotion,
Bharo hamāre meṁ jñān shakti.	Fill us with powerful wisdom.
Narak nāśak ho krūs dhārī,	You are the hell-destroyer, the cross-bearer
Dayā karo he dayālu yīśu.	Show us mercy, merciful Jesus.

(Number 329; anonymous composer)

Hindi Christian *bhajans*, like their *bhakti* counterparts, use vernaculars and mix and match terms from a variety of linguistic contexts. Consider Hymn 511 in *Ārādhănā ke Gīt*:

Terī nazar ke pyāse haiṁ hum,	We thirst for your gaze,
Tujhse duā yah karte haiṁ hum.	That you look upon us, we beseech you.
Tū hai hāmī, tū hai svāmī,	You are our advocate, you are our master,
Tū hai prem apār.	You are love unbound.
Tū hī dān, tū hī mān,	You are the gift, you are the honor,
Tū hai jag kā ādhār.	You are the foundation of the world.
Tū hai śakti, tū hai ***bhakti***,	You are power, you are devotion,
Tū hai tāraṇăhār.	You are savior.

(Number 511; lyrics and tune by D. M. Daniel)

The song is listed as hymn of *ārādhănā (bhakti)* and exemplifies the linguistic mixing of languages and concepts that occurs when *bhakti* traditions and

Christian worship come together. *Nazar* is an Urdu word via Arabic. *Hāmī* is Arabic in origin and *Svāmī* and *Apār* are Sanskritic in origin. *Hāmī* is an Arabic loan-word that means 'supporter' or 'advocate.' It is sometimes also conflated with the Arabic *ḥāmī*, which means 'to confirm' something, as in *ḥāmī bharănā* (to agree with, to assent to).[118] In the next verse, *mān* and *ādhār* are borrowed from Sanskrit. Finally, Sanskrit provides *śakti*, *bhakti*, and *tāraṇăhār*, which respectively mean power, devotion, and one who enables a crossing over. The combination of *nazar*, *hāmī*, *svāmī*, *bhakti*, and *tāraṇăhār* in the Hindi hymnal asks a singer of the hymn to perform a type of multilingualism where understanding the full meaning of the hymn depends on facility with a range of linguistic terms in Urdu, Hindi, Arabic, and Sanskrit. Hindi Christian hymns share other ideas with *bhakti* traditions.[119] A recurring theme in popular Hindi Christian hymns, for instance, recalls sacrifice and surrender. A devotee brings herself to Christ, surrenders, seeks, shelter, and receives freedom or *mukti* from time and death. Consider these examples:

I.

Dil merā le le, pyāre yīśu,	Take my heart, O dear Jesus,
tūne ise banāyā hai,	You are the one who has made it,
ismeṁ tu apnā ghar banā le,	Make in it [now] your own house,
jiske liye hī yah banāyā hai.	For this only it was made.
Pavitr ātmā kā yeh ho bhavan,	May the Holy Spirit[120] live here,
agni ke baptismā se,	By the baptism of fire,
har jagah, har samay dūṁ gavāhī,	Everywhere, always, may I witness,
jaisā yeh usne sikhāyā hai.	Just as He has taught this.
	(Number 311; anonymous composer)

II.

Yīśu tu ne kiyā nihāl, jab maiṁ śaraṇ meṁ terī āyā.
Jesus, you freed me, when I came under your refuge.

Yīśu ākar tere dwār, barkat pāī beśumār,
kripā terī huī apār, mere dil kā mail miṭāyā.

Jesus, having reached your door, countless blessings I received,
Your mercy was unbound, as it cleaned my dirty heart.

. . .

Jo terī śaraṇ meṁ āe, vah pāpoṁ se bac jāye,
man meṁ pāvan ātmā āe, isko maiṁne hai ājmāyā.

He who comes to your refuge, from his sins he is saved,
He receives the Holy Spirit, in this witness I have shared.

Hai dās terā viśvāsī, kāṭī tūne kāl kī phāṁsī,
dhan-dhan amar lok ke vāsī, darśan maiṁne terā pāyā.

Your believer is a servant, you have cut the noose of time,
Blessed-blessed those in heaven, your vision I have received.
(Number 282; lyrics and tune by Premdas)

In the context of *bhakti* and of Hindu religious vocabulary, *pāp* refers to sin, evil, wickedness, or a wrong.[121] In *bhakti*, one turns to God to seek liberation from the effects of sin, which are generally understood as forms of self-attachment, mistaken desires, or evil acts. The effects of such evil and sin can keep one bound to life and the cycle of rebirths. As a describer of sin and evil, the word *pāp* – along with its antonym *puṇy* (meritorious, auspicious) – functions in both Christian and Hindu circles. It is common in Hindi hymns to beseech Christ for safety and a personal relationship:

Bolo jay milkar jay	Sing his praise, join his praise
bolo jay yīśu kī jay.	Sing his praise Jesus' praise.
Bolo jay, jay, jay.	Sing his praise, praise, praise.
Prem tere kī yahī rīt:	Tis' the nature of your love:
Man meṁ bhar de terī prīt,	Fills one's heart with your love,
tere prem ke gāyeṁ gīt.	We sing songs of your love.
Khidmat apnī le mujh se,	Take from me your service [Lord]
is mandir meṁ tū hī base,	In this temple may you stay,
jag me terā nām phaile.	May the world hear your name.

(Number 47; anonymous composer)

With *bhakti* literature, Christian hymns further share an erotic terminology. Mirabai is well-known for her love-filled songs directed at Krishna, her playmate and lover.[122] Christian hymns recall the lover's relationship that exists between Christ and his *bhakt* in comparable terms and suggest a two-way relationship in which a devotee surrenders to Christ and is at the receiving end of Christ's love. Consider this Hindi translation of a German Lutheran hymn:

Maiṁ prem apār ko nit sarāhtā	I always praise the love unbound
jo yīśu tujh se prakaṭ hai,	That appears from you, O Lord,
aur apne ko samarpit kartā	And I surrender myself
tujh ko jo merā premī hai.	To you who's my lover [Lord].

Tū mujhse kaisī prītī rakhtā!	How it is that you love me!
Man terā mujhko cāhtā hai.	You are in love with me.
Is prem se sab prabhāvit hotā	This love changes everything
vah jo kuch mere bhītar hai.	That which is inside of me.
He prem asēm jo swarg se āyā	O love unbound who came from heaven
maiṁ terā hūṁ, tū mujh ko bhāyā.	I am yours and in love with you.

(Number 7; original German, lyrics by Gerhard Tersteegen, tune by Dimitri Bortniansky, Hindi translator unknown)

The lovers' relationship described in Hymn 7 does not exist in a vacuum. It complements communal forms of worship. The relationship of *bhakt* communities to the singer saints of India is complicated. *Nirguna bhakti*, Hawley and Juergensmeyer note, is not readily hospitable to institutions, temples, priests, and structures. The resistance of *nirguna* poets to organized religion typified in the poetry of Kabir was particularly attractive to those seeking to escape structures of caste and creed.[123] Kabir's critique of Hinduism and Islam on one hand and his relationship with a community of listeners and yogis who rejected Hindu hierarchies on the other, however, reflects the very concrete ways in which society and politics impact religious practices.

Christian devotion is imprinted with the Christological core embedded in Hindi hymns. As one consequence of this imprint, Christian Hindi hymns are clearly not devotionally 'layered' with primary and secondary deities as can be found in *bhakti bhajans*. While local healers and saints do figure in devotional schemes, Hindi Christian sources are distinct from *bhakti* devotionals in their exclusive devotion to Jesus. The Christological core has also led to the dominance of *saguna* forms of devotion rather than *nirguna* forms of devotion in the body of Hindi devotionals.[124] Key features of *nirguna* and *saguna* devotions like longing, community, refuge, love, and surrender are nevertheless part of some of the most well-known Hindi Christian hymns.

Bhakti traditions pay attention to the relationship between teacher and disciples. In concrete terms, the values and practices of a worshipping community are passed down from teacher to teacher. Such teachers depend on their community of disciples to manifest the teachings and devotion to God. The worshipping community is the site of religious expressions, growth, and transmission. The Kabir *panth* has valued the transmission of faith and worship from *gurus* to disciples.[125] Mira's songs are best experienced in "the company of other worshippers."[126] Or, in the words of a famous Hindi Christian hymn:

Dhanyavād sadā prabhu khrist tujhe	We give thanks to you always Jesus Christ,
tere sanmukh śīś navāte haiṁ,	We bow our heads before you,
hum terī Ārādhănā karne ko	To worship you [and sing your praise]
mandir meṁ tere āte haiṁ.	We gather in your temple.

Dhany vīrom̐ kā is maṇḍlī ke,	Give thanks for the brave ones of this church
tere nām par jo balīdān hue,	Those who martyred in your name,
hum unke sāhas tyāg ko le	Taking on their valor and sacrifice
nity āge baṛhte jāte haim̐.	We keep on moving [boldly] ahead.

(Number 22; original Hindi, lyrics by M. R. Utarid, tune by Goodwin R, Utarid)

Hindi Christian hymns and *bhakti* devotionals echo a variety of themes. These themes include a strong personal bond between God and devotee, a two-way relationship with mutual obligations, personal devotion in the context of and as part of larger communities of worship, and a certain exclusivity in a devotee's focus on a supreme deity who meets her need for love and salvation. The cultural milieu of Hindi Christian works has been shaped by ideas other than the motifs found in *bhakti* traditions.

The Indian subcontinent has a long history of Christian scholarship and this history can be traced to India's earliest Christian communities in the first century CE. Early trade routes and later colonial expansions brought converts in contact with Christian communities outside the subcontinent. Hindi Christian literature exists as part of this Christian milieu in the subcontinent. However, it seems that Indian Christian scholarship has minimally interacted with Hindi Christian materials. While the influence of Western authors on Hindi Christian writers is evident, Hindi Christian writers have for the most part ignored Indian Christian scholarship in other languages. Hindi Christian writers may have engaged their Western predecessors but a study of Hindi Christian materials reveals that Indian Christian scholarship in other languages has not been an influential partner of Hindi Christian writing in the way Western scholarship has. Let us look at two examples.

The bibliography of Dayal's popular Hindi-language textbook on Christianity (published in 2005) presents a list of 74 books. Eleven of the 74 are by Indian authors. Western sources dominate the list, led by the works of D. M. Baillie, Karl Barth, Emil Brunner, Mircea Eliade, David Ford, John Hick, John McQuarrie, Reinhold Niebuhr, Karl Rahner, and Paul Tillich. Only five of the 11 Indian-authored books are in Hindi. In a widely-used Hindi-language textbook, then, only 6.7 percent sources are in Hindi. Other Hindi-language textbooks do not fare any better. The 23-book bibliography of Masih and Peter's *Prabhu Yeśu kī Jīvanī aur Sevākāry* (2007) lists only one Indian author – the rest are from the West. All its sources are in English. The 30-book bibliography of Khan's Christian ethics, *Khristīy Nītiśāstr* (2009), lists only two books by Indian authors (one by H.H. Titus, another by Joseph Vadakumcherry). Again, all its sources are also in English. What explains this state of affairs? Are Hindi Christian writers generally unaware of Indian Christian sources in English or other languages? Do Hindi Christian authors have limited access to translated editions of non-Hindi sources (assuming they are restricted to the use of Hindi)? Are non-Hindi sources from India unhelpful and hence underutilized on purpose?

An analysis of the interactions between Indian Christian theology and Hindi Christian scholarship sheds light on these questions. Missionary theologians like Robin Boyd, William Barclay, and John Webster were aware of local theological works and found in Indian Christian theology a familiarity with their personal ideas and vocabulary. A sense of familiarity created the impression that Indian Christian theologies were vernacular expressions of their Western concepts. Boyd laments this perceived state of affairs in his 1969 dissertation on Indian Christian theology. The question of whether Boyd and his compatriots had understood Indian theology on its own terms was yet to emerge as a necessary query. Rather, the conventional wisdom of the day understood Indian Christianity as an echo of missionary expressions. Capturing the popular point of view, Boyd writes:

> There is no doubt that to an outside observer the Church in India seems to be dominated by Western attitudes and modes of thought. In church architecture, church organization, church services, church music and church publications, Western forms and attitudes still seem to predominate. . . . Again, the teaching given in theological colleges throughout India has been, and still is, dominated by Western theology, as a glance at any syllabus will show. The result is that the preaching of the average Indian minister or evangelist reflects the Western theological categories in which he has been trained.[127]

Western categories did not influence Indian Christianity exclusively. Sanskrit motifs and upper-caste Hinduism also shaped Indian Christian works in English. In the nineteenth and twentieth centuries, many of the pioneers of Indian Christian thoughts were upper-caste Hindu converts or Hindu reformers like Krishna Mohan Banerjee (1813–1885), Pandita Ramabai (1858–1922), Brahmabandhab Upadhyay (1861–1907), Keshub Chandra Sen (1838–1884), and A. J. Appasamy (1848–1926). Their influence led to what Arvind Nirmal has called a Brahmanic turn in Indian Christian theology. Nirmal explains:

> Broadly speaking, Indian Christian theology in the past has tried to work out its theological systems in terms of either *advaita Vedanta* or *vishishta advaita*. Most of the contributions of Indian Christian theology in the past came from caste converts to Christianity. The result has been that Indian Christian theology has perpetuated within itself what I prefer to call the 'Brahmanic' tradition. . . . To speak in terms of traditional Indian categories, Indian Christian theology, following the Brahmanic tradition, has trodden the *jnana marga*, the *bhakti marga* and the *karma marga*. In Brahma Bandhav Upadhyay, we have a brilliant theologian who attempted a synthesis of Sankara's *Advaita Vedanta* with

> Christian theology. In Bishop A.J. Appasamy, we have a *bhakti marga* theologian who tried to synthesize Ramanuja's *Vashishtha Advaita* with Christian Theology. In M.M. Thomas we have a theologian who has contributed to theological anthropology at the international level and who laid the foundation for a more active theological involvement in India – the *karma marga*. In Chenchiah we find an attempt to synthesize Christian theology with Sri Aurobindo's 'Integral Yoga'.[128]

Banerjee, who joined the Church of England post-conversion and was an ordained minister and professor at Bishop's College in Calcutta, interpreted Christ as the true *prajāpati* (Lord and Creator) and the true *puruṣ* (both human and divine).[129] Ramabai came from a Maratha Brahmin family and post-conversion tried to combine her Hindu upbringing with her experience of the Holy Spirit.[130] The influence of Sanskrit and the Vedas was not new to nineteenth and twentieth century Indian Christian thought. Roberto de Nobili (1577–1656) learned Tamil and Sanskrit, adopted the life of a *sanyāsi*, tried to establish a seminary with Sanskrit as the medium of instruction, and experimented with Sanskrit as a liturgical language in the church.[131] Other followed in his enculturated footsteps. Evaluations of Indian Christian thought by Hindi authors have faulted it in both its Westernized and Sanskritic content.[132]

Hindi Christian literature is neither Brahmanic in construct nor Vedantic in content. It reflects a general distaste for Sanskritic ideas and idioms. It embraces a commitment to economic development, social mobility, and the abolition of caste- and gender-based discriminations. The demography of Hindi Christianity – made up mostly by Dalits, tribal, and rural converts[133] – partly explains this outcome. Hindu reformers of the nineteenth century wanted to identify ideas like love, equality, and grace as shared motifs with Hinduism in their quest to reform caste practices and gender relations. M. M. Thomas, V. S. Azariah, and Paul D. Devanandan spoke for many Christians in newly-Independent India when they invited church communities to dedicate themselves to nation building, interfaith harmony, and close alliances with civil society. S. J. Samartha (1920–2001), George M. Soares Prabhu (1929–1995), Dhyanchand Carr (1938–), Renthy Keitzar (1936–2000), Aruna Gnanadason (1949–), Monica Jyotsna Melanchthon (1962–), and James Massey (1943–), among others, have produced works that address the needs of church and society, tribal issues, inter-religious dialogue, gender empowerment, ecumenism, Dalit rights, and ecological care.[134] Hindi Christian authors have been cautious in their engagement of Brahmanic and upper-case ideas.

Debates over the religious meaning of 'Hindi' have shaped the development of Hindi Christian ideas in the context of Hinduism and India. The term's reference to a language was not an issue. Rather, the controversy centered on whether 'Hindi' meant 'Hindu' or 'Indian' when used by Christian authors writing in Hindi. The question played out in the editorial decision over the Hindi title of a translated book. The story unfolds in C.W. David's introduction to Boyd's *An Introduction to Indian Christian Theology* in 1976 and his subsequent introduction to Benjamin Khan's *Bīsvīṁ Śatābdī ke Pramukh Dharmavijñānī* ("Major Christian Theologians of the Twentieth Century") in 1990. In the 1970s, David was the editor-in-chief of the Hindi Theological Literature Committee, Khan a prominent Hindi Christian author, and Boyd a well-respected scholar of Christianity in India. David sparked the conversation when he decided to change the title of the Hindi version of Boyd's book to "Christian Theology in India" instead of maintaining Boyd's original "An Introduction to Indian Christian theology." Explaining his decision, David wrote: "There can be no such thing as Indian Christian theology" because "Christ is universal, beyond every nation."[135] That Christ was universal, however, was not the only argument against describing Boyd's book as a study of Indian Christian theology rather than as a study of Christian theology in India. David preferred a particular feature of Boyd's work and wanted to promote that feature as the core "Indian" aspect of Indian Christian thought.

Two strands dominate Boyd's account of Indian Christianity. One strand focuses on Hindu contributions to the development of Christian thought in India. Boyd draws upon a number of Hindu reformers to explain the content of Indian Christianity and his study is colored by interactions between upper-caste Hindu converts and reformers and emerging Indian Christian scholarship. Boyd's reliance on Hindu-Christian encounters to introduce Indian Christianity gave the impression that Indian Christian thought was, generally speaking, Hindu Christian thought. To balance a reliance on Hindu modes of thinking, Boyd explained Indian Christian thought as the "search for truth" intrinsic to India's religiosity and not specific to any one religious tradition. To tangle with truth was at the heart of "true religious enquiry." In the artful Hindi translation of Boyd's argument, what made Indian Christianity Indian was a Christian's "*saty ke sāth ulajhnā*" ("struggling with truth"), where the truth is Christ. Boyd reminded his readers that the idea of struggling with or searching for truth was a domestic idea, with a rich history, and transcended religions. "To tangle with truth, which is the demand of true religious enquiry, is not a foreign idea for the Indian tradition."[136]

Indian Christian thought is made Indian by its search for truth/Truth. Locating the search for truth at the heart of Christian thought made it truly Indian. Such a Christianity would embrace ethics, engage philosophy, avoid repeating Hindu thoughts, and save Indian Christian thought from merely parroting Western works. "In India today," Boyd explained,

> there is the need for a conduct-based, witness-giving theology. . . . It seems that before becoming the congregation's systematic theology or Indian doctrines it is important to tangle with the Christian revelation

and biblical witness in order to understand their internal meaning and structure.[137]

David sought to promote the struggle for truth in Boyd's account of Indian Christianity and wanted to minimize Boyd's dependence on Hindu thought. To this end, David renames Boyd's work as 'Christian theology in India.' "The author," David explains, "has provided a 'definition of Indian Christian theology' in the thirteenth chapter of the book. We accept 'Indian Christian theology' in that sense."[138]

Other Hindi Christian authors picked up on David's discomfort with characterizing Boyd's work as an accurate depiction of Indian Christian thinking. Benjamin Khan uses theologies in English by Western authors of the twentieth century to introduce Western Christian thoughts to Hindi readers. Khan's methodology stands in contrast with Boyd's. Boyd used theologies in English influenced by Hindu-Christian debates to characterize Indian Christian thought. Khan's book is aimed at a broad Hindi Christian audience: seminarians, pastors, educators, authors, and general readers. He was motivated by a lack of good Christian sources available in Hindi. Khan explained,

> Many readers who go to seminary to study religion are maybe not competent enough in English to fully understand those books on Christian-literature that are written in English. In the same way, an average Christian also remains ignorant about schools of thought in Christian literature beyond the Bible because he does not have available in the mother tongue any book whose study allows him to learn about the primary schools of thought in Christian theology. I have been feeling this void for a very long time.[139]

Khan clarifies his intention to introduce Hindi readers to Western Christian thought in simple terms accessible to a general reader. "As far as language in concerned," he further writes, "I have tried to present the thoughts in very simple language."[140] Clarity regarding his task and sources allows David to encourage his readers to find new ways to present Christian theology in terms of India's context. He invites his readers to "think anew in the cultural context of India and to present Christian theology in terms of the religion and ethics here [in India's context]."[141]

"Indian theology" – a term Khan uses in *Bīsvīṁ Śatābdī ke Pramukh Dharmavijñānī* in 1990 – should introduce the incarnated, risen Christ in ways that makes sense to the developing world. "Jesus Christ," Khan argues,

> is this Word of God who incarnated, who united humans with God in his life, death, and resurrection. Such a presentation of this Christ is necessary that can be acceptable to today's human, who wants to be

> self-reliant on the basis of her intelligence and advances in science and who has attained maturity.[142]

Khan finds Boyd's work lacking in its presentation of Indian (Christian) theology. He explains:

> We have studied Boyd's 'Indian Christian theology.' At the same time, some works and a book have also been published on Dalit theology. It is our humble belief that writing Indian Christian theology in English can only lead to the false use of Indian categories of thought. It is our hope that in the near future Indian scholars and thinkers will emerge who will write systematic theologies that could be truly called Christian theologies.[143]

Khan's review of Boyd is harsh. It claims a schism between the English language and Indian thought that is rather hard to defend. Nevertheless, Khan's comments clarify the debate on the meaning of 'Christian' in Hindi Christian sources. The Hindu tinge of Boyd's Indian Christianity can be explained as a function of the paucity of Indian Christian sources that avoid Hindu categories. It is less a function of Boyd's methodology. Boyd's selection of Indian Christian sources takes him to the Hindu worldview. David and Khan find Boyd's portrayal of 'Indian Christian' thought problematic for different but overlapping reasons. Their discomfort is symbolic of the general suspicion with which Hindi Christian authors approach Indian Christian scholarship. The desire to Indianize and Hindify Christian claims without Hinduizing them is driving this suspicion.

Notes

1 What follows is found in Carey's 'Journal' and all quotes are from the original copy of the Journal held under copyright at the Angus Library, Regent's Park College, University of Oxford. Quotations are used with the permission of the Angus Library and Archive, Regent's Park College. The 'Journal' is also transcribed in the *Memoir of William Carey* by his nephew, Eustace Carey.

2 The work in Serampore depended on local clerks and assistants. Munshis and missionaries were not equals. Missionaries were *sahib* ("master") and munshis servants. For a study of *mumśīs* and their *sāhibs*, see Das, *Sahibs and Munshis* (1978).

3 Carey's 'Journal,' 11–12. A note on the Journal's front page reads: "A Journal kept by Mr. Carey from June 1793 (the time of his leaving Europe) to June 1975, with a Letter to Mr. Pearce in Oct. 1795."

4 Jonathan, *Biśap*, 71: "*[Śrī kṛṣṇa kānt] ek acche vidvān, ucc koṭi ke rājanītijñ aur rāṣṭrīy ekīkaraṇ evam sāmpradāyik samanvay kī kāmanā karne vāle netā haiṁ.*"

English translations and transliterations of Devanāgarī Hindi are mine, unless noted otherwise. Proper nouns are reproduced following common usage or published forms. As readers may lack access to Hindi source materials, the book includes English transliterations of all Hindi quotations. Translations attend to context and intent. As a result, in some cases the translations are not literal in nature. As an instance, *bolo* literally means 'say' (imperative). In the context of

Hindi Christian hymns, however, *bolo* is better translated as 'sing,' as in 'sing praise' rather than 'say praise.'

5 Jonathan, *Biśap*, 71: "*Masīhī samāj aur masīhī aguve sarvādhik prabuddh haiṁ. [Mānanīy rājyapāl kā āgrah thā ki] sab prakār kā masīhī śubh samācār pracāry kāry aur dharmparivartan svecchā se kam se kam pacās varṣoṁ ke liye band kar diyā jāe.*"

6 Jonathan, *Biśap*, 71: "*Śubh samācār pracār kā arth kyā hai? Kyā yah parameśvar ke prem ko dūsroṁ ke sāth bāṁṭnā hai?*"

7 Jonathan, *Biśap*, 71: "*Kyā hamne un logoṁ ko, jo kalīsiyā ke bāhar haiṁ, galat saṅket die haiṁ?*"

8 Bauman, *Pentecostals, Proselytization, and Anti-Christian Violence.*

9 Hasan, "The Myth of Unity," 185–186.

10 Fox, "Hindu Nationalism," 67–68.

11 Fox, "Hindu Nationalism," 71–72.

12 King, *One Language, Two Scripts*, 127–128, 144–145.

13 Pandey, *The Construction of Communalism*, 216–217.

14 Khalidi, "Hinduising India."

15 Raghavendra, *The Politics of Hindi Cinema*, xxvii–xxviii.

16 Doniger, *The Hindus*, 106–107.

17 Truschke, *Culture of Encounters.*

18 Orsini, *Before the Divide*; Hakala, *Negotiating Languages.*

19 They include, outside of India, Arun W. Jones (Dan and Lillian Hankey Associate Professor of World Evangelism, Candler/Emory) and Timothy C. Tennent (President, Asbury Theological Seminary). In India, key scholars who have engaged Hindi Christian materials include John H. Anand (Editor, Hindi Theological Literature Committee), Ravi Tiwari (Registrar, Senate of Serampore), and Din Dayal (Former Moderator, Church of North India).

20 Shukla, *Hindī Sāhity kā Itihās* and Hawley, *Three Bhakti Voices.*

21 Hawley and Juergensmeyer, *Songs of the Saints of India*; Hawley, *Three Bhakti Voices*; Thiel-Horstmann, *Bhakti in Current Research, 1979–1982*; Horstmann, *Bhakti in Current Research, 2001–2003*; Hopkins, *Singing the Body of God*; Malik, *Hindi Poetry Today*; Schomer, *Mahadevi Varma*; Schomer and McLeod, *The Sant Tradition of India*; and Hansen, *Grounds for Play*. Catalogues of Hindi literature are also available, from Blumhardt's colonial-era *Catalogues of the Hindi, Panjabi, Sindhi, and Pushtu Printed Books in the Library of the British Museum* (1893) to McGregor's *Hindi Literature of the Nineteenth and Early Twentieth Centuries* (1974).

22 Dandekar, *The Subhedar's Son*; and ibid., "Pilgrimage, Authority and Subversion."

23 This is not an exhaustive list but it captures the major types of Hindi Christian works.

24 Tiwari, *Hindī Bhāṣā kā Udgam*, 104ff.

25 Tiwari, *Hindī Bhāṣā kā Udgam*, 104: "*Ataḥ 'deśī bhāṣā' jan-bhāṣā kā hī nām hai aur jis kāl evam sthān meṁ jo bhāṣā is pad par āsīn rahī, vah is nām se abhihit huī.*"

26 Tiwari, *Hindī Bhāṣā kā Udgam*, 135.

27 Van der Veer, *Religious Nationalism*, 170.

28 Masica, *The Indo-Aryan Languages*, 27.

29 Quoted in Singh, *Hindī Bhāṣā*, 21.

30 Masica, *The Indo-Aryan Languages*, 50–51.

31 For what follows, see Chatterji, *Indo-Aryan and Hindi*, 6–28, 156–197.

32 Flood, *An Introduction to Hinduism*, 33–34.

33 McGregor, "The Rise of Standard Hindi," 115–117, 131.

34 Chatterji, *Indo-Aryan and Hindi*, 131–154.

35 McGregor, "The Progress of Hindi," 913–914, 945–948. See also Orsini, *Before the Divide*, 7.

36 Van der Veer, *Religious Nationalism*, 166.
37 Tiwari, *Hindī Bhāṣā kā Udgam*, 147.
38 For instance, see Pollock, *The Language of the Gods*.
39 Monier-Williams, *A Sanskrit-English Dictionary*, 493.
40 Tiwari, *Hindī Bhāṣā kā Udgam*, 440.
41 Masica, *The Indo-Aryan Languages*, 27.
42 McGregor, *The Oxford Hindi-English Dictionary*, vii.
43 Dalmia, *The Nationalization of Hindu Traditions*.
44 Orsini, *Before the Divide*; Shackle and Snell, *Hindi and Urdu since 1800*; Hakala, *Negotiating Languages*.
45 Dalmia, *The Nationalization of Hindu Traditions*.
46 Orsini, *The Hindi Public Sphere 1920–1940*.
47 McGregor, "The Progress of Hindi," 913.
48 www.censusindia.gov.in/Census_Data_2001/Census_Data_Online/Language/Statement1.htm. India's national population in 2001 stood at 1.028 billion (www.censusindia.gov.in/Census_Data_2001/). Data from the 2011 Census has not been released yet.
49 Studies of vernacular Christian materials in cognate languages like Awadhī will further enrich this study of Hindi Christian literature, but such studies are beyond the scope of this work.
50 Office of the Registrar, "Statement-1: Abstract of Speakers' Strength," 6.
51 Office of the Registrar, "Part-1: Distribution of the 22 Scheduled Languages," 24.
52 Office of the Registrar, "Statement-7: Growth of Scheduled Languages," 16.
53 Office of the Registrar, "Statement-5: Comparative Speakers' Strength," 18.
54 KPMG, "Indian Languages," 7.
55 KPMG, "Indian Languages," 2.
56 Christopher Shackle and Rupert Snell identify the area across North India from Rajasthan to Bihar as the 'Hindi area.' Shackle and Snell, *Hindu and Urdu Since 1800*, 13.
57 Masica has a similar, if dated, map: he places the Union Territory of Delhi and the Indian states of Uttar Pradesh, Bihar, Madhya Pradesh, Rajasthan, Haryana, and Himachal Pradesh in the 'Hindi area.' Masica, *The Indo-Aryan Languages*, 9.
58 Ethnographic and textual data from field research in 2010–2011, partly funded by the South Asia Institute at Harvard, covered central and north Indian collections, including those at the Hindi Theological Literature Committee (Jabalpur) and Indian Society for Promoting Christian Knowledge (Delhi). I collated literature on translation history and theories concerning Hindi scriptures and conducted interviews with practitioners and scholars in Delhi, Nagpur, Jabalpur, and Damoh. A research assistant from India visited and accessed the archives of the Methodist publishing house in Lucknow and the Lutheran publishing house in Chhindwara responsible for considerable Hindi Christian literature in the region.
59 The Committee was led by Rev. Dr. John H. Anand, who served as the Committee's Editor and Publisher. Anand is an ordained priest of the Church of North India. Born of a Muslim mother and a Hindu father, both of whom were Dalits, Anand converted to Christianity under the influence of an American Methodist missionary. Formally trained in Hindi literature and theology, Anand has approximately sixty books to his credit. He has served as Editorial Secretary of both the Indian Society for the Promotion of Christian Knowledge and the Bible Society of India and as professor at Satyaniketan Theological College. Anand has translated the New Hindi Bible from the original Hebrew and Greek for the Bible Society of India. He has also translated the Book of Worship of the Church of North India and The Ecumenical Hindi *Pavitr Bāibil* (Holy Bible).
60 See, for instance, Kunnatholy, *St. Thomas Christians*.
61 Evans, *Kaise Pāyā Muktidātā*, 10–11.

62 Hooper, *A Welshman in India*, 162.
63 Eck, *Banaras*.
64 For what follows, see Dalmia, *The Nationalization of Hindu Traditions*.
65 Dalmia, *The Nationalization of Hindu Traditions*, 108.
66 Dalmia, *The Nationalization of Hindu Traditions*, 110.
67 Dalmia, *The Nationalization of Hindu Traditions*, 144.
68 *Conference on Urdu and Hindi Christian Literature*, 46.
69 http://scholar.harvard.edu/files/rakeshpeterdass/files/hindi_catalogue_1917.pdf.
70 http://scholar.harvard.edu/files/rakeshpeterdass/files/hindi_theological_writings_bibliography_H.T.L.C.pdf.
71 England et al., *Asian Christian Theologies*.
72 England et al., *Asian Christian Theologies*, 331–332.
73 England et al., *Asian Christian Theologies*, 401.
74 England et al., *Asian Christian Theologies*, 272–273.
75 England et al., *Asian Christian Theologies*, 217.
76 Amaladoss, "Foreword 1," xvi.
77 England et al., *Asian Christian Theologies*, xxiv.
78 Bauman and Young, *Constructing Indian Christianities*, xiii.
79 Sinha, *Masīhī Ācaraṇ*, ii (*kh*): "*Hindī masīhī sāhity kā durbhāgy hai ki uske pāṭhak bahut kam hai. . . . Hindī bhāṣiyoṁ se āgrah hai ki ve jāgeṁ aur acchī pustakoṁ ko paḍhne se apnī badnāmī ko dūr kareṁ aur prabuddh hoṁ.*"
80 *Ārādhănā ke Gīt*, iii: "*Masīhī gīt sangrah meṁ vartamān bhāratīy racnāoṃ kī kamī, kliṣṭ pāścāty racnāoṃ kā ādhiky, aur saral, spaṣṭ aur vartamān pracalit bhāṣā kā abhāv khalne lagā thā.*"
81 *Ārādhănā ke Gīt*, i.
82 *Ārādhănā ke Gīt* [Music Edition], iii.
83 Anand's Preface in Sinha, *Masīhī Ācaraṇ*: "*Hindī kśetroṁ ke thiyolājikal kalejoṁ ke prinsipal, carc ke biśap, pāsṭar, prakāśan saṃsthāeṁ, hamārī pustakoṁ ke vitrak, borḍs, miśnarī saṃsthāeṁ hamārī bharsak madad kartī haiṁ.*"
84 Raj, "The Ganges, the Jordon, and the Mountain," 41.
85 San Chirico, "Between Christian and Hindu," 23–28.
86 Narayanan, "Afterword: Diverse Hindu Responses," 260.
87 Dempsey, "Lessons in Miracles from Kerala," 128–133.
88 Flood, *An Introduction to Hinduism*, 14.
89 Cf., Assmann, *Monotheismus*, 10; cited in Malinar, *The Bhagavadgītā*, 7, 238.
90 Malinar, *The Bhagavadgītā*, 7–9, 237–238.
91 Nasr, *The Study Quran*, 664–665.
92 Ernst, *Following Muhammad*, 118.
93 Lumbard, "The Quranic View of Sacred History," 1766–1769.
94 Raj and Dempsey, "Introduction," 5.
95 Raj and Dempsey, *Popular Christianity in India*; Young, *India and the Indianness of Christianity*; Bauman and Young, *Constructing Indian Christianities*.
96 Mosse, *The Saint in the Banyan Tree*, 27–28, 284.
97 Bowen, *Religion in Practice*, 125.
98 Hawley and Juergensmeyer, *Songs of the Saints*, 7.
99 Eck, *Darśan*, 16.
100 Schelling, *The Oxford Anthology of Bhakti Literature*, xvi.
101 Monier-Williams, *A Sanskrit-English Dictionary*, 743. For the dates, see Doniger, *The Hindus*, 693.
102 Lipner, *The Face of Truth*, 112–115; Bartley, *The Theology of Rāmānuja*, 78–79.
103 Bartley, *The Theology of Rāmānuja*, 79.
104 Schelling, *The Oxford Anthology of Bhakti Literature*, xvii–xix.
105 Kulandran, "Christian Faith and Hindu Bhakti," 118–121.
106 Hawley, *Three Bhakti Voices*, 105. Translated by Hawley.

107 Scott, "Hindu and Christian *Bhakti*," 12.
108 Scott, "Hindu and Christian *Bhakti*," 21–22.
109 Schelling, *The Oxford Anthology of Bhakti Literature*, xiv.
110 Chakrabarty, *Provincializing Europe*, 231–232 and Raychaudhuri, *Europe Reconsidered*, 88–89, cited in Pinch, "*Bhakti* and the British Empire," 167.
111 Pinch, "*Bhakti* and the British Empire," 176–177.
112 Pinch, "*Bhakti* and the British Empire," 178–179.
113 Jones, *Missionary Christianity*, xx–xxi.
114 Jones, *Missionary Christianity*, 8–16.
115 Jones, *Missionary Christianity*, 275.
116 Hymn numbers are from *Ārādhǎnā ke Gīt*.
117 *Ārādhǎnā ke Gīt*, "Topical Index," 1.
118 McGregor, *The Oxford Hindi-English Dictionary*, 1069.
119 For an analysis of the interplay of *bhakti* motifs and social hierarchies in Tamil Christian hymns, see Israel, *Religious Transactions in Colonial South India* (2011). Israel's work on Tamil hymns is also summarized in a 2014 article, "Authority, Patronage and Customary Practices."
120 'Holy Spirit' is the typical Hindi translation of *pavitr ātmā*.
121 McGregor, *The Oxford Hindi-English Dictionary*, 623.
122 Hawley and Juergensmeyer, *Songs of the Saints of India*; Hawley, *Three Bhakti Voices*.
123 Hawley and Juergensmeyer, *Songs of the Saints*, 42–45.
124 *Nirguna* forms of devotion address God without qualities, form, or attributes (from *nir-guna*, without qualities or attributes). *Saguna bhakti* is directed to God with attributes and qualities (from *sa-guna*, with qualities or attributes).
125 Hawley and Juergensmeyer, *Songs of the Saints*, 44–47.
126 Hawley and Juergensmeyer, *Songs of the Saints*, 129.
127 Boyd, *An Introduction to Indian Christian Theology*, 1–2.
128 Nirmal in Massey, *Indigenous Peoples, Dalits*, 215. To note, by "caste converts" Nirmal means upper caste converts.
129 Banerjee, *The Relation Between Christianity and Hinduism*, cited in England et al., *Asian Christian Theologies*, 211–212.
130 Ramabai, *A Testimony*, cited in England et al., *Asian Christian Theologies*, 212–213.
131 Rajamanickam, *Roberto de Nobili on Adaptation* and Arokiasamy, *Dharma, Hindu and Christian*, in England et al., *Asian Christian Theologies*, 206–207.
132 Thomas, "Introduction," v.
133 See, Clarke, *Dalits and Christianity* and Massey, *Dalits in India*.
134 England et al., *Asian Christian Theologies*, 189–192.
135 David's preface in Boyd, *Bhārat meṁ Masīhī Dharmavijñān*, ix: "*Bhāratīy khristīy dharmavijñān jaisī koī cīz nahīṁ ho saktī [kyoṁki] khrist sarvalaukik hai, kisī bhī rāṣṭr se pare hai.*"
136 Boyd, *Bhārat meṁ Masīhī Dharmavijñān*, 162: "*Saty ke sāth ulajhnā, jo sacī dharmasaiddhāntikī kī māṁg hai, bhāratīy paramparā ke liye videśī bāt nahīṁ hai.*"
137 Boyd, *Bhārat meṁ Masīhī Dharmavijñān*, 163: "*Bhārat meṁ āj vyāvahārik, sākṣī dene vāle dharmavijñān kī āvaśyakatā hai . . . Esā pratīt hotā hai ki kalīsiyā kā vyavavastit dharmavijñān athavā bhāratīy viśvāskathan banne ke pahle yah āvaśyak hai ki khristīy prakāśan aur bāibalī sākṣy se uljhā jāe tāki unke āntarik arth aur āntarik saṃracanā ko samjhā jā sake.*"
138 David's preface in Boyd, *Bhārat meṁ Masīhī Dharmavijñān*, ix: "*Lekhak ne pustak ke terhaveṁ addhyāy meṁ 'bhāratīy khristīy dharmavijñān kī paribhāṣā' dī hai. Us arth meṁ ham 'bhāratīy khristīy dharmavijñān' ko svīkār karte haiṁ.*"

139 Khan, *Bīsvīṁ Śatābdī ke Pramukh Dharmavijñānī*, xi: "*Bahut se pāṭhak jo semanarī meṁ dharm adhyayan ke liye jāte haiṁ ve śāyad aṁgrezī bhāṣā meṁ itne nipuṇ nahīṁ hote ki masīhī-sāhity par aṁgrezī meṁ likhī pustakoṁ kā pūrī samajh ke sāth adhyayan kar sakeṁ. Isī prakār sādhāraṇ masīhī bhī bāibal ke atirikt any masīhī sāhity kī vicārdhārāoṁ se anabhijñ rahtā hai kyoṁki use mātṛbhāṣā meṁ koī eisī pustak upalabdh nahīṁ jis ke adhyayan se vah masīhī dharmavijñān kī pramukh vicārdhārāoṁ ko paḍh sake. Is riktatā ko maiṁ kāfī lambe samay se mahasūs kar rahā thā.*"

140 Khan, *Bīsvīṁ Śatābdī ke Pramukh Dharmavijñānī*, xii: "*Bhāṣā kā jahāṁ tak sambandh hai, maiṁne vicāroṁ ko bahut saral bhāṣā meṁ vyakt karne kā prayās kiyā hai.*"

141 David's preface in Khan, *Bīsvīṁ Śatābdī ke Pramukh Dharmavijñānī*, ix: "*[P]reraṇā bhī prāpt hogī ki ve bhārat ke saṃskṛtik pariveś meṁ nayā cintan kareṁ aur yahāṁ ke dharm aur karm siddhānt kī vicār koṭiyoṁ meṁ masīhī dharmavijñān ko prastut bhī kareṁ.*"

142 Khan, *Bīsvīṁ Śatābdī ke Pramukh Dharmavijñānī*, 211: "*Yah īśvar kā śabd yīśu masīh hai jo dehadhāri huā, jisne apne jīvan, mṛtyu aur punarutthān meṁ manuśy kā īśvar se milāp karāyā. Is masīh ka eisā prastutikaraṇ āvaśyak hai jo āj ke manuśy ko, jo apnī buddhi aur vijñān kī naī naī khojoṁ ko dvārā ātm nirbhar honā cāhtā hai aur paripakv avasthā ko prāpt kar cukā hai, māny ho.*"

143 Khan, *Bīsvīṁ Śatābdī ke Pramukh Dharmavijñānī*, 213–214: "*Hamne bāuyaḍ ke granth 'inḍiyan kriściyan thiyāuloji' kā adhyayan kiyā. Idhar dalit dharmavijñān par bhī kucch lekh aur ek pustak prakāśit huī hai. Hamārī vinamr mānyatā hai ki aṁgrezī meṁ bhāratīy khristīy dharmavijñān likhne meṁ bhāratīy vicār koṭiyṁ kā jūṭhā prayog hī ho saktā hai. Hamārī āśā hai ki nikaṭ bhavisy meṁ bhāratīy vidvān evam cintak paidā hoṁge jo vyavasthit dharmavijñān likheṁge jise vāstav meṁ masīhī dharmavijñān kahā jā sakegā.*"

References

Amaladoss, Michael. "Foreword 1." In *Asian Christian Theologies: A Research Guide to Authors, Movements, Sources*. Volume 1: *Asia Region 7th – 20th Centuries; South Asia; Austral Asia*, edited by John C. England, Jose Kuttianimattathil, John Mansford Prior, Lily A. Quintos, David Suh Kwang-sun, and Janice Wickeri. Delhi: Indian Society for Promoting Christian Knowledge, 2002.

Ārādhănā ke Gīt [Songs of Worship]. Lucknow: Lucknow Publishing House, 2009 [1975].

Arokiasamy, Soosai. *Dharma, Hindu and Christian, According to Roberto de Nobili: Analysis of its meaning and its use in Hinduism and Christianity*. Rome: Editrice Pontificia Universita Gregoriana, 1986.

Assmann, Jan. *Monotheismus und Kosmotheismus: Ägyptische Former eines 'Denkens des Einen' und ihre europäische Rezeptionsgeschichte*. Heidelberg: Winter, 1993.

Banerjee, Krishna Mohan. *The Relation Between Christianity and Hinduism. Papers for Thoughtful Hindus*. Madras: The Christian Literature Society, 1892.

Bartley, Christopher J. *The Theology of Rāmānuja: Realism and Religion*. London: Routledge, 2002.

Bauman, Chad M. *Pentecostals, Proselytization, and Anti-Christian Violence in Contemporary India*. New York: Oxford University Press, 2015.

Bauman, Chad M. and Richard Fox Young, eds. *Constructing Indian Christianities: Culture, Conversion and Caste*. New Delhi: Routledge, 2014.

Blumhardt, James Fuller. *Catalogues of the Hindi, Panjabi, Sindhi, and Pushtu Printed Books in the Library of the British Museum*. London: British Museum, 1893.

Bowen, John R. *Religion in Practice: An Approach to the Anthropology of Religion*, fourth edition. Boston: Pearson, 2008.

Boyd, Robin H.S. *An Introduction to Indian Christian Theology*. Madras: The Christian Literature Society, 1975 [1969].

Boyd, Robin H.S. *Bhārat meṃ Masīhī Dharmavijñān* [An Introduction to Indian Christian Theology]. Jabalpur: Hindi Theological Literature Committee, 1976 [1969].

Carey, Eustace. *Memoir of William Carey*. London: Jackson and Walford, 1836.

Carey, William. 'Journal.' Regent's Park College, Oxford: Angus Library and Archive, 1795.

Chakrabarty, Dipesh. *Provincializing Europe: Postcolonial Thought and Historical Difference*. Princeton: Princeton University Press, 2000.

Chatterji, Suniti Kumar. *Indo-Aryan and Hindi: Eight Lectures, On the History of the Aryan Speech in India and on the Development of Hindi (Hindusthani) Delivered before the Research & Post-Graduate Department of the Gujarat Vernacular Society in 1940*. Ahmedabad: Gujarat Vernacular Society, 1942.

Clarke, Sathianathan. *Dalits and Christianity: Subaltern Religion and Liberation Theology in India*. New Delhi: Oxford University Press, 1998.

Conference on Urdu and Hindi Christian Literature held at Allahabad, 24th and 25th February, 1875. Madras: The Christian Vernacular Education Society, 1875.

Dalmia, Vasudha. *The Nationalization of Hindu Traditions: Bhāratendu Hariśchandra and Nineteenth-Century Banaras*. Ranikhet: Permanent Black, 2010 [1997].

Dandekar, Deepra. "Pilgrimage, Authority and Subversion: Anonymous Marathi Christian Didactic Literature in Nineteenth Century India." *Zeitschrift für Indologie und Südasienstudien* 35 (2018): 39–60.

Dandekar, Deepra. *The Subhedar's Son: A Narrative of Brahmin Christian Conversion from Nineteenth-Century India*. New York: Oxford University Press, 2019.

Das, Sisir Kumar. *Sahibs and Munshis: An Account of the College of Fort William*. New Delhi: Orion Publications, 1978.

Dempsey, Corinne G. "Lessons in Miracles from Kerala, South India: Stories of Three 'Christian' Saints." In *Popular Christianity in India: Riting Between the Lines*, edited by Selva J. Raj and Corinne G. Dempsey. Albany: State University of New York Press, 2002.

Doniger, Wendy. *The Hindus: An Alternative History*. New York: Penguin Books, 2009.

Eck, Diana L. *Banaras: City of Light*. New York: Columbia University Press, 1999 [1982].

Eck, Diana L. *Darśan: Seeing the Divine Image in India*. New York: Columbia University Press, 1998.

England, John C., Jose Kuttianimattathil, John Mansford Prior, Lily A. Quintos, David Suh Kwang-sun, and Janice Wickeri, eds. *Asian Christian Theologies: A Research Guide to Authors, Movements, Sources*. Volume 1: *Asia Region 7th – 20th Centuries; South Asia; Austral Asia*. Delhi: Indian Society for Promoting Christian Knowledge, 2002.

Ernst, Carl W. *Following Muhammad: Rethinking Islam in the Contemporary World*. Chapel Hill: The University of North Carolina Press, 2003.

Evans, Thomas. *Kaise Pāyā Muktidātā, Bhayaharṇ Dās kā Itihās* [How I Found the Savior, or the Shepherd Convert of Monghyr]. Benares: Medical Hall Press, 1877.

Flood, Gavin. *An Introduction to Hinduism*. Cambridge: University of Cambridge Press, 1996.

Fox, Richard G. "Hindu Nationalism in the Making, or the Rise of the Hindian." In *Nationalist Ideologies and the Production of National Cultures*, edited by Richard G. Fox. Washington, D.C.: American Anthropological Association, 1990.

Hakala, Walter N. *Negotiating Languages: Urdu, Hindi, and the Definition of Modern South Asia*. New York: Columbia University Press, 2016.

Hansen, Kathryn. *Grounds for Play: The Nautanki Theatre of North India*. Berkeley: University of California Press, 1992.

Hasan, Mushirul. "The Myth of Unity: Colonial and National Narratives." In *Contesting the Nation: Religion, Community, and the Politics of Democracy in India*, edited by David Ludden. Philadelphia: University of Pennsylvania Press, 1996.

Hawley, John S. *Three Bhakti Voices: Mirabai, Surdas, and Kabir in Their Time and Ours*. New Delhi: Oxford University Press, 2005.

Hawley, John. S. and Mark Juergensmeyer. *Songs of the Saints of India*. New Delhi: Oxford University Press, 2004 [1988].

Hooper, David, ed. *A Welshman in India: A Record of the Life of Thomas Evans, Missionary*. London: James Clark & Co., 1908.

Hopkins, Steven P. *Singing the Body of God*. New York: Oxford University Press, 2002.

Horstmann, Monika, ed. *Bhakti in Current Research, 2001–2003*. New Delhi: Manohar Publishers, 2006.

Israel, Hephzibah. *Religious Transactions in Colonial South India: Language, Translation, and the Making of Protestant Identity*. New York: Palgrave Macmillan, 2011.

Israel, Hephzibah. "Authority, Patronage and Customary Practices: Protestant Devotion and the Development of the Tamil Hymn in Colonial South India." In *Constructing Indian Christianities: Cultures, Conversion and Caste*, edited by Chad M. Bauman and Richard Fox Young. New Delhi: Routledge, 2014.

Jonathan, Franklin C. *Biśap: Dāyitv, Darśan aur Mūly* [Bishop: Vocation, Vision and Value]. Jabalpur: Hindi Theological Literature Committee, 1994.

Jones, Arun W. *Missionary Christianity and Local Religion: American Evangelicalism in North India, 1836–1870*. Waco: Baylor University Press, 2017.

Khalidi, Omar. "Hinduising India: Secularism in Practice." *Third World Quarterly* 29, no. 8 (2008): 1545–1562.

Khan, Benjamin. *Bīsvīṁ Śatābdī ke Pramukh Dharmavijñānī* [Major Christian Theologians of the Twentieth Century]. Jabalpur: Hindi Theological Literature Committee, 1990.

King, Christopher R. *One Language, Two Scripts: The Hindi Movement in Nineteenth Century North India*. Delhi: Oxford University Press, 1994.

KPMG in India and Google. "Indian Languages – Defining India's Internet: A Study by KPMG in India and Google." April 2017. Accessed at https://assets.kpmg/content/dam/kpmg/in/pdf/2017/04/Indian-languages-Defining-Indias-Internet.pdf.

Kulandran, Sabapathy. "Christian Faith and Hindu Bhakti." *Indian Journal of Theology* 6, no. 4 (October–December 1957): 118–121.

Kunnatholy, Abraham. *St. Thomas' Christians in Madhya Pradesh: A Historical Study on Apostolic Church of St. Thomas*. Bangalore: Asian Trading Corporation, 2007.

Lipner, Julius J. *The Face of Truth: A Study of Meaning and Metaphysics in the Vedāntic Theology of Rāmānuja*. Albany: State University of New York Press, 1986.

Lumbard, Joseph. "The Quranic View of Sacred History and Other Religions." In *The Study Quran, A New Translation and Commentary*, editor-in-chief Seyyed Hossein Nasr. New York: HarperOne, 2015.

Malik, Keshav. *Hindi Poetry Today*. New Delhi: Indian Council for Cultural Relations, 1985.

Malinar, Angelika. *The Bhagavadgītā: Doctrines and Contexts*. New York: Cambridge University Press, 2007.

Masica, Colin P. *The Indo-Aryan Languages*. Cambridge: Cambridge University Press, 1991.

Massey, James. *Dalits in India*. Delhi: Indian Society for Promoting Christian Knowledge, 1995.

Massey, James, ed. *Indigenous Peoples, Dalits: Dalit Issues in Today's Theological Debate*. Delhi: Indian Society for Promoting Christian Knowledge, 1998.

McGregor, Ronald S. "The Rise of Standard Hindi and Early Hindi Prose Fiction." *Journal of the Royal Asiatic Society of Great Britain and Ireland*, no. 3/4 (October 1967): 114–132.

McGregor, Ronald S. *Hindi Literature of the Nineteenth and Early Twentieth Centuries*. Wiesbaden: Otto Harrassowitz, 1974.

McGregor, Ronald S., ed. *The Oxford Hindi-English Dictionary*. New Delhi: Oxford University Press, 1993.

McGregor, Stuart. "The Progress of Hindi, Part 1: The Development of a Transregional Idiom." In *Literary Cultures in History: Reconstructions from South Asia*, edited by Sheldon Pollock. Berkeley: University of California Press, 2003.

Monier-Williams, Monier. *A Sanskrit-English Dictionary, Etymologically and Philologically Arranged, with special reference to Cognate Indo-European Languages*. Delhi: Motilal Banarsidass Publishers 2005 [1899].

Mosse, David. *The Saint in the Banyan Tree: Christianity and Caste Society in India*. Berkeley: University of California Press, 2012.

Narayanan, Vasudha. "Afterword: Diverse Hindu Responses to Diverse Christianities in India." In *Popular Christianity in India: Riting Between the Lines*, edited by Selva J. Raj and Corinne G. Dempsey. Albany: State University of New York Press, 2002.

Nasr, Seyyed Hossein, editor-in-chief. *The Study Quran, A New Translation and Commentary*. New York: HarperOne, 2015.

Office of the Registrar General & Census Commissioner, India. "Statement-1: Abstract of Speakers' Strength of Languages and Mother Tongues – 2011." Ministry of Home Affairs, Government of India, 2018.

Office of the Registrar General & Census Commissioner, India. "Statement-5: Comparative Speakers' Strength of Scheduled Languages – 1971, 1981, 1991, 2001 and 2011." Ministry of Home Affairs, Government of India, 2018.

Office of the Registrar General & Census Commissioner, India. "Statement-7: Growth of Scheduled Languages – 1971, 1981, 1991, 2001 and 2011." Ministry of Home Affairs, Government of India, 2018.

Office of the Registrar General & Census Commissioner, India. "Part-A: Distribution of the 22 Scheduled Languages-India/States/Union Territories – 2011 Census." Ministry of Home Affairs, Government of India, 2018.

Orsini, Francesca. *The Hindi Public Sphere 1920–1940: Language and Literature in the Age of Nationalism*. New Delhi: Oxford University Press, 2009 [2002].

Orsini, Francesca, ed. *Before the Divide: Hindi and Urdu Literary Culture*. New Delhi: Orient BlackSwan Private Limited, 2010.

Pandey, Gyanendra. *The Construction of Communalism in Colonial North India*, third edition. New Delhi: Oxford University Press, 2006 [1990].

Pavitr Bāibil, arthāt Purānā aur Nayā Dharm Niyam [Holy Bible, i.e., the Old and New Religious Testaments]. Bangalore: Bible Society of India, 2004.

Pinch, Vijay. "Bhakti and the British Empire." *Past & Present* 179 (May 2003): 159–196.

Pollock, Sheldon. *The Language of the Gods in the World of Men: Sanskrit, Culture, and Power in Premodern India*. Berkeley: University of California Press, 2006.

Raghavendra, M.K. *The Politics of Hindi Cinema in the New Millennium: Bollywood and the Anglophone Indian Nation*. New Delhi: Oxford University Press, 2014.

Raj, Selva J. "The Ganges, the Jordon, and the Mountain: The Three Strands of Santal Popular Catholicism." In *Popular Christianity in India: Riting Between the Lines*, edited by Selva J. Raj and Corinne G. Dempsey. Albany: State University of New York Press, 2002.

Raj, Selva J. and Corinne G. Dempsey. "Introduction: Between, Behind, and Beyond the Lines." In *Popular Christianity in India: Riting Between the Lines*, edited by Selva J. Raj and Corinne G. Dempsey. Albany: State University of New York Press, 2002.

Raj, Selva J. and Corinne G. Dempsey, eds. *Popular Christianity in India: Riting Between the Lines*. Albany: State University of New York Press, 2002.

Rajamanickam, S. *Roberto de Nobili on Adaptation*. Palayamkottai: De Nobili Research Institute, 1971.

Ramabai, Pandita. *A Testimony*. Maharashtra: Kedgaon, 1917.

Raychaudhuri, Tapan. *Europe Reconsidered: Perceptions of the West in Nineteenth-Century Bengal*. Delhi: Oxford University Press, 1988.

San Chirico, Kerry P.C. "Between Christian and Hindu: *Khrist Bhaktas*, Catholics and the Negotiations of Devotion in the Banaras Region." In *Constructing Indian Christianities: Culture, Conversion and Caste*, edited by Chad M. Bauman and Richard Fox Young. New Delhi: Routledge, 2014.

Schelling, Andrew, ed. *The Oxford Anthology of Bhakti Literature*. New Delhi: Oxford University Press, 2011.

Schomer, Karine. *Mahadevi Varma and the Chhayavad Age of Modern Hindi Poetry*. Berkeley: University of California Press, 1983.

Schomer, Karine and W.H. McLeod, eds. *The Sant Tradition of India*. Berkeley: Graduate Theological Union, 1987.

Scott, David S. "Hindu and Christian *Bhakti*: A Common Human Response to the Sacred." *Indian Journal of Theology* 29, no. 1 (January–March 1980): 12–32.

Shackle, Christopher and Rupert Snell. *Hindi and Urdu since 1800: A Common Reader*. New Delhi: Heritage Publishers, 1990.

Shukla, Ramchandra. *Hindī Sāhity kā Itihās* [History of Hindi Literature]. Delhi: Malik and Company, 2007 [1965].

Singh, Suraj Bhan. *Hindī Bhāṣā: Sandarbh aur Saṃracanā* [Hindi Language: Context and Structure]. Delhi: Sahitya Sahkar, 1997.

Sinha, Yunus Satyendra, trans. *Masīhī Ācaraṇ* [The Christian Character, by Stephen Neill]. Jabalpur: Hindi Theological Literature Committee, 2008 [1956].

Thiel-Horstmann, Monika, ed. *Bhakti in Current Research, 1972–1982*. Berlin: Dietrich Reimer Verlag, 1983.

Thomas, Madathilparampil Mammen. "Introduction." In Robin H.S. Boyd, *An Introduction to Indian Christian Theology*. Madras: The Christian Literature Society, 1975 [1969].

Tiwari, Uday Narayan. *Hindī Bhāṣā kā Udgam aur Vikās* [The Birth and Growth of Hindi Language]. Allahabad: Lokbharit Prakashan, 2009.

Truschke, Audrey. *Culture of Encounters: Sanskrit at the Mughal Court*. New York: Columbia University Press, 2016.

Van der Veer, Peter. *Religious Nationalism: Hindus and Muslims in India*. Berkeley: University of California Press, 1994.

Young, Richard Fox, ed. *India and the Indianness of Christianity: Essays on Understanding – Historical, Theological, and Bibliographical – in Honor of Robert Eric Frykenberg*. Grand Rapids: William B. Eerdmans, 2009.

2 The making of a genre

The politics of Hindi

On November 1, 1956, eight new states came into being in Nehru's India. This reflected Nehru's failure. But the politics of language had won. Territories were reorganized into new states on linguistic grounds. The states were a defeat of Nehru's vision but a victory of popular will. Indians have always been obsessed with languages.[1] The languages of the Indo-European family were distinct from other languages on the land mass, such as Tamil and other South Indian languages that form part of the family called Dravidian, which were distinct from other language families like Chinese and Semitic (Hebrew, Arabic). Some of the Indian languages mixed with each other. Hinduism, born of diverse language groups, was such a mixture. The *Rig Veda* incorporates words and ideas from the Indus Valley Civilization, Vedic culture, Adivasis or "original inhabitants" of India, Munda speakers (of the Austro-Asiatic language family), and Dravidian languages. In other cases, these languages lived side-by-side without blending; not quite a melting pot but a tossed salad of sorts. Linguistic traditions fostered one another.

A tradition of linguistic multiplicity has continued through the various ebbs and flows of Indian civilization. The earliest evidence of inscriptions are the edicts of the Mauryan emperor Aśoka.[2] The earliest script in Indian history is the pictographs of the Indus Valley Civilization, but that language remains undeciphered. Aśoka's edicts are phonetic and rely on words, not pictures, to communicate meaning. They display both multilingualism and a 'national' policy on language. The edicts are in four different scripts and three different languages. The scripts are *kharoṣṭhī*, *brāhmī*, Greek, and Aramaic. The languages are Prākrit, Greek and Aramaic. The different scripts and languages suggest there were different audiences for the inscriptions. The edicts are not translated into local languages. Inscriptions in Karnataka, for instance, are in Prākrit, which was not the local language. Mauryan administrators were expected to translate and explain the edicts to locals. Prākrit terms were imported to explain ideas difficult to translate in the language of the inscription's audience. One Aramaic inscription, for instance, uses Prākrit loan words and ideas written in Aramaic. This suggests a form of bilingualism since the audience must be familiar with both the Prākrit term and its Aramaic meaning.

By the tenth century, various languages had emerged.[3] Punjabi, Hindi, and Bengali were emergent, just as Tamil and other Dravidian languages were gaining strength. The emergence of Muslim rule in the tenth century brought Arabic as a written script while Persian remained the languages of speech. Persian became the lingua franca of the Indo-Muslim empire. By the eleventh century, Persian had taken a backseat to a mix of Persian and Old Punjabi and with the capture of Delhi by the Mughals in 1192, the seeds for Hindu and Urdu were planted. The local speech of Delhi, Khaṛī Bolī or "standing speech," along with many loan words from Persian, became the lingua franca of northern India. Hindi and Urdu are Persianized names. Muslim rulers referred to the local language of Indians as *hindī* ("of the Indus," 'Indian language') or *hinduī* ("of the Hindus," "Hindu language'). Urdu got its name from Mughal Delhi, known as *Urdū-e mu'allā*, and was born of a combination of a Turkish loan word (*urdū* or "camp") and Persian and Arabic modifiers. By the fifteenth century, the script of Hindi was mostly the Western Hindi dialect of Braj-bhāṡā ("language of the Braj," Krishna's home town). Muslims gave the names Hindavī, Hinduī, Hindī to the Khaṛī Bolī dialect, which became the basis of colloquial Hindustani and literary Urdu.[4] Even as Persian gradually gained prominence during Muslim rule in India from the eighth century to its heyday between the thirteenth and eighteenth centuries, a form of *rekhta* or gibberish or mixed language was present in the Sufi communities of the Delhi Sultanate in the thirteenth century and the Mughal rule in the late seventeenth and early eighteenth centuries.[5] *Rekhta*, a mixture of Persian and Urdu words, expressed a form of bilingualism, where even if a language like Persian or Sanskrit was dominant, it could not crowd out local linguistic expressions from the courts and other places.[6]

European rule fostered linguistic reorganization. Portuguese missionaries were the first Christians to reach India and continued using Hindi-Urdu loan words in speech. Some loans words live on in modern Hindi: *padre* became *pādrī* ("priest") and *egreja* became *girjā* ("church"). By the end of the eighteenth century, Urdu had replaced Persian within the Muslim community as the language of communications. While the British continued to use English as their main language throughout their time in India, they had recognized the gap between their preferences and the Indian languages that were in wide use. To bridge this gap the British established the Fort William College in 1800, aiming to teach Indian languages to British officers.

Strife between religions catalyzed linguistic reorganizations. The British missionary-linguist John B. Gilchrist was perhaps the first to align Indian languages with religions. Professor of Hindustani at Fort William College, Gilchrist suggested that Urdu and Hindustani, in the Persian script, was the language of north Indian Muslims while Hindi in the Devanagari script the language of north Indian Hindus.[7] As Hindu-Muslim relations increasingly frayed in the nineteenth and twentieth centuries, Hindustani faded out and Hindu and Urdu were torn asunder. Hindustani, an amalgam of Hindi and Urdu, was the lingua franca of northern India for much of its history. Under the influence of religious contests, the nineteenth century saw the emergence of parallel movement. A movement arose to ground Hindi more firmly in Sanskrit. Modern Hindi is an offspring of Sanskritized Hindi. In parallel, a movement arose to ground Urdu in Persian. By the late nineteenth century, 'purified Hindi' and 'purified Urdu' began to circulate in literary circles.[8] By the time the twentieth century was in full stride and independence bloomed, the question of languages took center stage.

"The most controversial subject in the Constituent Assembly was language."[9] The assembly met between 1946 and 1949. The Indian National Congress, poised to govern independent India, had a well-defined policy on languages. Congress had committed to linguistic provinces in 1917. The Nagpur Congress of 1920 cemented this principle in official policy. Mahatma Gandhi supported this policy. As did Nehru. By India's independence, however, Nehru had changed his mind. He worried that a nation just partitioned on the basis of religion was at high risk of disintegrating into civil strife if states were reorganized on the basis of languages. Disruptive forces had come to fore due to the partition, and linguistic provinces could further weaken a feeble India. The unity of India would be better served if states were organized in a way that kept within them communities with different languages and cultures. Gandhi did not agree with Nehru's change of opinion but agreed that the nadir of partition was not the best backdrop to linguistic organizations. He advised patience till the nation calmed down. Nehru was concerned with the question of a national language as well. Which one should it be?

Nehru considered Hindustani "the only possible all-India language."[10] So did Gandhi. English-speaking Indians separated themselves from the masses. Congress, with its all-India scope, could not conduct affairs in provincial languages. And if Congress wanted to avoid a dependence on English, the choice "must be Hindustani."[11] But 'Hindustani' could not mean Hindi without Urdu or Urdu without Hindi. Congress specifically used the word Hindustani and not Hindi to define the national language.[12] Hindustani meant Hindi and Urdu in spoken form and the Devanagari and Arabic scripts in written form.[13] It was already spoken by millions and understood by millions more. It was relatively easy to learn. There was the issue of script, but there was no reason why both Devanagari and modified Arabic could not be promoted.

Gandhi was very invested in promoting Hindi and Urdu speech and scripts equally. In 1942, he proposed an association to promote Hindi and Urdu jointly and equally. He hoped this would finally lead to a "natural fusion of the two becoming a common interprovincial speech called Hindustani." This Hindustani would not be Hindi + Urdu but "Hindustani = Hindi = Urdu."[14]

Earlier in 1938, Gandhi had disparaged attempts to separate the two parts of Hindustani:

> I know that there are some who dream that there shall be only Urdu or only Hindi. I think it will always remain a dream and it is an unholy dream. Islam has its own peculiar culture, so has Hinduism its own. India of the future will be a perfect and happy blend of both.[15]

Hindustani united all India, politically and religiously. Nehru agreed with Gandhi on the preeminent case of a combined Hindi-Urdu Hindustani to be India's national language. "To consider Hindi as the language of the Hindus and Urdu as that of the Muslims is absurd," Nehru wrote in 1937, well aware that while the Muslims may have brought the Persian script of Urdu, Urdu was "of the very soil of India and [had] no place outside India."[16] Rising national consciousness in the second half of the nineteenth century created an "absurd" split between Hindi and Urdu. First it was Hindu nationalism that latched on to (Sanskritized) Hindi and then it was Muslim nationalism that latched on to (Persianized) Urdu.[17]

The Constituent Assembly recognized the question of language and tried to pause the drive for linguistic organization. It appointed a three-person committee to address the question of language. Members included Nehru (a Kashmiri Pandit from the north), Vallabh Bhai Patel (a Gujarati speaker from the west), and Pattabhi Sitaramayya (a Telegu-speaker from the south). The committee recommended against linguistic reorganization arguing that separatist and disruptive tendencies should be discouraged.[18] After much debate, the Assembly chose Hindi as the official language of the Union of India. The constitution ratified this arrangement on January 26, 1950. A 15-year grace period was added to smooth relations between Delhi and the states: Hindi would not be imposed – imposition would be a mistake, Nehru thought – but English would be used along with Hindi as the language of communication between the central government and the states. It was Gandhi's dream that Hindustani one day replace English as the language of interprovincial communication and the educated classes. This would bring all Indians closer together.[19] Gandhi's dream remained just that. In modern India, English is safely entrenched due to a triple advantage: it is the language of global mobility, social mobility, and national mobility. Hindi faces more resistance than English outside the northern and central regions of India.

In 1965, Nehru tried to expand the grace period afforded to English. That attempt proved problematic because Hindi still retained its status as the official language under the Official Languages Act of 1965. By 1965, opponents of Hindi had geared up to oppose its continued national place. Effigies of the Hindi demoness were burned in Tamil Nadu and other states.[20] But the problems with Hindi did not start in 1965. Even 1948 and 1949 saw a revival of language-based movements among speakers of

Kannada, Marathi, Malayalam, and Gujarati. A struggle in the Sikh state for a separate Punjab brought language and religion together. The gradual decline of Nehru's attempts to devolve linguistic reorganizations of states in free India reached its nadir with the passage of The States Reorganization Act of 1956.

Religion and language have cohabited in India since its emergence as a collection of peoples. Through India's history, this relationship has been symbiotic, each force fostering the growth and development of the other. According to Keay, the earliest modern vernacular of Hindustan emerged in the tumult between the Mughal rulers and Hindu kingdoms in the twelfth and thirteenth centuries. In Rajasthan's poetry, local expressions found new life under alliances with Mughal rulers. Keay notes, the rise of the worship of Ram in the early parts of the fifteenth century further propelled vernacular literature.[21] Language is one axis of contest in India. "Because they are so many, and so various, the people of India are also divided."[22] The other axes include caste, religion, and class.[23] Language is second only to caste, but above religion and class as a site of conflict. Given the fusion of language and religion in India, and the emergence of the notion that 'a particular language belongs to a particular religion,' Hindi Christian works present a different equation of languages with religions. At this point, it is pertinent to describe the general body of works that has helped me unearth the particular ways in which Christian authors have claimed Hindi for Christians. Such a description is necessary given the novel nature of this study of Hindi Christian works. In what follows, I sketch the contours of Hindi Christian literature and identify key ideas in the literature. Who are some of the influential Hindi Christian authors today? What are the key attributes of Hindi Christian works? How do important Christian works in Hindi examine the value and function of Hindi to 'Indianize' Christianity and make it *deśī*? These questions guide this chapter.

Congregations and Christians who use Hindi constitute a small portion of the religious makeup of India. Nearly 40 percent of Indians speak a form of Hindi, and Christians constitute around 3 percent of the national population. Among the roughly 30 million Christians in India, Hindi-speaking churches account for less than a fourth of Indian Christians. Though a small part of the Christian population, Hindi-using Christians have produced and continue to produce a steady stream of religious materials.[24] Yet there are no obvious collections of Hindi Christian sources. Leonard Theological College (1922) in Jabalpur, Madhya Pradesh, and the Luther W. New Jr. Theological College (1987) in Dehradun, Uttarakhand, teach in Hindi and English and have a small collection of books in Hindi. There is a general paucity of Hindi Christian sources. New Theological College has bemoaned the paucity of quality Hindi sources and translations. "The Church in the 'Hindi Belt' is in dire need of quality publications in Biblical Studies, Theology, Church History and other related fields. Even basic Christian books in these fields are not available in Hindi."[25] The Hindi Theological Literature

Committee produces a small but steady stream of publications, but it lacks a library or central collection.

Sources to study Indian Christian ideas are readily available to a researcher. Christian literature from India has been codified in many places. These include colonial collections, missionary archives, and institutional libraries. Collections are available with seminaries like Leonard Theological College, Gurukul Theological Seminary, and Yale Divinity School. Recent collections come from ecumenical groups like the National Council of Churches in India, Christian Conference of Asia, and World Council of Churches. Publications on Indian Christianity and global mission provide helpful bibliographies.[26] Collections of Hindi Christian sources are rare and limited when compared to those of non-Hindi sources. To address this state, in 2010 I requested the Hindi Theological Literature Committee to compile an updated list of Hindi Christian works. The Committee compiled a list of 1,181 books in a "Comprehensive Catalogue." The catalogue is the first comprehensive update to the list compiled by missionary agencies in 1917. The 1917 list was published by the Christian Literature Committee of the Uttar Pradesh and Mid-India Missionary Councils and the North India Christian Tract and Book Society and was titled "A Descriptive and Classified Catalogue of Hindi Christian Literature." It listed publications up to 1917 and included a "Report on Protestant Hindi Christian Literature" by Edwin Greaves.

The 2010 catalogue includes new sections on science, ethics, and the history of Christianity in South Asia. The catalogue differs in composition and tenor, too. The earlier list has long sections on apologetics, missionaries, mission fields, and refutations of other religions. Its content reflects editorial concerns dominant in missionary colonies. The 2010 catalogue has sections on religion, history of Christianity, ethics, social action, and interfaith relations. It reflects twenty-first century sensibilities by a religion vying for good relations with its neighboring faiths in a democratic nation. Across 14 categories, 490 books were listed in 1917. By 2010, the catalogue had expanded to 1,181 books. Interestingly enough, less than a third of the 1917 listings appear in the 2010 list. In 1917, just one Indian author was listed among 32 authors in the theology section. By 2010, more than half the theologians listed were Indian (32 out of 56). Biblical studies like translations, commentaries, and concordances constituted the largest segment of each catalogue – 24 percent in 1917 and 32 percent in 2010. Both lists pay attention to ethics and guidebooks for proper living. Christian ethics makes up roughly 10 percent of the 2010 list. Seventy-five advice books (15 percent) for Christian men, women, and children were listed in 1917. Titles of selected books shed light on the tenor of the compendium. They include *Ābhuṣaṇ kā lobh* ("The Love of Jewelry"), *Gālī Denā* ("Cursing"), *Haridāsī, Ek Kahānī Madyapān ke Pariṇām ke Viṣay Meṁ* ("A Story on Drunkenness") *Kristiy Mātā* ("A Christian Mother"), *Kumār Śikṣā* ("On Raising Good Boys"), and *Prakāśit Prabhā* ("True Faith"). No book on ethics appears in both lists. Each entry is unique.

Comparisons between the 1917 and 2010 lists identify interests that have shifted over time and interests that have remained stable through the century that separate the catalogues. Sections on religion, Bible, Christian history, theology, and ethics populate both lists. They include biographies, Bible studies, hymnbooks, textbooks, and critical essays. They address parents, converts, theologians, ethicists, liturgists, hymnists, historians, administrators, and general readers. They teach ethics, faith, and identity through biographies, stories, and 'manuals.'

The 2010 catalogue is a comprehensive account of Hindi Christian sources. Yet it codifies sources published by 'formal' institutions like seminaries, denominational presses, and ecumenical bodies. Both lists are dominated by mainline publishing houses like the Indian Society for the Promotion of Christian Knowledge, the Christian Literature Society, Lucknow Publishing House, and the Hindi Theological Literature Committee. Both lists are limited in scope and a study of Hindi Christian sources needs to look beyond them.

The catalogues generally neglect local hymns, sermons, testimonials, and conversion accounts in Hindi. They ignore media like songs, music videos, CDs, feature films, and the many plays that are popular in towns and villages. Finally, they overlook 'marginal' materials like self-published books, unpublished hymns and liturgy, and publications by independent presses and non-mainline churches. The 2010 list is at the moment one of the most comprehensive lists of Hindi Christian literature and is as such a valuable resource for research. Yet its contribution needs to be matched by that of field research. The corpus of Hindi Christian sources includes works by lay and ordained authors, hymnodists, women and men, church leaders, school teachers, college professors, social workers, missionaries, government officials, farmers, and hospital chaplains. Its forms include poems, plays, hymns, sermons, theologies, ethics, biblical commentaries, stories, testimonies, and conversion accounts. This body of work can be organized into two major genres.

Types of Hindi Christian works

Hindi Christian works present two major types of Christian commentary. *Doctrinal* works explore Christian history, draw on creeds, and explicate the language of Christianity. They cover claims about God, creation, Christ, salvation, sin, and eschatology. Their audience is primarily scholars, seminarians, pastors, teachers, and church leaders. Didactic stories about and from the life and work of Jesus also abound. Among evangelistic communities, they include conversion accounts and apologetic works. *Narrative* works include short stories, poems, songs, films, and plays that aim to shape faith and discipleship. Such accounts explore biblical sources and help produce textual studies, sermons, and sermon outlines. The question of ethics captivates a substantial number of Hindi Christian sources that provide instructions and guidelines for social actions. These contain instructions to particular groups like pastors, preachers, leaders, youth ministers, bishops, women, men, and children. They also offer general instructions on Christian discipleship. A persistent attention to an Indian and Hindi form of Christianity that is not Hinduized permeates these types of publications.

Doctrinal accounts and Hindi

The past 50 years have seen a number of theological works that present Christianity in Hindi terms.[27] *Masīhī Dharm Vijñān kā Paricay* ("Introduction to Christian Theology") by Bishop Din Dayal[28] is one such example. Dayal's theology focuses on language in two ways. First, the content of theological language is important. Second, the form of language matters. When engaged in theology, it is necessary to exhibit great care in the language used, concepts employed, and claims made. Particular care is necessary when translation is at play and meaning is being carried across linguistic frameworks. Theology does not possess static content but rather should ground its experiments in available expressions. Writing in Hindi or choosing Hindi as the form of Christian expression raises certain theological issues. 'Modern restatements' (*ādhunik punarkathan*) are best served when they avoid sloppy "Indianizations" (*bhāratīyakaraṇ*).[29] The Chalcedonian definition of the two natures of Jesus Christ may be immersed in the worlds of Greek and Roman philosophy.[30] Yet restatements of Chalcedon in Hindi must employ both care in expression and caution in content. Dayal is skeptical of the ability of Chalcedon's language regarding the hypostatic union of Christ's divine and human nature to carry over into Hindi. The Greek of Chalcedon cannot be easily transferred (*translatus*, past participle of *transferre*) to Hindi. Yet a theology that glosses over the form of relationship between Jesus and God proposed by Chalcedon would fail to preserve the complexity of Christ's personhood and therefore fall short of an important Christian witness.[31] Dayal's hesitancy to embrace Indianizations stems from his insistence that Christian claims are inter-connected. "[T]he doctrines of creation, salvation and the final end are connected with each other."[32] Descriptions of relationship between Christ's humanity and divinity affect the stories one can write about his resurrection and salvific work.

Underlying Dayal's caution is a theory that language can be theological in nature. Theology, he writes, has three specific functions. First, it should try to reveal the Christian faith in ordinary language (*sāmānya bhāṣā*). Second, where theology presents itself as a technical language (*prāvidhik bhāṣā*), it should be able to express and reflect the quotidian faith and practices of Christians. Finally, theology should be intelligible to people. Dayal's underlying argument is clear: theological language should be faithful (presumably to scripture, church, and tradition), clear, and accessible. The necessary interplay of theological claims requires of theology a degree of clarity, coherence, and care. 'Theology' is translated in Hindi as *dharm vijñān*, which literally means 'religious science,' or the science of religion. Playing on the word *vijñān* (science), Dayal explains: "If theology is a type of science then like a science it should possess clarity, and harmony [*sāmañjasyatā*,] and comprehensiveness [*vyāpakatā*] are important in its explanations."[33]

Theology is a way to use ordinary language in extraordinary and analogical (*sādṛśyamūlak*) ways that are grounded in Scripture and history.[34] Hence, Dayal critiques Indian theologians like Sadhu Sundar Singh and Appasamy when they present Christ as an *avătār* in Hindu terms. Dayal draws the line at *avătār*. He refuses to use '*avătār*' to translate 'incarnation.' To communicate the Christian idea of Christ's divine-human form, Dayal exclusively prefers the Hindi term *dehdhāraṇ* (discussed later) in place of the Brahmanic Hindu *avătār*. Unlike the idea of *avătār* in Hinduism, Dayal argues, Christ is the sole incarnation of a God who comes to save and not to destroy the wicked.[35] Translators of the Hindi Bible have formalized this difference by using *dehadhāraṇ* (taking on flesh, en-fleshing) instead of *avătār* to communicate the Christian idea of incarnation.

Dayal's theology seeks to impart Christian truths by explaining church doctrines but other forms of theology in Hindi exist. One such form is theology through the conceptual arts in media like poems, hymns, and theater. *Masīh Merī Manzil* ("Christ My Destination") by Shivraj Kumar Mahendra, a first-generation Christian convert ordained in 2008 by the Christian Evangelical Assembly, is one such example.[36] The collection of poems addresses the nature of sin, church, discipleship, and worship. Like Dayal, Mahendra's task is pedagogical and theological in nature. His poems are interconnected, uses colloquial Hindi, and cover a wide range of topics common to Christian theology, liturgy, and worship. His poems are geared toward new converts who may be new to the faith and those who are seeking to rejuvenate their faith through poetry. He explains,

> The occasion for the publication of *Masīh Merī Manzil* is very important. It represents an expression of joy, thanks, and gratitude on my completion of 12 years in Christian faith and service. It also marks my ordination. Along with that, it testifies to God the Father's unlimited mercy, love, grace, forgiveness, blessings, care, and constant encouragement. . . . It is my hope and prayer that the collection of poems presented [here] will encourage Christian sisters and brothers, especially those who are new in faith, and will be found useful for the glory of Christ the Lord.[37]

In the poem *Ārādhănā kā Samay* ("Time of Worship"), Mahendra offers that the time of worship is a time of thanksgiving and openness. Come as you are, bring gifts, bring praise, bring your troubles, pray for help, and come in holiness. The poem *Parameśvar kā Sevak* ("Servant of God") brings together a collection of commitments taken by a person who decides to become a disciple of God.[38] One of the poems, *Usne Kahā Thā* ("He Had Said"),[39] uses a series of contrasts to explain human sinfulness and God's response to it: Christ wants us to be bold, but we stumble around with fear and despair; he asks us to witness, but our (sinful) acts do not bear that out; he wants us to liberate the captive, but we are slaves to our desires; he asks us to rejoice (in unity), but we cling to old divisions. Mahendra writes:

Usne kahā thā krūs uṭhākar calne
Inhe dekho ye apnī lāś dho rahe haiṁ.

He had said: pick up the cross and walk
Look at them! They haul around their dead bodies.

Usne kahā thā prārthanā meṁ jāgte rahne
Inhe dekho ye din-dahāṛe so rahe haiṁ.

He had said: be alert in prayers
Look at them! They are asleep in broad daylight.

Usne kahā thā kal kī cintā na karne
Inhe dekho ye parsoṁ kı fikr meṁ ro rahe haiṁ.

He had said: do not worry for tomorrow
Look at them! They wail in worry for the day after tomorrow.

Usne kahā thā jākar cele banāne
Inhe dekho ye to khud cele nahīṁ ban pā rahe haiṁ.

He had said: go and make disciples
Look at them! They themselves have failed as disciples.

Another poem, *Kalīsiyā* ("Congregation"),[40] imagines an ideal church. An ideal church is a group of believers who share certain things in common. A church is a company of castes, a caretaker of divine plans, a homestead for the scorned, and a bearer of grace. Mahendra writes, for example:

Viśvāsiyoṁ kī sangati hai	A group of believers
Sab jātiyoṁ kī sadgati hai	A company of castes
Masīhiyoṁ kī manḍalī kalīsiyā	A society of Christians, the church
Īśvarīy parivār kī pragati hai.	It is the progress of the divine family.
Tiraskritoṁ kī naī svīkriti hai	A new acceptance of the scorned
Bahiṣkṛtoṁ kī naś anukṛti hai	A new imitation of the outcast

Dīn dukhiyoṁ kī manaḍalī kalīsiyā	A society of the wretched, the church
Īśvarīy anubhūtiyoṁ kī abhivyakti hai.	It is an expression of divine compassion.
Gumanāmoṁ kī naī pahacān hai	The new identity of the unknown
Nāummīdoṁ kā nayā armān hai	The new longing of the hopeless
Āśādhāriyoṁ kī manaḍalī kalīsiyā	A society of hopefuls, the church
Īśvarīy protsāhan kī khān hai.	It is a treasury of divine grace.

Mahendra's attempt to neutralize caste is noteworthy. Indian Christianity has a long-standing problem with caste. Many Indian Christians come from lower-class and lower-caste backgrounds. Caste-based discrimination within churches is a widespread and ongoing concern for Christians in India. Christians in India remain "pinned" to their local culture, language, birth *(jāt)* and caste.[41] It is also a long-standing issue. Riots broke out in 1858 when British administrators in Travancore allowed Christian women converts to cover their upper bodies in contradiction to the local traditions that permitted only upper caste women to cover the upper part of their bodies. The Christian response is illuminating. A compromise was proposed. Christian converts should be allowed to cover their upper bodies but with a "simple restriction." They should not imitate the dress styles of the upper caste. Upper caste converts could dress differently than lower caste converts and lower caste converts should not the dress in stylings of upper caste women. This would allow the society and church to function in peace.[42] Rather, Indian Christianity contains a multitude of clan and caste relationships.

The tolerance of caste-discrimination within the church was part of missionary strategy. The alliance between British administrators and Christian missionaries was strategic. British administrators wanted to maintain peace in the colony. Social arrangements were accepted and promoted toward comity. Christian missionaries were sympathetic to colonial goals. Missionary schools were not segregated but education was caste- and clan-based. Upper caste children were taught in separate classrooms. Men and women sat separately in churches. Upper caste converts were treated differently than lower caste converts. Churches were generally monochromatic. Syrian Christian churches were populated and managed by Syrian Christians. Dalit churches were populated by Dalits. Church management was reserved for the privileged. When a missionary was not in charge, upper caste converts were. The management of Indian churches remained in upper class and upper caste hands from the beginning of missionary enterprises in India. This state of affairs is gradually changing. Church leadership after the British Raj has increasingly reflected church memberships. Christian contribution to nation building after India's independence in 1947 is partly responsible for a sea change in church management. Church demographics can explain changes in the make-up and management of churches. This explanation has its limits. The turn in Christian leadership from the elite to those previously on the margins has lagged considerably behind the turn in Christian demographics from upper caste, urban populations to lower caste, rural populations.

John Anand echoes Mahendra's vision of an ideal Christianity. Where Mahendra tries to tackle ongoing caste-based discrimination with the church, Anand has turned his attention to a more recent health crises within Indian Christianity, due to the refusal of the Indian church to address sensitive topics like AIDS. Anand has criticized the churches' negligence of people with AIDS. His play on the topic captures the plight of HIV-positive church members.[43] In the opening scene a character dies of AIDS and no one wants to touch the body. The doctors want the body immediately removed from the hospital and the nurses and ward boys refuse to handle the corpse. Stigma persists and misinformation abounds: AIDS is transmitted through sex with many partners and the person with AIDS must, therefore, have been promiscuous. AIDS can be passed via touch, so handling an AIDS patient, whether dead or alive, is life-threatening. There is no cure for AIDS; once you contract it, you are as good as dead. We soon find out the patient was a woman. Within no time, the local 'community leader' is threatening the doctors and nurses. Remove her from here. Take her away. The story gets more complicated. She was a convert: a Hindu who became a Muslim, and now neither community wants her. Neither does the hospital, nor her neighbors. Another character says she is giving words to what everyone is thinking: these homosexuals, druggists, prostitutes, fornicators! They are a stigma to humanity and should be put away.

As the play unfolds, it becomes clearer that many of the invectives are being hurled by Christians. Some Hindus and Muslims join these Christians. Other Hindus and Muslims in the play are sympathetic to the deceased. Eventually, a nun cares for the dead body and takes it in without fear of contagion or stigma. This act of compassion leads to repentance on the part of the abusers. Anand's play does not chastise one religion over another. Rather, each religion represented in the play has both sympathetic and judgmental characters. The lead character starts off as a Christian in some sympathy with the abusers but gradually finds some sympathy for the patient. The play ends without a clear resolution regarding his position on how to treat the AIDS-bearing body. In his play, Anand has captured the attitude of Christians toward AIDS. For some, it is the mark of immorality and therefore bearers of AIDS do not deserve sympathy. For others, like the nun in the play, God gives opportunities to serve everyone. For yet others, they remain on the fence. The lead actor's unresolved attitude toward AIDS-bearers captures the church's unresolved position on the treatment of AIDS patients.

Theology seeks not only to educate but also to animate faith and guide discipleship. Didactic interests are central to Christian story telling in Hindi. Hindi Christian materials frequently use biblical accounts of the life and ministry of Jesus to translate faith and traditions into practices and modes of discipleship. Two types of narratives dominate this genre of literature: stories from the Gospels and personal conversion accounts. Stories in these sub-genres offer different messages to their listeners and readers. Biblical accounts recall the story of Christ and his disciples. Conversion accounts ground those stories in contemporary times and places, thus allowing Christians the tools to live in discipleship.

Narrative accounts and Hindi

Komal Masih and Christopher Peter rely on canonical Gospels and first-century sources to re-construct Jesus's life and ministry.[44] The four Gospels constitute the "most important" ("*sabse mahatvapūrṇ*") Christian sources to reconstruct Jesus's life and ministry. "About the life and ministry of Jesus the most important Christian sources are (Matthew, Mark, Luke, and John)."[45] Redaction criticism ("*sampādakīya ālocanā*") and form criticism ("*rūp ālocanā*") inform us that the Gospels are redacted and edited accounts of the life of Jesus.[46] But the Gospels, especially in Matthew and Luke, offer "sufficient historical information" (*paryāpt aitihāsik jānkārī*) to allow us to tell the story of Christ's life, ministry, and death.[47]

Masih and Peter echo narrative theologians such as Hans W. Frei and Ronald F. Thiemann. Frei writes: "A man's being is the unique and peculiar way in which *he himself holds together* the qualities which he embodies – or rather, the qualities which he is."[48] Further,

> A man . . . is what he *does* uniquely, the way no one else does it. . . . In that kind of passage from free intention into action, ordering the two (intention and act) into one harmony, a free man gains his being. He becomes what he is; he gains his identity.[49]

For Frei, the self-agency to self-claim makes identity self-referential:

> A person's identity is the total of all his physical and personality characteristics referred neither to other persons for comparison or contrast nor to a common ideal type called human, but *to himself*. . . . A person's identity is the self-referral, or ascription to him, of his physical and personal states, properties, characteristics, and actions.[50]

In similar vein, Thiemann explains that

> a person's identity is constituted by the intentions he or she carries into action. Actions are appropriately described as enacted intentions, and intentions are rightly described as implicit actions. Identity-description is nothing more or less than the description of characteristic intention-action patterns across a chronological sequence.[51]

Hence, personal identity means "characteristic patterns of intention and action." For Frei and Thiemann, a person's identity is linked to and revealed through what the person intends to do and what she does. A link between intentions and actions underlies the identification of a person's identity. Intended actions when enacted persistently over time provide the characteristic patterns of behavior that allow the identification. Personal identity in this account is very much the result of self-manifestation.

Masih and Peter turn to Gospel accounts of the speech-acts of Jesus to discover the "personality" ("*vyaktitv*") of Jesus. "Studying the parables of Jesus, we find important and interesting information concerning the individual personality of Jesus."[52] In sympathy with position of Frei and Thiemann, Masih and Peter offer that to tell the story of Jesus is not merely an exercise in sharing information but also an exercise in teaching and learning. Stories about Jesus ought to be didactic, they assert, since the chief protagonist of those stories, Jesus, draws attention to certain values and ways of being aimed toward a robust relationship with God. The Gospels show us the life and ministry of Jesus and tell us what he taught his disciples to do. Hindi Christian narrative accounts then build on the Gospel model to both show and tell, to share and teach. "According to the Century Dictionary a parable is such a story that can be true and that is said to teach some ethical truth."[53] Unlike the works of Frei and Thiemann, however, the works of Masih and Peter attend to the necessity of and challenges inherent in using Hindi to Indianize Christianity.

Stories about Jesus are the subject of poems, films, plays, and novels. *Kavitā meṁ Śubh Sandeś* by Sarojini Arya is a good example of this genre.[54] *Kavitā meṁ Śubh Sandeś* (or "Good News in Poetry") is a remarkable collection of 77 poems that narrate the story of Jesus's life, death, and resurrection based on the Gospel of Matthew. Hindi Christian songs – informative and didactic – are widely available among Christian communities in central and north India. Christian hymns, which include missionary imports like Martin Luther's *A Mighty Fortress is Our God* translated in Hindi[55] and local entrants like Sabir Chimmanlal's *Dil kā Badalnā Cāhiye* ("The Heart Should Change")[56] share space with commercial Christian songs. Commercial songs are generally non-denominational in content and are released by music labels to capitalize on key events in the Christian calendar like Good Friday, Easter, and Christmas. They cover Christian missions, praise and worship, revival meetings, and church planting events. Audio compact disks and cassettes are quite popular in rural areas and widely available during key seasons. The commercial viability of such songs routinely attracts top-level recording artists, musicians, and studios around the country. Shaan, Udit Narayan, Sadhana Sargam, and Kavita Krishnamurthy are some of the few mainstream, popular, Bollywood playback singers who have recorded Christian Hindi songs and albums for general release.

Like their narrative and poetic counterparts, Hindi Christian songs narrate diverse ideas. They speak of God's unending love, Christ's ministry, the Kingdom of God, creation, human frailty, discipleship, refuge in God, and joy in Christ. Like others of its genre, as an instance, *Dil Merā Le Le, Pyāre Yīśu* ("Take my Heart, O Dear Jesus),[57] a very popular hymn, presents Christ as the sole object of a Christian's desire. Worldly attachments clutter the heart and lead it away from devotion to Christ. Turn to Scripture, the hymn then instructs, and let the Spirit reside in you:

Dil merā le le, pyāre yīśu,	Take my heart, O dear Jesus,
tūne ise banāyā hai,	You are the one who has made it,
isameṁ tū apnā ghar banā le,	Make in it [now] your own home
jiske liye hī yah banāyā hai.	For this only it was made.
Duniyā kī sab cījeṁ nikālkar,	Having cleansed all worldly things,
ise pāk aur sāph ab kar,	Make it now pure and clean,
gandagī gunāhoṁ kī sab dhokar,	Having cleansed all dirt of sins,
us khūn se jo bahāyā hai.	By that blood which you have shed.
Padhtā hūṁ meṁ jab pavitr vacan,	When I read the Holy Word,
prabhu-pās jāne kā sādhan.	The way to approach the Lord. . . .
Pavitr ātmā kā yah ho bhavan,	May the Holy Spirit live here,
āgni ke baptismā se,	By the baptism of fire,
har jagah, har samay duṁ gavāhī	Everywhere, always, may I witness
jaisā yah usne sikhāyā hai.	Just as He has taught this.

The final type of narrative account that deserve attention is *sātvāṇī*, or the 'seven sayings' of Jesus on the cross. The seven sayings are (as found in the New Revised Standard Version, henceforth NRSV): (1) Father, forgive them; for they do not know what they are doing. [Lk. 23:34] (2) Truly I tell you, today you will be with me in Paradise. [Lk. 23:43] (3) Woman, here is your son. . . . Here is your mother. [Jn. 19:26–27] (4) My God, my God, why have you forsaken me? [Mt. 27:46] (5) I am thirsty. [Jn. 19:28] (6) It is finished. [Jn. 19:30] (7) Father, into your hands I commend my spirit. [Lk. 23:46]. *Sātvāṇī*s offer a revealing look at forms of scriptural interpretation in Hindi churches. Each of the seven savings is read and preached on during Good Friday services. The performance of each *vāṇī* sandwiched between hymns and prayers. In effect, scriptural interpretation becomes a liturgical act. In the Evangelical Lutheran Church in Madhya Pradesh, each *vāṇī* is read aloud, followed by a brief reflection, a specific hymn set to each *vāṇī*, and a short prayer. Each coda – reading, reflection, hymn, prayer – is timed to ensure the end of the seventh coda ends coincides with 3 p.m. on Good Friday, an estimate of Jesus' time of death.

Individual Gospel accounts of Jesus's pronouncements on Calvary are arranged chronologically to reproduce the timeline of Christ's death on the cross. The seven verses are deployed as individual pieces of a scriptural puzzle that must be properly arranged to create a portrait of Jesus's dying acts. Given the role of structure in the ways the Gospels present this sequence of events, the liturgical arrangement of the seven sayings of Jesus has also been standardized across Hindi Christian churches. This standardization, in turn, reflects a common tradition within Hindi Christianity from which different interpreters draw. S. W. Prasad's *Krūs kā Bhed* ("Mystery of the Cross"), John Henry Anand's *Śubh Śukravār kī Ārādhănā* ("Good Friday's Liturgy"), and Udit Sona's *Antim Sāt Vacan* ("Final Seven Sayings") each identify and arrange the seven sayings in the same order.[58] Standardization has meant the ritual of *sātvāṇī* is generally recognizable and immediately familiar across a variety of Hindi-speaking churches.

The "seven sayings" constitute a creative exercise of polyvalent Christology. Anand notes that the Greek original for "It is finished" is *tetelesataī*, which is a word used by merchants for transactions.[59] Sins are our debt before God and debts, by their nature, suggest that a repayment is involved. "All types of sin," Anand argues, "are also our debt toward God. God cannot accept us till this debt is not paid."[60] Christ pays the debt and "completes" the "battle" against sin and evil. He re-establishes our relationship with God. "What was completed? What was finished?" Anand asks. "The battle against sin, the battle against evil. Our relationship with God was re-established."[61] Where Anand uses mercantile language to present a transactional account of the Cross, Sona uses the idea of just recompense to portray Christ's death as a sacrificial event.

Christ's sacrifice ends all sacrifices. It "ended sin" by removing sin from the world. "Only after" this work does Christ complete the work of justice and, in doing so, destroy Satan's power.[62] Prasad agrees with Sona that Christ's death and resurrection end the need for any more attempts to reconcile us with God. But unlike Anand and Sona, Prasad suggests that the work of Christ does not "finish" with his death. "No, the resurrected Lord, seated in heaven close to His Father at His [Father's] right hand is working for you and for me" to help humans continue their relationship with God.[63] Annual enactments of *sātvāṇī*, then, represent the sorts of careful, textual, and liturgical analyses that have made a deep and lasting place within the general community of Hindi Christians in central India. *Sātvāṇī* constitute a theological and liturgical act that weaves together from different Gospels a cogent account of Jesus's life and ministry as found in his sayings on the cross. In addition to *sātvāṇīs*, other forms of biblical commentaries are also popular and readily available. Two such examples include Benjamin Khan's *Māno Yā Na Māno Prabhu Yīśu Ko Jāno* ("Believe or not, Know Jesus Christ") and E. D'Mello's *Īśvāṇī kā Sāthī* ("Companion of God's Voice").

In *Māno Yā Na Māno*, Khan offers a patient reading of the Gospel of John in the context of the other three gospels employing many familiar tools of biblical commentary. He begins by clarifying his methodology: the work will draw on the Gospel of John to present both the speech and acts of Christ and John's insights into the salvific work of Christ as the eternal Word of God. Further, as the oldest 'standard' gospel, the Gospel of John also helps fill the gaps in the first three gospels – even as Khan acknowledges that the gospels are but partial accounts of Jesus's 33 years and there were other gospels that vied for attention in the early church. In other words, Khan's commentary presents itself as a theological commentary on the Gospel of John that seeks to present a complex (yet limited) sketch of the person and work of Christ. Khan writes:

> I have followed the path of the gospel penned by Saint John to write this story of the life of Jesus Christ. [This is] because . . . the fourth gospel presents a holistic picture of the life of Jesus Christ in which we see not only a sequential account of external events but we also see the way in which each internal link of the sketch of Jesus Christ the Savior is joined together. And this gospel fulfills the gaps we see in the accounts of the other gospels.[64]

Commenting on John 1:19 (when the Jewish leaders question John the Baptist) he writes: "Hope in the Kingdom of God was the heart of the Jewish faith and the central message of the Old Testament."[65] John the Baptist was preaching the imminence of this kingdom and asking Jews to repent. Thousands of Jews flocked to him. "A common man, preaching repentance and starting a new tradition of baptism, was not only attracting thousands to himself but was also forcing the religious leaders to find out who is this person?"[66] This is what brought the Jewish priests and Levites to John the Baptist and gave him the chance to declare the imminent arrival of Christ. Or, commenting on John 10:22–42, Khan explains a change in Jesus's attitude toward the publicity around his speech and acts. The Jesus of the earlier chapters of John is cautious.

> The danger was that, having seen his miracles and knowing that [Jesus] was the expected savior [literally, "the savior to come"], people may forcibly capture him and declare him the king of the Jews, and in doing so incite a new uprising in the land.[67]

During the Feast of Dedication that brought him to Jerusalem, however, Jesus makes a very public claim regarding his relationship with God (John 10:30) and faces the ire of the Jewish people. Khan concludes his commentary on the Gospel of John with reflections on the episode of doubting Thomas in John 20:24. Verse-based commentaries exist along with sermons and reflections on key biblical verses. D'Mello's collection of stories exemplifies this type of creative re-telling of biblical verses, where relatable stories ground selected verses and their main lessons. The following two short stories demonstrate D'Mello's approach:

> *I.*
>
> Prasad was the village chieftain for many years. During his administration he severely persecuted Catholic priests and nuns. Poor people disliked him too. Once he fell very ill. He expressed his desire to be admitted for treatment only to the Catholic hospital in the city and not to any other hospital. When asked for his reason, he said, "Catholics do not seek revenge against others, treat others with fairness, and forgive [those who have wronged them] because they are followers of Christ."[68]
>
> *II.*
>
> Sampat had become a Christian. His relatives did not like this. One day both his brothers came to his place and said to him, "Why did you become a Christian? What does our religion lack? Do you know who Jesus was, who were his parents? . . ." Sampat patiently listened to his brothers' questions and after thinking about them said, "Before becoming a Christian I used to act in wicked ways, my children used to be afraid of me, I did not have food in my house, my wife was unhappy . . . since I have accepted Christ, I have stopped drinking, there is peace in my house, children have food to eat, we live in peace. For me Christ is alive. We are living according to his teachings; there is prayer and worship in the house. We have found a new life in Christ.[69]

The stories combine biblical lessons with actionable wisdom. The first story, as per D'Mello, is a commentary on Eph. 4:32: "And you too forgive one another." ("*Āp bhī ek dusre to kṣamā kareṁ.*") A bully is the protagonist. The readers are asked to discern how to treat a bully. In the story, in time of serious need the bully turns to those he previously tormented because he knows that as Christians they will still treat him with kindness. The story does not say whether the bully is reformed post-need, but the moral of the story seems to be to forgive those who have erred against you. The second story is an account of Jn. 6:35: "I am the Bread of Life." ("*Jīvan kī Roṭī Maiṁ Hūṁ.*") In the retelling, the new life of a recent convert draws our attention to the real impact that accepting Jesus can produce on one's life. As the story goes, the protagonist stops drinking, takes care of his family, keeps his wife happy, and leads a worshipful household. The story speaks to quotidian issues (alcohol-induced family-wide sorrow) and offers Christianity as the cure. Hindi commentaries on the Bible comes in many shapes. This diversity in commentaries – structured reconstructions (*sātvāṇīs*), textual analyses (Khan's *Māno Yā Na Māno*), and creative adaptations (D'Mello's short stories) – reflects the wide range of approaches Hindi Christian authors have adopted toward the reception of the Bible in Christian communities. Across this diversity, however, a theme persists: Hindi is to be promoted as a language of Christianity in India.

Along with doctrinal works, narrative accounts, textual commentaries, and hymnbooks, another popular form of Hindi Christian work focuses on advice for faithful living. These guidebooks vary in form and content. There are, for instance, systematic presentations of Christian ethics, tracts against community ills like alcoholism, gambling, and casteism, advice on nurturing children, resources for new converts, guidelines for church leaders (both lay and ordained), and systems of ethical concepts and applications. In light of the deep relation between faith and action in Christ's life, Hindi sources argue, ethics and theology are inseparable. Christ lived and taught a certain way of being and speaking in the world. His words and deeds show us what must be done in faithful discipleship. Khan explains:

> There is a close relationship between Christian ethics and theology. Christian ethics depend on theology in two ways: (1) Christian ethics obtains its material from the life, teachings, and the personality of Jesus Christ. (2) It is the task of Christian ethics to provide a moral exposition of Christian principles or faith. From this perspective, ethics serves theology. Christian ethics reflects on Christian materials of faith [literally, "faith-stuff"] in the context of [the] vow and Christian people and the Christian community.[70]

Ethics relates to theology in two ways. First, the stuff of Christian ethics comes from the words and deeds of Jesus – and his disciples. Second, the job of Christian ethics is to translate Christian faith into practice in an ever-changing world. Christian ethics explores the stuff (*sāmagrī*) of Christian faith in the context of a commitment (*saṅkalp*) to Christ and to Christian community (*samāj*) in the world. Christ commands ("*ādeś*") love of God and neighbor.[71] Christ desires that we live faithfully in the love, mercy, and invitation of God. A biblical site to explore the relationship between mercy and faithfulness is, Khan suggests, the Sermon on the Mount (or on the Plain, if you happen to be reading Luke).[72] A Christian is asked to exhibit Christ-like values: faith in God, love of God and neighbor, and responsible actions.[73] Faith and action compete in the Bible, and Khan notes the dissonance between James (2:24–26) and Paul (Romans 3:38). Yet he writes, if works had no value to God, then Christ's life would lack purpose and would be wasted ("*vyarth hai*"). "Paul only wants to show that if works led to liberation then Christ's descent and sacrifice would be wasted. He is rather emphasizing that which God has done for humans," Khan writes.[74] A common translation of *vyarth* is 'useless.' However, in the context of Khan's argument, 'wasted' would be a more accurate translation.

Khan asserts that Christ saves and teaches. Christ enacts in word and deed the imminent Kingdom of God. But in addition to this didactic function, Christ's incarnation, death and resurrection also constitute an act of saving. His death and resurrection point to the healing of our separation from God. The salvific function of Christ's life, death, and resurrection addresses human sin in our separation from God and the didactic function of Christ's life, death, and resurrection addresses human sin in our human response to God. These roles of Christ are complementary. Since these functions go hand-in-hand, for a Christian, faith in Christ is incomplete without discipleship of Christ. An important purpose of faith is discipleship and vice-versa. Faith and discipleships are useful in their own ways to a Christian. Without the other, in other words, each aspect lacks an important "close relationship" (*ghaniṣṭh sambandh*). The speech-acts of God in Christ, Khan explains, are both the measure and beacon of life. Interpreting Matt. 5:20, Khan argues, "From this it is clear that no one other than God is good, and God alone is the source and measure of ethics."[75] Drawing from Dietrich Bonhoeffer's *Ethics*, Khan asks: what does it mean to be a Christian? What does it mean to be a member of a church? What shapes a Christian life? What is the responsibility of a Christian to the world? For Bonhoeffer, to be a Christian is to be a human, to be in relation, and in being so to regain one's true human nature. Christ is the example of a (true) human life. A Christian lives in the world and in the church as a new human transformed in Christ.[76]

In additional to analytical works like Khan's, ethical insights are also available in practical handbooks on Christian living. One such handbook is a collection of short stories compiled by Edward D'Mello for parents, teachers, and pastors. Through short stories, D'Mello shares advice on how to overcome failure (*Parvatārohī*, "The Mountain Climbers," and *Akṣamatā*, "Incapacity"), purify the mind and body (*Safāī*, "Cleaning"), manage quarrels (*Jhagṛā*, "The Fight"), handle praise (*Suvikhyāt*, "Popular"), and serve each other (*Bhalā Kāry*, "Good Works").[77] For Khan and D'Mello, ethics and theology go hand in hand, principles being practiced in service to Christ.

Christ's restorative and didactic missions are interrelated. Masih and Peter ground their Christology in what they call a "realistic" ("*yathārthavādī*") perspective on Christ. The Gospel of Mark, our earliest source on Christ's life,[78] grounds Jesus in his joys, struggles, and desires. They note that in Mark Jesus scolds (1:25), takes pity (1:41; 6:34), feels tired (4:38), gets angry (8:17–21; 9:19), despairs (7:34), forgives (12:15), worries (14:33), and feels weak (14:38; 15:21). "The Christ of the Gospel according to Mark is a common human like you and us."[79] The Gospel is generous also in its descriptions of Jesus's sense of his relationship with God. The author of the Gospel uses 'Christ' multiple times and describes Jesus as the 'Son of God.' This aspect of Jesus's being matters since Christ's restorative mission depends on his being one with God. "In Mark 1:1," Masih and Peter explain, "the divinity of Jesus is not in his being called Christ but is in his being the 'Son of God'."[80] He saves because he is the incarnated Son of God. "Jesus, because he is the Son of God, is one with God from a spiritual perspective."[81] What does "spiritual" mean, in the context of Jesus's being?

Jesus's relationship with God, in Masih and Peter's construction, stems from his oneness in spirit rather than from the union of nature. Body and human nature, even if of Jesus, cannot obtain the Kingdom of God; so, while

Masih and Peter are willing to accept the physical resurrection of Jesus, they reject a bodily physical ascension to heaven. "The physical resurrection of Jesus is acceptable [to us] but a physical ascension cannot be accepted because flesh and blood cannot inherit the Kingdom of God (1 Cor. 15:50). Therefore, the principle that Paul has presented can be accepted more easily."[82] Rather, "by a supernatural and mysterious process," they write, "the dense, physical body of Jesus is transformed into a subtle, spiritual body. In the end, Jesus ascends in this subtle, spiritual body."[83] Masih and Peter use the Hindi word "*sthūl*" to explain the physical body of Christ. "*Sthūl*" can be translated as "apparent" or "outward."[84] However, it is evident from Masih and Peter's argument that they do not intend to suggest a Docetic interpretation of Jesus's physical body. The Son incarnates to liberate from sin and to proclaim the imminent Kingdom of God. God's agency is at the forefront of Masih and Peter's soteriology.[85] Jesus's restorative mission, which is primarily a function of his divinity, makes possible the conditions for his speech-acts. Key to their soteriology, however, is the inseparability of Jesus's didactic and salvific missions. Drawing on the Gospel of Mark they write: "Jesus Christ incarnated to do two great things. First, to proclaim the imminence of the Kingdom of God. . . . According to Mark, Christ's second work is – liberation."[86] Christ comes to preach the Kingdom of God, a time when God's justice and righteousness will rule peoples' hearts.[87]

Unlike Masih and Peter, Khan places the onus of Christ's restorative mission on his humanity. For Khan, only a human could "compensate" for human sin. God really forsakes Jesus on the cross. Khan considers Jesus to be fully divine and fully human, yet he chooses to focus on Christ's humanity as the medium of salvation. It is Christ's humanity that allows us to connect with God. On the cross, Christ's human nature bears the effects of sin. Christ's humanity becomes the medium of our salvation. Christ's death breaks the power of death and sin, and humans can now live in new ways. Khan explains,

> God is holy, holy, holy and Jesus was sinless. For us [Jesus] became sin. Sin and holiness cannot be together. Due to this reason there was not a rupture in the relation between the Father and the Son but separated from the Father, surrounded by the forces of sin, to sacrifice himself for the salvation of humans, Jesus was hanging alone on the cross.[88]

Khan further adds, "Only a human could recompense for the sin of humans." A didactic force pulsates through the story of Christ. Jesus Christ's life and ministry consists in "doing his father's work": to proclaim the imminent Kingdom of God. This kingdom stands for a new way of relationships with God and fellow-humans. According to Khan, this difference between Jesus's self-understood mission – to preach a form of human relationship with God and fellow-humans – and the expectations of the Jewish leaders of Jesus's time – for a Jewish political establishment – was "a primary reason" for disagreements between Jesus and the leaders.[89] As a God-man ("*Īśvar-manuṣy*") Jesus knew his mission and taught an ethical truth.[90] The new revelation ("*nayā prakāśan*") of Christ put God first and proclaimed how God helps humans walk on the path of ethical completeness.[91]

Responsibility to witness

Christ's restorative and didactic missions create the conditions for a robust human response to Christ's work. Sometimes the link in Hindi Christian materials between "being saved" and "accepting Christ" is so strong that a Christian life may come across as a necessary condition for Christ's presence. In the words of the hymn *Dil Merā Le Le, Pyāre Yīśu* ("Take my Heart, O Dear Jesus"), for instance, only a clean and uncluttered heart can hold Christ.[92] An emphasis on the relationship between the restorative and didactic elements of the gospel is not unique to Hindi Christian materials and can also be found in English works that address Christianity in India.[93] The relationship between holiness and presence is a particular (though not exclusive) feature of Hindi Christian works. As an instance, the anonymous hymnist of Hymn 409 in *Ārādhănā ke Gīt* lists a litany of tasks incumbent on a devotee of Christ who wants to "climb the holy mountain and be there forever":

> *Tere ghar meṁ, he prabhū! Kaun surakṣit rahegā*
> *Kaun pavitr parvat par caḍh ke sadā rahegā.*
>
> In your house, O Lord! Who will be safe?
> Who will climb the holy mountain and be there forever?
>
> *Sīdhī cāl kā calnevālā, dharm ke kām kā jo kartā,*
> *Apne man se sac boltā, cuglī nahīṁ kartā.*
>
> One who walks the straight path, one who does the works of faith,
> Who tells truth with his mind, and never tells tales.
>
> *Aur jo kisī dūsre se burāī nahīṁ kartā*
> *Na apne paḍosī kī vah nindā kabhī suntā.*
>
> And who does not do evil to another,
> Nor suffers those who scorn his neighbor.
>
> *Jis ke lie burā puruṣ hai nikammā ṭhahrā,*
> *Par yahovā ke ḍarvaiyoṁ kā vah ādar kartā.*
>
> For whom a bad person is useless,
> But who respects those who fear God.

Vacan de, phir hāni dekhe, taubhī na badaltā,
Kisī ko udhār se de kar kabhī byāj na letā.

Having given his word, then seeing a loss, even then does not change,
Having given a loan to someone does not charge interest.

Nirdoṣ ke satāne nimitt ghūs na kabhī letā,
Aisā kām jo kartā hai, sadā hī rahegā.

Never takes a bribe that will harm the innocent,
One who does such deeds, will remain [there] forever.

In this hymn, theology and ethics go hand in hand: to speak of the acceptance of Christ – as one who finds herself in the Lord's home – is to speak of concrete discipleship. Only those who live by certain ethical ideas – some of which are mentioned in the hymn – will find safety in the house of the Lord. One who does not cheat or lie, who respects God's people, tells the truth, is true to his word, does not charge interest on loans (in other words, helps others financially without expecting monetary benefits in return), does not harm the innocent – even though, it seems, the hymnist accepts briberies as a regular state of affairs – will climb the holy mountain and stay there forever. Hindi Christian short stories echo the purpose of human ethics, the responsibility to serve the needy, to be honest, and to witness even when facing persecution. D'Mello's collection, as mentioned previously, comprises didactic stories that illustrate these principals through common-sense interpretations of biblical verses. In one particular story, the responsibility to live an ethical life – in this case, by serving the poor – trumps spending time with Christ:

> He was the resident of a religious house. It was his job [literally, "duty"] to help the poor who gathered at the temple door for assistance. One day, as he was getting ready to leave for work, Christ appeared to him in a vision. He now had to choose whether to stay with the Christ who had appeared or to do his duty to help the poor. He chose to fulfill his duty. It had become dark by the time he returned to his room after helping the poor. As soon as he lit the lamp, Jesus appeared again. Seeing Jesus, he was overcome with joy. Jesus said to him, "If you had not gone to fulfill your duty, I would have left from this place."[94]

A few things are noteworthy. The choice between spending time with Jesus and helping the poor is dramatic. From the resident's response to seeing Christ again – "[s]eeing Jesus he was overcome with joy" – it is clear that he did not think less of spending time with Christ and was very happy that he could now spend time with Jesus at the end of the day. In the context of the story, not only is the resident happy to see Jesus again but is happier – "overjoyed" – to encounter Jesus in the night now that he has fulfilled his day-job of assisting the poor. In the morning, however, fulfilling the duty was more important. The story suggests the resident faced a risky decision: the story implies Jesus's reappearance depended on the resident's choice. Jesus's reappearance is a reminder of another lesson from the story: service to others and fellowship with Jesus are not contradictory ways to be Christian. The biblical verse that accompanies the story makes this clear: "And the king will answer them, 'Truly I tell you, just as you did it to one of the least of these who are members of my family, [a] you did it to me'." (Matt. 25:40; NRSV) Service (in the day) makes fellowship (in the night) more enjoyable. In the story's chronology, service precedes fellowship with Christ. The story tells its readers that our actions influence how Christ relates to us. D'Mello's title for this story is, "I Would Have Left" (*Maiṁ Calā Jātā*). As Christ puts it, "I would have left if you had not left for work." It is important to fulfill one's religious duty; even further, doing so endears one to Christ. Another account, titled "Truth" (*Saccāī*), is an interpretation of Psalm 26:2: "Prove me, O Lord, and try me; test my heart and mind" (NRSV). The story goes:

> A new servant was being tested. While paying the salary, the master gave 10 ten-rupee notes and slipped in an extra 10 rupee note. When the servant counted the money, an extra 10-rupee note was found. He said to the master, "There is an extra 10 rupees. Take these." The master praised the honesty of the servant and asked him to keep the 10 rupees.[95]

Then there is *Param-Prasād* ("The Eucharist"), the story of practicing the Eucharist while such a practice could lead to state-authorized persecution. The story is an interpretation of John 6:58: "This is the bread that came down from heaven, not like that which your ancestors ate, and they died. But the one who eats this bread will live forever" (NRSV).

> A communist government ruled the nation. Christians were strictly prohibited from following their faith. A priest was using coded language to contact Christians. He used to inform people where to meet him, like on the side of roads, while selling goods, or while selling newspapers. When Christians bought goods from him he would pass on the Holy Communion to them [hidden] in the goods. Believers would take those elements home and would conduct the ritual of the Eucharist with their families [in the safety of their homes]. Where there is a will, there is a way.[96]

'Param-Prasād' can be literally translated as "supreme propitiatory offering." D'Mello's use of 'param-prasād' to mean 'Eucharist' is revelatory for a few reasons. First, it is a (polytraditional) concept drawn from Hindu practices and vocabulary: *prasād* refers to the food offered to idols or a gift, boon, or blessing one receives as a result of the offerings to idols.[97]

Second, *param-prasād* is not a commonly-used word for the Eucharist or the elements of the Eucharist among Hindi-speaking Protestant Christians; the 'normal' Protestant Christian word for the Eucharist in Hindi is *prabhu-bhoj* (literally, "meal of the Lord," a translation of "Lord's Supper"). However, *param-prasād* is regularly used in Catholic circles in India. Finally, a literal translation of *param* (best, highest, supreme) could suggest Christians are making a comparative claim vis-à-vis the *prasād* of Hindus; one is *param-prasād* while the other is just *prasād*. Such a comparative interpretation is, however, faulty because, in Catholic circles, *param* is taken to mean "holy." So, in functional terms, *param-prasād* refers to the "holy *prasād*" rather than to a comparatively better (supreme or highest or best) *prasād*.

In Hindi Christian materials, certain basic responsibilities and practices emerge as part and parcel of accepting Christ as one's savior. In "Truth," for instance, the master-servant relationship readily brings to mind the call to discipleship every Christian will face. Our master – Christ – recognizes our truthfulness and rewards us for our ethical choices. The presentation of a basic Christian value – honesty – in a story on the relationships of servants to masters also reflects, I would offer, D'Mello's attempt to ground his lesson in a phenomenon – the exchange of money between servants and householders – which is commonplace in most Indian families that can afford to hire home-helpers. In other words, by using the servant-householder relationship as his medium, D'Mello deploys a very familiar relationship to anchor his message. Concrete forms of religious responsibilities and practices – like keeping the Eucharist, the subject of *param-prasād* – are available to a Christian through Scriptures and the interpretive attempts of the Christian communities to which a person belongs. Christ's restorative mission is inseparably tied to a didactic mission, which points a believer to discipleship. To be "saved from sin" implies concrete ethical injunctions to refrain from ills like drunkenness and gambling, and to be good parents, live uprightly, be gracious, work diligently, and witness to Christ. Responsible living is embedded in Hindi Christian literature, appearing in a variety of materials addressed to general and specific groups like children, women and men, pastors, bishops, lay leaders, and evangelists. The shape and function of Christian discipleship in India is the focus of chapter 4.

Notes

1 For this paragraph, I rely on Doniger, *The Hindus*.
2 For the edict's languages, see Thapar, *Reading History from Inscriptions*.
3 Shackle and Snell, *Hindi and Urdu Since 1800*.
4 McGregor, "The Rise of Standard Hindi," 114.
5 Aquil, *The Muslim Question*, 1, 2, 133–136. See also Eaton, "Sufi Folk Literature," 120–121.
6 Thapar, *The Penguin History of Early India*, 470; Aquil, *The Muslim Question*, 134–135.
7 Orsini, "Introduction," 3.
8 Guha, *India After Gandhi*, 130.

9 Guha, *India After Gandhi*, 128, 189–208.
10 Nehru, *The Unity of India*, 244.
11 *Collected Works*, "National Language" (*Young India*, 10–2–1927), 38:104.
12 *Collected Works*, "Note to Amritlal T. Nanavati" (On or before July 5, 1946), 91:241.
13 Urdu script uses a modified form of Arabic that includes additional letters that represent sounds exclusive to Persian and/or Urdu. Naim, *Introductory Urdu*, 15.
14 *Collected Works*, "Hindi + Urdu = Hindustani" (*Harijan*, 8–2–1942), 81:486.
15 *Collected Works*, "Hindustani, Hindi and Urdu" (*Harijan*, 29–10–1938), 74:126.
16 Nehru, *The Unity of India*, 247.
17 Orsini, *The Hindi Public Sphere 1920–1940*.
18 Guha, *India After Gandhi*, 192.
19 *Collected Works*, "Hindi + Urdu = Hindustani" (*Harijan*, 8–2–1942), 81:486.
20 Guha, *India After Gandhi*, 394.
21 Keay, *A History of Hindī Literature*, 8–9.
22 Guha, *India After Gandhi*, 1.
23 Guha, *India After Gandhi*, 8–9.
24 Recent projects include a ten-volume Pastors Pulpit Bible Commentary in Hindi in 2011–2014. I advised the Editorial Board of the Pastors Pulpit Bible Commentary series. In 2010, the second edition of *The Oxford Hindi Dictionary of the Christian Church* was printed. This is the official Hindi translation of *The Oxford Dictionary of the Christian Church* (ed. F.L. Cross and E.A. Livingstone) under license from Oxford University Press.
25 www.ntcdoon.org/index.php/publications
26 For instance, see Sugirtharajah, *Asian Faces of Jesus*, and Chhungi. *Theologizing Tribal Heritage*.
27 Dongre, *Prem Īśvarīy* (1960); Chauhan, *Viśvās Caṭṭān* (1962); Yesudas, *Kṛpā Mārg* (1965); Zahir, *Svarg aur Uske Uparānt* (1968); Lall, *Susamācār-Pracār* (1970); Khan, *Sacchī Śānti* (1971); Singh, *Masīhī Ādhyātmik Śikṣā* (1975); and, Dayal, *Masīhī Dharm Vijñān* (2005).
28 Bishop Dayal was born in 1925 in a Christian family in north India (Uttar Pradesh). He received his Bachelor of Arts from Allahabad University in 1949 and a Bachelor of Divinity from Leonard Theological College, Jabalpur, in 1952. He was ordained in 1953. He served as Chaplain at the Allahabad Agricultural Institute and was missionary in South Africa from 1955–1964. He completed a Master of Theology from Pittsburgh Seminary in 1965 and served as pastor in India from 1965–1970. In 1970, he was elected Moderator of the North India Synod of the United Church of Northern India, a founding member of the Church of North India. Dayal served as Bishop of the Lucknow Diocese, Deputy Moderator, and Moderator of the Church of North India. He retired in 1990.
29 Dayal, *Masīhī Dharm Vijñān*, 148–149.
30 Dayal, *Masīhī Dharm Vijñān*, 144. For an excellent history of the formula of Chalcedon, see Chadwick, *The Early Church*, especially 200–212. For the text of the Chalcedonian statement, see Hardy, *Christology of the Later Fathers*, 371–374.
31 Dayal, *Masīhī Dharm Vijñān*, 142.
32 Dayal, *Masīhī Dharm Vijñān*, 170: *[S]ṛṣṭi, uddhār aur antim samāpan ke siddhānt ek dūsre se juḍe hue haiṁ.*
33 Dayal, *Masīhī Dharm Vijñān*, 3–4. "*Yadī dharm vijñān ek prakār kā vijñān hai to vijñān ke samān usme spaṣṭā honī chāhie, aur uskī vyākhyā me sāmañjasyatā aur vyāpakatā āvashyak hai.*"
34 Dayal, *Masīhī Dharm Vijñān*, 31.
35 Dayal, *Masīhī Dharm Vijñān*, 148–149.

36 Mahendra earned degrees in social science, theology, translation, divinity, and Hindi. He has translated five books into Hindi – on interreligious relations, history of the Indian church, prayer, and the ecumenical movement – and managed *Jīvan Darpaṇ* ("Life Mirror"), a Christian radio program, from 2002 to 2004. Biography from Mahendra, *Masīh Merī Manzil*, 70–73.

37 Mahendra, *Masīh Merī Manzil*, xv–xvii: "*Masīh Merī Manzil ke prakāśan kā avasar atyant mahattvapūrṇ hai. Yah masīhī viśvās aur sevakāī meṁ mere 12 varṣ pūre karne ke ānand, dhanyavād aur ābhār kī abhivyakti ko darśātā hai. Yah mere abhiṣek (ārḍineśan) ko bhī cinhit kartā hai. Iske sāth hī, mere ab tak ke safar meṁ param pitā parameśvar kī asīm krupā, prem, anugrah, kṣamā, āśiṣ, dekhbhāl aur satat protsāhan kī gavāhī bhī detā hai. . . . Merī āṣā aur prārthanā hai ki prastut kavītā-saṅgrah masīhī bahno-bhāiyo ke lie, viśeṣakar unke lie jo viśvās meṁ nae hai, protsāhan kā kāraṇ hogā aur prabhu parameśvar kī mahimā ke lie upayogī siddh hogā.*"

38 Mahendra, *Masīh Merī Manzil*, 25, 30.

39 Mahendra, *Masīh Merī Manzil*, 55–56.

40 Mahendra, *Masīh Merī Manzil*, 38–39.

41 Frykenberg, *Christianity in India*, 458.

42 Fernando and Gispert-Sauch, *Christianity in India*, 239–242.

43 Anand, *O Mṛtyu!*

44 Komal Masih was born in Uttar Pradesh. He earned a Bachelor of Divinity and Master of Theology from Leonard Theological College, Jabalpur, in 1960. After serving as a parish priest for two years in the Methodist Church of India, he joined as professor the Bareilly Theological Seminary (1962–1965) and North India Theological College (1967–1976). He obtained a Master of Sacred Theology degree from Wesley Theological Seminary in Washington, DC (1965–1967). He then served as District Superintendent of the Muradabad Conference of the Methodist Church, and from 1981–82 as Vice-President of the Hindi Theological Literature Committee.

Christopher B. Peter was also born in Uttar Pradesh. He completed a Bachelor of Theology from North India Theological College in 1973 and completed a Bachelor of Divinity from Leonard Theological College in 1975. He was ordained a pastor of the Methodist Church in 1974. From 1976–1979, he taught the Old Testament at North India Theological College. He earned a Master of Theology in 1981 from United Theological College, Bangalore and rejoined North India Theological College as a professor in 1981.

45 Masih and Peter, *Prabhu Yeśu kī Jīvanī aur Sevākāry*, 9: "*Yīśu ke jīvan evaṃ sevā kāry ke sambandh meṁ sabse mahatvapūrṇ khristīy srot haiṁ (mattī, markus, lūkā aur yūhannā).*"

46 Masih and Peter, *Prabhu Yeśu kī Jīvanī aur Sevākāry*, 3.

47 Masih and Peter, *Prabhu Yeśu kī Jīvanī aur Sevākāry*, 19.

48 Frei, *The Identity of Jesus Christ*, 5. Emphasis added.

49 Frei, *The Identity of Jesus Christ*, 12.

50 Frei, *The Identity of Jesus Christ*, 95.

51 Thiemann, *Revelation and Theology*, 90.

52 Masih and Peter, *Prabhu Yeśu kī Jīvanī aur Sevākāry*, 133–134: "*Yīśu ke dṛṣṭāntoṁ ko paḍhkar hameṁ yīśu ke nijī vyaktitv ke viṣay meṁ bhī mahatvapūrṇ va rocak jānkārī miltī hai.*"

53 Masih and Peter, *Prabhu Yeśu kī Jīvanī aur Sevākāry*, 133: "*Sencurī ḍikśanarī ke anusār dṛṣṭānt ek aisī kathā hai, jo sac ho saktī hai aur jo kisī naitik saty kī śikshā dene ke lie bolī jāi.*"

54 Arya was a research assistant in India's Ministry of Education, Assistant Director at the Bureau of Indian Standards, and a Joint Director at India's Home

Ministry. She has published 11 Hindi books on education, science and technology, handicrafts, and stories of the Bible. She was awarded the Hindi Millennium Award for her various contributions to Hindi literature. (Biography from Arya, *Kavitā meṁ Śubh Sandeś*)

55 *Ārādhǎnā ke Gīt*, Number 70.

56 *Ārādhǎnā ke Gīt*, Number 310.

57 *Ārādhǎnā ke Gīt*, Number 311.

58 For the order, see note 36.

59 In *An Intermediate Greek-English Lexicon* (798), Liddell and Scott note that *teleou* can represent both "to complete" and "to pay what one owes."

60 Anand, *Śubh Śukravār ki Ārādhǎnā*, 45: "*Sab prakār ke pāp bhī parameśvar ke prati hamārā karj haiṁ. Parameśvar hameṁ tab tak svīkār nahīṁ kar saktā jab tak yah karj cuktā nahīṁ ho jātā.*"

61 Anand, *Śubh Śukravār ki Ārādhǎnā*, 47: "*Kyā pūrā huā? Kyā samāpt huā? Pāp ke viruddh yuddh, burāī ke viruddh yuddh. Parameśvar se hamārā sambandh punah sthāpit huā.*"

62 Sona, *Antim Sāt Vacan*, 54–55.

63 Prasad, *Krūs kā Bhed*, 24: "*Nahīṁ, prabhu jīuṭhakar apne pitā ke pās svarg meṁ uske dāhine hāth baiṭhā mere aur āpke liye kāry kar rahā hai.*"

64 Khan, *Māno Yā Na Māno*, xiii: "*Maiṁne yīśu masīh ke jīvan kī is kahānī ko likhne meṁ sant yūhannā dvārā racit susamācār ke mārg par calā hūṁ. Kyoṁki . . . cauthā susamācār yīśu masīh ke jīvan kā ek viśāl citr prastut kartā hai jismeṁ hum keval bāhy ghaṭanāoṁ ko silsilevār hī nahīṁ dekhte varan uddhārkartā yīśu masīh ke citr ke āntarik rūp kī pratyek kaḍī ko āpas meṁ juḍe hue dekhte haiṁ. Aur yah susamācār any susamācāroṁ kī ghaṭanāoṁ meṁ jo darāreṁ dikhāī detī haiṁ unkī pūrti kartā hai.*"

65 Khan, *Māno Yā Na Māno*, 52: "*Parameśvar ke rājy kī āśā yahūdī dharm kā hṛday thī aur purāne niyam kī śikṣā kā kendr bindu.*"

66 Khan, *Māno Yā Na Māno*, 53: "*Ek sāmāny vyakti paścāttāp kā pracār kartā huā aur baptismā kī ek naī paramparā kā śubhārambh kartā huā, na keval hazāroṁ ādmiyoṁ ko apnī or kheṁc rahā thā balki isne dhārmik netāoṁ ko bhī majbūr kiyā ki ve patā lagāyeṁ ki yah vyakti kaon hai?*"

67 Khan, *Māno Yā Na Māno*, 144: "*Khatrā yah thā ki unke āścaryakarm dekh aur yah jān ki āp hī āne vāle masīhā haiṁ to ho saktā thā ki log unheṁ zabardastī pakaḍ yahūdiyoṁ kā rājā ghoṣit kar dete aur deś meṁ ek vidroh kī āg bhaḍak uṭhatī.*"

68 D'Mello, *Īśvāṇī kā Sāthī*, 53: "*Prasād kaī sāloṁ se sarpanc banā rahā. Uske śāsan ke samay usne kaitholikoṁ ke yājak ko va dharmabahinoṁ ke bahut hī satāyā thā. Garīb logoṁ ko uske prati nafrat bhī thī. Ek bār vah bahut bīmār paḍ gayā. Usne yah icchā prakat kī ki use śahar ke kaitholik aspatāl meṁ hī ilāj ke lie bhartī kiyā jāy aur any kisī aspatāl meṁ nahīṁ. Kāraṇ pūchne par usne batāyā, "kaitholik log kisī kā pratiśodh nahīṁ karte, īmāndārī se ilāj karte haiṁ aur ve īsā ke anuyāyī hone ke kāraṇ kṣamā kar dete haiṁ.*"

69 D'Mello, *Īśvāṇī kā Sāthī*, 91: "*Sampat īsāī ban gayā thā. Uske sambandhiyoṁ ke yah acchā nahīṁ lagā. Ek din uske donoṁ bhāī uske yahāṁ āye aur bole, "tum kyoṁ īsāī ban gaye ho? Hamāre dharm meṁ kyā kamī hai? Tumheṁ mālūm hai īsā kaun the, uske māṁ-bāp kaun the? . . ." Sampat ne śānt hokar apne bhāiyoṁ ke praśn sune aur sockar kahā, "īsāī banne ke pūrv maiṁ durācār kartā thā, mere bāl-bacce mujhse ḍarte the, mere ghar meṁ khāne kā anāj nahīṁ thā, merī aurat dukhī thī . . . jab se maiṁne īsā ko svīkār kiyā hai, maiṁne dārū pīnā choḍ diyā hai, mere ghar meṁ ab śānti hai, baccoṁ ko bhar-pet khānā miltā hai, ham pyār se jīte haiṁ. Mere lie īsā jīvit haiṁ. Unki śikṣā ke anusār hum jī rahe haiṁ, ghar meṁ prārthanā, bhajan-kīrtan hotā hai. Hameṁ īsā se nayā jīvan milā hai.*"

70 Khan, *Khristīy Nītiśāstr*, 16–17: "*Khristīy nītiśāstr kā dharmavijñān ke sāth ghaniṣṭh sambandh hai. Do rūpoṃ meṁ khristīy nītiśāstr dharmavijñān par ādhārit hai: (1) Khristīy nītiśāstr apnī viṣay sāmagrī yīśu khrist kī jīvanī aur śikśā tathā vyaktitv se prāpt kartā hai. (2) Khristīy nītiśāstr kā kāry yah hai ki khristīy siddhāntoṃ yā viśvās kī naitik vyākhyā kare. Is dṛṣṭikoṇ se nītiśāstr dharmavijñān kā sevak hai. Khristīy nītiśāstr saṅkalp aur khristī jan aur khristī samāj ke sandarbh meṁ khristīy viśvās-sāmagrī par vicār karatā hai.*"

71 Khan, *Khristīy Nītiśāstr*, 65–66.

72 Khan, *Khristīy Nītiśāstr*, 76.

73 Khan, *Khristīy Nītiśāstr*, 165–176.

74 Khan, *Khristīy Nītiśāstr*, 170: "*Paulus to keval yah dikhānā cāhtā hai ki yadi karm dvārā hī mukti hai to fir masīh kā avatarit honā aur balidān vyarth hai. Vah to jo īśvar ne manuṣy ke lie kiyā us par jor de rahā hai.*"

75 Khan, *Khristīy Nītiśāstr*, 63: "*Isse yah spaṣṭ hai ki parameśvar ke sivāy aur koī śubh nahīṁ, aur parameśvar hi naitikatā kā srot evam māpadaṇḍ hai.*"

76 Khan, *Khristīy Nītiśāstr*, 159–162.

77 D'Mello, *Īśvāṇī kā Sāthī*, 3, 6, 9, 15, 67.

78 Masih and Peter, *Prabhu Yeśu kī Jīvanī aur Sevākāry*, 168.

79 Masih and Peter, *Prabhu Yeśu kī Jīvanī aur Sevākāry*, 173: "*Markus racit susamācār kā yīśu hamāre-āpke samān ek sādhāraṇ manuṣy hai.*"

80 Masih and Peter, *Prabhu Yeśu kī Jīvanī aur Sevākāry*, 174: "*Mar. 1:1 me . . . yīśu kī divyatā uske Masih kahlāe jāne meṁ nahiṁ varan 'parameśvar kā putr' hone meṁ hai.*"

81 Masih and Peter, *Prabhu Yeśu kī Jīvanī aur Sevākāry*, 177: "*Yīśu parameśvar kā putr hone ke kāraṇ parameśvar ke sāth ādhyātmik dṛṣṭikoṇ se ek hai.*"

82 Masih and Peter, *Prabhu Yeśu kī Jīvanī aur Sevākāry*, 131: "*Yīśu kā daihik punarutthān to svīkāry hai parantu daihik svargārohaṇ ko svīkār nahiṁ kiyā jā saktā kyoṁki māṁs aur lahū parameśvar ke rājy ke adhikārī nahīṁ ho sakte (1 kur. 15:50). Ataḥ paulus ne jo siddhānt prastut kiyā hai vah adhik saraltāpūrvak svīkār kiyā jā saktā hai.*"

83 Masih and Peter, *Prabhu Yeśu kī Jīvanī aur Sevākāry*, 131: "*Yīśu kā sadeh punarutthān to huā parantu ek alaukik v rahasyapūrṇ proses ke dvārā uskī sthūl bhautik deh sūkśm ātmik deh meṁ parivartit ho gai. . . . Antataḥ sūkśm ātmik deh meṁ yīśu kā svargārohaṇ huā.*"

84 McGregor, *The Oxford Hindi-English Dictionary*, 1046.

85 Masih and Peter, *Prabhu Yeśu kī Jīvanī aur Sevākāry*, 133–147.

86 Masih and Peter, *Prabhu Yeśu kī Jīvanī aur Sevākāry*, 177: "*Markus racit susamācār ke anusār prabhu yīśu masīh do mahān kāry karne ke lie dehadhārī huā. Pahalā kāry hai – parameśvar ke rājy ke nikaṭ hone kī ghoṣaṇā (1:15) . . . Markus ke anusār masīh kā dūsrā kāry hai – chuḍautī.*"

87 Masih and Peter, *Prabhu Yeśu kī Jīvanī aur Sevākāry*, 138.

88 Khan, *Māno Yā Na Māno*, 191–192: "*Parameśvar pavitr pavitr pavitr hai aur yīśu niṣpāp thā. Hamare lie pāp banā. Pāp aur pavitratā donoṁ sāth nahīṁ ho sakte. Is kāraṇ pitā aur putr ke madhy āpsī riśtoṁ meṁ darār hī nahīṁ āī parantu pitā se pṛthak ho pāp kī śaktiyoṁ se ghirā huā manuṣy ke uddhār ke lie apnā balidān dene ke lie yīśu akelā hī krūs par laṭkā huā thā. Manuṣy ke pāp kī kshatipūrti manuṣy hī de saktā thā.*"

89 Khan, *Māno Yā Na Māno*, 33.

90 Khan, *Māno Yā Na Māno*, 45.

91 Khan, *Māno Yā Na Māno*, 89–90.

92 *Ārādhănā ke Gīt*, Number 311.

93 Amaladoss, *The Asian Jesus*; Premkumar, "The Commonwealth of Dalits and Tribals."

94 D'Mello, *Īśvāṇī kā Sāthī*, Story 68, 33–34: "*Vah maṭhvāsī thā. Uskā kām maṭh ke dvār par jo bhī garīb madad ke lie āye uskī sahāyatā karnā thā. Ek din jaise hī vah kām ke lie nikal hī rahā thā ki īsā ne use darśan diye. Use ab cunnā thā ki vah darśan meṁ dikhe īsā ke sāth rahe yā garīboṁ kī madad ke lie kartavy par lage rahe. Usne kartavy pālan karnā cun liyā. Garīboṁ kī madad kar jab vah apne kamre meṁ lauṭā to aṁdherā ho calā thā. Jaise hī usne dīp jalāyā īsā ā khaḍe hue. Īsā ko dekhkar vah ānand se fūlā na samāyā. Īsā ne usse kahā, 'agar tum kartavy pālan ke lie nahīṁ nikalte to maiṁ yahāṁ se calā jātā'.*"

95 D'Mello, *Īśvāṇī kā Sāthī*, Story 122, 60: "*Naye naukar kī parīkṣā ho rahī thī. Mālik ne pagār dete samay das-das rupaye ke noṭ diye aur us rakam meṁ das rupaye kā ek noṭ adhik rakhā. Naukar ne paise gine to das rupaye kā ek noṭ adhik niklā. Vah mālik se bolā, 'das rupaye adhik haiṁ. Inheṁ lījie.' Mālik ne naukar kī saccāī kī praśaṃsā kī aur un das rupaye apne pās rakhne ko kahā.*"

96 D'Mello, *Īśvāṇī kā Sāthī*, Story 178, 87: "*Deś meṁ samyavād kī sarkār thī. Īsāiyoṁ ko dharm pālan karnā sakht manā thā. Sāṅketik bhāṣā dvārā ek yājak īsāiyoṁ se sampark kiyā karte the. Vah logoṁ ko sūcit karte the ki ve unse kis jagah mileṁ, jaise saṛakoṁ ke kināre, sāmān becte hue yā samācār patr becte. Īsāi log jab unse sāmān kharīdte to ve sāmān ke sāth param-prasād rakhkar de dete. Viśvāsī us prasād ko upne ghar le jākar apne privāroṁ meṁ param-prasād svīkār karne kī vidhi racte. Jahāṁ cāh vahāṁ rāh.*"

97 McGregor, *The Oxford Hindi-English Dictionary*, 666.

References

Amaladoss, Michael. *The Asian Jesus*. Maryknoll: Orbis Books, 2006.

Anand, John Henry. *Śubh Śukravār kī Ārādhănā: Prabhu Yeśu ke Antim Sāt Śabd tathā Pahāṛī Upadeś* [Liturgy of Good Friday: The Final Seven Words and the Sermon on the Mount of Christ Jesus]. Delhi: Indian Society for Promoting Christian Knowledge, 1993.

Anand, John Henry. *O Mṛtyu! Kahāṁ Hai Terā Ḍaṁk?* [O Death! Where is Thy Sting?]. Lucknow: Lucknow Publishing House, 1994.

Aquil, Raziuddin. *The Muslim Question: Understanding Islam and Indian History*. Gurgaon: Penguin Books, 2017 [2009].

Ārādhănā ke Gīt [Songs of Worship]. Lucknow: Lucknow Publishing House, 2009 [1975].

Arya, Sarojini V. *Kavitā meṃ Śubh Saṃdeś* [Good News in Poetry]. Delhi: Indian Society for Promoting Christian Knowledge, 2003.

Chadwick, Henry. *The Early Church*, revised edition. London: Penguin Books, 1993 [1967].

Chauhan, B.P. Singh. *Viśvās Chaṭṭān* [Ground of Faith]. Delhi: M.S.S, 1962.

Chhungi, Hrangthan, ed. *Theologizing Tribal Heritage: A Critical Re-look*. Delhi: Indian Society for Promoting Christian Knowledge, 2008.

Collected Works of Mahatma Gandhi. Edited by the Indian Ministry of Information and Broadcasting. New Delhi: Publications Division, Government of India, 1958.

Dayal, Din. *Masīhī Dharm Vijñān kā Paricay* [An Introduction to Indian Christian Theology]. Jabalpur: Hindi Theological Literature Committee, 2005.

D'Mello, Edward. *Īśvāṇī kā Sāthī* [Companion of God's Voice]. Pune: Ishvani Kendra, 2007.

Dongre, Pushpa. *Prem Īśvarīy* [Divine Love]. Lucknow: Lucknow Publishing House, 1960.

Doniger, Wendy. *The Hindus: An Alternative History*. New York: Penguin Books, 2009.

Eaton, Richard M. "Sufi Folk Literature and the Expansion of Indian Islam." *History of Religions* 14, no. 2 (1974): 117–127.

Fernando, Leonard and G. Gisspert-Sauch. *Christianity in India: Two Thousand Years of Faith*. Gurgaon: Penguin, Viking, 2004.

Frei, Hans W. *The Identity of Jesus Christ: The Hermeneutic Bases of Dogmatic Theology*. Eugene: Wipf & Stock Publishers, 1997 [1974].

Frykenberg, Robert Eric. *Christianity in India: From Beginning to the Present*. New York: Oxford University Press, 2008.

Guha, Ramachandra. *India After Gandhi: The History of the World's Largest Democracy*. New York: Harper Perennial, 2008.

Hardy, Edward Rochie, ed. *Christology of the Later Fathers*. Louisville: Westminster John Knox Press, 1954.

Keay, F.E. *A History of Hindī Literature*. Calcutta: Association Press, 1920.

Khan, Benjamin. *Māno Yā Na Māno Prabhu Yīśu Ko Jāno: Prabhu Yīśu Masīh kī Jindagī kī Kahānī* [Believe or not, Know Jesus Christ: The Story of the Life of Jesus Christ]. Delhi: Indian Society for Promoting Christian Knowledge, 2003.

Khan, Benjamin. *Khristīy Nītiśāstr* [Christian Ethics]. Jabalpur: Hindi Theological Literature Committee, 2009 [1981].

Khan, Jordan C. *Sacchī Śānti kī Khoj* [Search for True Peace]. Delhi: M.S.S., 1971.

Lall, Moti. *Susamācār-Pracār Darśan aur Vyaktigat Pracār-Kary* [Personal Evangelism]. Jabalpur: Hindi Theological Literature Committee, 2008 [1970].

Liddell, H.G. and R. Scott. *An Intermediate Greek-English Lexicon, founded upon the seventh edition of Liddell and Scott's Greek-English Lexicon*. Oxford: Oxford University Press, 1889.

Mahendra, Shivraj K. *Masīh Merī Manzil* ("Christ my Destination"). Delhi: Indian Society for Promoting Christian Knowledge, 2008.

Masih, Komal and Christopher Peter. *Prabhu Yeśu kī Jīvanī aur Sevākāry* [The Life and Ministry of Jesus]. Jabalpur: Hindi Theological Literature Committee, 2007.

McGregor, Ronald S. "The Rise of Standard Hindi and Early Hindi Prose Fiction." *Journal of the Royal Asiatic Society of Great Britain and Ireland*, no. 3/4 (October 1967): 114–132.

McGregor, Ronald S., ed. *The Oxford Hindi-English Dictionary*. New Delhi: Oxford University Press, 1993.

Naim, Choudhri Mohammed. *Introductory Urdu*, Volume I, revised, third edition. Chicago: University of Chicago, 1999.

Nehru, Jawaharlal. *The Unity of India: Collected Writings 1937–1940*. New York: The John Day Company, 1942.

Orsini, Francesca. "Introduction." In *Before the Divide: Hindi and Urdu Literary Culture*, edited by Francesca Orsini. New Delhi: Orient BlackSwan Private Limited, 2010.

Prasad, S.W. *Krūs kā Bhed: Krūs se Sāt Vacanoṁ par Ādhārit Laghu Pustikā* [Mystery of the Cross: A Short Book Based on the Seven Sayings from the Cross]. Lucknow: Lucknow Publishing House, 1991.

Premkumar, R. Daniel. "The Commonwealth of Dalits and Tribals: Towards the Re-Positioning of the Church's Ecumenical Agenda in India Today." In *Ecumenism: Prospects and Challenges*, edited by Vinod Victor. Delhi: Indian Society for Promoting Christian Knowledge, 2001.

Shackle, Christopher and Rupert Snell. *Hindi and Urdu since 1800: A Common Reader*. New Delhi: Heritage Publishers, 1990.

Singh, C.K. Paul. *Masīhī Ādhyātmik Śikṣā* [Christian Doctrines]. Ranchi: The Department of Evangelism and Literature, Gossner Evangelical Church, 1975.

Sona, Udit. *Antim Sāt Vacan: Yīśu Dvārā Kahe Gaye Antim Vacanoṁ par Manan* [Final Seven Sayings: Reflection on the Final Seven Sayings by Jesus]. Delhi: Indian Society for Promoting Christian Knowledge, 2010.

Sugirtharajah, Rasiah S., ed. *Asian Faces of Jesus*. Maryknoll: Orbis Books, 1993.

Thapar, Romila. *Reading History from Inscriptions*. Kolkata: K. P. Bagchi & Company, 2002.

Thapar, Romila. *The Penguin History of Early India: From the Origins to AD 1300*. Gurgaon: Penguin Books, 2015 [2002].

Thiemann, Ronald F. *Revelation and Theology: The Gospel as Narrated Promise*. Eugene: Wipf & Stock, 1985.

Yesudas, G.D. *Kṛpā Mārg* [The Way of Grace]. Bombay: The Christian Literature Society, 1965.

Zahir, Alfred. *Svarg aur Uske Uparānt* [Heaven and Beyond]. Allahabad: N.I.C.T.B.S., 1968.

3 Linguistic choices

The politics of religion is intertwined with the politics of language in India. Political contests over languages make up a substantial part of India's history.[1] Given its ability to unite and consolidate, linguistic affinity is ideological. Ideologies function as "sub-national, national or cross-national identifier[s] of populations contesting for or protecting non-religious, usually political or socioeconomic, interests."[2] In India, languages act as identifiers of populations and tools to contest and protect political and socioeconomic interests. Ramachandra Guha notes India's long history of loyalty to linguistic and cultural traditions accounting for the strength of its regional identities.[3] The alignment of Hindi with Hindu and Urdu with Muslim influenced India's partition in the middle of the nineteenth century.[4]

At India's independence, 'Hindi imperialism' was acutely felt in areas that spoke other languages. Jawaharlal Nehru and other secularists considered the State's non-alignment with languages and religions a cardinal policy. But this approach invited trouble.[5] Sardar Vallabh Bhai Patel, India's first Deputy Prime Minister, struggled to unite India's many linguistic and cultural groups.[6] Patel, whom Nehru tasked to convince the various principalities to join the newly formed nation, struggled frequently with the question of language: would India have one language? How could we accept the tyranny of Hindi or English in our region? While Hindi was spoken widely in the north of India, southern Indians spoke languages like Tamil or Telugu or Malayalam. Oriya in the east, Punjabi and Gujarati in the west, in addition to the hundreds of tribal languages and local dialects, created a tapestry of deep and dominant regional cultures. The Indian National Congress maintained a multilingual policy during its one-party rule, fully aware that imposing a national language would lead to civil divisions. During the independence movement, Gandhi and Nehru promoted Hindustani as the shared national language across the nation. After independence, Nehru's position on the matter shifted. By the time Congress passed The States Reorganisation Act in 1956, the party had conceded the fact that India would be organized on the basis of linguistic states. India remains conflicted on the issue of an official language. Hindi may be a national language, at least according to Article 343 of the Constitution, but for all practical purposes one is better off using English outside the Hindi belt. Hindi is just a part of the national fabric of India, not the entire cloth.

Political contests over language are part of India's history. Yet, as Sunil Khilnani[7] and Ashutosh Varshney[8] have shown, language has not played a powerful role in destabilizing India's democracy. Rather, linguistic loyalties have led to influential political alignments. On one hand, linguistic organization after independence prevented language-based regional power centers from tearing the young nation apart. On the other hand, linguistic identities account for some part of the gradual shift of political power from central governments to regional rule. Language has, Varshney writes, led to a proportionally minor amount of communal violence compared to other motivators. Compared to religion and caste, language has accounted for a share of communal violence that is disproportionate to the size and influence of languages in India.[9]

Languages in India are repositories of strong group identities and culture. Language helped consolidate political power and ideologies. The Hindi movement of the nineteenth century exacerbated the politics of language and religion. Christopher R. King has shown that the Hindi movement was part of a "process of multi-symbol congruence" of language, religion, and nationalism that transformed old equations: "Urdu = Muslim + Hindu and Hindi = Hindu + Muslim" became "Urdu = Muslim and Hindi = Hindu."[10] Christian materials in Hindi challenge the claims for such alignments. Hindu nationalists may have adopted Hindi and produced slogans like "Hindi, Hindu, Hindustan," but their legacy and politics have shared public space with the centuries-old legacy and politics of the Christian use of Hindi.

While it is possible to speak of a Sanskrit, Urdu, or English cosmopolis,[11] when Christian authors write in Hindi, they are participants in an ongoing history of linguistic and religious alignment that continues at the national and regional levels. Christian missionaries found an active language scene when they reached the Hindi-speaking regions of the Central Provinces. Hindi and many dialects were integral to local cultures and linked to local pride in food, dress, history, and community. Consequently, Christian missionaries found it natural and necessary to turn to locally prevalent languages in their attempts to function as preachers, teachers, and translators. Hindi authors and translators in Independent India have continued this tradition of writing and producing Christian texts in Hindi. However, such practices should also be understood in light of the challenge they pose to cultural and religious narratives that seek to align a language primarily with one religion over others. To the extent that Hindi-language Christian literature exists diachronically and synchronically across India's history and geography, it does not constitute a break from the cultural communication and self-understanding of Christian writers and hymnodists in other Indian languages.[12] But it does signify a radical embrace of the lingua franca for the sake of educating the population and communicating a religious message.

The lineage of contemporary Christian writings in Hindi stretches back to Christian works in vernacular Hindi produced by missionaries and the publication houses of missionary societies in central and northern India. This lineage can be recognized in the type of language used over a span of nearly a hundred years. Consider the following three versions of Matthew 1:18[13] in Hindustani and modern Hindi that span 95 years:

> *Yīśu khrīṣṭkā janm is rītise huā. Uskī mātā mariyamkī yūsaphse manganī huī thī par unke ekaṭṭhe honeke pahile vah dekh paḍī ki pavitr ātmāse garbhăvatī hai.* ।
>
> (Hindi New Testament, 1909)[14]

> *Yīśu masīh kā janm is prakār se huā: yīśu kī mātā mariyam kī maṁgnī yūsaph se huī thī, par unke milan ke pūrv vah pavitr ātmā se garbhăvatī pāī gai.* ।
>
> (Hindi New Testament, 1988–89)[15]

> *Ab yīśu masīh kā janm is prakār se huā, ki jab us kī mātā mariyam kī maṁgnī yūsaph ke sāth ho gaī, to unke ekaṭṭhe hone se pahile vah pavitr ātmā kī or se garbhăvatī pāī gai.* ।
>
> (Hindi New Testament, 2004)[16]

Readers and speakers of modern standard Hindi will be able to understand the birth story of Jesus written in these three different types of Hindi without any specialized skills.[17] This is not surprising. By the late nineteenth and early twentieth centuries, Khaṛī Bolī -based Hindustani was in widespread use in central and northern India. Hindustani had been taken beyond its home in northern India through merchants and due to the reach of the Mughal Empire.[18] From the early nineteenth century, John B. Gilchrist at the Fort William College was promoting Hindustani prose based both on Persian and Khari Boli-based registers.[19] In turn, Gilchrist was building on nearly a half-century of Hindi-language publications by mission centers in central and northern India.[20]

Through its various phases, vernacular Christian literature has sought to transmit ideas to those of different cultures and languages. Like Syrian and Catholic attempts to communicate in other linguistic regions, Hindi-speaking Christians exercised great care and deliberation when attempting to carry across – *trans-latio*[21] – ideas between Christianity and Hinduism. Without conceptual equivalence, translations needed selective distance from local contexts and interpretive mobility. Care and mobility aptly describe key features of Hindi language Christian literature. Two case studies elaborate on the translation strategies of Hindi Christian writers. The first case study deals with the creation of neologisms. The second examines the deployment of polytraditional words as bridge words. The case studies in translation that concern this chapter help explain some of the important ways in which Hindi-speaking Christians have deployed translation choices.

This chapter deals with Hindi-language Protestant Christian literature produced by Christian publishing houses in central and north India. This literature is mostly generated by the Hindi Theological Literature Committee, Lucknow Publishing House, and the Indian Society for Promoting Christian Knowledge. With the incorporation of the Indian Society for Promoting Christian Knowledge as an independent and autonomous body under the Societies Registration Act of 1860[22] and the formation of the Hindi Theological Literature Committee in 1954, Indian Christian literature in general and Hindi Christian literature in particular acquired powerful sponsors. Today, the Committee is the largest producer of Hindi Christian literature and Christian materials and the Indian Society is its national and international distributor. Based respectively in Jabalpur (Madhya Pradesh), Lucknow (Uttar Pradesh) and Delhi, these agencies have produced most of the Hindi-language Christian texts in the region.[23]

Christian uses of Hindi

Hindi's relation to Christianity can be traced back to the use of Hindi as a language of instruction by missionaries who settled in the eastern and central parts of colonial India. The Serampore trio – William Carey, Joshua Marshman, and William Ward – of the Bengal-based Baptist Missionary Society (1792) were at the forefront of this trend. Reports of missionary activities shed light on the type of activities in which early Baptist missionaries were involved. On November 25, 1800, a Hindu named Fakira approached the Mission for 'examination' as a Christian – a process through which non-Christians were tested on their readiness to become Christian. However, as the story goes, after his exam Fakira returned to his village and never came back. As a result, a certain Krishna Pal, a carpenter from the suburbs of Serampore, ended up being the first convert of the Bengal Mission. The Periodical Account of the Indian Mission to its London Headquarters in 1801 includes Fakira's story, as reported by John Sutcliff, based on the personal diary of Daniel Brunsdon. Sutcliff, a Baptist minister in Olney, North Buckinghamshire, mentored William Carey and other missionaries including Brunsdon, who wrote him the account from India:

> *This has been a memorable day indeed! The first Hindoo, named Fakīra, came before the Church. His answers were ready, simple, and satisfactory. He has for some time heard brother Thomas at Beerbhoom; and is lately come down to us at Serampour. Brother Carey interrogated him in Bengallee, and afterwards interpreted, as the Sisters could not understand all his answers. I can only note down a few questions and answers. Q. How do you expect salvation? A. From the mercy of God in Christ. Q. How came you first to think about God and your soul? A.*

> *From hearing Mr. Thomas speak God's word, and the gospel; I thought nothing about it before. Q. If we should not be willing to receive you, what do you intend to do? Will you go back to your old way of living, and serve the debtahs? A. No! If you do not receive me, I will take my book, and go about telling the Hindoos of this great Saviour; and if you do not give me any thing to eat, God will. – Every one was well satisfied with what he said. The meeting closed with prayer by brother Carey in Bengallee, and by brother Thomas in English.*[24]

Bible translations, Christian instruction, and language training informed early forms of contact between Hindi language and Christian ideas. The Serampore trio soon realized the value of using Hindi as a language for secular and theological instruction. Hindi language training in missionary schools provided a platform for Christian instruction. At the same time, the commitment to proselytize was supported by the use of local languages like "Bengallee" (Bengali) and Hindustani.

The Baptists in Serampore were not the only ones producing Christian literature in Hindi. By 1912, such texts had come to be catalogued in the survey of vernacular Christian literature published by the National Missionary Council for India (now the National Council of Churches in India). This catalogue was expanded and republished in 1917. North Indian poets like Tulsīdās and Kabīrdās had "proved the capabilities of Hindi to convey religious truths" and missionaries of the time claimed that what was possible in verse was also possible in prose.[25] And so, in addition to references to 490 Christian works in Hindi, the 1917 catalogue also listed 13 publishing houses located throughout central and north India.[26] There was the Methodist press in Lucknow. Ranchi was home to a Lutheran press and an Anglican one. The Baptists published from Calcutta. Mhow hosted a Presbyterian publishing house and Jabalpur hosted a publishing house of the Disciples of Christ church. German Lutheran missionaries from Berlin had reached Ranchi in Chotanagpur in 1845 and over the next century many mission agencies shaped the region: the Gossner Evangelical Lutheran Mission, the Society for the Promotion of the Gospel, the Scottish Free Church Mission, and the Dublin University Mission. Publications and translations by missionaries paid attention also to tribal dialects and languages. By 1939, for instance, the British missionary Clemet F. Moss devised a written script for the Gondi language and used it to introduce Christianity to the Gondi tribes in Padhar in the Central Provinces. Moss, a medical doctor, shaped Gondi, translated parts of the Gospels into Gondi, and established Padhar Hospital. His work among the Gonds has been chronicled by Robert C. Ruark, a journalist who wrote accounts of his visits to Moss in Padhar.[27]

Vernacular materials covered a range of topics. Among the 490 publications listed in the 1917 Hindi language catalogue, 21 had Indian authors while the rest were penned by non-Indian missionaries. The largest set of publications (59 books) dealt with Hinduism. Titles included *Bhāg kā*

Brittānt ("What is Fate"), *Dharma Kasauṭi* ("Touchstone of Religion"), *Shāstra Parikshā* ("The True Shatras") and *Pāp Shodhan Siddhānt* ("The True Atonement").[28] These books sought to refute Hindu objections to Christianity, to 'expose' the insufficiency of Hindu soteriology, and to compare Hinduism unfavorably to Christianity. In addition to books confronting Hinduism, the catalogue recorded biblical commentaries, biographies of Jesus and Paul, concordances, synoptics, dictionaries, interpretive aids, works on theology and catechisms, collection of sermons, church histories, apologetics, prayer books, devotionals, hymnbooks, books on health and hygiene from a Christian perspective, missionary biographies, guidebooks for men, women, and children, school textbooks, magazines, and periodicals.

Catholic missions and publications were also widespread. In 1534, for instance, the Episcopal See of Goa was created and Catholic missionaries were sent to minister to local Christians – Portuguese soldiers and merchants, Armenians in Mughal courts – and to preach to non-Christians. In north-central India, Agra was the focal point of Jesuit work dating to the time of Akbar's reign (1556–1605 CE).[29] In 1579, Akbar invited Jesuit Fathers from Goa to his court in Agra, and in 1620, during the reign of Jahāngīr, Akbar's eldest son, Jesuit missionaries were invited to Patna and they established a church there in addition to the one they had established in Agra.[30] Belgian Jesuit Catholic missionaries first reached Chotanagpur in central India in 1868, preceded in the east by the Jesuit Mission in Bengal.[31]

From the earliest stages it was clear that Hindi served as a 'bridge' language: its instruction at the influential College of Fort William gave civil servants and missionaries a linguistic foothold among the local public and running schools in Hindi provided the missionaries a valuable means to support their mission. Described as an important center of Indian Studies due to its pioneering work, the College's influence on the development of Indian literature has been questioned. The College community itself produced works limited to grammar books, dictionaries, fables, and historical narratives and translated books into English for the benefit of students and administrators. The College published 130 books, the largest number of which were in Hindustani or Urdu-Hindi (37), followed by Sanskrit (24), Arabic (20), Bengali (18), Persian (18), and Marathi (6). There were two books in Chinese and one each in Burmese, Kannada, Oriya, Punjabi, and Telugu.[32] The College, however, also served as a substantial patron of authors and poets in a variety of Indian languages. It supported the development of Indian literature for practical purposes like school education. The influence of the College in the area of school education in vernaculars is generally recognized in studies on the College of Fort William.[33] Social purposes like school-age literacy and administrative ease were not the only reasons for using Hindi. Religious education and the composition of Christian communities were also a factor.

Early charters of the College of Fort William stressed ethical formation in addition to civil training under the belief that "the solution to Indian social problems lay in its evangelization."[34] The educational interests of British civil servants and missionaries complemented each other to a certain extent. British administrators held the administration responsible for the moral and material progress of Indians through education and left religious teaching largely to Christian missions. But through the persistence of Scottish missionaries like Alexander Duff and John Wilson, British administrators cooperated with missions. In the early decades of the nineteenth century, the East India Company government in Punjab and Uttar Pradesh had started to provide monetary support to mission-sponsored education. By the early twentieth century, schools managed by Christian missions received financial and administrative support as part of the government's wide educational program.[35] Translations of the Bible and the Gospels into Hindi accompanied the work of such schools, and many early Christians saw themselves in service of education, health, and social development as much as they were committed to evangelizing and raising local churches. The use of Hindi, then, as along with bringing practical benefits, was also driven by religious education. Usage was also given a boost as a result of the serious challenges presented to the ecclesiastical interests of missionaries by other catalysts. Particular among these catalysts was a strong pull on the use of vernaculars exerted by the changing demographics of an increasingly Indianizing Christianity.

The use of Hindi by missionaries was controversial. Influential missionaries like Alexander Duff disagreed with the move to use vernaculars to transmit Christianity. For certain missionaries, languages and religions were intertwined. Preceding Hindu nationalists today, Christian missionaries contended that religion, culture, and language could not be separated from each other. Evangelism ought not just to preach the gospel but also to shape colonial India in light of Christian *or* Western values (and, yes, these values were interchangeable).[36] Which language, these missionaries asked, would

> prove the most effective instrument of a large, liberal, and enlightened education? – the best primary medium of conveying the literature, science, and Christian theology of Europe to those who by their instruction and example are to be the teachers and guides of their countrymen?[37]

While Carey and his ilk – whom Duff dismissed as "Orientalists and Christian philanthropists" – chose vernaculars and translations, for Duff and his Scottish partners only English could be the "most effective medium of Indian illumination – the best and amplest channel for speedily letting in the full stream of European knowledge" in India. Dubbed "Anglomaniacs" by their critics, these missionaries argued that language was not simply a way to communicate but also a repository of religion, culture, and values. English was Christian while Bengali and Sanskrit were Hindu. Just as someone acquiring Sanskrit would "become indoctrinated into a false system [Hinduism]," a person who acquires English would be "perpetually brought in contact with the *new ideas*, the *new truths*, of which [English] terms are the symbols and representatives."[38] Despite its intensity, this debate over vernaculars did not sway Christians away from using Hindi. The changing shape of Christian demographics in India partly accounts for the staying power of a multitude of languages among Christians in India.

Missionary Christian communities drew people from a wide demographic, the majority coming from lower castes and classes that were subject to social, religious, and economic discrimination.[39] This resulted in the increased use of vernaculars for Christian worship and liturgy, the support for and acceptance of Indian missionaries, and alignment with India's Independence movement.[40] Indigenization and the use of vernacular language became rallying issues for central Indian churches, a growing number of whose members shared lower socioeconomic status and Dalit backgrounds. The increasing number of 'backward' converts was in turn a reflection of both mission needs and geographic realities. Most missionary activity started in the cities, which were better supplied and connected due to transport and communication networks, and gradually extended to surrounding villages and towns. The introduction of the railways further increased connections between cities and facilitated missionary work in rural areas.[41]

After 1862, Anglican missionary work, which had started in Calcutta, Secunderabad and Meerut, spread to smaller towns like Itawa, Jhansi, Gwalior, Orcha, Sagar, Ranipur, and Mahu. By 1881, the Presbyterians had extended their missionary work to areas in Farukhabad, Punjab, and North India,[42] covering vast Hindi-speaking regions. In central India, Gond kings ruled various kingdoms in what is now Madhya Pradesh and eastern Maharashtra. Chhindwara and Nagpur became centers of Gond rule and in 1679 Father Philip de Faria was sent from the Catholic mission in Patna to Nagpur.[43] Catholic ministers knowledgeable in Hindi[44] were serving at Sardhana-Meerut (c. 1820),[45] Jabalpur (1845),[46] Kamptee (1849),[47] Chhattisgarh (1852),[48] and Thana (c. 1865),[49] among other Hindi-speaking regions. They set up churches, schools, and convents that taught English and Christian principles in Hindi. By 1931, five of every six Indian Christians were rural.[50] Growth in the Indian church was driven by Dalit leaders and communities. 'Large-scale conversions'[51] among Dalits were initiated by Dalit leaders.[52] In Punjab the Christian population grew from 3,912 in 1881 to 395,629 in 1931, mostly due to conversion by lower-caste Chuhra leaders who then convinced members of the community to convert. In Uttar Pradesh, Mazhabi Sikhs and their leaders near Moradabad approached local Methodist missionaries in 1859. In Andhra Pradesh, the Malas converted in the thousands in the 1840s–1880s, so did the Madigas and Sudras.[53] By 1931, Uttar Pradesh had a Christian population of 173,077, most of whom were Dalits. In Madhya Pradesh, on the other hand, most of the converts were people from the Gond and Bhil tribes.

Given this demographic context, the use of vernaculars in general, and Hindi in particular, served the Indian church quite well. Vernaculars proved an efficient means to connect people to the Gospels. The same applied to Hindi and its cognates because the ways in which people encountered Christian ideas were gradual and by no means clear-cut. In many cases new Christians continued to live in their communities (be they villages, towns, or cities), interact with their neighbors, face caste-based discrimination, and as research by Sebastian Kim has shown,[54] negotiate the ground between their first religious tradition (which in most cases was a form of Hindu, Dalit, or tribal traditions) and Christianity.

When a language is presented as fully descriptive of a religious tradition, it can reify that tradition's values and claims. Claims of syncretism and reification in the study of religion, Tony Stewart argues, stems from the association of languages with religions – like Sanskrit and Hindi with Hindus, Urdu with Muslims, and Marathi with Brahmins – and from the construal of monolithic religions under terms like "Christian," "Hindu," and "Muslim." India's linguistic legacy of terms that seek conceptual equivalence[55] across religious traditions belie the claim that expression in different religious traditions constitute mutually exclusive zones of communication. Rather, vernaculars and translations appear as attempts to negotiate bridges and 'excess' across religious traditions rather than to transmit meaning across religious traditions without change, as if what was transmitted and what was received were photocopies of each other. Vernacular religions in India represent ongoing negotiations that signal certain linguistic strategies. These translation strategies cannot be characterization as either seeking assimilation within or distance from the broader religious languages of the regions in which those negotiations are taking place. For instance, Richard Eaton's study of Sufis in the Deccan sheds light on the gradual adoption of Islamic theologies and practices among the Dakani-speakers of the region.[56] Tony Stewart similarly highlights the casual and ongoing way in which religious communities interacted and adapted to each other in Bengal.[57]

In similar vein, Hindi-language Christian literature contains borrowed or adapted ideas, neologisms, and creative thinking. Consider the debate over how to address Jesus. On one hand there is the nonhonorific address. It is colloquial, relatable, common in vernaculars, and quotidian. It is exemplified in Hindi hymns with lyrics like *yīśu, yīśu! pyāre yīśu! tū hī merī āśā hai* ("Jesus, Jesus, you [the nonhonorific *tū*] alone are my hope").[58] Nonhonorific divine address – useful when trying to communicate the Gospels in the vernacular and in oral rather than written form – has a counterpart in honorific divine addresses in translations of the Hindi Bible, which, unlike their predecessors, have sought to create conceptual parity with the honorific way in which neighboring Hindus address gods. Compare, for instance, the highlighted references in these translations of Matthew 5:1–2:

> *yīśu bhīḍako dekhake parbatpar caḍh* ***gayā*** *aur jab vah* ***baiṭhā*** *tab śiṣy* ***us*** *pās āye* | *aur vah apnā muṃh kholake unheṃ upadeś dene* ***lagā*** |
>
> (1909 Hindi New Testament; with nonhonorific references)[59]

> *jansamūh ko dekhakar yīśu pahāḍ par caḍh* ***gae*** *| jab vah* ***baiṭh gae*** *tab śiṣy* ***unake*** *samīp āe | yīśu in śabdoṃ meṃ unheṃ upadeś dene* ***lage*** *|*
>
> (1988–89 Hindi New Testament; with honorific references)[60]

Or, the differences in these highlighted translations of Luke 4:14–16:

> *yīśu ātmākī śaktise gālīlko fir* ***gayā*** *aur* ***uskī*** *kīrti āspāske sāre deśameṃ fail gaī | aur usne unkī sabhāomeṁ upadeś* ***diyā*** *aur sabhne* ***uskī*** *baḍāī kī | tab vah nāsaratko* ***āyā*** *jahāṃ* ***pālā gayā thā*** *aur apnī rītipar biśrāmke din sabhāke gharmeṃ jāke paḍhaneko* ***khaḍā huā*** *|*
>
> (1909 Hindi New Testament; with nonhonorific references)[61]

> *yīśu ātmā kī sāmarthy se bhar kar galīl pradeś* ***lauṭe*** *aur* ***unkā*** *nām āspās ke sāre pradeś meṃ fail gayā | vah sabhāgṛhoṃ meṃ upadeś* ***dete the*** *aur sab log* ***unkī*** *praśansā karte the | yīśu nāsarat nagar meṃ* ***āe****, jahāṃ* ***unkā pālanpoṣaṇ huā thā****| vah apnī rīti ke anusār viśrām-divas par sabhāgṛh meṃ* ***gae*** *| vah dharmśāstr paḍhane ke lie* ***uṭhe*** *|*
>
> (1988–89 Hindi New Testament; with honorific references)[62]

The shift from non-honorific to honorific language in Matthew 5:1–2 and Luke 4:14–16 is conspicuous when the 1909 and 1988–1989 versions are compared. The older version of the Hindi Bible uses terms like (*caḍh*) ***gayā***, ***baiṭhā***, (*dene*) ***lagā***, and ***khaḍā huā*** – "he climbed," "sat," "started giving," and "stood up" respectively – in forms reserved for references to actions by someone younger or less honored than the reader. The 1909 version uses possessive pronouns like ***uskī*** – "his" – in forms used to refer to those less honored than the reader. In the newer version of the Hindi Bible, these words take on honorific conjugations like (*caḍh*) ***gae***, ***baiṭh gae***, (*dene*) ***lage*** and ***uṭhe***,[63] along with the honorific personal possessive ***unkī*** in place of the non-honorific ***uskī***. Other such linguistic shifts and strategies are also evident in Hindi Christian literature.

Dehadhāraṇ in Hindi Christian literature

One of the influential debates in Hindi-language Christian theology has revolved around the merits and shortcomings of using the term *avătār* to present the relationship between Jesus and God. How to translate 'incarnation'? Can *avatar* capture what Christians are trying to communicate? Given the familiarity of the concept in Indian culture, scholars have compared *avătār* with incarnation.[64]

Early Hindu reformers found the idea of Jesus as *avătār* appealing. Ramakrishna Paramahamsa (1836–1886) and his disciple Swami Vivekananda

(1863–1902) considered Jesus to be an *avătār* of God. According to Ramakrishna, an *avătār* is someone who has a deep, personal experience of God. For Ramakrishna, Jesus fit the bill. His disciples, especially Vivekananda, ascribed the same designation to Ramakrishna. Of Jesus and Ramakrishna, Vivekananda wrote:

> The Word has two manifestations, the general one of Nature, and the special one of the great Incarnations of God – Krishna, Buddha, Jesus and Ramakrishna. Christ the special manifestation of the Absolute is known and knowable. The Absolute cannot be known; we cannot know the Father, only the Son.[65]

These Hindu thinkers were not alone in calling Jesus an *avătār*.

Christian uses of *avătār* have a long history in India. In the seventeenth century Roberto de Nobili used the term cautiously to affirm that Christ, unlike the other *avătār*s, is the true incarnation of God.[66] *Avătār* generally meant 'descent' or 'manifestation.' Many Christian authors have argued that their tradition shared certain claims about *avătār*s: the embodiment of God in human form, a direct experience of God in this life, and personal devotion to an embodied deity. Yet, as Michael Amaladoss notes,[67] Indian Christians also adapted the idea to include features particular to Christian claims: that Jesus did not come in power but rather as a suffering servant (according to the *Bhagavad Gītā*, Krishna reveals his cosmic form, whereas Jesus in the New Testament refuses an entreaty to do so); God's humanity in Jesus did not disappear after Jesus's death, but it endures in time and eternally; and Jesus's humanity leads all humanity to salvation. These features explained why Jesus was "a special incarnate avatar."[68]

Others have tried to bring Christ closer to other *avătār*s, especially to Krishna. For Ovey N. Mohammed,[69] the Christ of the New Testament can be compared to the Krishna of the *Bhagavad Gītā*: he is the "true God and true human" who saves graciously. Based on a lengthy analysis of soteriology in the *Bhagavad Gītā* and in the New Testament, Mohammed writes in unmistakably Christian idioms that "God takes the initiative in reconciling us to Godself by becoming incarnate in Krishna and Jesus."[70] In a similar vein, Vengal Chakkarai,[71] a Vaiṣṇavite convert to Christianity, has argued that *avătār* rather than guru is most suitable to translate the concept of incarnation as it expresses the intimate union between God and human as "no mere theophany but a permanent, mediating union."[72]

Sadhu Sundar Singh,[73] a Sikh convert to Christianity, has also used *avătār* and incarnation synonymously.[74] Father Camille Bulcke, in his much-used English-Hindi Dictionary, translates 'incarnate' as *dehadhārī* or *śarīrădhārī* (one who takes on or holds or puts on a body) and 'incarnation' as *dehadhāraṇ*, *avătāraṇ*, and *avătār*.[75] More recently, after a careful survey of the arguments on both sides and a credible assessment of *avătār* in Advaitā,[76] Steven Tsoukalas has argued for the "interchangeability" of '*avătār*' and 'incarnation,' albeit with substantial caveats. Substantial enough that he proposes neologisms to translate 'incarnation' into Sanskrit rather than adopt the readily available term *avătār*. Tsoukalas hopes to retain the familiarity of *avătār* and maintain the uniqueness of Christ in order to find common ground that "enhances evangelistic/interreligious relations." Yet Tsoukalas concludes that each term – '*avătār*' and 'incarnation' – falls short in light of the other's religio-philosophical context. To bridge the gap, he proposes *īśvarāvatāraviśeṣaivapūrṇamanuṣya* ("a full human being [arising] from a unique specific/particular descent of the Almighty") or *īśvarāvatāra viśeṣaivamanuṣyasatya* ("a real human being [arising] out of a unique specific/particular descent of the Almighty") to communicate the Christian idea of incarnation in Sanskrit.[77] Nevertheless, both of Tsoukalas's neologisms include and build on the term '*avătār*.' In this approach, he is in the company of Indian scholars. As one Indian theologian has put it, "the term avatar is the closest Hindu equivalent to the Christian idea of incarnation."[78]

But another strand in Indian Christian theology questioned the interchangeability of *avătār* and incarnation, both in general and in the specific case of comparisons between Krishna and Christ. An 1801 account from the early days of the Baptist Missionary Society in Bengal reports that Hindus "often confound the names of Kreeshnoo and Christ, which they pronounce Creestoo." Alarmed by this trend, Joshua Marshman (1768–1837), a prominent member of the Serampore trio and a key collaborator with William Carey on Bible translations, composed a three-page poem in Bengali to correct this increasingly common error. The first page of the poem is presented here as a sample from the 1801 report:

> *The* DIFFERENCE*:*
>
> Or, *Kristnoo* and *Christ* compared.
> THE words of love, dear Hindoos, now attend:
> *Kreeshnoo* and CHRIST as one, why apprehend?
> Examine coolly, I'll propose the test,
> Who ne'er examines justly ranks a beast.
> In cool discussion he who God appears,
> His followers be, dismissing all your fears.
> To kill a tyrant, *Kreeshnoo* man became;
> CHRIST took our nature sinners to redeem.
> One country's welfare, *Kreeshnoo*'s highest aim;
> CRHIST [sic] as their Saviour may all nations claim.
> *Kreeshnoo* could earthly good alone procure;
> But CHRIST hath heavenly glory made secure.
> His own enjoyment merely *Kreeshnoo* sought,
> He ne'er for sinners felt one anxious thought;
> Midst crowds of wanton nymphs, in sport and play,
> And idle mirth, he spent the live-long day.
> CHRIST to the blind gave sight, speech to the dumb,

And even rescued from the darksome tomb;
He his own pleasure ever did forego,
And spent his life t' abolish sinners' woe.
Who thus in love and rich compassion shone,
Dear brethren judge, he must be God alone.[79]

Conflating Krishna with Christ was a matter of deep concern, and care was taken in this early stage of the Protestant mission to separate the two and present one as "God alone" against the other. Poems such as the one by Marshman above signified gaps in translation: attempts to borrow terms and concepts wholesale across contexts could lead to misinformation and confusion. The use of *avătār* led to a loss in transmission; incorrect information was being communicated. Conflating Krishna with Christ (ignoring key differences between them), treating them as interchangeable saviors, and in doing so relegating Jesus to one savior among many, undermined a core Christian claim: that only Jesus Christ could save. Keshab Chandra Sen, who feared the rise of a Brahminical version of Christianity, vehemently opposed using *avătār* for incarnation, calling such use "the lie of Christian avatarism."[80] Brahmabandhab Upadhyaya, proposing a form of *advaitin* Christology, seemed to argue that there was only one descent, that of Christ, in which the Supreme Brahman became incarnate.[81]

In line with such thought, Din Dayal adds an important corrective in *Masīhī Dharmvigyān kā Paricay* (An Introduction to Christian Theology), published in 2005. The official English title on the copyright page of the book reads: "An Introduction to the Indian Christian Theology." The copyright holder, the Hindi Theological Literature Committee, felt it necessary to qualify 'Christian Theology' with 'Indian,' which is absent from the original Hindi title. The change sheds light on the strategy of the Hindi Theological Literature Committee to mark and market its publications as 'Indian.' Marketing aside, the addition of 'Indian' to the title had other motives. Expressing Christian theology in Hindi claimed Hindi for Christianity in India. Yet, to call Christian theology 'Indian' also meant clarifying that 'Indian' does not mean 'Hindu.' To 'Indianize' Christianity is not to 'Hinduize' it. Resistance to *avaˇtār* in Hindi-language Christianity, and Indian Christianity at large, is a case in point. It stems from fears that the use of *avaˇtār* compromises the uniqueness of Christ and dilutes Christian claims when they copy Hinduism. Dayal's corrective is to make explicit the fact that socioeconomic factors also affected the resistance to *avaˇtār*: Christian converts from lower caste and Dalit backgrounds sought distance from mainstream Hindu theology. As a consequence, missionaries translating the Bible and the 'Good News' into Hindi sought an identifiable Christian vocabulary separate from that of the Hindu elite.

Given the competing claims on the suitability of the term *avătār* as a synonym for incarnation, then, Hindi translators created a neologism. Unlike

Indian Christian theologians who synced Hindu and Christian ideas at the turn of the twentieth century, Hindi Bible translators consistently ignored *avătār* and chose *dehadhāraṇ* (*deh* "body" + *dhāraṇ* "to possess") to translate *ὁ λόγος σὰρξ ἐγένετο*[82] in John 1:14 ("the logos became flesh," from the verb *γίνομαι*, "to become," which the New Revised Standard Version translates as "the Word became flesh").

Dehadhāraṇ has been translated as 'embodied' or 'incarnation,' but I suggest that the best translation is one that preserves the active nature of the act of embodiment (that Jesus Christ embodies) and focuses on the one who embodies. *Dehadhāraṇ* in this construction is specific to Christ (as the translators intended), points to his 'taking birth' (and not a passive reference to his 'being born'), and hints at his taking and having a real and physical body. In the words of a popular Urdu-Hindi translation of "Hark! The Herald Angels Sing": Jesus "wore Adam" (literally: "wore the clothes of Adam"; *pahanā ādam kā libās*).[83] A *dehadhārī* is one who is bodily or possesses a body (*śarīrī*)[84] and is a living creature (*prāṇī*).[85] Dayal's book is an example of the preference for *dehadhāraṇ* in Christian theology in Hindi that is also evident in the Hindi Bible and in Hindi-language Christian hymns, poems, and other literature.

Dayal lists four objections to the use of *avătār* in Christian contexts. First, he notes that Hindus speak of many *avătārs* while Christians hold that Christ is differentiated by a triple mark: contra plurality, Christ is "Lord forever, unique, and embodied" (*khrist sadā ke lie advitīy dehadhārī prabhu hai*).[86] Second, the historicity of Hindu *avătār*s is not "important" (*mahatva*) to Hindu scholars and in some cases is contested; Christ, on the other hand, was a "historic man" (*aitihāsik puruṣ*).[87] Third, there is a "huge difference" (*bhārī antar*) in the objective of Hindu *avătār*s and the *dehadhāraṇ* of Jesus Christ: *avătār*s seek the destruction of evil and the wicked (consider Krishna in the Gita) while Christ comes to save sinners and those in need of redemption.[88] Finally, and here Dayal's attention to the body of Jesus shapes his case, "Hindu *avătār* is Docetic" (*Hindū avătār rūpābhās [Docetic] hai*).[89] Viṣṇu appears in human form on earth. Such Docetic claims were also made of Christ in early Christianity, but theologians of that time – and here Dayal is drawing his argument mostly from Chalcedon's declaration of Christ's dual nature – strongly opposed such an idea. Given these differences, though avătār can be found in Indian hymns in other languages,[90] Hindi-speaking Christians by and large have not accepted the word. As Dayal rightly notes, every Hindi Bible of the Bible Society of India has used *dehadhāraṇ* to translate John 1:14.

Objections to *avătār* among Hindi Christian sources are not limited to Dayal. The influential Indian evangelist Richard Howell also objects to *avătār* in *Parivartan* ("Conversion"), his treatise on Christian evangelism.[91] Howell objects to *avătār* in terms of both theology and language. Howell provides a list of eight objections. Howell echoes the four objections raised by Dayal: Christ is a unique incarnation, historic, a savior and not a destroyer, and fully human. To these arguments, Howell adds a few more. *Avătārs* are different from other human beings in degree only and not in type. On the bodily nature of Christ, Howell's gloss is different than Dayal argument. Dayal claims *avătār* language is docetic. Howell tries to argue that a fully human *avătār* would get caught in the karmic cycle and will need liberation from the effects of karma. The presentation of Krishna's bodily form in the Gita provides a counterpoint to the ways in which Dayal and Howell interpret the body of an *avătār*. The Gita suggests that Krishna possesses a type of special body. Krishna's body is material but above the vicissitudes of karma, attachment, and ignorance. To the extent that Krishna's body is material yet possesses unique features, the Gita shares common ground with Dayal and Howell when they ascribe a special body to Christ and explain that he was fully human *yet* without sin. In the Gita, Krishna distinguishes his lower and higher material nature (*prakṛti*). Based on an analysis of this claim, Steven Tsoukalas concludes that Krishna is "sinless" because his body lacks a "connection with *prakṛti* as it relates to *triguṇātmikā* [the material nature of ordinary humans]," but since "human beings' material [lower] nature comes from the eternal [higher] *prakṛti* that is indwelled by Viṣṇu," there is identification of Krishna with humanity.[92] Howell further claims that Christ is not an *avătār* because *avătārs* emerge from the supreme Atman (*viśv ātmā*) and return to it lacking an independent existence of their own. Then there is the claim regarding history. According to Howell, Hindu *avătārs* share knowledge acquired from history while Christ gives heavenly knowledge. The argument seems to be that Hindu religious *gurus* and teachers, many of whom claim to be reincarnations, pass on knowledge acquired from history, having learned from their earthly teachers (e.g., Gita 4:1–4). Christ, on the other hand, imparts heavenly knowledge not learned from the past but drawn from His relation with the Father. Finally, according to Howell, *avătārs*, including those cases where a *guru* claims to be liberated, promise and teach "realization of the self" (*svayaṁ ka anubhav*) but Christ calls humanity to a new birth, freedom, and fellowship with the living God. Howell's objections are rather imbalanced: they ascribe complex theology to Christian claims while present Hindu ideas in reductive and contrasting terms. In doing so, Howell's objections seem more rhetorical and self-confirming in nature than grounded in a deep understanding and independent study of Hindu theology.

Howell's concern with *avătār*-as-a-Christian-term is linguistic in nature too. Word choices matter to Howell. Words possess history and meaning in particular contexts and can be both beneficial and harmful. His analysis of the appropriateness of *dehădhāraṇ* or *avătār* follows a longer discourse on the adequacy and virtue of words. Poorly chosen and hurtful words harm God's mission. They can also confuse others and result in undesirable responses. So, Howell encourages Christian to avoid words like "ignorant" and "idol worshippers" when speaking to non-Christians. Such words "do not express love," are "without merit" (*ayogy*), and "generate opposition" (*virodhī bhāvănā utpann karne vāle*).[93] Not only can poor words harm relations, they also can confuse Christians and non-Christians alike. *Avătār* is one such word. Of *avătār* and other such *ayogy* words he writes: "Those words that help us progress, come, let us attempt to take the words of our mission from the thought-world of Holy Scripture."[94]

The preference for *dehadhāraṇ* and its grammatical forms is evident in the near exclusive occurrence of the word in Hindi Christmas hymns. The primary Hindi hymnal, *Ārādhănā ke Gīt* (Songs of Worship), published in its most recent edition in 2009 by a joint committee of the Madhya Pradesh Christian Council and the Methodist Church in Southern Asia for use in Madhya Pradesh, Uttar Pradesh and Bihar, presents forty-seven songs for Advent and Christmas. In every case where incarnation is referenced in these hymns – barring one in the chorus of number 110: *le līnhā khrist avătārā, manāo khuśī* (Christ has become incarnate, Rejoice!) – we find *deh dhāraṇ* or *dehadhārī* or *dehadhār* (numbers 77, 86, 90, 92, 93, and 98). Consider the Hindi translation of a favorite hymn among Lutheran churches: "O Come, All Ye Faithful."[95] The original text is attributed to John Francis Wade (1711–1786) and was translated in part (stanzas 1, 3–4) by Frederick Oakeley in 1814; *Ārādhănā ke Gīt* does not list its Hindi translator.[96] Presented here are the English and Hindi translations of the chorus, stanza 1, and stanza 4:

O come, all ye faithful, Joyful and triumphant! O come ye, o come ye to Bethlehem; Come and behold him, born the king Of angels;	*ab āo viśvāsiyo* *jay jay karate āo* *ab āo hum caleṃ baitlaham ko* *caranī meṃ dekho mahimā* *kā rājā;*
O come, let us adore him, O come, let us adore him, O come, let us adore him, Christ, the Lord.	*ab āo hum sarāheṃ* *ab āo hum sarāheṃ,* *ab āo hum sarāheṃ* *khrist prabhu ko.*
Yea, Lord, we greet thee, Born this happy morning; Jesus, to thee be glory giv'n! Word of the Father, now in flesh Appearing.	*āmīn! prabhu dhany ho* *trāṇ ke lie janmā* *he yīśu ho terī anant mahimā,* *pitā kā vacan ab dehadhārī* *huā.*

Other variations to express the incarnation of Christ elaborate on the theme: "wore the clothes of Adam" (*pahanā ādam kā libās*; number 88), "having taken on a human body" (*manuṣy deh vah dhāraṇ kar*; number 90), "lives among us" (*madhy hamāre nivās*; number 95), "humbled in the form of a man" (*ādamī kī sūrat meṃ huā pastahāl*; number 96), "God has become man" (*huā hai khudā insān*; number 107), "who is born of/the son of Mary" (*jo mariyam kā jāyā hai*; number 114), "left heaven, became human" (*choḍā āsamān, banā iṃsān*; number 118), and "God has come down to earth having become human" (*utar āyā jahāṃ meṃ ab khudā iṃsā ban ke*; number 122). It is further the case that, in support of Dayal's argument, biblical verses that speak of Christ's descent to earth, like John 3:13, have been translated using *utarā* to highlight the act of descent in clear distinction from words for 'appear' or 'seem' (Greek: δοκέω), like *darśan* in John 21:14 ("This was now the third time that Jesus appeared to the disciples"), *dikhāī* in 1 Corinthians 15:5 ("and then he appeared to Cephas"), or *pragaṭ* in Hebrews 9:26 ("he has appeared once for all at the end of the age"). Forms of *utarā* are also used in Genesis 28:12 ("and the angels of God were ascending and descending"), Exodus 34:5 ("The Lord descended in the cloud"), Mark 1:10 ("the Spirit descending like a dove on him"), John 1:51 ("the angels of God ascending and descending upon the Son of Man"), and Ephesians 4:9 ("he had also descended into the lower part of the earth"). While the debate between *dehadhāraṇ* and *avătār* among Indian Christians writing in English seems yet unsettled, Hindi authors and churches have repeatedly chosen the former over the latter. What explains this choice? I suggest that the preference for *dehadhāraṇ* among Hindi-speaking Christians is fueled by the desire to use a distinct Christian vocabulary in service of a recognizable Christian identity amidst their (mostly) Hindu neighbors.

For Hindi authors, like many English writers before them, differentiating Christ from *avătār*s like Krishna and Ram was important. There were significant differences between the concepts of *avătār* and incarnation such that they did not allow any easy interchangeability. D. P. Sham Rao, writing on *guru* traditions in India, spoke for many Christians when he wrote,

> We cannot . . . ignore the concepts of *avatara* and *guru* which have molded the Indian religious consciousness. But we cannot use *avatara* and incarnation as interchangeable terms, nor can Christ be understood merely as a *guru*. But the concepts are relevant starting points and need to be studied in depth by Indian Christian thinkers.[97]

Avătār, Sham Rao notes, was not the only term available to translate the idea of Christ's human descent. Indian authors have deployed a host of ideas to communicate incarnation. Jesus has been described as *antaryāmin*, *Cit* (of *Satchitānandā*), *Satyāgrahi* (Mohandas Gandhi), Dancer,[98] Drum,[99] and, a *Parambhakta* (in complete harmony of thought and purpose with God) who inspires *bhakti*,[100] among others. Hindi Christian sources do not reflect an affinity for these proposals and, as discussed earlier, reveal a considerable preference for *dehădhāran*.

Despite the preference for *dehadhāraṇ* in Christian literature in Hindi, a certain level of comfort with polytraditional religious vocabulary is also evident in the Hindi Bible and other Hindi Christian works. Polytraditional words convey ideas and function in more than one religious tradition.

Intentional linguistic semblance occurs when a religious group deploys a word or idea that is recognizably part of the vocabulary of another religious group. Take, for instance, the frequent use in the Hindi Bible of *mandir* (a temple, palace, abode, dwelling, or figuratively, the body[101]), a term that Hindi-speaking Christians would readily recognize as one used also by Hindus to refer to temples. *Mandir* appears in 1 Samuel 3:3, Matthew 4:5, Matthew 12:6, John 2:21, 1 Corinthians 3:16, Ephesians 2:21 (*pavitr mandir* for "holy temple"), and Revelation 21:22. *Pavitr sthān* (1 Corinthians 3:16) or *pavitr bhavan* (Psalms 11:4) or *pavitr mandir* (Ephesians 2:21) is sometimes deployed as an alternative to *mandir* to refer to the innermost part of a temple as distinct from the whole temple enclosure when the original Hebrew or Greek so demands, for example, to translate *ναός θεοῦ* in 1 Corinthians 3:16.[102] Unlike the unsuitability of *avătār* as a substitute for *dehadhāraṇ*, however, *mandir* functions along with other available options like *bhavan* (2 Chronicles 2:12: "who will build a temple for the Lord"), and *pavitr bhavan* (Psalms 11:4: "The Lord is in his holy temple").

Polytraditional words are not unique to the Hindi Bible and appear in Hindi Christian poems. In her poems on the Gospel of Mark, for instance, Sarojini Arya replaces *yīśu* (Christ) with *prabhu* (Lord or God) and *khudā* (Urdu: God) with *parameśvar* (Supreme Lord[103]) to present the Good News (*śubh saṃdeś*) to readers of any religion or community. Arya explains, "I have tried to make this presentation universal and broad in such a way that a reader of any religion/community can read it. I have also tried to keep it close to our culture and have used the word 'lord' for 'Jesus' and the word 'supreme lord' for 'God'."[104] God is not transcendent, or *nirguṇ*, in Arya's construction, neither does her work minimize its evangelical intent; yet her willingness to liberate God from Christian specific references suggests comfort with a pan-religious vocabulary. Comfort with pan-religious vocabulary is evident in the use of polytraditional words in Hindi Christian hymns. *Darśan* (number 18), *mandir* (numbers 22, 47, 66, 193, 330, 406), *bhakti/bhakt* (numbers 29, 374), māyā (number 285), *mukti/muktidātā* (numbers 44, 78, 193, 284), *śifā* (number184), *dharm* (numbers 27, 224), *īmān* (numbers 27, 213, 287), *khidmat* (numbers 47, 377), and *pāk* (numbers 73, 148, 185, 437) make frequent appearances in Hindi-language Christian hymns.[105]

Christian works in Hindi reveal creative range and theological mobility. While *dehadhāraṇ* emerged as a distinct neologism, *avătār* has also found a place in Hindi-language Christian discourses. While Hindi hymns have sought distinct translations, they are also replete with pan-religious terms and ideas. Resistance to the explanatory power of *avătār* can be traced to its limited ability to express incarnation through Christian eyes and due to a robust sense of distinction between the process described in incarnation and that described in *avătār* theology. Here, the translation choice serves to distinguish and mark-out ideas. In other instances, however, the use of polytraditional words in Christian hymns and literature in Hindi serves to equate and mark-in ideas. Here, words do not serve one tradition in specific ways but function within and between multiple religious traditions. Amidst mobility, however, some of the religio-linguistic choices demonstrate a certain amount of stability. *Dehadhāraṇ*, as shown previously, is remarkably consistent across Hindi-language Christian religious literature and devotionals. Similarly, polytraditional words like *mandir* and *īmān* find regular use across such texts. A careful study, then, of religious language and translation choices by Hindi-speaking Christians demonstrates the complex and dynamic nature of Christian-Hindu relations in a context where markers of religious identity are functional and shared. It brings to light some of the many subtle and rich developments found in Protestant Christian literature in central and north India that seek to function across religiously diverse and idiomatic Hindi worlds.

Notes

1 Doniger, *The Hindus*; Khilnani, *The Idea of India*; Varshney, *Battles Half Won.*
2 Nandy, *Time Warps*, 62.
3 Guha, *India After Gandhi.*
4 King, *One Language, Two Scripts*, 173–176.
5 Nandy, *Time Warps*, 73–76.
6 Guha, *India After Gandhi*, 118.
7 Khilnani, *The Idea of India.*
8 Varshney, *Battles Half Won.*
9 See the riot database in Varshney, *Ethnic Conflict and Civic Life.*
10 King, *One Language, Two Scripts*, 15.
11 Pollock, *The Language of the Gods*, 11–12.
12 Cf. Pollock, *The Language of the Gods*, 21.
13 "Now the birth of Jesus the Messiah took place in this way. When his mother Mary had been engaged to Joseph, but before they lived together, she was found to be with child from the Holy Spirit" (NRSV).
14 *Dharmăpustak kā Antbhāg*, [or, The New Testament in Hindi], 2.
15 *Hindī Bāibil* ("Hindi Bible"), 1–2.
16 *Pavitr Bāibil* ("Holy Bible"), 1.
17 Cf. Allen, *Ocean of Inquiry*, 12.
18 Shukla, *Hindī Sāhity kā Itihās*, 299–301.
19 Shukla, *Hindī Sāhity kā Itihās*, 301; Das, *Sahibs and Munshis*, 18.
20 Anand, *Pāścāty Vidvānoṁ kā Hindī Sāhity*, 78–80.
21 Kraput, "Postcolonialism," 177.
22 The London-based Society for Promoting Christian Knowledge was formed on March 8, 1698. Its missionary activities led to the formation of the Indian Society for Promoting Christian Knowledge in 1710. Under the Societies Registration Act of 1860, Indian Society for Promoting Christian Knowledge constituted itself as a self-governing body independent of the London-based Society for Promoting Christian Knowledge. On October 15, 2010, Indian Society for Promoting Christian Knowledge celebrated its tercentenary in India.
23 Textual data from field research, partly funded by the South Asia Institute at Harvard University, covered central and North Indian collections, including those at the Hindi Theological Literature Committee, the Indian Society for Promoting Christian Knowledge, and Lucknow Publishing House, a Methodist publishing house.
24 Yale Digital Library Collection, digcoll 183956, page 106.

25 Greaves and Mukerji, *A Descriptive and Classified Catalogue*, iii–iv.

26 The American Tract Society, Allahabad; Baptist Mission Press, Calcutta; Bengal Sunday School Union, Calcutta; Christian Literature Society, Allahabad; Christian Mission Press, Jabalpur; Canadian Presbyterian Mission Press, Rasalpur, Mhow; Calcutta Tract Society, Calcutta; Epworth League Office, Lucknow; Gossner Evangelical Lutheran Mission Press, Ranchi; Methodist Publishing House, Lucknow; North India Christian Tract and Book Society, Allahabad; Punjab Religious Book Society, Lahore; and the Society for the Propagation of the Gospel Mission Book Depot, Ranchi. (Greaves and Mukerji, *A Descriptive and Classified Catalogue*, v).

27 Ruark *El Paso Herald*; Ruark, *Spokane Daily*; and, Ruark, *Winona Daily*.

28 English titles as given in the 1917 catalogue. Greaves and Mukerji, *Descriptive and Classified Catalogue*, 17–21.

29 Sharma, *Christian Missions in North India*, 16.

30 Moget, *Vagabonds for God*, 1.

31 Tete, *Constant Lievens*, 13–15. See also, Mahto, *Hundred Years of Christian Mission.*

32 Das, *Sahibs and Munshis*, 154–164; Augustine, *Fort William*, 166–168.

33 Das, *Sahibs and Munshis*, ix, 112–118.

34 Das, *Sahibs and Munshis*, 8.

35 Mayhew, *Christianity and the Government of India*, 160–161. Mayhew (1878–1948), a Classics master at Eton in the 1920s and an educator in the Colonial Education Service, was director of Public Instruction, Central Provinces, India. An Oxford graduate, he was first assigned to Madras in India in 1903, was deputy director of Public Instruction in Madras by 1907, and by 1916, at age 38, was appointed director of Public Instruction in the Central Provinces (Whitehead, *Colonial Educators*, 149–153).

36 Ingleby, *Missionaries, Education and India.*

37 Duff, *India, and India Missions*, 518.

38 Duff, *India, and India Missions*, 519–520.

39 Sahu, *The Church of North India*, 9.

40 Sahu, *The Church of North India*, 101–103.

41 Dayal, *Uttar Bhārat aur Pākistān meṃ Masīhī Dharm*, 151.

42 Dayal, *Uttar Bhārat aur Pākistān meṃ Masīhī Dharm*, 170.

43 Tete, *Constant Lievens*, 2.

44 Tete, *Constant Lievens*, 57.

45 Different dates are claimed for the start of the Catholic church in Sardhana. Sardhana's Catholic Basilica, *The Church Basilica of our Lady of Graces*, lists two possible dates for the beginning of the church: 1809 and 1820 (www.sardhanachurch.org/TheChurch-Basilicaof.aspx; accessed April 10, 2015). Sharma lists the completion of the church in 1821 (Sharma, *Christian Missions in North India*, 58). According to Sharma, the church's beginning must have preceded 1821.

46 Moget, *Vagabonds for God*, 101.

47 Moget, *Vagabonds for God*, 49.

48 Moget, *Vagabonds for God*, 126.

49 Moget, *Vagabonds for God*, 57.

50 Hutton, *Census of India*, 423, cited in Webster, *The Dalit Christians*, 73.

51 Webster is critical of the term "mass movement," popularized by Pickett's *Christian Mass Movement in India* (1933), whose distinguishing features are a group decision in favor of Christianity and the "consequent preservation of the converts' social integration" (Pickett, *Christian Mass Movements in India*, 22). Webster argues the conversions were neither the product of group think nor did they succeed in preserving the converts' social integration. He prefers "large-scale conversions" to highlight the personal choice central to the act of conversion and the converts' move from an assigned social hierarchy to a "new 'mixed' community of unclear social status" (Webster, *The Dalit Christians*, 45).

52 Webster, *The Dalit Christians*, 47.
53 Webster, *The Dalit Christians*, 48–50.
54 Kim, *In Search of Identity*, 35–36, 190–200.
55 Stewart, "In Search of Equivalence," 269–270.
56 Compare Richard M. Eaton's 1974 study of the expansion of Indian Islam in "Sufi Folk Literature and the Expansion of Indian Islam," *History of Religion*, 127. Eaton contends that the Sufis of the Deccan made "no conscious effort" to gain non-Muslim followers and hence cannot be called missionaries seeking conversions akin to that of the nineteenth- and twentieth-century Christianity movement in India. He describes "conversion," which has been aligned with Christian missionary activity, as a sort of "self-conscious, sudden and total change of belief" and hence "inadequate" to describe the "process" by which Sufis of the Deccan found non-Muslim followers. Rather than a sudden conversion to Islam, these followers are "still undergoing a gradual process of Islamic acculturation" (Eaton, "Sufi Folk Literature, 127). This study of Hindi Christians questions Eaton's ascription of Christian conversion as sudden and total change. Gradual acculturation – in theology, practice, and liturgy – better explain the ongoing transformation of Hindi-language Christian communities in India.
57 Stewart, "In Search of Equivalence," 261–262.
58 *Ārādhǎnā ke Gīt*, Number 267.
59 *Dharmputstak kā Antbhāg*, 9–10.
60 *Hindī Bāibil*, 6.
61 *Dharmputstak kā Antbhāg*, 175.
62 *Hindī Bāibil*, 101–102.
63 The transition is in the concluding vowel, from *gay-ā*, *baiṭh-ā*, (*dene*) *lag-ā*, and *khaḍ-ā hu-ā* to *ga-e*, *baiṭh ga-e*, (*dene*) *lag-e* and *uṭh-e*.
64 See, for instance, Sheth, "Hindu Avatar and Christian Incarnation."
65 Vivekananda, *The Complete Works*, 7:1; see also Amaladoss, *The Asian Jesus*, 21–24.
66 Thangaraj, *The Crucified Guru*, 75.
67 Amaladoss, *The Asian Jesus*, 117.
68 Amaladoss, *The Asian Jesus*, 121.
69 Mohammed, "Jesus and Krishna," 11. Mohammed, a Jesuit, is professor of systematic theology at Regis College, the Jesuit School of Theology at the University of Toronto. Mohammed has published on Ignatian spirituality and the *Bhagavad Gītā*, Hinduism, and spirituality and on the theology of religions and interfaith hermeneutics.
70 Mohammed, "Jesus and Krishna," 22.
71 Chakkarai, *Jesus the Avǎtār*, 5–6, 48. Chakkarai (1880–1958) was from a wealthy Chettiar family in Madras. After practicing law (1908–1913) he joined the Danish Mission in Madras. Inspired by Mahatma Gandhi, in 1917 he joined the Home Rule Movement. He was a theologian and wrote *Jesus the Avǎtār* and *The Cross and Indian Thought*. He was also an influential public figure and was elected mayor of Madras (1941), chairman of the All-India Trade Union Congress (1951), and member of the Legislative Council (1954) (England et al., *Asian Christian Theologies*, 224–225).
72 Boyd, *An Introduction to Indian Christian Theology*, 170; Thangaraj, *The Crucified Guru*, 76.
73 Singh, *Wisdom of the Sadhu*, 63–69. Singh (1889–1929) was born in a well-to-do family of Jat Sikhs. His mother deeply influenced his early religious life and introduced him to Sanskrit and Hinduism. His mother's death in his teens left him spiritually troubled and in urgent need to connect with God. This struggle lasted for two years, when at the age of sixteen, on a cold December night in 1904, Singh saw Yesu (Jesus) in a vision. He was baptized on his sixteenth birthday and soon thereafter became an itinerant preacher of the gospel in the mode of one

who renounces the world. He travelled extensively throughout North India, visited Tibet regularly, and preached far and wide in Ceylon, Japan, China, France, Switzerland, England, and the United States. His works – mostly pamphlets and letters – include *At the Master's Feet*, *Reality and Religion*, *Visions of the Spiritual World*, and *With and Without Christ*. (Riddle, *The Vision and the Call*)

74 Boyd, *An Introduction to Indian Christian Theology*, 98; Heiler, *The Gospel of Sâdhu Sundar Singh*, 95–98.

75 Bulcke, *Aṁgrezī-Hindī Koś*, 413.

76 Tsoukalas compares chapter 4 of the Bhagavad Gītā (with Krishna's *avătār*) and commentaries on it by Śaṅkara and Rāmānuja with notions of incarnation in Orthodox Christianity to reach his conclusion. (Tsoukalas, *Kṛṣṇa and Christ*, 117–130)

77 Tsoukalas, *Kṛṣṇa and Christ*, 225–228.

78 Thangaraj, *The Crucified Guru*, 27.

79 Yale Digital Library Collection, digcoll 184118, page 318.

80 Sen, quoted in Boyd, *Introduction to Indian Christian Theology*, 81.

81 Boyd, *Introduction to Indian Christian Theology*, 81.

82 Greek text from Aland, *Novum Testamentum Graece*, 247.

83 *Ārādhănā ke Gīt*, Hymn 88.

84 McGregor, *The Oxford Hindi-English Dictionary*, 945.

85 Bahri, *Rājapāl Hindī Śabdakoś*, 407.

86 Dayal, *Masīhī Dharmvigyān kā Paricay*, 148.

87 Dayal, *Masīhī Dharmvigyān kā Paricay*, 148.

88 Dayal, *Masīhī Dharmvigyān kā Paricay*, 149.

89 Dayal, *Masīhī Dharmvigyān kā Paricay*, 149. English word in original.

90 Tsoukalas points to Telugu hymns that use *avătār*. Tsoukalas, *Kṛṣṇa and Christ*, 225.

91 Howell, *Parivartan*, 194–195. At the time of publication of *Parivartan*, Howell was President of the Evangelical Fellowship of India (EFI). Founded in 1951 as a national alliance of evangelical Christians, EFI trains missionaries to witness the good news, seeks to transform India, and advocates for the poor and marginalized. Its legal arm (the Christian Legal Association) advocates on behalf of the rights and freedom of Christian converts and institutions.

92 Tsoukalas, *Kṛṣṇa and Christ*, 165.

93 Howell, *Parivartan*, 170–171.

94 Howell, *Parivartan*, 171: *Jo śabd hameṁ āge baḍhne meṁ sahāyak hai āie ham apne miśan ke śabdoṃ ko pavitr śāstr kī vicārădhārā se lene kā prayatn kareṁ.*

95 *Evangelical Lutheran Worship*, number 283.

96 *Ārādhănā ke Gīt*, number 86.

97 Sham Rao, *Five Contemporary Gurus*, 46; cited in Thangaraj, *The Crucified Guru*, 87.

98 Amaladoss, *The Asian Jesus*, 147ff.

99 Clarke, *Dalits and Christianity*.

100 Appasamy, *The Theology of Hindu Bhakti*; also see Boyd, *An Introduction to Indian Christian Theology*, 121.

101 McGregor, *The Oxford Hindi-English Dictionary*, 780.

102 Abbott-Smith, *A Manual Greek Lexicon*, 300.

103 A title of Viṣṇu or Śiva. McGregor, *The Oxford Hindi-English Dictionary*, 604.

104 Arya, *Kavitā meṃ Śubh Saṃdeś*, xiv–xv: "*Maine is prastuti ko is tarīke se sārvajanik aur vyāpak banāne kā pyrays kiyā hai, tāki kisī bhī dharm/samudāy ke pāṭhak ise paḍh sakate haiṃ. Maine ise apnī saṃskṛti ke nikaṭ bhī rakhane kā prayās kiyā aur "prabhu" śabd "yīs'u" ke lie aur "parameśvar" śabd "khudā" ke lie istemāl kiyā hai.*"

105 Hymns from *Ārādhănā ke Gīt*.

References

Abbott-Smith, G. *A Manual Greek Lexicon of the New Testament*. New York: T & T Clark, 2001 [1921].

Aland, Barbara, Kurt Aland, Johannes Karavidopoulos, Carlo M. Martini, and Bruce M. Metzger, eds. *Novum Testamentum Graece*. Stuttgart: Deutsche Bibelgesellschaft, 1993 [1898].

Allen, Michael S. *The Ocean of Inquiry: A Neglected Classic of Late Advaita Vedānta*. Doctoral dissertation, Harvard University, 2013.

Amaladoss, Michael. *The Asian Jesus*. Maryknoll: Orbis Books, 2006.

Anand, John Henry. *Pāścāty Vidvānoṃ kā Hindī Sāhity* ["Western Contribution to the Hindi Language and Literature"]. Jabalpur: Hindi Theological Literature Committee, 2011 edition.

Anand, John Henry and Ramdutt Vashisht. 1988. *Merā Paṛosī Merā Bhāī* [My Neighbor My Brother]. Delhi: Indian Society for Promoting Christian Knowledge.

Anand, John Henry and S.K. Warne, trans. *Sampreṣaṇ: Arth aur Abhyās* [Communication: Meaning and Practice]. Jabalpur: Hindi Theological Literature Committee, 1995.

Anderson, Walter K. and Sridhar Damle. *The Brotherhood in Saffron: The RSS and Hindu Revivalism*. Delhi: Vistaar Publications, 1987.

Appasamy, A.J. *The Theology of Hindu Bhakti*. Bangalore: Christian Literature Society, 1970.

Ārādhǎnā ke Gīt [Songs of Worship]. Lucknow: Lucknow Publishing House, 2009 [1975].

Arya, Sarojini V. *Kavitā meṃ Śubh Saṃdeś* [Good News in Poetry]. Delhi: Indian Society for Promoting Christian Knowledge, 2003.

Augustine, M.L. *Fort William: Calcutta's Crowning Glory*. New Delhi: Ocean Books, 1999.

Bahri, Hardev. *Rājpāl Hindī Śabdakoś* [Rajpal Hindi Dictionary]. Delhi: Rajpal & Sons, 2010.

Boyd, Robin H.S. *An Introduction to Indian Christian Theology*. Madras: The Christian Literature Society, 1975 [1969].

Bulcke, Camille. *Aṁgrezī-Hindī Koś, An English-Hindi Dictionary*. Ranchi: Catholic Press, 2007 [1968].

Carey, Eustace. *Memoir of William Carey*. London: Jackson and Walford, 1836.

Carey, William. 'Journal.' Regent's Park College, Oxford: Angus Library and Archive, 1795.

Chakkarai, Vengal. *Jesus the Avătār*. Madras: Christian Literature Society, 1926.

Clarke, Sathianathan. *Dalits and Christianity: Subaltern Religion and Liberation Theology in India*. New Delhi: Oxford University Press, 1998.

Das, Sisir Kumar. *Sahibs and Munshis: An Account of the College of Fort William*. New Delhi: Orion Publications, 1978.

Dayal, Din. *Uttar Bhārat aur Pākistān meṁ Masīhī Dharm: Pratham Śatābdī se Bīsvīṁ Śatābdī ke Ārambh Tak* [The History of Christian Religion in North India and Pakistan: From the First Century to the Beginning of the Twentieth Century]. Jabalpur: Hindi Theological Literature Committee, 1997.

Dayal, Din. *Masīhī Dharm Vijñān kā Paricay* [An Introduction to Indian Christian Theology]. Jabalpur: Hindi Theological Literature Committee, 2005.

Dharmpustak kā Anthbhāg, arthāt Mattī au Mārk au Lūk au Yohan Racit Prabhu Yīśu Khrīṣṭ kā Susamācār, aur Preritoṃ kī Kriyāoṃ kā Brittānt, aur Dharmopdeś aur Bhaviṣydvāky kī Patriyāṃ, jo Yūnānī Bhāṣā se Hindī meṃ kiye gaye haiṃ [or, The New Testament in Hindi]. Boston: Massachusetts Bible Society, 1909.

Doniger, Wendy. *The Hindus: An Alternative History*. New York: Penguin Books, 2009.

Duff, Alexander. *India and India Missions: Including Sketches of the Gigantic System of Hinduism, both in Theory and Practice; also, Notices of Some of the Principal Agencies Employed in Conducting the Process of Indian Evangelization*. Edinburgh: John Johnstone, 1839.

Eaton, Richard M. "Sufi Folk Literature and the Expansion of Indian Islam." *History of Religions* 14, no. 2 (1974): 117–127.

England, John C., Jose Kuttianimattathil, John Mansford Prior, Lily A. Quintos, David Suh Kwang-sun, and Janice Wickeri, eds. *Asian Christian Theologies: A Research Guide to Authors, Movements, Sources*. Volume 1: *Asia Region 7th – 20th Centuries; South Asia; Austral Asia*. Delhi: Indian Society for Promoting Christian Knowledge, 2002.

Evangelical Lutheran Worship. Minneapolis: Augsburg Fortress, 2006.

Greaves, Edwin and N.K. Mukerji, eds. *A Descriptive and Classified Catalogue of Hindi Christian Literature: Published Up To 1916–17*. Allahabad: North India Christian Tract and Book Society, 1917.

Guha, Ramachandra. *India After Gandhi: The History of the World's Largest Democracy*. New York: Harper Perennial, 2008.

Heiler, Friedrich. *The Gospel of Sādhu Sundar Singh* (trans. Olive Wyon). Delhi: Indian Society for Promoting Christian Knowledge, 2009 [1924].

Hindī Bāibil: Purānā aur Nayā Niyam [Hindi Bible: Old and New Testament]. Bangalore: Bible Society of India, 1988–89.

Howell, Richard. *Parivartan: Masīh se Milāp* [Conversion: A Meeting with Christ]. New Delhi: Evangelical Fellowship of India, 2006.

Hutton, J.H. *Census of India, 1931. Vol. I – India. Part I – Report*. Delhi: Manager of Publications, 1933.

Ingleby, J.C. *Missionaries, Education and India: Issues in Protestant Missionary Education in the Long Nineteenth Century*. Delhi: Indian Society for Promoting Christian Knowledge, 2000.

Khilnani, Sunil. *The Idea of India*. New York: Farrar, Straus and Girous, 1999.

Kim, Sebastian C.H. *In Search of Identity: Debates on Religious Conversion in India*. New York: Oxford University Press, 2003.

King, Christopher R. *One Language, Two Scripts: The Hindi Movement in Nineteenth Century North India*. Delhi: Oxford University Press, 1994.

Krupat, Arnold. "Postcolonialism, Ideology, and Native American Literature." In *The Post- Colonial Studies Reader*, edited by Bill Ashcroft, Gareth Griffiths, and Helen Tiffin. New York: Routledge, 2006 [1995].

Mahto, S. *Hundred Years of Christian Missions in Chotanagpur since 1845*. Ranchi: The Chotanagpur Christian Publishing House, 1971.

Mayhew, Arthur. *Christianity and the Government of India: An Examination of the Christian Forces at Work in the Administration of India and of the Mutual Relations of the British Government and Christian Missions, 1600–1920*. London: Faber & Gwyer, 1929.

McGregor, Ronald S., ed. *The Oxford Hindi-English Dictionary*. New Delhi: Oxford University Press, 1993.

Moget, Francis. *Vagabonds for God: A Story of the Catholic Church in Central India, 1846- 1907*. Bangalore: S.F.S. Publications, 1990.

Mohammed, Ovey N. "Jesus and Krishna." In *Asian Faces of Jesus*, edited by R.S. Sugirtharajah. Maryknoll: Orbis Books, 1993.

Nandy, Ashis. *Time Warps: Silent and Evasive Pasts in Indian Politics and Religion*. New Brunswick: Rutgers University Press, 2002.

Pavitr Bāibil, arthāt Purānā aur Nayā Dharm Niyam [Holy Bible, i.e., the Old and New Religious Testaments]. Bangalore: Bible Society of India, 2004.

Pickett, Jarrell Waskom. *Christian Mass Movements in India: A Study with Recommendations*. New York: Abingdon Press, 1934.

Pollock, Sheldon. *The Language of the Gods in the World of Men: Sanskrit, Culture, and Power in Premodern India*. Berkeley: University of California Press, 2006.

Riddle, Thomas E. *The Vision and the Call: A Life of Sadhu Sundar Singh*. Delhi: Indian Society for Promoting Christian Knowledge, 2004 [1997].

Ruark, Robert C. *El Paso Herald Post*, Wednesday, May 09. UNC Digital Archives, Folder 273: Scan 85, 1962.

Ruark, Robert C. *Spokane Daily Chronicle*, May 10. UNC Digital Archives, Folder 273: Scan 85, 1962.

Ruark, Robert C. *Winona Daily News*, Sunday, May 13. UNC Digital Archives, Folder 273: Scan 85, 1962.

Sahu, Dhirendra Kumar. *The Church of North India: A Historical and Systematic Theological Inquiry into an Ecumenical Ecclesiology*. Frankfurt: Peter Lang, 1994.

Sham Rao, D.P. *Five Contemporary Gurus in the Shirdi (Sai Baba) Tradition: A Study of Shri Sai Baba of Shirdi, Shri Upasani Baba of Sakuri, Shri Sati Godavari Mata of Sakuri, Shri Meher Baba of Ahmednagar, and Shri Satya Sai Baba of Puttaparthi*. Madras: The Christian Literature Society, 1972.

Sharma, Raj Bahadur. *Christian Missions in North India, 1813–1913: A Case Study of Meerut Division and Dehra Dun District*. Delhi: Mittal Publications, 1988.

Sheth, Noel. "Hindu Avatara and Christian Incarnation: A Comparison." *Philosophy East and West* 52, no. 1 (2002): 98–125.

Shukla, Ramchandra. *Hindī Sāhity kā Itihās* [History of Hindi Literature]. Delhi: Malik and Company, 2007 [1965].

Singh, Sundar. *Wisdom of the Sadhu: Teachings of Sundar Singh*, edited and compiled by Kim Comer. Walden: Plough Publishing House, 2000.

Sinha, Yunus Satyendra, trans. *Masīhī Ācaraṇ* [The Christian Character, by Stephen Neill]. Jabalpur: Hindi Theological Literature Committee, 2008 [1956].

Stewart, Tony K. "In Search of Equivalence: Conceiving Muslim-Hindu Encounter Through Translation Theory." *History of Religions* 40, no. 3 (February 2001): 260–287.

Tete, Peter, ed. *Constant Lievens and the History of the Catholic Church in Chotanagpur*. Ranchi: Archbishop's House, 1993.

Thangaraj, M. Thomas. *The Crucified Guru: An Experiment in Cross-Cultural Christology*. Nashville: Abingdon Press, 1994.

Tsoukalas, Steven. *Kṛṣṇa and Christ: Body-Divine Relation in the Thought of Śaṅkara, Rāmānuja and Classical Christian Orthodoxy*. Milton Keynes: Paternoster, 2006.

Varshney, Ashutosh. *Ethnic Conflict and Civic Life: Hindus and Muslims in India*. Delhi: Oxford University Press, 2002.

Varshney, Ashutosh. *Battles Half Won: India's Improbable Democracy*. New York: Penguin, 2014.
Vivekananda. *The Complete Works of Swami Vivekananda*. Almore, 1931.
Webster, John C.B. *The Dalit Christians: A History*. Delhi: Indian Society for Promoting Christian Knowledge, 2009 [1992].
Whitehead, Clive. *Colonial Educators: The British Indian and Colonial Education Service, 1858–1983*. London: I. B. Tauris, 2003.
Yale Digital Library Collection, digcoll 183956.
Yale Digital Library Collection, digcoll 184118.

4 Shaping identity

Hindi Christian authors are invested in the public image of Christianity in India. Commentary on public perceptions of Christians is prevalent in two types. In one form, Hindi Christian works are attuned to the ways in which Christians self-represent their religion to others and the ways in which Indian Christians are represented in public forums by others. This type of commentary has two foci: proper Christian ethics and proper portrayals of Christians in mass media like television and films. Debates on ethics cover topics like discipleship and guidebooks for Christians. Debates on media have focused on the proper language of mass communication and the proper form of Christian serials on television. These debates are the focus of this chapter. The other type of Hindi Christian commentary studies the role of Christians in Indian society. This commentary has taken a few complementary paths. There is focus on the promotion of interfaith relations. Explicit appeals to the minority position of Christians has fostered efforts to encourage relations with people of other faiths. The Hindu majority is a recurrent goal of Christian outreach on nation building, economic development, and communal peace. Interfaith dialogue has emerged as an important tool in this regard. Commentary on 'gentle' evangelism complements Christian investments in multifaith relations. As an instance, Hindi Christian sources reflect on the language of evangelization. What is being said? How is it being said? How does evangelization effect interfaith relations? Reviews of Christianity and society are the focus of the next chapter.

Identity is a form of communication. Religious expressions are a particular form of mass communication. Lawrence Babb and Susan Wadley provide a helpful model to study any such impact. In the context of the relationship between religion and mass communication, Babb and Wadley propose that religion can be understood in one of two ways. Religions can be understood as holding places, as "reservoirs that retain" the most expansive range of self-expressions in beliefs, rituals, records, ceremonies, icons, and other important manifestations of the religion. As reservoirs or repositories, religions communicate information to insiders and outsiders alike, though there may be greater focus on exchange of information within groups. A religion, as a system of communication, can also serve as a signal tower and socially transmit its content. A recurrent form of social transmission is public acts of rituals, prayers, and storytelling. Given the coded nature of religious symbols, some information is attenuated outside the group. Nevertheless, information flows out. Transmitters alter information and put their stamp on it. Some media are more conducive to standard messages than others. Texts, television, and films tend toward standardization. Spoken words, sung exchanges, and local appeals tend to inject variety in religions. The emergence of religion as a dominant theme on India's state television, Doordarshan, impacted public perceptions of Christians in India and as a result, Hindi Christians reacted to those portrayals.[1] Before examining etic images of Christians, I turn to self-portrayals by Hindi Christians. Discipleship is the main topic of Hindi Christian self-portrayals. In this chapter, I explain the context in which Christian guidebooks on ethics and life emerged. I sketch the proper Christian life as described in four important Hindi Christian guidebooks. I identify the central attributes of such a life. In Hindi Christian sources, Christian life is a public calling of sorts: it is important to transmit Christ in ways that serve the public good and contribute to the nation. Questions regarding the propagation of religion are, then, adjudicated in relation with commentary on the privileges and obligations of citizenship in India.

The milieu of Hindi Christians fosters sustained ethical thinking. *Bhakti* beliefs and practices, as noted earlier, permeate the religious landscape occupied by Hindi Christians. Similarly, public commentaries on *dharma* abound. Local newspapers carry daily columns on 'life lessons.' These columns are a recurring feature of newspapers in the region like *Dainik Bhāskar* and *Dainik Jāgaraṇ* in Hindi and *The Hindu* in English. Advice on proper living in Christian contexts appears in the form of commentaries on discipleship. Hindi Christian works explain the need for proper discipleship in two ways. Christian discipleship is traditionally understood as a necessary response to faith in attempts to attenuate any separation of 'faith' from 'works.' Benjamin Khan, author of one of the authoritative Hindi texts on Christian ethics, draws extensively on Dietrich Bonhoeffer's account of Christian life to explain the necessary connection between theology and ethics. Discipleship can also be understood as the public face of religion. Transmission is in Christianity's DNA. Hindi Christian works distinguish the need to evangelize from the need to convert. The former practice is generally accepted. The latter practice is up for debate. Discipleship is a medium to present religion in the best light. So, just as Hindu sources present "*Ram-Sita kī joḍī*" as the archetype of a perfect marriage,[2] Christian sources present Jesus as the model of virtues and actions.

The notion of discipleship orients the formation of proper faith and practice and provides a framework to form, grow, and spread faith. I have found Dietrich Bonhoeffer's comments on discipleship helpful to Hindi Christian works on discipleship. Another helpful source is the study of medieval monastic life by Talal Asad.[3] Virtues develop through repetitive acts, Asad argues, and the community provides the support structure that helps turn habits into virtues. Faith is expressed in the speech and acts of individuals. But these expressions acquire their shape and content from their religious milieu. They are also formed through guided and public repetitions of ritualized behaviors. Religious communities, then, establish the conditions for faith(ful) attitudes and practices. As a source of ideas on discipleship, Bonhoeffer's comments on it are as fertile as Asad's comments on the role of communities. Like Asad, Bonhoeffer explores the place of virtues, community, and public witness as a shaper of ethics. Bonhoeffer has the additional advantage of being studied by Hindi Christian authors like Benjamin Khan. Khan engages Bonhoeffer in *Khristīy Nītiśāstr* (a 1981 work on Christian ethics) and *Bīsavīṁ Śatābdī ke Pramukh Dharmavijñānī* (a 1990 work on theology). Bonhoeffer insists there can be no Christianity without personal discipleship. He writes:

> Discipleship means adherence to Christ, and, because Christ is the object of that adherence, it must take the form of discipleship. An abstract Christology, a doctrinal system, a general religious knowledge on the subject of grace or on the forgiveness of sins, render discipleship superfluous, and in fact they positively exclude any idea of discipleship whatever, and are essentially inimical to the whole conception of following Christ. With an abstract idea it is possible to enter into a relation of formal knowledge, to become enthusiastic about it, and perhaps even to put it into practice; but it can never be followed in personal obedience. Christianity without the living Christ is inevitably Christianity without discipleship, and Christianity without discipleship is always Christianity without Christ.[4]

Hindi Christian guidebooks echo Bonhoeffer's commitment to personal obedience and concrete discipleship. For the guidebooks, Christ is not just a messenger (of God's grace) but also a model to emulate. This argument is the crux of *The Cost of Discipleship*, which was written to re-affirm the basis of human relations in Christ rather than in any nation, creed, or family.[5] Only Christ, the Mediator between all relationships, could call Christians to discipleship and loyalty. The argument was counter-cultural and explosive. The original 1937 German was titled simply *Nachfolge* ("discipleship") but the first English translation in 1948 was titled *The Cost of Discipleship*. By 1948, the personal cost to Bonhoeffer of his primary allegiance to Christ had become clear. But in 1937, the Führer Principle was ascendant, Nationalist Socialism had gained power, Adolf Hitler was Reich Chancellor, Nazi intimidation was gaining steam, many German Christians had aligned with Hitler, and church opposition to the "Reich church" was quite small.[6]

Humans are connected via Christ the Mediator. As such, the link with Christ precedes all other ties. And discipleship of Christ precedes all loyalties. Bonhoeffer's account of discipleship repudiated the "illusion" of "direct relation" with the world, an illusion that had led many Christians in Germany to align with a leader other than Christ. Discipleship was, then, a public declaration of allegiance against the demands of the world. It was 'costly' because it rebuffed the demands of other powers and did so in a very public way. Followers of Jesus, Bonhoeffer explains, "are a visible community."[7] Discipleship is a public act because good works should be signposts to God. And signposts, by their very nature, are of minimal use when hidden from others. "Jesus does not say that men will see God; they will see the good works and glorify God for them. The cross and the works of the cross, the poverty and renunciation of the blessed in the beatitudes, these are the things which will become visible."[8] Bonhoeffer's theology of the visible affirms the importance for Christian ideas to be concretely perceptible. Hindi Christian guidebooks insist that Christian discipleship should be public. They affirm the public and communicative functions of Christian ethics. The public, communicative, and concrete nature of proper Christian discipleship reflects the public, communicative, and concrete life of Christ in history. "The Body of Christ takes up space on earth. That is a consequence of the Incarnation."[9] A Christian may hide light (read, life) under a bushel, but she is called to shine.

Crucial differences remain between Bonhoeffer's notion of discipleship and that found in Hindi Christian guidebooks. For instance, *The Cost of Discipleship* distinguishes between visible and invisible aspects of discipleship. While a Christian is called to serve publicly, Bonhoeffer asserts that such service must be in "separation from the world, [in] our transcendence of its standards, and [in] our extraordinariness."[10] Christian righteousness, the source of (visible) Christian public service, should be hidden from (or, invisible to) ourselves.

> Our task is simply to keep on following, looking only to our Leader who goes on before, taking no notice of ourselves or of what we are doing. We must be unaware of our own righteousness, and see it only in so far as we look unto Jesus. . . . Thus we hide the visible from ourselves in obedience to the word of Jesus.[11]

Such a "separation" is not meant as a call to renounce the world. Nor is it a call to create isolated communities. It is, rather, recognition of an "extraordinary" way of living and to beware the temptation to seek a Christian social order. Hindi Christian works ascribe to disciples the responsibility of transforming social orders.

Discipleship

Early Hindi Christian guidebooks were translations of works by Western missionaries. A Hindi translation of Williams Barclay's *Through the Year* was published as *Viliyam Bārkle ke Sāth Dainik Masīhī Ācaraṇ* ("Daily

Christian Conduct with William Barclay"). The original daily readings appeared in 'Orbiter Visa' and 'Seen in Passing' in *British Weekly* from 1952.[12] C. W. David, former editor of the Hindi Theological Literature Committee, translated the originals. Barclay was a prolific writer and influential preacher. Barclay's devotionals were popular among Hindi pastors who liked the devotionals for their ability to express the great truths of the Bible in simple and comprehensive ways. As Anand noted in his preface to David's translation, "Dr. William Barclay is among those few biblical scholars who have brought the great truths of the Bible to general readers of the world in simple words."[13] A Hindi translation of Stephen Neill's *The Christian Character* was published in 1956 as *Masīhī Ācaraṇ* ("Christian Conduct"). Translated by Pastor Yunus Satyendra Sinha, the book went through multiple prints as it gained popularity. Its second edition, prepared in 1960, was republished ten years later in 1970. A third run of the second edition in 2008 added another 1000 copies of *Masīhī Ācaraṇ* for use among Hindi-speaking Christians.

While not a guidebook by design, one of the first Hindi texts to gain popularity, *Masīhiyoṇ kā Parameśvar*, combined doctrinal commentary with ethical insights and instructions on Christian discipleship. A Hindi translation of Neill's *The Christian's God* by C.W. David (the original English and its Hindi translation were both published in 1954), *Masīhiyoṇ kā Parameśvar*, gained so much popularity that it saw two reprints in its first year and was re-issued in a new edition each year thereafter. "[H]aving commissioned a Hindi translation by Dr. C. W. David of the English book *The Christian's God*," Anand notes, the "book became so popular that in no time it was reprinted twice within the year. From there on it was published in a new edition every year."[14] The immense popularity of *Masīhiyoṇ kā Parameśvar* inspired other Hindi-loving missionaries in the region to band together and support the work of the North Indian Theological College and the Hindi Theological Literature Committee in Bareilly (Uttar Pradesh).[15]

The popularity of such works grew with the evolution of Hindi Christian readership. The general support for Hindi Christian works has grown over the last half century. Hindi Christian works acquired a national sponsor in 1957 in the Hindi Theological Literature Committee. But 15 years later, C. W. David, its editor at the time, bemoaned the relative paucity of Hindi readers. "It is the misfortune of Hindi Christian literature that it has very few readers," he wrote. "This literature has received from neither the church nor the Indian community any praise or special encouragement." He appealed to his audience: "Hindi speakers are requested to awaken and, by reading good books, to remove their shame and be enlightened."[16] Reliable data on the growth of Hindi Christian readership are not available. Yet there are signs of growth. The 2010 catalogue more than doubled the listing of Hindi Christian works. Similarly, perceptions of Hindi Christian readership have changed. In 1970, David agonized over the unpopularity of Hindi Christian literature. But in 2008, Anand, his successor, could be upbeat on the future of Hindi Christian publications. Anand proudly notes: "H.T.L.C. [Hindi Theological Literature Committee] has published nearly 150 small and big books. [And] by the grace of God H.T.L.C. wants to increase this number to 200 in the next two to three years." Where David bemoaned the lack of institutional support in 1970, by 2008 Anand claimed widespread support for Hindi Christian materials:

> [T]he Principals of theological colleges, church bishops, pastors, publication houses, distributors of our books, boards, and missionary organizations from the Hindi regions are giving us their full support. We are confident and hope that their love toward us will continue in the future.[17]

Intra-communal support has acted as catalyst to the popularity of Hindi Christian guidebooks. But larger social realities also explain the popularity of such resources. Consider the religious advice column that has appeared since 1964 in *The Hindu*. The columns provide operational wisdom drawn from Hindu scriptures, traditions, and teachers. Here is a sample of advice that is offered:

> From womb to tomb of a person, about 40 religious rites have been prescribed (Samskaras) for the prosperity, happiness and sound health of a human being.
>
> (June 18, 1976)[18]

> Some of the commands in the text of the Lord are he who acts thoughtlessly or with a bad intention, invites misery; do not give up the path of righteousness out of greed or selfishness; do not utter words which may hurt others; never keep the company of those, who, under the pretext of devotion and preceptorship, indulge in hypocrisy and immoral activities; do the vocation befitting your station in life; avoid dealing with the wicked, those who deceive and the fraudulent, always see the good in others and not their faults; respect saints and study scriptural texts with reverence; to undo sins committed, by mistake, adopt expiatory measure as per the scriptural directives. Supplement devotion with righteous conduct and never give up faith in the Lord out of fear of slander by the unscrupulous and the ignorant.
>
> (January 5, 1990)[19]

> The Ramayana pervades our cultural life; every character has been presented to the reader in such a way that he or she can mould his or her future in a proper manner.
>
> (May 17, 1991)[20]

> To avoid getting involved in worldly activities and refrain from indulging in prohibited acts, those who rely on scriptural authority have been

asked to abide by the Law of Virtue. . . . When any clarification is necessary people can seek their guidance or from those who are well versed in them.

(April 16, 1996)[21]

God has provided mankind with numerous methods to realise the goal of life, to ensure a smooth journey here and enjoy peace of mind. The prescribed daily religious exercises are easy to be adopted and can be carried out without much effort. Taking bath early, performing certain minimal acts, visiting temples and paying obeisance to the Almighty and preceptors are not difficult. Observance of austerities is also not rigid.

(October 19, 1996)[22]

Then there are the columns on dharma:

God has prescribed a Constitution for mankind and if its laws are violated, naturally He will be unhappy. . . . [E]very man, to the extent possible and with sincerity, should follow the injunctions contained in the Sastras. He should abide by the Law of Dharma, undertake to carry out the specific duties enjoined upon him and refrain from doing prohibited acts.

(January 20, 1982)[23]

Among the many forms of spiritual duties is the ceremony to appease the chief of the celestials (Indra), to ensure that Nature lavishes her bounty on humanity. Service to God and other deities associated with Him, in any form, is deemed as service to society . . . [further] prayers and observances of austerities like "Sankranti" festivals are needed.

(January 16, 1991)[24]

The duties assigned in the scriptures should be carried out by men and women. . . . Freed from passion, anger and fear, absorbed in God, taking refuge in Him, purified by spiritual knowledge, they seek His grace.

(November 25, 1992)[25]

Only the observance of the guidelines contained in the scriptures would promote discipline. To know what these are, the Epics and Puranas are being expounded in temples and other places, so that all would know their significance. Listening to them also indicated besides people's rights, their responsibilities too. Spiritual education should hence be imparted at various levels.

(November 20, 1993)[26]

To fulfill one's dharma is to act according to the "duties [one is] assigned in scriptures." Scriptures speak of many duties, which the advice columns conveniently summarize and simplify: for instance, do not act with bad intentions, mind your words, seek God, and perform the appropriate rites. Instructions on dharma in specific contexts are also available. Characters in the Ramayan, Mahabharat, and Gita reappear as models of virtues and actions. Rama, for instance, gives up his birth-right as the first-born to rule and goes into exile to keep a promise made by his father to his mother. In the Gita, Arjun follows Krishna's instructions and battles his cousins so as to fulfill his duty as a warrior. Hindi-language dailies regularly publish religious advice columns. *Dainik Jāgraṇ*, for instance, publishes the *Adhyātm* ("spirituality") column every day. Bhopal-based *Dainik Bhāskar*, one of the most popular newspapers among Hindi readers, publishes religious advice under a frequent column called *Jīvan Mantr* ("life counsel").

Christian authors have produced a variety of guidebooks in Hindi. A set of seven guidebooks shed light on the ideas that recur in Hindi Christian guidebooks on discipleship. *Masīhī Ācaraṇ* (translated from Stephen Neill), *Viliyam Bārkle ke Sāth Dainik Masīhī Ācaraṇ* (translated from William Barclay), and Dayal's *Vyaktigat Manan-Cintan* ("A Diary of Private Prayer") provide resources for spiritual growth. *Merā Paṛosī Merā Bhāī* ("My Neighbor, My Brother") by John Anand and Ramdutt Vashisht, and *Samprêṣaṇ tathā Mukti kā Śubh Sandeś* ("Communication and the Good News of Salvation") by John Anand explore Christian discipleship that is attuned to interfaith relations. *Striyoṁ kā Parameśvar ke Sāth Calnā* ("Walking of Women with God") by Winifred Paul and *Mahilā Dharmavijñān Pāṭhy-Pustak* ("Women's Theological Text-Book") by Elizabeth James explore the role of women. *Pāstarī Vidhyā* ("Pastoral Insights") by Daniel Patlia and *Biśap: Dāyitv, Darśan aur Mūly* ("Bishop: Vocation, Vision and Value") by Franklin Jonathan guide women and men who are tasked with leading churches. *Susamācār-Pracār Darśan aur Vyaktigat Pracār Kāry* ("Sharing the Good News and Personal Evangelism") by the popular evangelist Moti Lall speaks to evangelical work in multifaith contexts. These books are characterized by a combination of practical insights and theological reflections in service of readily applicable best practices. These books share certain attributes. They provide tools for the formation of Christian beliefs and practices. They present Christian ideas within society-at-large with an eye toward public witness. They are communicative and formative in intent, symbolic and instrumental in content, and personal and communal in scope. Certain features of these guidebooks are conspicuous.

A primary concern of Hindi Christian guidebooks is the public nature of Christian discipleship. Public discipleship, Lall explains, is a central feature of Christian witness. A Christian is called to public, personal, witness:

> It is compulsory for every Christian to give witness, for a believer who has accepted Christ Jesus as his personal savior. He may not be able to give a big discourse, [or] he may hesitate to speak in a big assembly, but he will not be afraid to give his personal testimony before individual

> people. Sometimes this can lead to great success. This is what is special about personal evangelism.[27]

A Christian life is a life of words and actions. A Christian's behavior matters. In opposition to attempts at Christian communication that seek to belittle, dismiss, or denounce other faiths, Indian Christian leaders like Lall and Richard Howell insist that denigrating other faiths should not be part of preaching the good news. Just as Howell speaks about the benefits of using respectful and non-derogatory language and claims when speaking with people of other faiths, Lall insists that evangelism should not destroy or refute a religion or belief:

> It should be especially remembered in evangelism that a person's religion or belief should not be refuted. It is easy to refute and it is possible that we easily defeat another in debate. But this will be of no benefit. A brother said to me, 'a Christian evangelist roundly defeated a believer in the *sanātan dharm* in a debate and from that point I became opposed to the Christian faith.' It is not our job to denigrate anyone. It is our job to use our witness to help a person meet Christ so that Christ may help her in her state.[28]

For Lall, good evangelism occurs in the space created by relationships and friendships where the interlocutors can trust and hear each other with respect and patience. Lall writes (emphasis original):

> **When a Christian explains the truth of the good news to another person in a one-on-one conversation, and presents her life experiences to the other person with trust, then the listening friend understands the good news and believes [it]. If any questions arise, they can address them cordially. Reading and explaining verses from the Bible starts affecting the listener's heart. In the end the listener accepts Jesus as her savior. This is personal evangelism. Personal evangelism is to meet people one-on-one.** Christ has used the parable of the lost sheep in Luke 15:1–7 to explain that the shepherd puts in much effort to search for one sheep, and finds it. Similarly, one who engages in personal evangelism spares no pain and effort in helping one person meet God.
>
> Understand the benefit of personal evangelism also in this. Many people are indeed affected by preaching in the market or in the crowd but [they] ask the preacher many questions of meaning to showcase their wisdom, ability, or religiosity, to expose the preacher as a fool or as a preacher of a false faith. Indeed, many people will buy books and tear them and throw them. But I have seen that when you meet those same people separately, talk to them, their attitude changes.[29]

Lall's preferred outcomes from such encounters, however, differ from some of the other outcomes championed by Hindi Christian authors. For Anand

and Vashisht, as an instance, interfaith contacts should lead to a comparative reorientation of Christian theology.

> The purpose of this study [on interfaith relations] is not to present information on people of other faiths. On the contrary, its purpose is to increase our understanding about our neighbors as members of active living faiths. Their doctrines and speech-acts should be integral parts of Christian theological reflections on the world and society. In other words, this study is a call to Christians to make the religious beliefs of their neighbors a part of Christian theological understandings and reflections. Till now Christian thought has not taken this seriously. But when the beliefs of our neighbors tell us about the ways in which we believe and understand our doctrines, it becomes essential that we accept the challenge to imagine our beliefs in new ways or dimensions. In doing so, we will be able to learn new things about our neighbors in new ways and will be able to live with them in a more intimate or closer society. This is most needed in our country.[30]

They ask, since Christianity is not the only religion with a missionary impulse, how should Christian evangelists react to the missionary needs of other faiths?

> Followers of many world religions believe that they have been commanded to give witness of their faith. Preaching faith is considered a responsibility in Islam, because the message of Islam is considered to be universal. Teachings of Buddhism also insist on this. The Buddhist path is considered to be salvific for all. But Buddhist missions are aware that they do so with deep love and a concern for humans and with respect for the religious beliefs of others . . . [Hindus also] declare that the message of the sages of India should immediately reach the world, because without it "the world will be destroyed." . . . As Christians we have many times thought of ourselves as givers of a message and others as receivers. We have thought of witness as a monologue. So how should we react to the statements of peoples of other faiths, since their statements about preaching to the world reflect a similarly strong zeal, dedication, and sense of responsibility?[31]

Christianity's minority status in India poses particular challenges and has elicited specific responses in Hindi Christian guidebooks. Attempts to narrate India as a Hindu nation have portrayed Christianity as anti-cultural or, as Lall puts it, as 'culture-destructive' or 'culture-hostile.' As a result, state agencies and religious groups have taken upon themselves the task to restrict and reverse Christian activities (the post-Modi uptick in *ghar wāpsī*, or "homecoming," campaigns a recent symptom of this underlying cause). Lall writes:

> In the last fifty years many nations have gained freedom from imperial powers. They are independent now. Gaining independence is a good thing. But independence has led to a sharp increase in nationalistic feelings which has in turn led to attempts in nations to promote culture, etc. The Christian faith is called destructive of culture. As a result, foreign preachers who used to come have been banned by saying that they need not come. Local churches have neither the numbers nor the resources to maintain their work, let alone expand it. Various types of government pressures have forced weak believers to leave congregations and return to their old faiths.[32]

Under assault, Hindi Christian authors like Anand and Lall have argued that the Christian witness in India must be sensitive to the way it communicates its message – as Lall writes, "It is not our job to denigrate anyone." Further, the Christian witness in India should speak to its context and be contextually intelligent – as Anand asks, "How should we react to the statements of peoples of other faiths?" This witness, in other words, should use language and idioms that speak to its audience; and, it should communicate through actions even as it communicates through words. Anand, who has spent nearly 30 years promoting Hindi Christian literature, provides particularly valuable insights into the ways in which the relationship of religion and language has affected the content of Hindi Christian guidebooks on Christian witness. Anand draws special attention to the impact of public perception on religious communication. It is helpful to quote him in detail on the subject.

> We have received the good news of salvation in written form: the holy Bible. This is the word of God for us. This is our 'ultimate authority.' We must implement this ultimate authority in our lives before sharing it with others. Commentary does not attract people, but behavior (does). . . .
>
> The Hindi area of 21st century north India presents us with a serious problem. When I share the good news of salvation, my listener, audience, reader is a non-Christian, especially my Hindu neighbors. . . .
>
> From the perspective of language, the Christian community of north India is like Trishanku: whenever the Christian character in a Hindi film speaks a language, we can understand this fact. Our foreign brothers have taught us that Hindi is the language of the Hindus, and Urdu that of the Muslims. And English [of the] Christians. . . . A Christian religious leader can be only a cassock-wearing Roman Catholic Father.
>
> The Hindi Bible that you hold was translated in 1905 by the Presbyterian missionary of Allahabad, Dr. S. H. Kellogg [Samuel Henry Kellogg]. 100 years ago, Hindi was only a spoken language used in some districts of Uttar Pradesh and the Mahakaushal region of Madhya Pradesh. Dr. Kellogg translated according to the situation 100 years ago. Today

> the situation is completely different. Hindi is the national language – a language of contact used in Akashwani [India's radio broadcaster], Doordarshan, newspapers, magazines from Srinagar to Kanyakumari [north to south], Kuch-Saurashtra to Arunachal Pradesh [west to east]. Its vocabulary and form have completely changed. The meanings of key words have changed and new words have been introduced into Hindi to express new ideas.
>
> If a communicator does not use the language understood by a receiver of the 'good news of salvation,' the good news becomes bad news [and] meaning is lost.[33]

In the Ramayan, Trishanku enters heaven while alive in bodily form with the help of the great sage Vishwamitra. Due to a prior curse on Trishanku, however, the Lord of the Gods Indra refuses him a stay in heaven and tosses him out. As Trishanku falls from heaven, he prays to Vishwamitra, who suspends him between the two worlds of heaven and earth and places seven saints and numerous stars in the sky to accompany Trishanku, who is destined to live between the world above (heaven) and the one below (earth). Like Trishanku, Hindi Christians are caught between two worlds, the world of Hindi-India and the world of English-foreign.

The Hindi Christian community is neither here nor there because it views itself as part of the Hindi cultural world while public representations in the popular imagination ascribe it to the cultural world of English and by extension the foreign West. The gap between self-perception and popular imagination is the target of Hindi Christian angst. This gap is grounded in language politics. The mis-association, Anand argues, of language with religions where 'Hindi is for Hindus,' and ambivalence toward local cultural idioms, have complicated the self-representation of Christians in the Hindi belt. The concern with public depictions of Christianity is driven, it seems, by a desire to present Hindi Christianity in a credible and recognizable way as both Christian in content and Hindi in expression in a way that asserts for Christianity a very Hindi 'home-base.' Guidebooks by Hindi Christian authors on communication are, as we have seen in the case of Lall's *Susamācār-Pracār Darśan*, Anand's *Samprêṣaṇ*, and Howell's *Parivartan*, particularly rich sources to understand the public concerns of Hindi Christian authors.

The effect of social location on the shape of discipleship can be discerned in discourses on the role of women in Hindi congregations. The struggle between patriarchy and equality has shaped commentaries on proper Christian living. Elizabeth Schüssler Fiorenza has argued that gender itself is marked through specific discourses.[34] Hindu women, Tracy Pintchman shows, "largely control" ritual and religious practices outside "Sanskritic, Brahminical Hindu environments," which remain largely the purview of Hindu males. Yet, their practices are "not isolated from social, cultural, domestic, or larger religious roles or frames of meaning."[35] Women and men are accorded different roles in Hindi Christian guidebooks. As a matter of fact, many guidebooks are gender-specific, aimed only at women or men. The guidebooks propose traditional gender roles as well as models of gender equality. Sometimes, both arguments compete in the same work. *Mahilā Dharmavijñān Pāthya-Pustak* by Elizabeth James is an example of this type of work.

In *Mahilā Dharmavijñān*, a section on *pastar kī dharmapatnī* ("The Pastor's Wife") opens the chapter on *mahilā kāry* ("women's work"). A pastor's wife should treat the community with love. She should be able to "comfort those in pain" and be "truthful, friendly and peaceful."[36] She should, further, support her pastor-husband in his responsibilities.[37] A section on *śahar aur dehāt meṁ mahilā kāry* (women's ministry in city and village) follows the section on the pastor's wife. In this section, James upends the gender relation described in the previous section. In a strategic use of scripture and tradition, she deploys insights from the early church to assert that that women and men are co-partners in church and society. It is worth quoting James at length:

> Women have played a major role in evangelism and in the life of the congregation. From the very beginning our Lord considered women equal to men in grace and ministry (see Jn. 4:7 ff.; Mk. 5:23 ff.; Lk. 10:38–42). It is acknowledged that the Lord did not send women like [he sent] the disciples with the power to perform miracles, but within the community of disciples they have played a special role to serve, accompany, and host (Lk. 8:2; Mk. 15:40 ff.). Some of those women were the first witnesses to the resurrection (Mk. 16:1). Women had a special place in Jesus's parables. The book of Acts and the epistles mention many women who assisted in preaching the good news (Acts 1:14; 12:12; 16:13 ff.; Rom. 16:1, 3; 1 Cor. 1:11; Col. 4:15; 2 Tim. 1:5; Philem. 4:2–3). Women managed various responsibilities in the congregation. For instance, Phoebe was a deaconess in the congregation in Cenchreae (Rom. 16:1); Priscilla instructed Apollos (Acts 18:24–26); Titus 2:3–5 mentions women presbyters; widows prayed ceaselessly (1 Tim. 5:5). It also appears that there were prophetesses in the early church (Acts 21:9). Saint Paul calls women 'my co-workers' (Rom. 16:3). It can be assumed that through our Lord Jesus Christ and due to the attitude of the early church toward women, the status of women in human society has been lifted up.
>
> According to this tradition, today women are serving congregations in numerous ways, including as pastors and presbyters in some congregations. Women have the right to vote in congregations; they serve the congregation in many ways, serve as Bible women [or, evangelists], women teach in schools, work in hospitals, are missionaries, assistant pastors, etc.
>
> Women have congregational, inter-congregational, and international associations and societies. It is a matter of much pride that those

> hostels, schools, hospitals and organizations that are in women's hands are excelling in many areas.[38]

Schüssler Fiorenza argues that the New Testament accounts reveal signs of "androcentric process of redaction" where the role of women in the early church appears to have been qualified.[39] James seems to overlook such critiques. Consider her translation of *diaconon* as *ḍīkanes* ("deaconess") in Hindi. "Deaconess" has been used as more than a gender-equivalent term. Rather it has been used to mean a lesser "servant" or "helper."[40] James's translation tilts in that direction. Old and new Hindi Bibles, James's most probable sources, lack *ḍīkanes*. The 1909, 1989, and 2004 translations all use *sevikā* (servant, female) for the Greek *diaconon*. Though the 1989 and 2004 Hindi Bibles were published after the publication of James's book in 1978, the consistency of *sevikā* across the three Hindi Bible versions suggests that it is the most likely word James would have encountered if she had referred to a Hindi Bible in 1978. On one hand, then, it can be argued that in her guidebook James elevates Phoebe's status by naming her a "deaconess" – a term with clerical resonance and one that connotes a communally-recognized position – rather than a "servant." Her departure from Hindi scripture is symbolic of a re-evaluation of women's role in churches. Such an interpretation is supported by her larger thesis in the section where she discusses Phoebe: women were influential leaders and teachers in the early church and women church leaders stand in this long tradition. On the other hand, when "deaconess" is understood as a demotion from "deacon," James is subject to Schüssler Fiorenza's critique.

Unlike Hindi translations of *diaconon*, translations of *prostasis* in Rom. 16:2 have undergone changes. According to the 1989 Hindi Bible, Phoebe provides the community and Paul with *sahāyatā* ("help"), but the 1909 and 2004 versions accord her a greater position in society as the *upkāriṇī* ("one who provides favors," or a benefactor) to congregants and to Paul (*bahutoṁ kī varan merī bhī upkāriṇī*). Changes in the status of Phoebe in the Hindi Bibles parallel similar developments in English-language depictions of her role. As an instance, the Revised Standard Version calls her a "deaconess" and a "helper" while the New Revised Standard Version calls her a "deacon" or "minister" and a "benefactor." Interestingly, translations of *sunergous mou* are consistent across the five Hindi Bible editions of the last century: *mere sahakarmī* ("my co-workers") is the term of choice in the 1909, 1989, and 2004 Hindi Bibles. In comparison, the English Revised Standard Version uses "my fellow workers" while the New Revised Standard Version uses "work with me" while translating Rom. 16:2.

James considers women co-participants in the ministry of preaching. As a result, *Mahilā Dharmavijñān Pāthya-Pustak* makes no distinction in the advice it offers women and men regarding preaching. Both are given the following tips:

- The best verses and topics are received when in prayer on one's knees.
- Never prepare the sermon first and then search for the verses.
- Present the weaker points first and save the stronger points for last.
- A sermon should be applicable to life and it should also have personal appeal.
- After preparing your sermon, practice it. Check your pronunciation, delivery, and biblical references. Write your sermon or prepare notes for it. Be of strong faith that God will bless your work.[41]

Preaching and communicating are the task of both women and men. Yet inequalities exist in practice and attitudes. Winifred Paul's *Striyoṁ kā Parameśvar ke Sāth Calnā* (2008) is a symptom of this tussle between 'imbalanced' roles and the sort of 'gender-shared' Christianity James describes. In her guidebook, Paul gives advice to Christian women in their capacity as wives and co-workers and, unlike James, ignores the leadership roles that Christian women have played in Indian congregations. Paul writes,

> Modern women are able in various ways. They are appropriate for various types of works. . . . They can serve the congregation by offering advice on congregational decisions, in the form of evangelists who win souls, by preparing the Eucharist, by teaching the good news to children, by running prayer cells, by leading the youth, by doing Sunday School work, by running the women's group, by visiting congregants who are ill, by caring for widows and orphans, by typing, by collecting gifts, by providing hospitality, and above all by smiling.[42]

Compared to James's description, Paul's vision is noticeably different. There is no reference to women pastors. Women play second-fiddle to men. They advise on decisions but are not decision-makers. They lead 'sub-groups' but do serve as pastors. Like James, Paul identifies women leaders in the Bible. But unlike James, Paul mentions them as historical details rather than as leaders in religious communities. Where James draws lessons from the early church to highlight women leaders, Paul gives women a backhanded compliment when she writes that "Jesus did not consider women untouchables."[43] The tussle between equality and patriarchy reflected in the guidebooks by James and Paul complicates models of Indian Christianity that present the religion as an egalitarian alternative to Indian society.[44] Paul's work, more than that of James, reflects this struggle. For instance, on one hand, she writes, Christian women should be obedient.[45] On the other hand, she "also has the right to obey God above humans."[46] Like James, Paul further argues that men and women serve certain social roles on earth, yet "there is no male and female in heaven. Gender differences are only on earth, there is no gender difference in heaven."[47] A Christian woman has "authority over her husband, children, and home"[48]; yet she "should not exert authority over men."[49]

Good works, or social ethics

While different in tone and content, the manuals of James, Paul, Anand, and Lall have a common feature: they seek to press Christian discipleship in the service of social goals. Hindi Christian guidebooks self-report three objectives: the formation of discipleship, public responsibility, and social witness. Anand and Lall use their guidebooks to comment on relations between Christians and their other-faith neighbors and to promote strategies to offer a 'friendly' Christian witness as a minority faith. In similar vein, James and Paul ask their readers to contribute to social development and community relations in India. A common interest underlies the difference in content. When read together, the works of Anand, Lall, James, and Paul reveal the desire to foster Christian character for public service. Or, Christian character "for the benefit of the church and the land of India," in the words of the publisher of these guidebooks.[50]

In her chapter on ethics, James proposes that the nature of Christian ethics is "two-fold." "Spirituality and ethics are deeply related"[51] (*gahrā sambandh hai*) and it is "necessary" (*āvaśyak*) for a Christian to be "certain" on the "principles that shape [her] behavior."[52] These behaviors, in turn, help a Christian fulfill her social obligations to community and nation. "[She] is responsible to her family, her society, [and] to her nation . . . ."[53] Christian ethics include social responsibilities. Christians with public rights are "ethically obligated to use them for the benefit of all." They are obligated to "respect life," to "not use wealth as an end but as a means to benefit others," to promote peoples' well-being," and to respect the truth, character, and social relations.[54] This list is non-religious in nature and James portrays Christian ethics as a reflection of general human rights and responsibilities. She explains:

> Society is the source of rights. Society endows people with rights along with some conditions. The condition is that those who have been given rights use them appropriately and do not use them to bring harm to others. The respect and value of a person are reflected in the rights available to a human in Christian ethics. These are the rights of a human: (1) the right to life and work, (2) the right to education. (3) The right to freedom. (4) The right to property. (5) The right to enter an agreement or contract.[55]

In James's view, Christian works must inform and contribute to the social contract. They should promote general human rights. Other Hindi Christian guidebooks echo this view. In *Vyaktigat Manan-Cintan* ("Private Reflections"), Din Dayal conflates Christian discipleship with social responsibility. He writes,

> Grant me that I do not break the promises made earlier, and that I do not fail to correct the mistakes I have made. Grant me that if I come

> upon a sojourner in need, I do not walk away. Grant me that I do not leave responsibilities unmet and that I do not allow a bad habit to take hold. Where my work may make the world a better place for others, where my words may uplift someone in pain or strengthen the weak in spirit, where my prayers may work to spread the kingdom of Jesus Christ, give me the ability to act, speak, and pray there.[56]

Christ is owed one's being and actions. Hindi guidebooks routinely emphasize the dependence of a Christian's witness on the creative power of God. As Dayal explains:

> Dear Father, protect me today. Keep all my thoughts and feelings today under control, direct my abilities. Instruct my wisdom. Take care of my will. Take my hands and make me quick to obey your commands. Take my eyes and keep them affixed on your eternal beauty. Take my mouth and make it a strong witness of your love. Make this day a day of obedience, spiritual joy, and peace. Make the words of this day a part of the kingdom of Jesus Christ, the savior.[57]

Where Dayal's prayer is directed to individual believers, Franklin Jonathan has asked church leaders to a special role as public communicators. Addressing bishops, he writes, "Among the people outside the church, among community at large, we are recognized by those works of our lives that are visible in our institutions, programs, and social work." "We should be recognized," he further explains, "by the ways in which we fulfill our obligations."[58] Probity in Christian witness is particularly incumbent on clergy because they represent the public leadership of Christian communities. Christians in India communicate their faith as members of a minority faith among people of larger faiths. As a result, Hindi Christian guidebooks have played special attention to the act of religious communication from a minority faith position. Anand, Dayal, James, Lall, Patlia, Paul, and Vashisht each speak to the particular ways in which being a minority should impact the life of Christian communities.

As a minority community, Patlia writes in *Pāstarī Viddhyā*, Christians must seek their well-being with care and love. "It is possible that due to the limitations put by the majority community [Christians] cannot fully enjoy their rights." In such contexts, he continues, Christians should "when needed resist with peace and love in such a way that even the greatest powers are defeated, a great testimony is presented, and the Kingdom of God is advanced."[59] "Peace" in this context should be understood as non-violence because Patlia has Gandhi's appropriation of Christian ideas like non-violent sacrifice in mind when commenting on particularly Christian ways to resist the curtailments on full social participation by minorities in secular and democratic societies like India where minorities share equal rights and privileges with other citizens.[60]

A minority community is not without means. It has equal rights and privileges in a democratic society. "Where there is the right to democratic freedom, a community, even if in the minority, possesses the freedom to fight for its civil rights."[61] Consequently, its minority status does not absolve it of its responsibilities and obligations as both a religious community with particular perspectives and a participant in the citizenry of the nation. Patlia wants Indian Christians to be robust citizens. He recognizes the limitations to public participation that can be placed on religious minorities. Yet, the recognition that the social witness and service of a minority can be affected by the scope of freedom to speak and act accorded to it does not prevent Patlia from commenting on particular ways in which a minority can witness its faith even as it works to participate fully in society and its politics and economics.

Similarly, *Masīhī Ācaraṇ*, the popular translation of Neill's *The Christian Character*, suggests attention to public perceptions of Christian activities – both church-oriented and evangelical – by peoples of other faiths. Neill's original work was written for a Christian audience quite different from India's Christian community. Yet C.W. David used his foreword in the Hindi translation to introduce the benefits of Christian education to India's emerging society by writing that "the acquisition and promulgation of Christian character [was] necessary for global welfare and development."[62] One reason for the popularity of *Masīhī Ācaraṇ*, it can be argued, was Neill's investment in (proper) Christian living and witness. As Neill noted, "even those who are not Christians are aware of the need for Christians to be like Christ. Many people in the world who are not Christians," he continued, "are well-aware of the behavior of Jesus Christ. They know that Jesus Christ was just, humble, pure, and truthful."[63] A Christian is called, then, to be like Christ because others have been saying to Christians that while "we cannot see Jesus Christ . . . we can see you."[64] David certainly recognized the value of this investment: "In this book is present a very beautiful and interesting enquiry of the ideal of Christian character, Christian virtues, and the rich source to acquire this ideal and these virtues."[65]

Neill's idea of evangelism ignored relations with people of other faiths. But Hindi Christian authors have paid close attention to Christian witness in minority contexts. This view is exemplified in the works of Richard Howell and John Anand. Christian witness, they argue, should be respectful and relational toward people of other faiths. It should recognize the value of other beliefs and practices. Respecting people of other faiths involves a certain approach to evangelism. Do not denigrate other faiths. Do not assert their inferiority to Christianity. Acknowledge the presence of truth in them. Christian witness should also be relational. It should build on relations rather than on apologetics or refutations. It should be open to learning from people of other faiths. One way to learn is to construct Christian claims that draw upon ideas in other religious traditions. Howell and Anand draw attention to the vocabulary of evangelism and invite Christian evangelists to use sensitive language and terms that can be hurtful and exclusive.

In his manual on evangelism, Howell asks his readers to use respectful words in their evangelism for people of other faiths and their beliefs. Do not call them "idolaters," or "people of darkness," Howell suggests. Refrain from using militaristic terminology like "enemy," "march," "war," "soldier," "victory," and "weapons" in mission work. Avoid language that minimizes women. Instead, focus on ideas like "family," "openness," "friendship," hope," "service," "peace," and "justice" when presenting Christian ideas.[66] The choice of words is not a tangential concern of evangelists. Rather, Howell invites Christians in general and evangelists in particular to "constantly examine their behavior and words."[67] In similar vein, Anand asks Christians to recognize the baggage associated with the English word "mission." The word suffers the burden of missionary history and aggression. Anand invites his readers to present the good news in an Indian vocabulary and suggests *dharm jāgăraṇ* ("spiritual awakening") as an alternative to "mission" and "conversion".[68] And finally, in his manual on Christian communication and preaching, Lall asks his readers to witness in the context of respectful and friendly relationships.

Hindi Christian guidebooks provide concrete applications of Christian ideals. They examine Christian actions in family, church, and society. They inculcate behaviors, attitudes, and actions that foster participation in public affairs. They explore the needs of Christian expressions in plural societies. They address notions of responsibility and witness. They assert the public nature of personal discipleship. They elevate the life of Jesus as a model of public virtues and actions. In their construction, Christian discipleship is the public expression of faith and a shaper of public affairs. Public depictions of Christianity by non-Christian raises another set of questions that concern the place of Christianity in the public imagination. Depictions of Christianity on Doordarshan, India's state television, is a case in point.

Mass religion

Rajiv Gandhi's government (1984–1989) changed the politics of television in India. Its decisions helped tie politics to religion in ways that have become impossible to disentangle. In the 1980s television in India was boring. I should know. I grew up on Doordarshan. Gandhi changed all that. And it began with the airing of the Hindu epic Ramayan on the state-run Doordarshan during prime time, 9 to 10 a.m. on Sunday. Doordarshan had the added distinction of being the dominant source of news and entertainment to the public and in many cases the only national source of news and entertainment outside national newspapers and the Hindi film industry. The first episode of *Ramayan*, the serialized presentation of the Hindu epic Ramayan, aired on 15 January, 1987. The serial ran for 78 episodes over a span of two years. Its last episode was telecast on July 31, 1988. The serial was immensely popular and influential. Its first episode drew a viewership of 24 percent; or, 24 percent of television households tuned in. By episode 11, it logged 50 percent television households. Episode 41 attracted 70 percent households. By the time of its conclusion, it drew more than 80 percent households. Viewers climbed from 40 million to 80 million in a few months. The serial *Ramayan* was also a commercial success. Two 20-minute advertising windows, during which commercial were shown, bookended each weekly episode. It turned the Sunday morning "soft spot" on television into prime time and earned around US $40 million in revenue every week for Doordarshan.[69]

State media has a political purpose. Its role is to promote "education, information and entertainment" for the purpose of the state's interest in projecting an image of leaders in control of the government and serving the nation by improving it.[70] India's state media explicitly sought to forge a "modern, national culture" by propagating a narrative of "development and national integration" in its programs.[71] This discourse, as noted later, served an additional explicit purpose: the promotion of Hindu culture as Indian culture.[72] Control, service, and development were at the heart of the image fostered by state-media in independent India. Control over media was itself a way to manage the image of rational, positive governance. Indira Gandhi, India's Prime Minister from 1966 to 1977 and then from 1980 to 1984, and Lal Krishna Advani, a leader in the government that followed that of Mrs. Gandhi's, kept leadership of the Ministry for Information and Broadcasting for themselves. The Ministry controlled the only national television broadcast (Doordarshan), the national radio broadcast (All India Radio), the Field Publicity Organization, and the Directorate of Advertising and Visual Publicity.

Commercial viability or the public success of programs broadcast was to an extent irrelevant in the era of state-run media.[73] As Rajagopal reports, state media was exclusively self-referential and apathetic of viewership. Its self-reference was evident in the content of its programs, most of which presented government leaders and the leaders of the political parties in power making speeches, cutting ribbons, presiding over public functions, and chairing meetings. Community receivers and television sets were severely underfunded and disappeared from government allocation after the Sixth Plan for 1980–1985. Most television and radio sets were privately owned and viewership negligible as a share of the population with access to broadcast signals. There were 2.8 million television viewers in 1983, 13.2 million in 1987, and between 42 and 47 million in 1994. The growth in viewership can be partly ascribed to the success of religion serials in the late 1980s. The initial jump in viewership after 1983 complemented a move toward commercially-viable and sponsored programs, beginning in 1984. The attitude toward viewership and commercial viability also started to shift in the mid-1980s. Producers were invited to submit proposals that met two objectives: promotion of educational messages – with an interest in programs that fostered unity, culture, and comity – and commercial success. The goal was to air programs that were "win-win": the government's interest in promoting its message would be paired with programs that relied less on government support.

The decision to telecast a religious epic during prime time was political. Purnima Mankekar has argued that it is "problematic" to characterize Doordarshan's decision as political and especially as part of the larger project of Hindu nationalism.[74] She explains that the decision to televise the Ramayan was made during an "ostensibly secular" Congress government, by a government bureaucrat, and that *Ramayan* was produced by a successful Hindi film producer and director, Ramanand Sagar. Yet the larger national political context in which the decision was made and the motives of key decision-makers cannot be ignored. Arvind Rajagopal has argued that Doordarshan's airing of a religious program broke with its secular history and a "Nehruvian taboo" on the secular and non-partisan nature of state agencies.[75] Doordarshan's decision to air *Ramayan* caused a stir for multiple reasons. More directly, there was the matter of religious preference. Doordarshan was promoting the Ramayan as a repository of Indian culture and deploying the state's apparatus to position Hindu vocabulary as India's vocabulary. There was further the matter of the politics of language. While Sagar was a producer of successful films in 'colloquial Hindi,' the *Ramayan* serial was crafted in highly-Sanskritized Hindi. The *Ramayan* serial fostered the sense that 'high' and 'pure' Hindi was Sanskritized and as such Hindu. The use of Sanskritic Hindi by the state's apparatus to promote an 'Indian culture' and national integration was not unique to Doordarshan or the 1980s. Nehru used to complain about the prevalence of Sanskritized Hindi in programs by All India Radio.[76]

The decision to telecast *Ramayan* would fall to S.S. Gill, secretary for information and broadcasting overseeing programming at Doordarshan. Why did Mr. Gill greenlight *Ramayan*? His reflections on his decision and reports on his goals leave room for uncertainty. He has argued that he wanted Doordarshan to help Indians build a shared sense of community. Serials of important stories from different religious traditions would help highlight India's religious diversity. That these different stories were aired on the state-owned and dominant television broadcaster during prime time would help foster a sense of unity and shared nationality among different religious traditions. Conflating culture with religion, Mr. Gill argued that the airing of religion serials would be a good way to promote Indian culture. In an op-ed in *The Indian Express* shortly after the *Ramayan* serial concluded its run, Gill explained his decision to air the *Ramayan* and took on his critics. It is helpful to quote him at length:

> It was in September 1985 that I officially approached Mr. Sagar to undertake this project and gave him some specific suggestions about the line of treatment. In this letter I proposed, 'Ramayan is not only a great epic of *Himalayan* dimensions, it is also a repository of our social and moral values. It does not purport to teach any religious orthodoxy

and its message it wholly secular and universal. Most importantly the real merit of a great epic like Ramayan lies in the fact that its message renews itself with every age and its symbols and metaphors acquire a fresh import and vitality in every era.' . . .

Right from the word go Ramayan was a runaway success and it ranks as the most popular serial ever telecast by Doordarshan. . . . The most serious charge levelled against this programme is that Ramayan is a Hindu scripture and its televising over the government owned medium amounts to blatant propagation of Hindu religion by the state. This, it is stated, compromises our secular credentials. It is further argued that having telecast Ramayan over Doordarshan, would the authorities agree to extend the same treatment to the Koran and the Bible?

On the face of it this is a very valid objection and deserves to be seriously examined. The first point to be noted in this connection is that, in the conventional sense, Ramayan is not a Hindu scripture. Strictly speaking it is not even a 'scripture.' It neither preaches any religion nor expounds any dogma, not propagates any orthodoxy. It lays no claim to being the revealed word of the gods or to monopoly of truth. It does not seek converts to any specific code of conduct, nor insist on a set of rituals or religious observances. It neither aims to establish a church nor a papacy. Though Valmiki's Ramayan is the original text, there are at least a dozen versions of Ramayan composed by different seers at different points of time and all of them are equally "authentic." Consequently, there is no 'authorized version' of Ramayan. . . .

In such a situation, to describe Ramayan as a Hindu scripture in the same sense as we refer to scriptures of the Judaic religions is a fallacy based on mixing categories. Ramayan is basically a secular epic which portrays a bewildering range of human relationships and socio-political situations. Its enduring appeal lies in the strength of its story-line and the delineation of its epic characters. One reason why it acquired the status of a scripture and Homer's Iliad and Odyssey remained only literary classics is that the action in Ramayan takes place in a moral universe, whereas the Greek epics are morally neutral. . . . Ram, Ravan, Sita, Laxman, Hanuman have the stark simplicity and elemental force of characters in a moral play. . . .

It is this unique combination of a gripping plot of cosmic dimensions teeming with hordes of sharply delineated characters, and its ingenious use as a vehicle for articulating the major individual and social issues of abiding concern from an essentially humanistic and ethical standpoint that explains the hold of Ramayan on the Hindu psyche. Over the ages Sita has served as a norm and a reference point while assessing the worth and character of a Hindu woman. Howsoever liberated a woman may be, she always carries a little Sita in her subconscious as a gentle censor and a guide. Ravan symbolises the unbridled arrogance of power and knowledge petrified into opaque evil in the absence of morality.

And Ram: the ideal son, the ideal brother, the ideal husband and the ideal ruler! . . .

[I]t is the Ramayan which has got woven into the warp and woof of the Hindu ethos and shaped the personal and social conduct of the Hindus over the past two thousand years. . . . In his search for an expressive metaphor to symbolise a welfare state of his dreams, Gandhiji could do no better than think of Ram Raj. You go to the countryside and see how frequently Ramayan is quoted in the commerce of daily life. You take away Ramayan from the consciousness of the Hindus and you leave them socially and morally maimed.

And despite Ramayan having permeated every pore and fibre of our culture and served as a bulwark of our social morality, our intellectuals cry wolf when this epic is televised as a serial by Doordarshan and describe it as an attempt to pander to the majority communalism.

When Peter Brooke produced an eight-hour stage version of Mahabharat, it won international acclaim. . . .

It is interesting to note that liberal Hindus feel quite embarrassed and guilty about the preponderance of their community in the Indian population, and they resort to all sorts of mental contortions to make amends for this "unfair" advantage. But the fact of the matter is that the Hindus do constitute 83 percent of the country's population and the Indian culture is essentially Hindu in its inspiration. Luckily, the diversity and catholicity of the Hindu religion makes life much easier for the minorities. There is no denying the fact that by and large Indian ethos is predominantly Hindu and Ramayan is its centre-piece. . . .

[The Ramayan program] was designed as a popular serial for the common folk to be broadcast over a mass medium. If medium is the message, then mass entertainment on television inevitably trivialises even the noblest of themes. An epic on TV does become a soap-opera to some extent. But when all is said and done, the Ramayan serial not only provided wholesome entertainment to millions of viewers, but also managed to highlight and reinforce some of the basic values of our culture.[77]

Gill explained his decision in moral terms. Ramayan reinforces the "basic values" of "our" culture. Hindu symbols are at the root of Indian cultural expressions and as such the characters of the Ramayan stand in as moral models for all Indians. The Ramayan is scriptural in so far is has a moral message rather than a religious one but in its scriptural form it has transcended any particular religion. Gill's views of both scripture and religion can be faulted for their limitations. The plurality of Ramayan versions and the story's universal nature is positively contrasted with the monolithic and orthodox scriptures of non-Hindu religions. The variety of hadiths, versions of biblical books, and ongoing debates over the meaning of texts is consumed under the imagined authority of authorized versions of other religions. Ramayan teaches Indians for the ages. Its world and its characters are flawless studies in behaviour, both to be emulated and to be avoided. The world of the Ramayan is the ideal India. It is *Ram Rajya*, where justice and peace prevailed, and prosperity abound, under the rule of an ideal king. Ideal India was – and should be – a *Ram Rajya*. After all, even Gandhiji himself, the father of the nation, could not find a better metaphor to describe ideal India. The characters of the Ramayan further represent ideal forms of behaviour and life. Sita an ideal woman and wife, Ravan an ideal villain, and Ram the ideal everything else. Follow Sita and Ram, do what they did, and avoid everything Ravan stands for. Ram's disloyalty to Sita, Ravan's ethical quandary, Sita's rejection of Ram, and Lakshman's violence against Ravan's sister[78] are irrelevant to Gill's construction of the Ramayan. The popularity of the Ramayan, the public influence of its characters, and the numerical dominance of Hindus in India was sufficient reason to declare India Hindu.

Gill's *Ramayan* is an example of the Hinduization of India. While Gill takes issues with some of Sagar's aesthetic presentation of Ramayan, his rationale to greenlight the epic for telecast echoes the rationale of Hindu nationalists of the Vishwa Hindu Parishad and the Bhartiya Janata Party. Gill's interest in Hindu-Indian epics did not end with the *Ramayan*. He was also interested in televising the Mahabharat, another great Hindu epic, for television and wrote a letter to Mr. B. R. Chopra encouraging him to serialize that epic for Doordarshan. Gill considered Hindu religion catholic and welcoming. Given this belief, why would it not be in the public interest to use state media to promote Hindu symbols and values to the nation? That those symbols and values transcended Hindu religion but stood for "our" Indian culture spoke to their national importance. In the context of Hindu-Muslim relations in the late 1980s, Gill's vision of an inclusive and nurturing Hinduism whose symbols, epics, and values were India's symbols, epics, and values was naïve at best, derelict at worst for a government official charged with public trust in a multireligious democracy, and partial even when given the benefit of the doubt. Hinduism, like Islam, has an inclusivist strand and an exclusivist strand. Secularism is the political form of the inclusivist strand. Hindu nationalism and Hindi-centricism is the political expression of the exclusivist strand. At the time of Gill's op-ed, exclusive Hinduism was dominant in public, legal, and government conversations.

In an interview with Mankekar in 1992, Gill argued that by introducing the viewers to the "best of all faiths" Doordarshan would make Indians proud of the "unity in diversity of India" and strengthen "national integration." Mr. Gill further recounted that he faced considerable resistance from fellow bureaucrats on his plans to telecast *Ramayan* but convinced them by proposing a larger plan to telecast epics from different religious traditions.[79] According to Mr. Gill, the plan was to air serial from different religious traditions. In practice, Hindu serials dominated the airwaves in the 1980s and early 1990s. *Ramayan* was followed by *Mahabharat*, *The Sword of Tipu*

Sultan, and a short-lived Christian serial, *Bāibal kī Kahānīyāṁ* ('Stories of the Bible'; more on this later). No serial inspired by the Quran or the Guru Granth Sahib was produced by the state media or aired on Doordarshan. Neither did any serial based on the epics and values of Jains, Buddhists, or India's other religious traditions appear on Doordarshan.

Gill's decision is grounded in the larger religion politics of the late 1980s. Quoting Asghar Ali Engineer, who reflected on the airing of *Ramayan* soon after its run concluded in 1990, Rajagopal has shown that the decision to telecast the *Ramayan* was a "political" decision. Gandhi had asked Gill about the desirability of aïring a Hindu epic on state television.[80] Gill decided to greenlight the *Ramayan* in a particular political context where Hindu-Muslim relations were fraying. It was a decision shaped by a government eager to raise its flagging political fortunes among the Hindu vote. Rajiv Gandhi was eager to show that Congress was not anti-Hindu.

The 1980s were a tumultuous time for Gandhi's Congress (I) and Hindu-Muslim relations in India. Gandhi's party was weakened and its reliance on "minority" votes frayed. Two important events in 1980s were influential in shaping Hindu-Muslim relations. First, the Supreme Court passed its decision on Shah Bano's appeal for alimony in 1985. Second, the Ram Janambhoomi-Babri Masjid issue erupted in the run-up to the Lok Sabha elections in 1989.[81] The latter issue catalyzed the former one and provided it context. The Ram Janambhoomi-Babri Masjid issue concerns the site of a place of worship. British policy of 'divide-and-rule' pitted Muslims against Hindus and divisions over control of the site emerged around 1855, just before the First War of Independence in 1857 (called the First Mutiny in accounts by the British rulers). At debate is whether on this particular site in modern-day Uttar Pradesh, a Muslim mosque or a Hindu temple should exist. What should exist is tied to what existed before, and the question of historic architecture is controversial. Muslims claim that a mosque, the Babri Masjid, has always stood on the site and is its rightful occupant. Hindu's claim that Ram was born on the site – it is the birth-place (*janam-bhoomi*) of Ram – and as such a Hindu temple belongs there. Further, Hindus claim a temple predated the Masjid, which was constructed at the site only after a Mughal Emperor destroyed a pre-existing temple that marked the birth-place of Ram. As such, restoring the temple is necessary. The question of whether a mosque or temple belongs on the site re-emerged a few years after India's partition.

India's Partition broke Muslim-Hindu relations. They were anyway at a breaking point before independence. By the end of 1946, there was a "collapse of faith" between the Indian National Congress and the Muslim League.[82] By August 1947, organized ethnic and religious cleansing was afoot on both sides of the newly-drawn border between India and Pakistan. Forced migration was in full swing. Planned violence defined the Partition and sat at its core.[83] Records of violence abound. In Hasilpur, approximately 350 people were gunned down. Children, women, and men were burnt alive, dismembered, raped, and had their bodies mutilated. In Bharatpur and Alwar, approximately 30,000 Muslims were killed and 100,000 forced to flee.[84] From September 18 to October 29, 1947, in a span of 42 days, 849,00 refugees entered India, and between August and November an additional 2.3 million refugees arrived. By November 1947, an estimated eight million people had been displaced in both directions.[85] In India, both the ruling Congress Party and the Hindu right (The Rashtriya Swayamsevak Sangh or the RSS and the Hindu Mahasabha) faced a political crisis in the refugee issue and tried to use it to their advantage. The Congress sought to gain their electoral loyalty while the Hindu right, which had played a role in partition-related violence,[86] sought to gain their trust.

Hindu-Muslim relations were on edge when the contest over the Babri Masjid and Ram Janambhoomi flared up again. Its immediate spark was lit on the night of December 22, 1949. The next day idols of Ram and Sita "miraculously" appeared on the site of the Babri Masjid. According to official reports by the local district magistrate, Hindu devotees entered the mosque "at night when the Masjid was deserted and installed a deity there."[87] Jawaharlal Nehru, the Prime Minister at the time, ordered the premises locked though did not remove the idols. The area remained locked till February 1986, when Rajiv Gandhi decide to open it to Hindus. The latter's decision was forced by religion politics.

On April 23, 1985, the Supreme Court of India ruled that Shah Bano, a divorcee, was owed alimony by her husband. In doing so, it overruled Muslim family law and affirmed that secular law and the rights granted therein supersede family law in India. Conservative Muslims were outraged a political storm gathered force.[88] There were protests and demonstrations against the court ruling across India. The Rajiv Gandhi Government felt a gathering threat and sought to appease the sentiments of Muslims by introducing a bill in Parliament to nullify the ruling. The Muslim Women (Protection of Rights on Divorce) Bill was enacted by Parliament in May 1986. It reaffirmed the place of family law in India and re-instated its primacy as the legal code through which family issues like alimony disputes would be settled.

Secularists, Muslims and Hindus alike, were livid at Gandhi's mockery of India's secular values. Hindu nationalists on the right were also livid, and argued that the supremacy of Muslim family law threatened India's integrity and Hindu culture. "Hindu nationalism has two simultaneous impulses," Varshney has argued: "building a united India as well as 'Hinduizing' the polity and the nation."[89] Gandhi perceived the threat to his Hindu support created by the Muslim Women Bill. To counter the latter, he decided to open the doors of Babri Masjid to Hindus. That the Masjid controversy and the Bill controversy were connected in Gandhi's decision is hinted at by the timing of each decision. The Bill was introduced in Parliament on February 25, 1986. To neutralize its effect on Hindu anger, the doors of the Masjid were opened to Hindus on February 1, 1986. Engineer reports that the timing was well-executed and television cameras were ready to televise the opening of the Masjid to Hindus in a pre-planned move. Gandhi's strategy to curry favor with both the Muslim and Hindu communities was a departure from the approach of his grandfather, Nehru, to religion politics.

Nehruvian secularism claims equidistance from all religions, concern for minority welfare, and a minimal role for religion in public affairs. In other words, the government should treat religions equally and keep them equally at a distance from its function and decisions. Gandhi flipped that script. Gandhi's secularism sought equal proximity to religions in an attempt to use religion as a political force. Varshney has described Rajiv Gandhi's brand of secularism as "unprincipled secularism" in light of its reliance on religion for electoral gains and the weakening of concern for minority welfare.[90] While Nehru sought equal distance from religions Gandhi sought equal proximity to religions. In relying on religions for electoral gain, Rajiv Gandhi was following in the footsteps of his mother, Indira Gandhi. As Prime Minister, Indira Gandhi had formed an alliance with a Sikh religious leader, Sant Bhindranwale, to defeat the Akali Dal, a secular party that was challenging Congress rule in Punjab.[91] Rajiv Gandhi's need for religion voters was in turn a function of the state of affairs of his Congress Party, which, by the 1980s, was out of ideas and organizational steam. Gandhi's embrace of religion politics sought to raise his flagging electoral fortunes at a time when the Hindu right was in ascendance and Muslim voters were becoming increasingly disenchanted with Congress rule.

Varshney draws a distinction between Nehruvian equidistance and Gandhian equiproximity.[92] Principles of secularism means the government does not favor any religion but maintains equal distance from them. Distance from religion means religion groups and organizations do not influence state policy and government actions. In theory, a state policy of equal proximity should also result in the equal treatment of all religions by the state. When the state moves close to one religion, it moves commensurately close to other religions. A balance results. In practice, however, religions do not have comparable electoral power. Numerical imbalances between religions, divisions internal to religions, and the geographic strength of religions affect electoral weight. In India, there is not one majority (Hindu) religion and many minorities. Rather, in terms of religions, and as a function of numerical strength and geographic distribution, India has one (Hindu) majority, one major minority (Islam), and many minor minorities like the Christian, Sikh, Jain, Buddhist, Parsi, and tribal religious traditions. Indira Gandhi used a regional strategy of state proximity with religion when she aligned Congress with religious Sikh in Punjab. Rajiv Gandhi may have taken his mother's strategy of state proximity to a national level, but his government did not do so with most, far less all, of India's religions. Varshney is right to note that Rajiv Gandhi's policy sought equiproximity in distinction from equidistance. However, Varshney does not address the limits of Rajiv Gandhi's attempts at equiproximity. Unlike his political pandering of Hindus and Muslims, Rajiv Gandhi did not attempt commensurate equiproximity with Christians or Jains or Buddhists. Given their limited numerical strength and electoral reach, the younger Gandhi ignored India's minor minorities.

Rajiv Gandhi's desire for a Hindu epic on state television must also be understood in the context of the relation between religion and state media in the 1980s. Religion was the explicit concern of state media at the time. Religious media complemented the language politics of the era. Both features of state media were shaped by their Nehruvian past and a desire to abandon it. Nehruvian secular demands tried to sanitize "public" by cordoning "community" from "secular." Under this model, religious programs were to be avoided.[93] This policy was formalized in a 1942 Conference of the Station Directors of All India radio. In practice, however, programs of religious music were common on All India Radio. Programs of different religions were aired on religion-specific days of the week: Muslim programs on Fridays, Hindu ones on Tuesdays. Religious festivals were also covered on radio. The 1942 policy ebbed the flow of religious programming on state media – television would emerge 30 years later, around 1975 – but by the mid-1950s devotional music was back in play. Most of the religious programs covered Hindu expressions. A meeting of All India Radio in the mid-1960s recommended phasing out devotional music, but successive governments chose to ignore the recommendation. As the next decade rolled in, religious programs had become a fixture of state media. During the Emergency in 1975, when Indira Gandhi's government invoked martial law, state media was regularly promoting religious content. As an instance, daily recitals of Tulsidas's *Ram Charitmanas* began during the Emergency. When a new government rode to power over the backlash against Emergency rule, the new Minister for Information and Broadcasting, Lal Krishna Advani, endorsed religious programs and continued their airing on All India Radio.

Government policy on religious programs also had to deal with the question of language politics, and Rajagopal has rightly argued that the religious bias of successive governments is quite apparent in the way state media was used to play language politics. The programming policy catered to Hindu or Muslim audiences in the name of impartial diversity. The language policy, on the other hand, favored Sanskritic Hindi for Hindus and Persian Urdu for Muslims. In-house radio and television programs tended to use Sanskritized Hindi, which was criticized for its distance from most north Indians, who spoke a language closer to Hindi-Urdu. Politics rather than popularity ruled the roost. Hence, B.V. Keskar, the Minister for Information and Broadcasting between 1952 and 1960, banned popular Hindi film music on All India Radio because he regarded film music steeped more in Muslim than in Hindu culture. Classical (Hindu) music was promoted instead.

The decision to air the *Ramayan* serial in Sanskritized Hindi must be situated in the context of religion politics and language politics that shaped governmental use of state-controlled media. *Ramayan* created a national audience in Sanskritic Hindi. In doing so, it was novel in many ways and a departure from both the state's impartiality toward religion and the loose federation of India's diverse regional cultures. For the first time, a fixed time of the week was set for religious programming, the program explicitly favored a single religion, the program was aimed at a national audience and not a regional one, and Hindi language was used for the entire nation.[94] A single religion's symbols and images were used as a stand-in for India's culture before a national audience. The substratum of Indian culture was Hindu and the Ramayan was a national story, not just a Hindu one. As Mankekar observes, each episode of the *Ramayan* began with the claim that its story was collated from diverse versions found around the nation.[95] Claiming a national provenance and the state's imprimatur, *Ramayan* established across a nation's diverse population the impression that India was Hindu, its great epics Hindu epics, and Delhi-centered Sanskritized Hindi its national language. Political parties in India were quick to cash-in on the influence of *Ramayan* (and the mostly Hindu religious serial that followed it).

Ramayan shaped the politics of religion and language in India. "After the screening of the Ramayan," Rajagopal notes, "Hindu myths and rituals began to be declared as legitimately belonging to the public arena."[96] Political groups claimed the Ramayan as India's primary symbol. Members of the secular Congress claimed the symbols and voice of the *Ramayan* serial as their own. Arun Govil, the actor who played the central character, Ram, campaigned for Congress across north India promising a *Ram Rajya* on behalf of the Congress Party if Congress was elected to power. Members of Hindu right like the Vishwa Hindu Parishad, Shiv Sena, Bajrang Dal, Rashtriya Swayamsevak Sangh also claimed the serial *Ramayan* as their symbol and voice. The Bhartiya Janata Party, a small electoral force in January 1987 when the serial began, used the serial to mobilize the Ram temple-Ramjanambhoomi movement and through that, its lagging fortune. Before the serial concluded, Vishwa Hindu Parishad had conducted ground-breaking ceremonies and a 'march to Ram's birthplace.' By June 1989, the Bharatiya Janata Party adopted the Ram temple as its main electoral platform.[97] Congress may have tried to appease the Hindus to increase its electoral power, but it was the Hindu groups that benefitted from Rajiv Gandhi's dalliance with Hindu nationalists. Before 1989, Hindu nationalists received less than 10 percent of the national vote. In 1989, this increased to 11.4 percent and in 1991 to more than 20 percent. Limited to a few pockets of support across north India, by 1991 the Bharatiya Janata Party had made inroads all over the nation. By 1991, it had 29 percent of the vote in Karnataka, 51 percent of the vote in Gujarat, and had formed governments in Uttar Pradesh, Madhya Pradesh, Rajasthan, and Himachal Pradesh. Today, the Bharatiya Janata Party rules in 22 of India's 29 states and has reduced Congress to a feeble opposition party. Importantly, riding the back of the Temple movement, the Bharatiya Janata Party had extended its reach from its traditional base (the urban trading community) to India's villages, small towns, youth, and growing middle class.[98]

The Ram temple movement lasted for three years in the lead-up to the national elections of 1989 and culminated in the destruction of the Babri Masjid in December 1992. Beginning in fall 1989, the Sangh family mobilized Hindu nationalists, middle class Hindus, small towns, and a large number of backward caste youth. The Mandal Commission's recommendations to expand reservations was a factor in the Sangh's political mobilization. However, the Sangh's central argument for electoral support revolved around the single issue of the Ram temple. Its most popular slogan during the 1989–1992 campaign was *Mandir Vahīṁ Banāyenge* ("We will build the temple right there!").[99] A popular version of the campaign went: *Rām Kasam, Mandir Vahīṁ Banāyenge*! ("I Swear by Ram, We will build the temple right there!"). A Hindu Temple would be built, yes; but more than that, a temple would be built that replaces the mosque, occupies its space, and displaces it for good! It is not enough to build a(nother) temple dedicated to Ram in Ayodhya. No. What is required is the demolition and displacement of the Babri mosque, a taking over of Muslim space by modern-day Hindu conquerors.

Communal coexistence was replaced by hardline communal exclusivism. The Ramayan serial exacerbated the trend toward communal exclusivism. It routinely denigrated non-Hindu identities and encouraged viewers "to equate Hindu culture with Indian culture."[100] Given this conflation, all non-Hindu ways of being appeared foreign. Since 'Hindu' was presented in cultural and not merely religious terms, non-religious Hindus could be Indian if they were culturally Hindu. Hence, Savarkar, the "ideological father of Hindu nationalism,"[101] could define a Hindu as "a person who feels united by blood ties with all those whose ancestry can be traced to Hindu 'antiquity,' and who accepts India – from the Indus River in the north, to the Indian Ocean – as his fatherland (*pitrubhu*)." Further, a person can be defined as a Hindu "only if he accepts India as a divine or holy land (*punyabhu*)," only if India is the 'cradle of his religion' and the land where he can find *moksha* or liberation.[102]

As Varshney notes, his definition meant Hindus, Sikhs, Jains, and Buddhists were triple insiders: India was their place in territorial, genealogical, and religious terms. Christians, Jews, Parsis, and Muslims could only be double insiders: their religions were not born in India and as such they could not claim this land as their "holyland."[103] The Ramayan serial presented culturally-other Indians as alien to India.[104] The Vishwa Hindu Parishad and parts of the Bharatiya Janata Party could then attempt to present Muslims as "demonic."[105] Given the state's preference to endorse uniformity because it can be easier to identify and control, many groups who claimed the Ramayan as their voice vehemently opposed any alternative presentations of the epic in the public sphere. Non-Brahminical versions and Jain versions were opposed. When the Maharashtra government tried to publish Dr. B. R. Ambedkar's chapter on the Ramayan, the Shiv Sena stopped it. Innovations were quashed by state support. The Shiv Sena again intervened and attacked a theatre that performed an interlocked play on Ram and Sita and Romeo and Juliet.[106] The Ramayan serial led to a realignment of religion, politics, and language in India's public sphere.

First aired on December 20, 1992, *Bāibal kī Kahānīyāṁ* debuted on the Sunday morning slot succeeding T.V. series like *The Ramayan*, *The Mahabharat*, and the Urdu-language *The Sword of Tipu Sultan*, three of the most popular Sunday morning television programs of the late 1980s and early 1990s at a time when a vast majority of the households did not have cable and Doordarshan serials were premier weekend programs. *Bāibal kī Kahāniyāṁ* aired for 15 episodes and discontinued in May 1993, before being revived for a short run in June 1996. Purnima Mankekar, an eminent media critic of Indian television, has shown that in the hands of state-appointed committees Doordarshan played a powerful role in promoting nation building and integration through prime-time programs (from 8:40 to 11:00 p.m. every evening and from 9:00 a.m. to noon on Sundays). Also known as 'National Programmes,' these prime-time broadcasts "were a major component of the effort to construct a pan-Indian 'national culture'."[107] *Bāibal kī Kahānīyāṁ*, then, represents the interest of the state in supporting a minority religious tradition, and its short life a reminder of the inability of its Christian and governmental sponsors to withstand market, cultural, and religious forces. Anand explains,

> The Doordarshan serial "Bāibil kī Kahāniyāṁ"[108] [Stories of the Bible] is another important example. The enthusiasm and excitement with which nearly 100 million viewers watched its first and second episode and turned off their T.V. sets in its third and fourth episodes. The reason was Arabic-Farsi laden Urdu. Our neighbors had asked us whether the language of the Bible was similar to that of the 'Quran'? What miscommunication. The good news became bad news. . . .
>
> I was talking to a senior official of Doordarshan regarding the script for the serial 'Bāibil kī Kahāniyāṁ.' Regarding the language she/he[109] said, 'Anandji, is such language appropriate for a national program?'
>
> The living good news of salvation should be communicated effectively to millions through a living language only. And for this a firm grasp ["complete knowledge"] of languages is important. If I am an inhabitant of the Hindi language, my region of work is the Hindi region [and] I should know the Hindi language. I should study it in its proper form.[110]

Anand is quite aware that Urdu-Hindi is not foreign to Christians and Christian communities in India. He was general editor of a Hindi-language introduction to Islam in 2004 that included a chapter on Jesus in the Qur'an[111] and edited an introduction to Christianity in India and Pakistan in 1994 that examined Christian schooling in Hindi, Urdu, and English in Lucknow.[112] In a popular translated textbook on communication and Indian Christian spirituality, Anand invites the readers to explore and adopt expressions of spirituality found in the many religious traditions in India.[113] Urdu was, in other words, not quite an 'other' or 'improper' language for Christians in north India. Further, the evidence from a linguistic analysis of the first four episodes of *Bāibal kī Kahānīyāṁ* suggests that there was more linguistic fluidity than Anand acknowledges.

The Hindi script of *Bāibal kī Kahānīyāṁ* used a wide range of loan words, including Sanskrit, Arabic, and Persian ones. The script of *Bāibal kī Kahānīyāṁ*, I would then offer, reflects a bold decision on the part of the producers and writers of the serial: Indian Christians are polyglots and should relate to a range of linguistic influences on the script. The first two episodes, as an instance, liberally sprinkle Sanskritic words in the narrator's voiceover and the characters' dialogues: *vṛkṣ*, *gyān*, *manuṣy*, *īśvar*, *ādimānav*, *vyāpt*, *nārī*, *ādeś*, *śāp*, all appear in the first two episodes. They also include *kaśtī* (boat), *khudā* (God), and *khāndān* (family), which are Persian loan words. In the second episode, Noah prays to his *khudā*. The third episode noticeably departs from the first two in script and tone. It relies frequently on *khudā* (which replaces *īśvar* has the divine name of choice) and other "Muslim" words – or words in the popular imagination most associated with Muslims in India – like *qabīlā* (Arabic, tribe), *be-aulād* (Persian, child-less), and *āqā* (Turkish, lord) and introduces numerous Urdu phrases and idioms. Given this diversity, then, one could argue that the writers and producers of *Bāibal kī Kahānīyāṁ* and the governmental managers at Doordarshan who approved it to air took an assimilative approach to the religious language of Christianity in India.

Explanations of the demise of *Bāibal kī Kahānīyāṁ* reveal tensions between etic and emic accounts of events. Anand attributes the serial's demise to a drastic decline in its popularity from millions of viewers to turned-off televisions due to the misapplication of culture to content – the use of Arabic-Urdu in a Christian program. Christian media accounts from the time further point to a controversy in Muslim-dominated areas on the depiction in *Bāibal kī Kahānīyāṁ* of prophets in human form. With a militant insurgency raging in Jammu and Kashmir, and bomb threats to Doordarshan offices and employees, the broadcaster decided to suspend *Bāibal kī Kahānīyāṁ* in 1993.[114] Mankekar, however, points to lackluster popularity of *Bāibal kī Kahānīyāṁ* among Indian audiences as the primary reason for its demise. Such a decline is, in her analysis, not linked to the language of the script. *Bāibal kī Kahānīyāṁ* failed to inspire loyalty, even among Christian viewers. Further, in Mankekar's narrative, *Bāibal kī Kahānīyāṁ* was rather uncontroversial in nature and content.[115]

Written in 1994 when *Bāibal kī Kahāniyāṁ* was taken off the air, Anand's comment expressed a timely concern. *Bāibal kī Kahānīyāṁ* was, after all, the first Christian serial to be aired by India's largest broadcaster in prime time and its short run did not particularly put Christian hearts and minds at ease with regards to the place of their foundational stories in the national religious narrative. Especially when compared to the success and influence of Hindu serials like *The Ramayan* and *The Mahabharat*, which lived on for many years in syndicated reruns, the quick demise of *Bāibal kī Kahānīyāṁ* readily stood out. Anand's view must, however, also be recognized for its pragmatic intent. His explanation that linguistic confusion cut the serial's life short hints toward the very real way in which religio-linguistic identities have practically functioned and continue to function in India. For a majority of Hindus, Urdu is the language of Muslims and English that of Christians. For many Christians – as reflected in Anand's view quoted earlier – Urdu is the cultural language of Muslims. Hence the perception of confusion among viewers by the use of Urdu instead of non-Urdu Hindi or of English in a Christian program.

Anand's concern with the introduction of 'Quranic language' in a Hindi Christian show stemmed from his lifelong interest in the Hindi-*karan* [or, Hindi-ization] of Christianity in India and from his desire to move Christianity away from its primary (and sometimes exclusive) association with English cultural worlds, as depicted most conspicuously in Hindi songs and Bollywood films. It stems partly also from an attempt to popularize and establish Hindi literature and resources among Christians in central and north India, a goal in which the Hindi Theological Literature Committee, under Anand's editorship, has particular investment and interest. The location of the discussion on the Christian use of Urdu on Doordarshan in a book on communicating the Good News further represents the desire among Hindi Christian authors to present an identifiable Christian witness with a distinguishable Christian vocabulary in their religiously plural context. Anand writes of the Christian witness,

> God has placed us Christians in a special situation: our neighbors are Hindu, Muslim, Jain, Buddhist, etc. Even their religion, faith, and culture are different. In faith we are living in a multifaith and multicultural context. On the other hand, as a minority religious community, how do we share the last commission of Jesus Christ with our neighbor?[116]

At the same time, however, Anand argues that Hindi Christians should not ignore their cultural context. A-cultural language in the Hindi Bible, he asserts, has also undermined the effectiveness and perception of the Hindi Christian witness. The earlier use of non-honorific language by Christians is a prime example of a disconnect between Hindi Christians and their cultural context.

> Another important thing: you use the honorific "you" for Christ the Lord in your conversations, in your prayer. This is our Indian culture. But when we read the Bible on Akashwani [India's national radio], Doordarshan [India's national TV], in public gatherings and use pronouns like you, your [in non-honorific form], we have to bow our head in shame. 'Jesus went,' 'Jesus said!' [in non-honorific forms].[117]

Certain concerns motivate Anand's opposition to the public use of non-honorific biblical language by Christians and the public use of Urdu in a national Christian serial. First, if Christianity is to be grounded in central India, it should use Hindi. Second, if Christians desire to be proud of their faith in public, they should be respectful of the cultural respect to divinities. Further, if Christians seek to establish themselves in public imaginations as members of a local religion and not a foreign one, they should embrace Hindi, reject English, and adapt Urdu (as needed). Finally, the embrace of Hindi as the language of religious expressions should be complemented by ways of being that present Christianity in positive and ethical ways. In other words, for Hindi Christian authors like Anand and Lall, public perceptions of Christianity are a function not only of the practice of religion but also of the language of religion.

Notes

1 Babb and Wadley, *Media and the Transformation of Religion*, 1–5, 191, 212.
2 Babb and Wadley, *Media and the Transformation of Religion*, 198.
3 Asad, *Genealogies of Religion*, 77–134.
4 Bonhoeffer, *The Cost of Discipleship*, 59.
5 Bonhoeffer, *The Cost of Discipleship*, 96.
6 Metaxas, *Bonhoeffer*, 140–143, 154, 172, 226, 262–263.
7 Bonhoeffer, *The Cost of Discipleship*, 117.
8 Bonhoeffer, *The Cost of Discipleship*, 119.
9 Bonhoeffer, *The Cost of Discipleship*, 248.
10 Bonhoeffer, *The Cost of Discipleship*, 155.
11 Bonhoeffer, *The Cost of Discipleship*, 158.
12 Barclay, *Through the Year*, 7.
13 Barclay, *Viliyam Bārkle ke Sāth*, I: "*Dr. Viliyam Bārkle un thoḍe se bāibil paṇḍitoṁ meṁ se haiṁ jinhoṇne bahut sahaj-saral śabdoṁ meṁ bāibil kī mahān saccāiyoṁ ko viśv ke sāmāny pāṭhkoṁ tak pahuṅcāyā hai. Bhāratīy pāsṭaroṁ meṁ Viliyam Bārkle bahut lokpriy haiṁ.*"
14 Anand's Preface in Sinha, *Masīhī Ācaraṇ*: "*[A]ṁgrezī pustak 'di kriściyans goḍ' kā hindī anuvād . . . Dr. Sī. Ḍablu. Ḍeviḍ ke karvākar . . . [y]ah pustak itnī lokapiry huī ki dekhte-dekhte ek hī varṣ meṁ ise do bār chāpnā paḍā. Āge calkar har varṣ iskā nayā saṃskaraṇ prakāśit hotā rahā.*"
15 Anand's Preface in Sinha, *Masīhī Ācaraṇ*.
16 David's Foreword in Sinha, *Masīhī Ācaraṇ*, ii (*kh*): "*Hindī masīhī sāhity kā durbhāgy hai ki uske pāṭhak bahut kam hai. Is sāhity ko na to kalīsiyā kī or se na bhāratīy samāj kī or se koī praśansā yā viśeṣ protsāhan prāpt hai. Hindī bhāṣiyoṁ se āgrah hai ki ve jāgeṁ aur acchī pustakoṁ ko paḍhne se apnī badnāmī ko dūr kareṁ aur prabuddh hoṁ.*"
17 Anand's Preface in Sinha, *Masīhī Ācaraṇ*: "*Hindī kśetroṁ ke thiyolājikal kalejoṁ ke prinsipal, carc ke biśap, pāsṭar, prakāśan saṃsthāeṁ, hamārī pustakoṁ ke vitrak, borḍs, miśnarī saṃsthāeṁ hamārī bharsak madad kartī haiṁ. Hameṁ viśvās aur āśā hai ki unkā prem hamāre prati bhaviṣy meṁ bhī banā rahegā.*"
18 *The Hindu Speaks*, 530.
19 *The Hindu Speaks*, 482–483.
20 *The Hindu Speaks*, 83.
21 *The Hindu Speaks*, 42.
22 *The Hindu Speaks*, 13.

23 *The Hindu Speaks*, 24–25.
24 *The Hindu Speaks*, 249.
25 *The Hindu Speaks*, 212–213.
26 *The Hindu Speaks*, 40.
27 Lall, *Susamācār-Pracār Darśan*, 62: "*Sākṣī denā pratyek viśvāsī ke lie anivāry hai, jis viśvāsī ne prabhu yīśu ko apnā nijī muktidātā grahaṇ kar liyā hai. Cāhe vah baḍe vyākhyān na de sakegā, cāhe baḍī sabhā meṁ kucch bolne se hickicāegā parantu nijī rūp se ek-ek jan ke āge apnī sākṣī dene se na ḍaregā. Kabhī-kabhī ismeṁ adhik safaltā bhī miltī hai. Vyaktigat pracār kī viśeṣatā yahī hai.*"
28 Lall, *Susamācār-Pracār Darśan*, 41: "*Susamācār pracār meṁ is bāt par viśeṣ dhyān rahe ki kisī ke dharm aur viśvās kā koī khanḍan na hove. Khanḍan karnā āsān hai aur ho saktā hai ki baḍī āsānī se ham bahas meṁ dūsre ko harā deṃ. Parantu isase koī lābh na hogā. Mujhe ek bhāī ne kahā, 'ek khristī pracārak ne ek sanātanī ko bahas meṁ burī tarah harāyā aur us samay se maiṁ khristīy dharm kā virodhī ho gayā.' Hamārā kām kisī kā khanḍan karnā nahīṁ hai. Hamārā kām yah hai ki apnī sākṣī se prabhu se kisī vyakti ko milāeṁ ki usī daśā meṁ prabhu yīśu uskī sahāytā kar sake.*"
29 Lall, *Susamācār-Pracār Darśan*, 59–60: "***Jab ek masīhī dūsre vyakti ko akele meṁ baiṭhkar bātcīt karke susamācār kā saty samjhātā hai, aur apne jīvan kā anubhav bharose ke sāth dūsre ke sāmne rakhtā hai tab susamācār śrotā mitr kī samajh meṁ ātā hai aur use viśvās ho jātā hai. Yadi koī praśn utpann hote haiṁ to ve mitratā se hal kiye jāte haiṁ. Bāībal ke pad kholkhol kar paḍhnā aur samjhānā, śrotā ke hriday par lāgū karnā hotā hai. Yahī vyaktigat pracār hai. Vyaktigat pracār ek-ek jan se milnā hai.*** *Prabhu ne lūkā 15:1–7 meṁ khoī huī bheḍ kā driṣṭānt dekar samjhāyā ki rakhwālā ek bheḍ kī khoj meṁ kitnā kaṣṭ uṭhātā hai, aur usko ḍhūnḍh kar lātā hai. Isī prakār vyaktigat pracār-kāry karne vālā ek ke pīche pariśram karne aur kaṣṭ uṭhāne meṁ āge baḍhtā hai, aur use parameśvar se milātā hai.*

Vyaktigat pracār kā lābh is bāt se bhī samajhie. Bājār v bhīḍ ke pracār meṁ kaī log susamācār pracār sunkar prabhāvit to hote hai parantu apnī buddhi, yogyatā, dharmaparāyaṇtā dikhāne ke lie pracārak se kaī prakār ke vyarth praśn karte hai, pracārak ko mūrkh aur jhūṭhe dharm kā pracārak dikhāte hai. Kaī log to pustakeṁ kharīdkar fāḍeṁge, fekeṁge. Parntu maine dekhā hai ki unhīṁ se alag meṁ milo, bāt karo, to ek dūsrī havā ho jātī hai."
30 Anand and Vashisht, *Merā Paṛosī*, 9–10: "*Is addhyayan kā uddeśy yah bhī nahī hai ki any dharmaviśvāsoṁ kī jānkārī prastut kare. Iske viprīt iskā uddeśy yah hai ki hum apne paḍosiyoṁ ke sambandh meṁ apne is bodh ko āge baḍhāe ki ve āj tak jīvit dharmoṁ ke mānne vāle log hai. Unke dharm siddhānt evam ācār-vyavhār jagat evam mānav samāj sambandhī masīhī logoṁ ke dharmavaigyānik cintan ke abhinn ang hone cāhiyeṁ. Dūsre śabdoṁ meṁ kahe to yah, ki yah addhayan masīhī logoṁ ko ek āvāhan hai ki ve apne paḍosiyoṁ ke dharm-viśvāsoṁ ko masīhī dharmavaigyānik bodh yā cetnā kā ang banāe. Ab tak masīhī cintan meṁ iske prati gambhīr driṣṭi nahīṁ apnāī gai hai. Par jab hamāre paḍosiyoṁ ke dharm-viśvās hameṁ is bāt kī jānkārī dete hai ki hum kis rūp meṁ apne dharmasiddhāntoṁ ko mānte aur samajhte hai, to hamāre liye yah anivāry ho jātā hai ki hum apne hī dharmaviśvās ke naye āyāmoṁ ko khojne kī cunautī prāpt kareṁ. Aisā karne se hum ek naye rūp meṁ apne paḍosiyoṁ ke sambandh meṁ nayī jānkārī bhī prāpt kay sakenge aur ek adhik ghaniṣṭ samāj meṁ hum unke sāth miljul kar rah sakenge. Hamāre deś meṁ iskī sabse baḍī āvaśyakatā hai.*"
31 Anand and Vashisht, *Merā Paṛosī*, 55: "*Vibhinn dharm paramparāoṁ meṁ bhī unke anuyāyī mānte hai ki unhe upne dharm viśvās ke liye sākṣī dene kā ādeś hai. Islām meṁ dharm pracār ek kartavy mānā gayā hai, kyoṁki islām kā sandeś sārvbhaumik mānā jātā hai. Bauddh dharm ke pāṭh meṁ bhī isī bāt par bal diyā gayā hai. Bauddh mārg ko aisā mānā gayā hai ki vah sab logoṁ ko*

mokṣ uplabdh karāegā. Par bauddh miśnoṁ ko yah āvhān hai ki ve gahan prem aur mānav kī cintā aur dūsroṁ ke dharm viśvāsoṁ ke prati ādar rakheṁ. [Hindu] āvhān karte hai ki bhārat ke riṣi-muniyoṁ kā sandeś sansār ko turant pahuṁcāeṁ, kyoṁki iske binā 'sansār kā vināś ho jaegā.' . . . Masīhī hone ke nāte humne bahudhā yah socā hai ki hum sandeś ke dene vāle hai aur dūsre log grahaṇ karne vāle. Humne gavāhī ko ekmukhī prakriyā hī mānā hai. To any dharm mānne vāle logoṁ ke uprokt kathanoṁ ke prati hamārī kyā pratikriyā hai, jab ki un kathanoṁ meṁ sansār ko gavāhī dene ke sambandh meṁ samān tīvr āgrah-bhāvanā, samarpaṇ aur dāyitv kī abhivyakti hai?"

32 Lall, *Susamācār-Pracār Darśan*, 57: "*Kaī deś picchle pacās varṣoṁ meṁ sāmrājy-vād se ājād hue hai. Ab ve svatantratā pā gae hai. Svatantratā pānā acchī bāt hai. Parantu is svatantratā ke sāth rāṣṭrīy bhāvanāe tīvr rūp meṁ kām karne lagī haiṁ jinke kāraṇ apne-apne deś kī sanskriti ityādi ko baḍhāne kā prayatn kiyā jā rahā hai. Masīhī viśvās ko sanskriti-ghātak batāyā jātā hai. Islie jo videś se pracārak āte the un par pratibandh lagā kar kah diyā gayā hai ki unke āne kī āvaśyakatā nahīṁ hai. Deś kī apnī maṇḍlī sankhyā v dhan meṁ itnī śaktiśālī nahīṁ hai ki apne kāry ko sambhāl sake, baḍhānā to asambhav hai. Kaī prakār ke sarkārī dabāv se nirbal viśvāsī maṇḍlī ko choḍ kar fir se purāne dharmoṃ meṁ cale jāte haiṁ.*"

33 Anand, *Samprêṣaṇ*, 32–34: "*Mukti kā śubh sandeś hameṁ likhit rūp meṁ hī prāpt hai: pavitr bāibil. Hamāre lie yah parameśvar kā vacan hai. Yah hamārī 'alṭīmeṭ athoriṭī' hai. Is alṭīmeṭ athoriṭī ko dūsroṁ par dikhāne ke pūrv hameṁ pahle apne jīvan meṁ apnānā hogā. Vyākhyā logoṁ ko ākarṣit nahīṁ kartī, par ācaraṇ. . . . 21-vīṁ śatābdī kā uttar bhārat kā hindī kṣetr, hamāre sāmne ek gambhīr samasyā hai. Jab maiṁ mukti kā śubh sandeś sunāne kī bāt kartā hūṁ tab mere śrotā, darśak, pāṭhak, gair masīhī, viśeṣakar mere Paṛosī hindū hote hai. . . .*

Uttar bhārat kā masīhī samāj bhāṣā kī driṣṭi se triśanku hai: kadācit hindī filmoṁ kā koī īsāī pātr jo bhāṣā boltā hai, usse hum is tathy ko samajh sakte haiṁ. Hamāre videśī bhāiyoṁ ne hameṁ sikhāyā ki hindī hinduoṁ kī bhāṣā hai, aur urdū musalamānoṁ kī. Aur īsāī aṁgrezī . . . Īsāī dharmaguru kesak pahanne vālā keval roman kaitholik fādar hī ho saktā hai.

Hindī bāibil jo āpke hāth meṁ hai uskā anuvād san 1905 meṁ ilāhābād ke presbīṭiri miśnarī ḍr. es. ec. kailāg ne kiyā thā. Sau varṣ pūrv hindī keval ek bolī thī jo uttar pradeś ke kucch jiloṁ aur madhy pradeś ke mahākośal kṣetr meṁ prayukt hotī thī. Ḍr. kailāg ne sau varś pūrv kī sthiti ke anurūp kāry kiyā thā. Āj stithi bilkul bhinn hai. Hindī rāṣṭr bhāṣā hai – sampark bhāṣā hai aur ākāśvāṇī, dūr-darśan, samācār-patroṁ, patrikāoṁ ke mādhyam se śrīnagar se kanyākumārī, kucch-saurāṭr se aruṇācal tak prayukt ho rahī hai. Uskī śabdāvalī aur rūp bilkul badal gae hai. Pramukh śabdoṁ ke arth badal gae aur nae-nae bhāvoṁ ko abhivyakt karne ke lie nae-nae śabd hindī bhāṣā meṁ ā gae haiṁ.

'Mukti kā śubh samācār' ghoṣit karte samay yadi sampreṣak us bhāṣā kā prayog nahī kartā jo sandeś grahaṇ karne vālā samajhtā hai to śubh sandeś aśubh sandeś ho jātā hai, arth kā anarth ho jātā hai."

34 Schüssler Fiorenza, *Jesus and the Politics of Interpretation*.

35 Pintchman, *Women's Lives*, 4.

36 James, *Mahilā Dharmavijñān*, 227: "*[S]amāj meṁ rahnevālī bahanoṁ se aur any sadasyoṁ se prem ke sāth vyavahār kar sake . . . dukhbharī kahāniyāṁ sun saktī hai aur dukhit hridayoṁ ko śānti de saktī hai . . . samarpit masīhī mahilā . . . saccī, mitratāpūrṇ aur śālīn . . . logoṁ kī bāt sunne, unko ucit smay par salāh dene, aur gopanīy bātoṁ ko man meṁ rakhne kī kṣamatā honī cāhiye.*

37 James, *Mahilā Dharmavijñān*, 228: *Pati ke samast dāyitv meṁ uskā saprem sāth de.*

38 James, *Mahilā Dharmavijñān*, 231–232: *Kalīsiyā ke jīvan aur pracār kāry meṁ striyoṁ kā bhārī hāth rahā hai. Hamāre prabhu ne ārambh se hī strī ko anugrah aur sevā meṁ puruṣ ke barābar mānā hai (dekhie yūhannā 4:7 kramik pad; markus 5:23 se āge; lūkā 10"38–42). Yah mānā ki striyoṁ ko celoṁ ke*

samān āścaryakarm karne kī sāmarth sahit prabh ne nahīṁ bhejā, parantu celoṁ ke samudāy meṁ sevā, sahāyatā aur ātithy satkār meṁ unkā viśeṣ bhāg rahā (lūkā 8:2; markus 15:40 se āge). Unmeṁ se kucch striyāṁ punurutthit khrist kī sarvpratham gavāh thīṁ (markus 16:1). Yīśu ke driṣṭāntoṁ meṁ striyoṁ ko mahatvapūrṇ sthān hai. Preritoṁ ke kām aur patriyoṁ meṁ anek striyoṁ kā ullekh hai jo susamācār pracār meṁ sahāyak thīṁ (preritoṁ ke kām 1:14; 12:12; 16:13 se āge; romiyoṁ 16:1, 3; 1 kurinthiyoṁ 1:11; kulussiyoṁ 4:15; 2 tīmuthiyus 1:5; filemon 4:2–3). Kalīsiyā meṁ striyāṁ anek prakār kī jimmedāriyāṁ sambhāltī thīṁ. Udāharaṇ ke liye, fībe kririvrayā kī maṇḍlī meṁ ḍīkanes thī (romiyoṁ 16:1); priskillā ne apullos kā praśikṣaṇ kiyā (pre. 18:24–26); tītus 2:3–5 meṁ presbiṭar mahilāoṁ kā ullekh hai; vidhvāeṁ parhit prārthanā kī sevā meṁ lagī rahtī thī (1 tīm. 5:5). Aisā pratīt hotā hai ki prārambhik kalīsiyā meṁ nabiyā bhī thī (pre. 21:9). Sant paulus striyoṁ ko 'mere sahakarmī' kahtā hai (ro. 16:3). Yah mānā jā saktā hai ki hamāre prabhu yīśu khrist ke dvārā aur striyoṁ ke prati prārambhik kalīsiyā kī abhivritti ke kāraṇ mānav samāj meṁ striyoṁ kā star ūṁcā huā hai.

Is paramparā ke anurūp āj mahilāeṁ kalīsiyā meṁ anek prakār se sevā kar rahī haiṁ, yahāṁ tak ki kucch kalīsiyāoṁ meṁ unko pādrī yā presbiṭar bhī banāyā gayā hai. Striyoṁ ko kalīsiyā meṁ matdān kā adhikār haiṁ; ve manḍalī meṁ anek rūpoṁ meṁ sevā kartī hai, bāibil vīmen pracār kāry kartī haiṁ, mahilāyeṁ skūloṁ meṁ śikṣā detī haiṁ, aspatāloṁ meṁ kāry kartī haiṁ, miśnarī haiṁ, sahāyak pādrī haiṁ, ādi.

Mahilāoṁ kī kalīsiyāī, antar-kalīsiyāī aur antarāṣṭrīy sabhāeṁ aur sangaṭhan haiṁ. Yah baḍe śrey kī bāt hai ki ve hosṭel, skūl, aspatāl aur saṃsthāeṁ jo mahilāoṁ ke hāth meṁ haiṁ kaī bātoṁ meṁ śreṣṭh haiṁ."

39 Schüssler Fiorenza, *Discipleship of Equals*, 159–161.
40 Schüssler Fiorenza, *Discipleship of Equals*, 157.
41 James, *Mahilā Dharmavijñān*, 234–235: "*Sab se acche pad aur viṣay vahīṁ hote haiṁ jo ghuṭnoṁ par prārthanā ke samay updeśak ko milte haiṁ . . . Yah kabhī na kariye ki āp updeś pahle taiyār kar leṁ aur tab pad ḍhūṇḍhate fireṁ . . . Āp ke jordār vicār binduoṁ ko ākhir meṁ aur kamjor vicār binduoṁ ko pahle rakhie . . . Updeś ko jīvan par lāgū karnā cāhiye aur usmeṁ vyaktigat apīl bhī honā cāhiye . . . Apne updeś ko soc lene ke bād updeś dene kā abhyās kījie. Āp ke uccāraṇ, abhivyakti, bāibal ke sandarbh ṭhīk se niścit hoṁ. Āp apnā updeś likh leṁ yā uske noṭs banā leṁ. Yah pakkā bharosā rakhie ki parameśvar āpke kām par āśiṣ degā.*"
42 Paul, *Striyoṁ kā Parameśvar ke Sāth Calnā*, 217: "*Ādhunik striyāṁ anek prakār se yogy hotī haiṁ. Vah kaī tarah ke kāryoṁ ke liye ucit rahtī hai . . . Vah kalīsiyā kī sammatiyoṁ par salāhakārī ke vibhāv meṁ, ātmā jītne kī upcārikā ke rūp meṁ, prabhubhoj taiyār karne ke lie, baccoṁ ko susamācār ke bāre meṁ batāne ke liye, prārthanā maṇḍaliyoṁ ko calāne ke lie, yuvā kī aguvāī karne ke dvārā, sanḍe skūl meṁ kāry karke, striyoṁ kī sangati ko calākar, kalīsiyā ke bīmāroṁ ke pā jākar, vidhavāoṁ evam anāthoṁ kī dekhbhāl karke, ṭankaṇ kāry (ṭāīping) karke, dān ekatrit karke, āgantuk satkārī hokar, aur in sabke ūpar muskurā kar, kalīsiyā kī sevakāī kar saktī hai.*"
43 Paul, *Striyoṁ kā Parameśvar ke Sāth Calnā*, 116: "*Masīh kī driṣṭi meṁ striyāṁ achūt nahīṁ thī.*"
44 Cf. Schüssler Fiorenza, *Discipleship of Equals*, 152, note 2.
45 Paul, *Striyoṁ kā Parameśvar ke Sāth Calnā*, 15.
46 Paul, *Striyoṁ kā Parameśvar ke Sāth Calnā*, 32: "*Uskā yah bhī adhikār hai ki manuṣy kī apekṣā parameśvar kī āgyā pālan kare.*"
47 Paul, *Striyoṁ kā Parameśvar ke Sāth Calnā*, 31: "*Svarg meṁ koī strīling athavā purling nahīṁ hai. Ling bhed keval is dhartī par hī hai, svarg meṁ koī ling bhed nahīṁ hai.*"

48 Paul, *Striyoṁ kā Parameśvar ke Sāth Calnā*, 31: "*Ek strī kā apne pati, bacce evam ghar ke ūpar adhikār hotā hai.*"

49 Paul, *Striyoṁ kā Parameśvar ke Sāth Calnā*, 132: "*Striyoṁ ko puruṣoṁ ke ūpar adhikār nahīṁ jamānā cāhiye.*"

50 David in James, *Mahilā Dharmavijñān*, xii: "*Kalīsiyā aur bhārat bhūmi ke kalyāṇ ke nimitt pustak ke lekhakoṁ aur sankalan kartī ke sāth hum bhī apne ārādhy prabhu yīśu khrist ke carṇoṁ meṁ ise samarpit karte haiṁ.*"

51 James, *Mahilā Dharmavijñān*, 103: "*Khristīy jīvan duhrā jīvan hai. Ismeṁ ādhyātmik aur naitikatā donoṁ kā gahrā sambandh hai.*"

52 James, *Mahilā Dharmavijñān*, 102: "*Pratyek khristīy jan ke liye yah āvaśyak hai ki vah apne ācaraṇ banānevāle siddhāntoṁ ko jāne aur unke sambandh meṁ use niścay ho.*"

53 James, *Mahilā Dharmavijñān*, 108: "*Parivār ke prati kartavy; samāj aur samudāy ke any logoṁ ke prati kartavy; deś ke prati kartavy.*"

54 James, *Mahilā Dharmavijñān*, 107–108: "*Adhikār jinke pās haiṁ unkā yah naitik dāyitv hai ki ve sab ke kalyāṇ ke liye uskā upayog kareṁ . . . jīvan ke prati ādar; ātmā-rakṣā; svāsthy rakṣā; ātm hatyā na karnā aur na dūsroṁ kī hatyā karnā . . . dhan ko sādhy rūp meṁ nahīṁ daran dūsroṁ kī bhalāī ke sādhan ke rūp meṁ arjit karnā cāhiye. Dūsroṁ kī sampatti kā ādar karnā cāhiye . . . buddhi, gyān, kauśal ādi kā vikās [karnā] . . . saty bolnā, apnī icchāoṁ, abhivṛttiyoṁ aur vāsnāoṁ par saṁyam rakhnā . . . ātm-nigrah aur ātm-sammān rakhnā, caritr aur sāmājik vyavasthā kā sammān karnā; gati tathā īmāndārī se kaṭhor śram karnā.*"

55 James, *Mahilā Dharmavijñān*, 107: "*Samāj adhikār kā srot hai. Kucch śartoṁ ke sāth samāj vyaktiyoṁ ko adhikār pradān kartā hai. Śart yah hai ki jinko adhikār die jāte haiṁ ve unkā ucit upayog kareṁ aur dūsroṁ ko asuvidhā na pahuṁcāne hetu unko kām meṁ leṁ. Khristīy nītiśāstr meṁ manuṣy ko jo abhikār prāpt haiṁ unmeṁ vyakti ke sammān evam mūly jhalakte haiṁ. Manuṣy ke adhikār ye haiṁ: (1) jīvan aur śram kā adhikār, (2) śikṣaṇ kā adhikār. (3) Svatantratā kā adhikār. (4) Sampatti kā adhikār. (5) Ikrārnāmā yā anubandh karne kā adhikār.*"

56 Dayal, *Vyaktigat Manan-Cintan*, 10: "*Var de ki maiṁ ne jo pahle pratigyāyeṁ kī haiṁ, unhe na toḍū aur jo galtiyāṁ kī haiṁ, unko binā sudhāre na choḍū. Var de ki yadi maiṁ kisī humrāhī ko sankaṭ meṁ dekhūṁ to katrā kar na calā jāūṁ. Var de ki maiṁ kartavy ko pūrā kiy bagair na choḍ dūṁ aur na kisī burī ādat ko kāyam rahne dūṁ. Jahāṁ merā koī kāry sansār ko manuṣyoṁ ke rahne ke lie behtar banā saktā hai, jahāṁ merā vacan kisī nirāś man ko protsāhan de saktā hai yā kamjor icchā-śaktivāle ko driḍh kar saktā hai, jahāṁ merī prārthanā muktidātā prabhu yeśu ke rājy ko vistrit kar saktī hai, vahāṁ mujhe karne, bolne aur prārthanā karne kī sāmārthy de.*"

57 Dayal, *Vyaktigat Manan-Cintan*, 34: "*Pyāre pitā, āj din bhar mere jīvan kī tū rakṣā karnā. Mere samast vicāroṁ aur bhāvanāoṁ ko niyantraṇ meṁ rakhnā, merī yogyatāoṁ kā sancālan karnā. Merī buddhi ko sikhānā. Merī icchā-śakti ko sambhālnā. Mere hāthoṁ ko lekar apnī āgyāoṁ kā pālan karne ke lie mujhe furtīlā banānā. Merī ākhoṁ ko lenā aur unheṁ apnī anant sundartā par lagā kar rakhnā. Mere muṁh ko lenā aur use apne prem kī gavāhī kā prabal vaktā banānā. Is din ko āgyāpālan kā din, ātmik ānand aur śānti kā din banānā. Is din ke kāryo ko muktidātā prabhu yeśu ke rājy kā hissā banānā.*"

58 Jonathan, *Biśap*, 22: "*Kalīsiyā se bāhar ke logoṁ meṁ, vistrt samudāy meṁ hamāre jīvan kā vah sevā pakṣ, jo hamārī saṁsthāoṁ, prayojanāoṁ, sāmājik kārykrmoṁ ke mādhyam seṁ vyakt hotā hai, hamāri pahcān kā cinh hai. Hamārī pahcān hamāre dāyitvoṁ ko . . . vahan karne se honī cāhiye.*"

59 Patlia, *Pāstarī Viddhyā*, 49–50: "*Sambhav hai ki vah bahusankhyak samudāy ke hathkaṇḍoṁ ke kāraṇ apne adhikāroṁ kā upayog [pūre] rūp se na kar sake. . .[par] āvaśyakatā paḍne par śānti aur prem kā aisā sangharṣ kar saktā*

hai ki mahān se mahān śaktiyāṁ bhī jhuk jāeṁ, uttam sākṣī utpann ho aur parameśvar kā rājy pragatiśīl ho sake."

60 Patlia, *Pāstarī Viddhyā*, 50.
61 Patlia, *Pāstarī Viddhyā*, 49: "*Jahāṁ gaṇtantrātmak svatantratā kā adhikār hai, vahāṁ ek samāj ko, cāhe alpsankhyak hī kyoṁ na ho, apne nāgrik adhikāroṁ ko prāpt karne ke lie sangharṣ karne kī pūrī svatantratā hai.*"
62 David's preface in Sinha, *Masīhī Ācaraṇ*, i (k): "*Masīhī ācaraṇ kī prāpti evam prasār viśv kalyāṇ evam pragati ke liye anivāry hai.*"
63 Sinha, *Masīhī Ācaraṇ*, 1: "*Ve log bhī, jo masīhī nahīṁ haiṁ, is bāt se paricit haiṁ ki masīhiyoṁ ko masīh ke samān honā hai. Sansār meṁ bahut log, jo masīhī nahīṁ haiṁ, prabhu yīśu ke caritr ko bhalībhaṁti jānte haiṁ. Unhe is bāt kā gyān hai ki prabhu yīśu nyāyapriy, namr aur śuddh ācaraṇ karne vālā tathā satybhāṣī jan thā.*"
64 Sinha, *Masīhī Ācaraṇ*, 2: "*Hum to prabhu yīśu ko dekh nahīṁ sakte, parantu hum āpko dekh sakte haiṁ.*"
65 David's preface in Sinha, *Masīhī Ācaraṇ*, i (k): "*Is pustak meṁ masīhī ācaraṇ kā ādarś, masīhī sadgun, tathā is ādarś evam in sadguṇoṁ ko apnāne ke sāmarth srot kā atyant sundar aur rocak vivecan kiyā gayā hai.*"
66 Howell, *Parivartan*, 170–171.
67 Howell, *Parivartan*, 171: "*Hameṁ lagātār apne vyavāhār aur bhāṣā ko jāṁcte rahnā cāhie.*"
68 Anand, *Samprêṣaṇ*, 6–7.
69 Rajagopal, *Politics after Television*, 84, 326.
70 Rajagopal, *Politics after Television*, 76–77.
71 Mankekar, *Screening Culture*, 5.
72 See also Mankekar, *Screening Culture*, 255.
73 Rajagopal, *Politics after Television*, 76ff.
74 Mankekar, "Epic Contests," 143.
75 Rajagopal, *Politics after Television*, 73.
76 King, *Nehru and the Language Politics of India*, 78.
77 Gill, "Why Ramayan on Doordarshan."
78 Scharf, *Rāmopākhyāna*.
79 Mankekar, "Epic Contests," 143.
80 Rajagopal, *Politics after Television*, 327.
81 Engineer, *Babri-Masjid*, 1ff.
82 Khan, *The Great Partition*, 62.
83 Khan, *The Great Partition*, 129.
84 Khan, *The Great Partition*, 135.
85 Khan, *The Great Partition*, 156.
86 Khan, *The Great Partition*, 176.
87 Quoted in Engineer, *Babri-Masjid*, 8.
88 Engineer, *Babri-Masjid*, 10–13.
89 Varshney, "Contested Meanings," 232.
90 Varshney, "Contested Meanings," 253.
91 Varshney, "Contested Meanings," 247.
92 Varshney, "Contested Meanings," 249.
93 Rajagopal, *Politics after Television*, 81ff.
94 Rajagopal, *Politics after Television*, 83.
95 Mankekar, "Epic Contests," 145.
96 Rajagopal, *Politics after Television*, 84, 117–118.
97 Also see, Rajagopal, "Ram Janmbhoomi," 1661.
98 Varshney, "Contested Meanings," 232–233.
99 Rajagopal, *Politics after Television*, 84, 161–162.

100 Mankekar, "Epic Contests," 140.
101 Varshney, "Contested Meanings," 230.
102 Andersen and Damle, *The Brotherhood in Saffron*, 33–34.
103 Varshney, "Contested Meanings," 230–231.
104 Pollock, "*Ramayan*," 264; referenced in Mankekar, "Epic Contests," 143.
105 Pollock, "*Ramayan*," 289.
106 Thapar, "The Ramayan Syndrome."
107 Mankekar, "National texts and gendered lives," 545–546.
108 Anand spelled the Hindi ("*Bāibil kī Kahāniyāṁ*") differently than Doordarshan did ("*Bāibal kī Kahāniyāṁ*") – with no difference in meaning.
109 The original Hindi pronoun (*unhone*) is gender non-specific.
110 Anand, *Samprêṣaṇ*, 35–36: "*'Bāibil kī kahāniyāṁ' dūrdarśan sīriyal ek aur mahatvapūrṇ udāharaṇ hai. Jis utsāh aur utsuktā se lagh-bhag 10 karoḍ darśakoṁ ne iskā pahlā-dūsrā epīsoḍ dekhā thā aur tīsre-cauthe epīsoḍ meṁ darśakoṁ ne apne-apne ṭī.vī. seṭ āf kar diye the. Kāraṇ arbī-fārsī se bojhil urdū. Hamare paḍosiyoṁ ne hum se pūchā ki kyā bāibil kī bhāṣā bhī 'kurān' kī bhāṣā jaisī hai? Kitnā galat Samprêṣaṇ huā thā. Śubh sandeś aśubh sandeś ban gayā thā. . . . 'Bāibil kī kahāniyāṁ' sīriyal kī pāṇḍulipi ke sambandh meṁ dūrdarśan ke uccādhikārī se bāt ho rahī thī. Bhāṣā ke sambandh meṁ unhoṁne kahā, 'ānand sāhab, kyā aisī bhāṣā rāṣṭrīy kārykram ke lie upyukt hai?'*

Mukti kā jīvit śubh sandeś jīvit bhāṣā ke mādhyam se hī karoḍoṃ logoṁ meṁ sārthak ḍhang se sampreṣit honā cāhie. Aur iske lie āvaśyak hai bhārat kī bhāṣāoṁ kā pūrṇagyān. Yadi maiṁ hindī bhāṣā kā nivāsī hūṁ, merā kāry kṣetr hindī bhāṣā kṣetr hai to mujhe hindī bhāṣā kā gyān honā cāhiy. Uskā vidhivat adhyayan karnā cāhie."
111 Bhajan and Khan, *Islām*, 234–246.
112 Dayal, *Uttar Bhārat aur Pākistān*, 201.
113 Anand and Warne, *Samprêṣaṇ*, 156–157.
114 Union of Catholic Asian News, "Bible series taken off national television after alleged Muslim threats," March 31, 1993.
115 Mankekar, "*Epic Contests*," 149, note 25.
116 Anand's preface in Khan, *Saṃvād*, I: "*Parameśvar ne hum-masīhiyoṁ ko ek viśeṣ sthiti meṁ rakhā hai: hamāre Paṛosī hindū, musalmān, jain, bauddh ādi haiṁ. Inkā dharm, viśvās, bhāṣā tathā sanskriti bhī bhinn hai. Vāstav meṁ hum bahudharm tathā bahusankriti ke pariveś meṁ rah rahe haiṁ. Dūsrī or alp-sankhyak dharmāvlambī samāj hone ke kāraṇ hum kis prakār apne Paṛosī ko prabhu yīśu kā antim ādeś sunā sakte haiṁ?*"
117 Anand, *Samprêṣaṇ*, 35: "*Ek aur mahatvpūrṇ bāt: āp apnī bāt-cīt meṁ, prārthanā meṁ prabhu parameśvar ke lie ādar sūcak sarvnām 'āp' kā prayog karte haiṁ. Yah hamārī bhāratīy sanskriti hai. Lekin jab hum ākāśavāṇī, dūrdarśan, lok sabhāoṁ meṁ bāibil paḍhte haiṁ aur tu, terā jaise sarvnāmoṁ kā prayog karte haiṁ, to lajjā se sir jhukānā paḍtā hai. 'Yeśu gayā', 'yeśu bolā!'.*"

References

Anand, John Henry. *Sampreṣaṇ tathā Mukti kā Śubh Sandeś* [How to Communicate Good News]. Lucknow: Lucknow Publishing House, 1994.

Anand, John Henry and Ramdutt Vashisht. 1988. *Merā Paṛosī Merā Bhāī* [My Neighbor My Brother]. Delhi: Indian Society for Promoting Christian Knowledge.

Anand, John Henry and S.K. Warne, trans. *Sampreṣaṇ: Arth aur Abhyās* [Communication: Meaning and Practice]. Jabalpur: Hindi Theological Literature Committee, 1995.

Anderson, Walter K. and Sridhar Damle. *The Brotherhood in Saffron: The RSS and Hindu Revivalism*. Delhi: Vistaar Publications, 1987.

Asad, Talal. *Genealogies of Religion: Discipline and Reasons of Power in Christianity and Islam*. Baltimore: The John Hopkins University Press, 1993.

Babb, Lawrence A. and Susan S. Wadley, eds. *Media and the Transformation of Religion in South Asia*. Philadelphia: University of Pennsylvania Press, 1995.

Barclay, William. *Through the Year with William Barclay, Devotional Readings for Every Day*, ed. Denis Duncan. London: Hodder and Stoughton1977 [1971].

Barclay, William. *Viliyam Bārkle ke Sāth Dainik Masīhī Ācaraṇ* [Through the Year with William Barclay, Devotional Readings for Every Day], trans. C.W. David. Jabalpur: Hindi Theological Literature Committee, 2010.

Bhajan, Sam V. and Benjamin Khan. *Islām: Ek Paricay* [Islam: An Introduction]. Jabalpur: Hindi Theological Literature Committee, 2004 [1974].

Bonhoeffer, Dietrich. *The Cost of Discipleship*. New York: Touchstone, 1995 [1937].

Dayal, Din. *Uttar Bhārat aur Pākistān meṁ Masīhī Dharm: Pratham Śatābdī se Bīsvīṁ Śatābdī ke Ārambh Tak* [The History of Christian Religion in North India and Pakistan: From the First Century to the Beginning of the Twentieth Century]. Jabalpur: Hindi Theological Literature Committee, 1997.

Dayal, Din. *Vyaktigat Manan-Cintan* [Personal Reflection]. Jabalpur: Hindi Theological Literature Committee, 2007.

Engineer, Asghar Ali, ed. *Babri-Masjid Ramjanambhoomi Controversy*. Delhi: Ajanta Publications (India), 1990.

Gill, S.S. "Why Ramayan on Doordarshan." *The Indian Express*, August 8, 1988: 8–9.

Howell, Richard. *Parivartan: Masīh se Milāp* [Conversion: A Meeting with Christ]. New Delhi: Evangelical Fellowship of India, 2006.

James, Elizabeth E., et al. *Mahilā Dharmavijñān Pāthya-Pustak* [Women's Theological Text Book]. Jabalpur: Hindi Theological Literature Committee, 2010 [1978].

Jonathan, Franklin C. *Biśap: Dāyitv, Darśan aur Mūly* [Bishop: Vocation, Vision and Value]. Jabalpur: Hindi Theological Literature Committee, 1994.

Khan, Benjamin. *Saṃvād: Kyoṁ aur Kaise, Masīhī Driṣṭikoṇ Se* [Dialogue: Why and How, from a Christian Perspective]. Jabalpur: Hindi Theological Literature Committee, 1994.

Khan, Yasmin. *The Great Partition: The Making of India and Pakistan*. New Haven: Yale University Press, 2007.

King, Robert D. *Nehru and the Language Politics of India*. Delhi: Oxford University Press, 1998.

Lall, Moti. *Susamācār-Pracār Darśan aur Vyaktigat Pracār-Kary* [Personal Evangelism]. Jabalpur: Hindi Theological Literature Committee, 2008 [1970].

Mankekar, Purnima. "National Texts and Gendered Lives: An Ethnography of Television Viewers in a North Indian City." *American Ethnologist* 20, no. 3 (1993): 543–564.

Mankekar, Purnima. *Screening Culture, Viewing Politics: An Ethnography of Television, Womanhood, and Nation in Postcolonial India*. Durham: Duke University Press, 1999.

Mankekar, Purnima. "Epic Contests: Television and Religious Identity in India." In *Media Worlds: Anthropology on New Terrain*, edited by Faye D. Ginsburg, Lila Abu-Lughod, and Brian Larkin. Berkeley: University of California Press, 2002.

Metaxas, Eric. *Bonhoeffer: Pastor, Martyr, Prophet, Spy, A Righteous Gentile vs. the Third Reich*. Nashville: Thomas Nelson, 2010.

Patlia, Daniel. *Pāstarī Viddhyā* [Pastoral Knowledge]. Jabalpur: Hindi Theological Literature Committee, 2008 [1968].

Paul, Winifred Irene. *Striyoṁ kā Parameśvar ke Sāth Calnā* [Walking of Women with God]. Delhi: Indian Society for Promoting Christian Knowledge, 2008.

Pintchman, Tracy, ed. *Women's Lives, Women's Rituals in the Hindu Tradition*. New York: Oxford University Press, 2007.

Pollock, Sheldon. "*Ramayana* and Political Imagination in India." *Journal of Asian Studies* 52, no. 2 (1993): 261–297.

Rajagopal, Arvind. "Ram Janmbhoomi, Consumer Identity and Image-Based Politics." *Economic and Political Weekly* (July 2, 1994): 1659–1668.

Rajagopal, Arvind. *Politics after Television: Religious Nationalism and the Reshaping of the Indian Public*. Cambridge: Cambridge University Press, 2001.

Scharf, Peter. *Rāmopākhyāna – the Story of Rāma in the Mahābhārata, And Independent-Study Reader in Sanskrit*. New York: RoutledgeCurzon, 2003.

Schüssler Fiorenza, Elisabeth. *Discipleship of Equals: A Critical Feminist Ekklēsiology of Liberation*. New York: Crossroad, 1993.

Schüssler Fiorenza, Elisabeth. *Jesus and the Politics of Interpretation*. New York: Continuum, 2000.

Sinha, Yunus Satyendra, trans. *Masīhī Ācaraṇ* [The Christian Character, by Stephen Neill]. Jabalpur: Hindi Theological Literature Committee, 2008 [1956].

Thapar, Romila. "The Ramayana Syndrome." *Seminar*, no. 353, January 1989.

The Hindu Speaks. *The Hindu Speaks on Religious Values*. Chennai: Kasturi & Sons Ltd., 1999.

Union of Catholic Asian News. "Bible series taken off national television after alleged Muslim Threats." March 31, 1993.

Varshney, Ashutosh. "Contested Meanings: India's National Identity, Hindu Nationalism, and the Politics of Anxiety." *Daedalus* 122, no. 3 (1993): 227–261.

5 Christians in India

Hindi Christian authors put Christian theology and ethics in service of specific social goals. I will examine these goals in this chapter. Each goal is backed by a strategy designed to present Christians in the best public light. To understand this strategy, I have found the works of three Hindi Christian thinkers to be particularly helpful because of the audience they address, their enduring influence on Hindi Christian education, and the unity with which they speak despite differences in context and subject matter. In *Khristīy Nītiśāstr* ("Christian Ethics") and *Saṃvād* ("Dialogue"), Benjamin Khan offers a Christian theo-ethical project that invites its Christian readers to learn from their Hindu neighbors in ways that promote interfaith dialogue. *Khristīy Nītiśāstr*'s primary audience was seminaries, seminarians, members of religious groups in universities and Christians in general. It was, hence, written as a textbook to provide a systematic exploration of Christian ethics based on a robust narrative account of Christ's life and ministry. Given its audience and its mission to shape Christian leaders in India, Khan's text does not present interfaith learning as a goal in itself. Such learning rather, Khan argues, must be put into practice in ways that promote interfaith relations, a goal that in turn shapes Christian theology and ethics.

In *Masīhī Dharm Vijñān kā Paricay* ("An Introduction to Indian Christian Theology"), Din Dayal examines the importance of Christian public relations in India's pluralist context. As previously noted, the official English name on the copyright page lists "An Introduction to the Indian Christian Theology." The Hindi title simply states '*Masīhī Dharm Vijñān kā Paricay*,' with no mention of it being Indian. Without this piece of editorial addition, the Hindi title would be translated as "An Introduction of Christian Theology."[1] Dayal's interest in public relation can be attributed to his career as a national leader with public responsibilities in the Church of north India, one of the largest Protestant denominations among Hindi-speaking Christians. Yet, as I will also show, his commitment to and views on Christian public witness should also be understood in light of his theology of God's self-revelation and the consequences of such a theology in a multi-religious context. Finally, in *Parivartan: Masīh se Milāp* ("Conversion: A Meeting with Christ") by Richard Howell, we find a text that is focused on the particular needs of doing evangelism as a religious minority. Howell makes a robust case for the impact of minority location on the languages and practices used by Christian evangelists in India.

If Christians are not just to profess but are also to propagate their faith in India, how must they present themselves to people of other faiths? What sort of identity do Hindi Christians seek? What are they hoping to achieve by presenting themselves in certain ways? These questions guide the writings of Khan, Dayal, and Howell and are examined in the following sections. Given the influence of Khan's work in Hindi Christian circles – his Christian ethics is a standard text in Hindi-language seminaries and currently in its third edition – and the pioneering nature of his work, I have paid considerable attention to his writings before I turn to the more recent works of Dayal and Howell in the first decade of the twenty-first century.

Interfaith relations: Benjamin Khan

Khan was born to a Methodist pastor and Christian homemaker in Haryana on September 3, 1927.[2] After schooling in (now) Pakistan, he studied philosophy (M.A.) at Punjab University and earned his doctorate in philosophy (*darśanśāstr*) from Agra University in 1962. A native speaker of Urdu, he gained expertise in English, Hindi, and Sanskrit, which he studied during doctoral research on the concept of dharma in Vālmīki's Rāmāyaṇa.[3] From 1952 he lectured on philosophy at Indore Christian College and from 1963–1986 he served as a professor with and the head of the department of philosophy at the College. He published and widely lectured on Indian philosophy and Gandhian thought and served as president of the Board of Studies in Philosophy, dean of the humanities faculty, and member of the University-wide executive committee of Indore University.

Khan made pioneering and original contributions to Hindi Christian literature.[4] These include an introductory book on Islam in 1974, *Khristīy Nītiśāstr* ("Christian Ethics"), *Bīsavīṁ Śatābdī ke Pramukh Dharmavijñānī* ("Prominent Theologians of the Twentieth Century), *Saṃvād* ("Dialogue"), and *Māno Yā Na Māno Prabhu Yīśu Ko Jāno* ("Know Jesus, Whether You Believe Him or Not"). Khan's book on Islam won an award from the Uttar Pradesh government. The state of Uttar Pradesh used to be a seat of power during the Mughal rule. It has one of the highest numbers of Muslims among the Indian States, and boasts many Islamic educational, architectural, and religious landmarks in cities like Lucknow, Aligarh, and Agra. Given the history of Islam in Uttar Pradesh, an award from the State Government for a book on Islam carried special recognition. Khan co-authored the book with Dr. Sam V. Bhajan. Bhajan earned an M.A. in Farsi from Punjab University and a Ph.D. in Islam from Tehran University. An expert in Islam and trained in Arabic, English, Farsi, Greek, Hindi, and Urdu, Bhajan later served as Director of the Hyderabad-based Henry Martyn Institute of Islamic Studies.[5] Throughout his career, Khan remained deeply committed to the practical applications of theology and considered *Khristīy Nītiśāstr* a Christian companion to his doctoral work on Hindu ethics.

> After the publication of my dissertation 'The Concept of Dharma in Valmiki Ramayana,' it was my heartfelt desire that I also write a book in Hindi on Christian ethics and from that time I have been engaged in a special study of this topic.[6]

And much like he did in his study of Hindu dharma, Khan begins his study of Christian ethics with a theological account of the state of and the need for ethics.

To understand the logic of *Khristīy Nītiśāstr*, it is helpful to examine *The Concept of Dharma in Valmiki Ramayana*. To understand *The Concept of Dharma*, in turn, it is helpful to recognize Khan's analysis of dharma. Khan's analysis of dharma functions as a prelude to his theological analysis of Christian ethical duties because Khan's commentary on the relation between Christian theology and ethics echoes his commentary on the relation between Hindu theology and ethics. Khan reads Vālmīki's Ramayan on dharma as a story on pragmatism. The story's characters frequently struggle with the question of how to act in order to fulfill the duties incumbent on them. In Vālmīki's Ramayan, for instance, King Daśaratha must banish his son Ram because he made a promise as King to do so to Kaikeyī, his wife, and a king is duty-bound to his word. Ram must obey his father and, even though the first-born heir to his father's throne, he must leave his inheritance and enter exile. Rāvanā must abduct Sita to avenge the dishonor to his sister, as his brotherly duty demands. Ram must rescue Sita, as his husbandly and royal duties demand. Ram must exile Sita out of duty to his subjects; Sita had spent time in the abode of another man, Rāvanā, as his captive and Ram's subjects doubted her purity when she returned. Sita, throughout the ordeal of being exiled with her husband, kept captive by Rāvanā, and exiled again by her husband, remains a faithful and dutiful wife who follows her strīsvadharma ("womanly duty"). Dharma, or "proper function, right action, or duty," permeates the Ramayan and is dependent on the social locations and positions in which the various characters find themselves. The story includes narrative conflicts where the characters act in less than ideal ways. Consider the mutilation of Śūrpaṇakhā, the slaying of Vālin, and the rejection of Sita by Ram, whose actions toward Sita are less than ideal.[7] There is also this scene from the later summary of the story of Ram in the Mahābhārata (at 3.265.22): when Rāvanā makes advances on his captive Sita, she reminds Rāvanā that she is the wife of another and he should refrain from such advances because he is the guardian of the quarter – and responsible for those who reside in it – and a sage's son who is duty-bound to proper action by his high birth.[8]

Khan's reading of dharma in the Ramayan is broadly on-point. But he does not examine the rhetorical nature of the story. The study of dharma in Hindu literature, Gavin Flood notes, is the study of "brahmanical self-representations and idealized images of gender roles" and the Ram and Sita of Vālmīkī's Ramayan are an ideal Hindu couple.[9] "He is honest, brave, the fulfiller of all his ethical responsibilities, and devoted to his wife, while she is modest, demure, virtuous, dedicated to her Lord and husband, yet strong in herself."[10] Khan does not acknowledge this rhetoric and how it compares to reality. He ignores episodes of deviations from dharma within the text.

Consider Sita's refusal of Ram. Sita has been liberated from the clutches of Rāvanā by Ram. Ram wants Sita to join him in Ayodhya. But Ayodhya's people cast doubt on Sita's virtue because she spent so much time as Rāvanā's captive. Sita professes her purity. Ram trusts Sita. Sita, after all, never lies. But Ram is caught between Sita's assertion and his peoples' suspicions. What is the virtuous Ram to do? Correct his people's assumptions and take Sita's word. Instead, he bends to public demand and exiles Sita. Time passes and Ram realizes he made a huge mistake. So, he goes to Sita in her exile and asks her to return to Ayodhya with him. Sita has none of it. She refuses to obey her husband. Instead, she calls on her mother, the Earth, to swallow her. Her mother duly obliges. Sita exerts her offence at Ram's distrust of her and ignores her duty to her husband as a good wife. Khan ignores such episodes in his reading of the Ramayan but presents dharma in the story as a straight-forward affair. Everyone does what is right.

Despite this lacuna, *The Concept of Dharma in Valmiki Ramayana* marked an important contribution to the study of Hindu ethics by a Hindi Christian scholar. Khan took the following lessons from the Ramayan on dharma. Dharma is the application of actions to values. One acts according to one's responsibilities. Values and actions are inseparable. Knowledge of values and commensurate actions is, however, not a sufficient means to ethical acts. Finally, dharma presupposes an active agent. It is not the imposition of an external value system on passive subjects. Precisely because proper actions can be difficult to discern due to conflicting dharmas, the actor has to discern which act is to be performed, which obligation must be fulfilled, and which goal must be achieved. Khan applies these insights from Ramayan-inspired dharma to his comments on Christian ethics. For Khan, the turn to *Khristīy Nītiśāstr* from *The Concept of Dharma* had two goals. Khan wanted to move from Hindu ethics to Christian ethics. He also wanted to write in Hindi. *The Concept of Dharma* remains Khan's only work in English. As noted previously, Khan desired to "write a book in Hindi" on Christian ethics. Why did he switch to Hindi when writing on Christian ethics, having written in English on Hindu ethics? Further, in which ways, if any, did the decision to write in Hindi affect the content of his Christian ethics? Before we turn to a comparative analysis of the content of *The Concept of Dharma* and *Khristīy Nītiśāstr*, then, a few notes on the choice of Hindi will help us identify the larger linguistic atmosphere within which Khan located *Khristīy Nītiśāstr* (and the other Hindi-language books that followed).

The desire to write in Hindi was partly practical. First, Hindi-language students for the Bachelor of Theology and Bachelor of Divinity degrees of the Senate of Serampore needed textbooks in Hindi. The Hindi Theological Literature Committee was tasked to publish these books. In response, the Committee launched a series of 'education books' and invited well-known scholars to contribute manuscripts. Both *Islām: Ek Paricay* (1974; Khan's first Hindi-language book) and *Khristīy Nītiśāstr* (1981) sought to meet the need of Hindi-medium seminary students. "It [was H.T.L.C.'s] request that, for the benefit of the Bachelor or Theology [B. Th.] and Bachelor of Divinity [B.D.] students of Serampore and on the basis of their syllabus, a book on Christian ethics be written."[11] Similarly, the book on Islam served an educational need. "[This] book has also been written to meet the needs of the B.Th. and B.D. students of Serampore Senate."[12] Second, both books, as mentioned earlier, were first works in Hindi written primarily for Hindi Christian readers.

The practical needs of Christian theological education, however, were not the only rationale for choosing Hindi. Both the publisher, Hindi Theological Literature Committee, and the author, Khan, were conscious of the fact that such books would serve two additional purposes. First, they would be accessible to the nation's vast Hindi-speaking population. As Bhajan and Khan write in their introduction to *Islām: Ek Paricay*, "It is our belief that our humble attempt will be valuable and a mile-post for all Hindi-language readers and seekers of truth."[13] Second, the contents of these books, in their pan-Hindi and extra-Christian reach, would hopefully bring about change in society-at-large beyond the mere sharing of knowledge regarding their respective topics. In his foreword to *Islām*, for instance, David hopes the book will "encourage seekers of truth" and "promote mutual dialogue and national unity."[14] Similarly, in his preface to *Khristīy Nītiśāstr*, Khan hopes his book would help his readers (both students and others) to develop character. Khan's commitment to interfaith relations in *Islām* and *Khristīy Nītiśāstr*, as explored in the following sections, should then, I would propose, be understood in light of his hope that writing in Hindi would reach a pan-Christian audience, shape society-at-large, and place Christian ideas and values in conversation with those held by people of other faiths. I turn to these topics now.

A person's dharma is tied deeply to a sense of one's place in life and that position's commensurate duties. "Dharma is relative" and "different for people at the several stages of development." "To a religious man," he continues,

> Dharma means the precepts found in the Vedas, and a strict adherence to them. To an ethical man, it is the voice of inner conscience that helps him distinguish between what is good and what is to be avoided. To a man on the street, it means customs and traditions. To a scribe it means law, secular or political, and to a philosopher, it means a metaphysical

> principle that binds and holds everything that sustains and nourishes, that principle of a thing in virtue of which it is what it is.[15]

Dharma is, Khan explains, "subject to time" and "a dynamic pragmatic principle operating in human situations and limited by human situations."[16] These stations in life, in turn, reflect the different levels of maturity or natural states in which a person finds herself. A person, then, is responsible for her actions, but proper actions are themselves a corollary of station in life. Knowledge of one's station in life (a theological task) creates the conditions for the possibility of commensurate and corresponding actions (*dharma*).

When turning to the task of Christian ethics 16 years later in *Khristīy Nītiśāstr*, Khan borrows ideas from *The Concept of Dharma*. He opens *Khristīy Nītiśāstr* with an examination of the place of theology in ethical discourse. Ethics cannot be separated from the task of religion:

> [A]n unbreakable bond exists between Christian religion and ethics, Christian theology and ethics and Christian faith and ethics. . . .
>
> [In Christianity] the primary principle is the reconciliation of a sinful human with God and this is possible by accepting the sacrifice of Christ. A human's true faith does not depend on her efforts, support, or religious works but on whether or not she had the experience of meeting (Reconciliation) with God. A person cannot become religious through her strength and efforts. This only generates pride in her. Having submitted before God, and having received strength [from God], a sinner can do ethical work. It is from this experience that in her life, her work and her relationships, a new change appears and she starts to live an ethical life. For this reason, Christian faith and Christian ethics are not separate but are undivided [or, single, being only one] and this is also true that in Christian faith we do not meet God by living an ethical life but having met God receive the strength [or, ability] to live an ethical life. In light of this presupposition, I am making a small attempt to write a book on Christian ethics.[17]

Theology and ethics are, for Khan, inseparable in the Christian context. They share an "unbreakable bond" ("*aṭūṭ sambandh*"). Christian ethics is not "separate" ("*pṛthak*") from Christian faith. Rather, Christian faith and Christian ethics are "undivided" ("*anany*") aspects of Christian reflection because there can be no ethics without one's experience of God and to experience God is to gain the ability, and hence the responsibility, to live ethically. The connection between theology and ethics shapes Khan's definition of "religious." A 'religious' person, Khan explains, has "the attitude and behavior that is necessary for the world or community; that virtuous conduct through which a community is protected and peace grows and through which one obtains swiftness in heaven."[18]

A few observations can be made on Khan's theology of Christian ethics. First, Khan's Christian ethics does not represent a contrast to ethical ideas in other faith traditions. Given their inter-faith context, rather, his writings reveal some of the ways in which interfaith relations and Christian witness in multifaith contexts have shaped Christian theological thought. As we have discussed earlier, Khan identifies his work as a comparative study to an earlier work on Hindu ethics. Ethical questions can find their "right answers" in the larger field of theological reflections that includes sources from other faiths. He writes,

> Religion calls God *sat, cit, ānand*. Some learned folks say *satyam-śivam-sundaram*. If this definition is accurate then it proves the unbreakable relation between ethic and religion, because the good (*śivam*, Good) that ethics studies, that is a property of God. Then we also know that we cannot give any correct answers to ethical questions till we do not discern what is the nature of a human, what is her[19] place in the universe, and what is the nature of the universe. Therefore, we reach this conclusion that from a logical and practical perspective there is a strong relationship between religion and ethics.[20]

Second, Khan's ethical project is part of a larger commitment to learning from and about other faith traditions in ways that further harmony and dialogue. When read together, Khan's *Khristīy Nītiśāstr* and *The Concept of Dharma in Valmiki Ramayana* offer an opportunity to engage in an interfaith dialogue that invites one to learn from other faith traditions in ways that affect an understanding of one's own faith tradition. Khan himself has not produced any work in this form of comparative reflection and cannot be called a comparative theologian. Yet *Khristīy Nītiśāstr* reveals Khan's invitation to learn from ideas and practices in other faiths.

Khristīy Nītiśāstr does not merely model a type of cross-faith learning. It proposes a larger purpose to interfaith learning. Cross-faith ethical learning seeks to improve society. Khan explains:

> Ethics is the common science to study what is good and bad in human character. Through its study we learn of human values and we also learn of what is appropriate and inappropriate behavior, of what is good and bad, in business, health, and in relations with each other.[21]

But reflections on ethics in pluralist contexts invite attention to goals beyond the study of right and wrong: they also seek to improve interfaith dialogue and harmony among people of different faiths. In his introduction to *Islām*, Khan then further writes:

> Nowadays there is a new movement afoot even among Christians whose goal is to establish a loving relationship between believers of the

various religions in the world. It is needed that adherents of different religions lovingly sit with each other to listen to each other and search for the ultimate truth together. Such a truth that fills the heart with that peace that gives rise to a new-human and that is full of love and hope. This new movement is called *saṃvād* (Dialogue). This does not mean that we cast dirt on each other, but that we sit in a loving environment and with patience and peace listen to and understand each other with compassion, learn from each other, and to the extent possible help each other for the betterment of society. To make this movement successful it is important that we are richly introduced to the beliefs and practices of other religions. For this reason, those books that present the beliefs, rituals, and ethics of different faiths in a proper way will certainly meet a big need of the times.[22]

Khan was writing about interfaith relationship at a time when positive interfaith relations had become an important Christian goal. Drawing from debates reflected in Acts 15, Galatians 2, and 1 Corinthians 7:12–16, the National Council of Churches in India adopted interfaith relations as a top priority in its earliest days as the Protestant Missionary Council in 1914. The Christian Conference of Asia had done so at its founding in 1957. The World Council of Churches created its Sub-unit on Dialogue with People of Living Faiths and Ideologies in 1971. Ecumenical history with interfaith relations stretches throughout the twentieth century. The need for interfaith relations generated heated debates at the 1928 (Jerusalem) and 1938 (Tambaran) missionary conferences. Paul Devanandan's address to the World Council of Churches Assembly in New Delhi in 1961 provided further impetus. Ongoing conversations about the need for Christians to build better interfaith relations led to the multifaith dialogue convened by the World Council of Churches in Lebanon in 1970. That same year, a meeting of the Central Committee of the World Council of Churches in Addis Ababa voted to establish a Sub-unit of the Council dedicated to interfaith relations.[23]

Christian organizations across India were investing in the dual goals of contributing to building India and to promoting interfaith relations. The history of Hindu-Christian interaction had entered a new phase. Missionary ambivalence toward non-Christian religions in the sixteenth to nineteenth centuries was exemplified in William Ward's and Alexander Duff's denigration of Hinduism and Robert de Nobili's adoption of Hinduism. By the eighteenth and nineteenth centuries, Hindu polemics against Christians were on the rise. By the late-nineteenth and twentieth centuries, a more positive approach to Hindu-Christian relations had started to take shape.[24] This approach was energized by Christian actions in the 1960s and 1970s. The National Council of Churches in India established the Christian Institute for the Study of Religion and Society in 1957 with the stated purpose to "facilitate Christian participation in nation-building and to promote interreligious dialogue."[25] Three years later, the Catholic Bishops' Conference of

India had declared inter-faith relations through dialogue a central goal and established a dialogue commission by 1966. Over the next three decades, Protestant, Roman Catholic, and Orthodox Christians in India would consolidate their inter-faith efforts.

A rationale for interfaith dialogue started to take form, and it was predominantly grounded in the desire to Indianize churches in India. Robinson notes that appeals to dialogue referenced the need for Indian Christians to understand their own identity as Indians, foster greater appreciation for India's many religions and cultures, and better realize the Indian identity of the church in India.[26] The focus on Hindu-Christian dialogue within the movement for interfaith dialogue was, for the most part, a reflection of the dominant religious group with which Christians interacted in the context of India. Endemic to efforts at dialogue was a certain understanding of the meanings of the term 'dialogue' and the goals of the activity of 'dialogue.' The term came to acquire a range of meanings among Christians in the twentieth century. 'Dialogue' involved conversations on religious claims and the search for truth, collaboration in the realm of public policy and practice, intra-Christian ecumenical debates on relations about religions, the theory and practice of life with neighbors of other faiths, and citizenship in a pluralist democracy.[27]

These types of dialogues share certain goals, primary among which is positive relations among people of different faiths, especially from the perspective of religious minorities. An asymmetry between Christian and Hindu interests in interfaith dialogue *qua* interfaith relations has influenced Christian attitudes toward such efforts. Nevertheless, on the Christian side there exists an unexamined assumption that interfaith dialogue is necessary, helpful, and important from the perspective of Christians as religious minorities in independent India. Another established assumption concerns the outcome of interfaith dialogues and asserts that dialogues inevitably foster peace. The notion that dialogue among practitioners of religions necessarily fosters interfaith relations is not without its detractors.[28] S.N. Balagangadhara asks important questions of the thesis that interfaith dialogues neutralize violence or, alternatively, foster peace.

Balagangadhara's critique rests on the idea that violence is probable when dialogues are asymmetrical. He notes, as an instance, how representations of religions can impact the shape and effect of dialogues. "Denying the experience of people whose religions" one talks about, he explains, can "inflict violence" on those talked about.[29] Who speaks for which religions, and how they speak about their and another's religion matters. In similar vein, dialogue can mitigate relations and foster antagonism when participants exert asymmetrical power in setting the terms of the dialogue as conversation or collaboration. The probability of harm to relations during dialogue increases when the dialogue is skewed or biased against the claims of some participants over others.[30] Robinson is sympathetic to criticism of such types of interfaith dialogue. He explains, as an instance, that dialogue should build on a "sympathetic understanding" of beliefs and practices as described by practitioners. Participants should take the claims of other participants seriously "even if it is difficult to enter into the plausibility structure of another religious tradition."[31] Authors like Robinson, and Khan (as noted later), are attuned to the form of critique of interfaith dialogue found in the reflections of Balagangadhara.

Khan's works reflect the interest of Hindi Christians to popularize interfaith relation. Khan's observations, then, are better understood as an acknowledgment of larger currents within the wider Christian family. It is relevant to note that *saṃvād* – as used by Khan, Dayal, and other Hindi Christian authors – takes on a positive tone to express conversations and dialogue that build relationships. *Saṃvād*'s root verb, *vād*, is usually understood as speaking, 'speech,' or in another popular use, a 'dispute' or 'controversy,' especially in the form *vād-vivād*.[32] *Saṃvād* does not necessarily imply a positive tone and can function as a reference, in a limited way, to 'speech together' (*saṃ vād*), discussions, debate, or dialogue.[33] As used in Hindi Christian literature, however, *saṃvād* predominantly functions as a reference to 'positive' dialogue (generally), and to interfaith dialogue more specifically in the context of Khan's works.

Finally, where interfaith learning became an invaluable resource and interfaith relations an important goal, ethics as the study of desirable (good) values and actions became for Khan the vehicle to present Christian witness as a social message in a multifaith context. The clearest expression of the link between social goals – harmony and dialogue – and Christian ethics is found in two places in Khan's corpus: his creative engagement of Bonhoeffer's *Ethics* in *Khristīy Nītiśāstr* (1981) and the summation of his life-long study of interfaith relations in his book on dialogue, *Saṃvād: Kyoṁ aur Kaise* ("Dialogue: Why and How," 1994). I will discuss these texts in detail, with supporting references to other relevant books by Khan.

Bonhoeffer's "religionless Christianity," which Khan translates as an instance of "secular theology," was an idea in response to the perception that God was being increasingly displaced as the foundation in key social discourses. Stated positively, the world was gaining greater "autonomy" from theology, which, Bonhoeffer observed, did not set conversations in society anymore. In theology, "reason is sufficient for religious knowledge." In ethics, "rules of life" have substituted the commandments. Politics have been "detached" from morality and built on "reasons of the state." Natural law has become the basis for law. Philosophers have provided alternatives in deism and pantheism. Natural sciences and physics have replaced the finite created world with an infinite self-sustaining one.[34] As Bonhoeffer put it in July 1944, the current state of divine affairs could be summarized as the attempt to speak of God *etsi deus non daretur* ("even if there were no God").[35]

The world had "come of age."[36] It was "conscious of itself and [of] the laws that govern its own existence" and had "grown self-confident."[37] During such a time, the challenge of the church was to speak of God in a world where God is not needed. Religionless Christianity provided a way ahead: the power of God in the world now diminished (in some discourses unnecessary), the church could invite people to look at the powerless and suffering God at the heart of the Bible. To the extent it points to the redeeming, incarnated, and this worldly Word,

> we may say that the development towards the world's coming of age outlined above, which has done away with a false conception of God, opens up a way of seeing the God of the Bible, who wins power and space in the world by his weakness. This will probably be the starting-point of our 'secular interpretation'.[38]

For Bonhoeffer, religionless Christianity was a call to rediscover the incarnate Word. It was also, in a very politically relevant way, a call to turn to the world and meet it in its particular needs and situations. A concrete, incarnated Christ existed at the heart of Christianity and, consequently, Christianity in an increasingly mature world had the renewed opportunity to (re)introduce Christ to the new world. "In Christ the reality of God meets the reality of the world and *allows us to share in this real encounter*. . . . Christian life is *participation in the encounter of Christ with the world*."[39] A real encounter happens in the concrete situations in which a Christian finds herself. Two aspects of Christian ethics are important in this regard: its concrete presence in a mature world, and its service as a worldly (penultimate) signpost to Christ. Not only are Christian ethics properly considered as *lived ethics*, they must also, crucially, be understood as "the penultimate in Christian life" that point toward and prepare the way for a person's encounter with Christ. Christ is the ultimate to which Christian ethics point and Christ is the ultimate from which the penultimate draws its foundation, form, and content.[40] Khan is a careful reader of Bonhoeffer and accurately identifies the Christology and worldliness that undergirds Bonhoeffer's Christian ethics.

The worldliness of Bonhoeffer's ethics plays a substantial part in Khan's use of Bonhoeffer in the Hindi Christian context. Bonhoeffer's *Ethics* receives substantial treatment in Khan's *Khristīy Nītiśāstr* and Bonhoeffer's *Ethics* and *Letters and Papers from Prison* receive sustained attention in Khan's *Bīsavīṃ Śatābdī ke Pramukh Dharmavijñānī*. Khan adapts Bonhoeffer's arguments on the role of Christian theology and ethics in the public realm by placing them in service of political engagement and building interfaith relations. Bonhoeffer was no stranger to interfaith relations and devoted substantial attention to the relation of the church to the Jews. Amidst an avalanche of anti-Jewish laws and restrictions, Bonhoeffer went farther than many of his fellow Christian leaders to declare that the church had an "unconditional obligation" to support and serve anyone who was a victim of state ordering whether they happened to be baptized or not in a clear reference to church obligations to protect the Jews from state persecution. By the spring of 1933, Metaxas reports, "Bonhoeffer was declaring it the duty of the church to stand up for the Jews."[41]

Khan finds Bonhoeffer particularly insightful because, in Bonhoeffer, Khan found a Western counterpart who asserted the worldliness of the church as a reminder of the lived nature of Christian ethics. Khan does not embrace Bonhoeffer's sense of a world 'without God.' For Bonhoeffer that meant the receding of God from public life. For Khan, however, God is not absent from the world; the challenge, rather, is to speak, in a public way of the God in whom Christians believe in light of the theological claims of people of other faiths. As a result, in his work Khan chose to highlight those sections of Bonhoeffer's *Ethics* where Bonhoeffer argues against the separation of the space of the church from that of the world (i.e., theological claims of "two spheres") and argues for the recognition of true humanity in the fulfillment of God's call to lived ethics in particular contexts – Khan wants the church to be active in the world and assert its lived nature and he wants Christian ethics to serve a larger purpose. In *Khristīy Nītiśāstr* (1981), Khan turns his attention to Bonhoeffer's views on the doctrine of "two spheres" that distinguishes between the "divine, holy, supernatural and Christian" and the "worldly, profane, natural, and un-Christian."[42] Paraphrasing Bonhoeffer, Khan writes:

> In his book 'Ethics,' Bonhoeffer, having accepted the commentary of Luther against the dualist [way of thinking] (Thinking in Term of Two Spheres), strongly critiques the natural and un-natural levels [or, spheres] of a human. . . . According to this dualism, ethics was also divided into two spheres . . . rules [or, laws] for those who are in the sphere of the natural and spiritual perfection for those who are religious, those who have decided to live a Christian life. . . .
>
> Bonhoeffer calls this dualism unrealistic and writes: 'A Christian, having accepted Christ, does not become the location of any duality but just as Christ is one, [she] too, having been liberated from dualities, becomes an undivided unity and does not live in two spheres [but] always in one sphere.' . . .
>
> Bonhoeffer writes that we should not consider this natural life as a life that is prior to accepting Christ but as a life that receives meaning through Jesus Christ.
>
> In summary we can say that Bonhoeffer gave new meaning and new value to the worldly life by stressing on the penultimate [or, on its penultimate nature]. In the same way, having demolished the two spheres or dualism, he proved that this world does not hinder one from accepting Christ but provides assistance in doing so.[43] A Christian should know that a Christian is a human and that particular human is human who has accepted the incarnated Christ.[44]

Bonhoeffer uses "supernatural" in *Ethics* to refer to the divine, holy, and spiritual in contrast to the worldly. Khan uses *aprākṛtik* to translate "supernatural." *Aprākṛtik* can mean "unnatural" or "not having to do with nature."[45]

Aprākṛtik, however, especially when backtranslated into English as "unnatural," does not sufficiently capture Bonhoeffer's basic thesis. Bonhoeffer does not present natural and supernatural as oppositional states couched in a faulty "two-sphere" way of organizing reality; using "unnatural," however, suggests a certain sense of mutual exclusiveness and oppositional relation ('a' functions as a negating prefix before prākṛtik in aprākṛtik) that is absent in Bonhoeffer's analysis. Further, Bonhoeffer's corrective to dualist thinking is a reaffirmation of the very this-worldly and human incarnation of the divine Word; the natural and supernatural cannot be sustained as exclusive categories in light of Christology. "The world, the natural, the profane and reason are now all taken up into God from the outset." Even further, "they do not exist 'in themselves' and 'on their own account'," but rather in Christ.[46] This interplay between the supernatural and natural is lost when the unnatural and natural are taken as the points of discussion. I believe a better Hindi translation would be *alaukik*, which is properly translated as "supernatural" or "transcendental."[47] Khan agrees with Bonhoeffer when the latter argues that "Ethical thinking in terms of spheres, then, is invalidated by faith in the revelation of the ultimate reality in Jesus Christ" and that "[t]here is no place to which the Christian can withdraw from the world, whether it be outwardly or in the sphere of the inner life."[48]

Since Christ is the sign of true humanity, Christian ethics takes its cues from the life of Christ, the true human in whom humanity finds its truth and fulfillment and toward whom the penultimate Christian ethical life points. Further, just as a Christian takes her cues from the life of Christ, so too the church, as a community of disciples, is called to take its ethical cues from Christ and to live in the world as the penultimate signpost to Christ. Khan explains:

> Christ is an example for human life. What he did, how he lived, how was his life; he lived among humans, he ate and drank with them, would sleep and rise up like them and would awaken a new humanity in them. This should be the ethical life of a Christian. Not far from the world but amidst the world, and this also should be the task of the church.[49]

Khan continues:

> The Church has a place in this world. The Church is a part of this world. The Church has a responsibility toward this world, [and] for this reason the Church is a community that is responsible to the world. It has to leap into this world, that does not believe in God. It cannot do anything by being far away from it.[50]

Here Khan is echoing Bonhoeffer, who argues that the church occupies a concrete space in the world as a witness to Christ:

> The Church does indeed occupy a definite space in the world. . . . It would be very dangerous to overlook this, to deny the visible nature of

> the Church, and to reduce her to the status of a purely spiritual force. For this would be to render ineffective the fact of the revelation of God in the world, and to transform Christ Himself into a spirit . . . the Church of Jesus Christ is the place, in other words the space in the world, at which the reign of Jesus Christ over the whole world is evidenced and proclaimed. This space of the Church, then, is not something which exists on its own account. It is from the outset something which reaches out far beyond itself, for indeed it is not the space of some kind of cultural association such as would have to fight for its own survival in the world, but it is the place where testimony is given to the foundation of all reality in Jesus Christ.[51]

Where Bonhoeffer speaks to a world increasingly without the need for God, Khan's reference to a world that "does not believe in God" should be understood as a reference to a context where people do not believe in God as understood by Christians rather than as a comment on the decreasing presence or absence of God in public discourses. This is because it is not Khan's purpose in *Khristīy Nītiśāstr* to argue (unlike Bonhoeffer) for the diminishing influence or absence of God in (Khan's) world. On the contrary, as discussed in following sections, the substantial influence of religion in public life in India features prominently in *Khristīy Nītiśāstr* as the context within which an Indian Christian is called to witness Christ and build interfaith relations. Despite these differences, Khan finds Bonhoeffer most appealing in the latter's insistence on the this-worldliness of Christian ethics and theology, a point Khan reiterates in his second engagement of Bonhoeffer in *Bīsavīṁ Śatābdī ke Pramukh Dharmavigyānī* ("Leading Theologians of the Twentieth Century"; 1990), published nine years after *Khristīy Nītiśāstr*.

In *Bīsavīṁ Śatābdī ke Pramukh Dharmavigyānī*, Khan is more direct in his insistence that the church is called to witness in the world and not away from it. Bonhoeffer writes, "It is not by ideals and programmes or by conscience, duty, responsibility and virtue that reality can be confronted and overcome, but simply and solely by the perfect love of God."[52] Quoting Bonhoeffer directly, Khan explains:

> Through ideals, programs, conscience, duty, responsibility and virtue we cannot face power nor can we overcome it. We can do this work through the love of God, through such a love that is not a general idea but is complete love.[53]

Further, Bonhoeffer describes this love as love of God in Christ, and calls it "living in the love of God."[54] Finally, this lived love, or the love of a God who lived in the world in Jesus,

> does not inspire a human to flee the world but rather empowers her to deal with all the troubles of the world, just as the body of Jesus Christ

> dealt with the fury of sin. It is also important for the Church that it put itself in harm's way for the sake of the world. A Christian, even while being in Christ is [still] based in the world.[55]

In Bonhoeffer's ethical writings and his letters and notes from prison, Khan finds a clear call for every follower of Christ and the church as the body of believers to take the world seriously and find place in it to preach the good news of presence rather than of absence. Khan writes, "Bonhoeffer . . . tells us that we must take this world very seriously. [We must] love it, live in it, and if needed even die for it. Our good news does not establish any escapist religion."[56]

Stated differently, Khan considers the call to a radical attention to the needs of the world Bonhoeffer's chief contribution to theology and ecclesiology.

> [Secular] theology certainly taught the church a new lesson. It was that the church give its full [and] active contribution to [address] the challenges and problems of the world. Just as the God of the Old Testament is fully involved in the spiritual, social and material aspects of the Israelites, in the same we need today such a God who provides spiritual and material support to all humanity in the world.[57]

Khan's theology, like Bonhoeffer's, asserts an active God present in the world in Christ, and consequently Khan's ethical writings call on Christians to be present and active in the world. Yet Khan and Bonhoeffer differ in revealing ways in how the church is called to be present and active in the world. Bonhoeffer properly relocates Christian discipleship and ethics within the world yet stops short of calling on the church to be shaped by the world. Khan, on the other hand, calls for Christian theology and ethics to be shaped by people of other faiths and invites Christians to place their lived ethics in service of interfaith relations. Dialogue, in this schema, becomes the primary expression of Christian service, and given the (particular) multifaith context within which Khan writes, interfaith relations emerge as special goals of a Christian theo-ethics.

The groundwork for such a project was laid in Khan's first Hindi Christian publication, his introduction to Islam (*Islām: Ek Paricay*), which he published with Sam Bhajan in 1974. In that book, Bhajan and Khan put the project to educate readers about Islam in service of interfaith relations. C. W. David highlighted this view in his foreword to *Islām*'s inaugural print in 1974 (emphases original):

> **Islam** is one of the main religions of the world. The number of followers of Islam currently in India is second to that of the majority Hindu believers. A majority of them lives in Hindi-speaking areas. According to the 1971 census, 45.3 crore[58] are followers of the Hindu religion, 6.1 crore Muslim, 1.4 crore Christian, 1 crore Sikh, 38 lakhs[59] Buddhist and

> 20 lakhs Jain. These numbers are presented here not to divide (literally, "separate"[60]) the nation but to explain the importance of the fact that in our nation there are different religious beliefs and religious ethics and that we should study each other, and even knowing that all religions are not the same we should respect the feelings of each other.
>
> There are three goals behind preparing ***Islām Ek Paricay*** out of which the authors have mentioned two also in their foreword: first, to assist with mutual dialogue (Dialogue); second, to meet the needs of B.Th. and B.D. students of the Serampore Senate; third, so that our nation, and especially Hindi-speakers, learn that even though religions are not similar, may the national and ethical life flourish in our nation and specially in Hindi-speaking regions.[61]

Khan returns to the theme of interfaith relations in *Khristīy Nītiśāstr* and *Saṃvād*. So, what is the way to interfaith relations in Khan's ethics? First, Christian love for neighbor should extend to non-Christian neighbors without the need to preach and propagate the faith. Second, given the social conditions in which an Indian Christian finds herself – i.e., living as a member of a religious minority in a democratic nation – Christian ethics must include robust participation in governance of communities to ensure that Christian values are brought to bear on politics and social policies. Finally, interfaith learning should be part of Christian discipleship in India.

First, Khan asks Christians to love their neighbors in their brokenness and complexity and not reduce them to what they do, how they live, whether they are religious or religious in the proper way, or their social standing. For a Christian, the first aspect or proper religiosity love of God. But Khan further explains:

> The second aspect of Christ's love rule is to love the neighbor. The neighbor is not some disembodied idea but a real truth. Christ did not command you to love humankind or humanity. That is why the topic of love is the neighbor. Who is my neighbor? Answering this question Christ offered a beautiful parable to present all the facets of a neighbor. We live in a world of formal relationships. We try [to find] what is this other person? In other words, what does this person do? . . . How many children does this person have? How is this person living her life? How happy or sad is this man? Is someone ill in her house? Etc. our introduction remains a surface introduction, i.e., what does he do? And we build a relationship on that basis. It is a matter of misfortune that we attempt to learn only one aspect (dimension) of her.[62]

In similar fashion, Khan suggests, we lose focus on the 'whole' neighbor when we exert our religious pride and "legalistic morality" against them for being improperly religious or irreligious:

> Some people take pride in their knowledge, wealth, physical beauty, race, etc. and this pride erects walls between human relationships. They prevent us from seeing the needs of our neighbors. Casteism in India and racism in some Western countries are examples of these. Christ calls our attention to another form of pride that was eating through the ethical and religious arrangements of his time like a termite. This was religious pride, or pride in being spiritual. [This religious pride] was hurt when they saw Jesus mingle with common people; drink and eat with them, and even touch them. . . . In the command to 'love your neighbor' Christ debunked all this legalistic morality [of the religiously proud] and, sitting with the poor and the sinners, demolished the wall that legalistic morality puts up between the religious and the unreligious.[63]

Loving one's neighbor involves turning to non-Christian neighbors. This is especially so because Christians in India find themselves in a religion-rich nation. He writes,

> [w]e Christians who live in India must be especially aware that even though India is a secular country nevertheless secularism does not imply the lack of religion [or, an irreligious nation]. Every person has the freedom to profess and propagate her own faith and has been commanded to respect another's faith.[64]

The source for such a command is not apparent at first. The source for Khan's reference to the freedom to profess and propagate religion is clearly Article 25 of the Constitution of India that reads: "Subject to public order, morality and health and to the other provisions of this Part, all persons are equally entitled to freedom of conscience and the right freely to profess, practice and propagate religion." No command to respect another's faith, however, exists in the country's constitution or in any part of the Indian Penal Code to the best of my knowledge. The 'command clause' seems to be Khan's editorial addition to the 'freedom clause' of Article 25. Nevertheless, this addition is very much in line with his larger argument: that an ethic by minority Christians in multifaith and secular India must include respect for people of other faiths. Even though India is a secular state, Khan explains, India is not "a-religious" (*a-dharm*[*ī*]). *Adharm* can mean both 'a-religious' and 'unrighteous/contrary to *dharm*.' McGregor, in his Hindi-English dictionary, notes only the latter meaning for *adharm*: unrighteousness, immorality, wickedness, sin, guilt, crime, irreligiosity, impiety.[65] In the context of Khan's argument, however, *adharm* is better translated as 'a-religious' or the 'lacking religion.' Khan, to elaborate, contrasts *adharm* with *dharmnirpekṣatā*, or a-religiosity with the religion-neutrality of the state (i.e., secularism), in the context of India's constitutional setup: India is a secular nation and not a nation that lacks religion. Further, "India's motto is 'Truth Alone Prevails,' i.e. only truth wins, and the meaning of truth in Indian philosophy is God." Finally, "[f]or a Christian, Christ is the truth,"[66] but every Indian Christian shares in the search for truth that exceeds religions.

What, then, must a Christian do to seek truth, as part of her call to love her neighbors, and in the socio-political context of a religiously diverse nation? Khan offers some "good practices" (*vyāvahārik subhāv*):

> First, claiming that he is a member of the Kingdom of God, a Christian should not run away from politics because he also is a member of the kingdom of the world.[67]
>
> Second, a Christian should not live in the country as a citizen with a negative attitude [or, as someone who only complains]. He should not just always complain that there is corruption in the country, [or that] law is weak. He should not blame this on others, he himself is also at fault because he has failed to make Christian values influential [in public life].
>
> Third, he should abandon such thinking that there is purity in politics or that politics is a pit of evil [literally, "the bowels of Satan"]. Politics is the mixture of the pure and the evil [literally, "devilish"] and it is the duty of a Christian to participate in politics and strengthen the forces of good.
>
> Fourth, a Christian should not become the pawn of a [political] party but should become a person who expresses his rights and vote according to Christ's teachings.
>
> Fifth, he should not always think that his perspective is the best. He should be humble.
>
> Sixth, a Christian should not think that solving only one problem will solve every problem of the nation. For instance, controlling population, eradicating gambling, etc. He should be engaged always in the task of strengthening social welfare, law, freedom, and security.[68]

In light of the responsibility Christians share with other citizens to ensure that truth prevails in matters of personal relations and affairs of the state, Khan encourages his readers to reject arguments against political involvement and to embrace their place in national governance among India's other religionists. It is a Christian's task not only to contribute to improving the nation but also to use her involvement in governance to share Christian values and to make them effective in the life of the nation.

Being a prophet who calls out injustice and wrongs is not enough; a Christian must also lead and affect change; a failure to affect change is a failure to participate. "Participation in politics," Khan declares, "is the responsibility of a Christian life."[69] Politics is neither dirty nor clean; it is complex and both and a Christian must encourage the good ("strengthen the forces of good"; "*śubh śakti ko prabal kare*") where things are bad. A Christian need not align herself to a political party. Khan does not ask Christians to reject political parties but to not become a "pawn" of parties. In other words, a Christian's affiliation to Christ's teachings and Christian values is independent of her political affiliations. It is relevant to observe here, that unlike political theologies that place an affiliation with Christ above that with political parties, Khan is quiet on the subject. He does not assert mutually exclusive relations to Christ and political parties. He seems, rather, to propose that a Christian use Christ's teaching as the standard to discern the way to exercise democratic rights and obligations. In other words, where party politics and Christian teachings align in a Christian's judgment, she can be loyal to both.

It is necessary to participate in politics and public affairs. This participation relies on positive interfaith relations. Interfaith dialogue and learning are the building blocks of interfaith relations. Interfaith dialogue leads to interfaith learning, which improve interfaith relations. Consequently, Khan elevates interfaith relations to a central goal of Christian theology and ethics in India. *Saṃvād* constitutes the fourth time that Khan writes on interfaith learning and relations following commentary, as discussed previously, in *Islām* (1974), *Khristīy Nītiśāstr* (1981), and *Bīsavīṁ Śatābdī ke Pramukh Dharmavijñānī* (1990). Khan makes his case with clarity:

> Contemporary communal intolerance, fanaticism and fundamentalism are producing such feelings of discord between followers of different faiths that our mutual relations have been polluted and we have started to view each other with disgust and doubt. Coexistence in such a situation has started to negatively affect our ethical, social and material values. Some people are engaged in fulfilling their political greed by misusing religion. Communal riots are gaining force and the minority community is living in fear. Falsities against each other's religions are being preached. Ethical values, especially the law is weak. Even some improper religious practices are rearing their heads. In such a situation 'interfaith dialogue' is becoming ever more necessary. Through this interfaith dialogue we can together attempt to stem the loss of ethics and the fall of religious values. Interfaith dialogue promotes not only the rooting up of biases but also the understanding among people of different faiths to live together. As we have previously seen, interfaith dialogue is the process through which we attempt to understand the practices, values and religious experiences of other faiths. If there is true intention behind this [process] then all distances are bridged and we come so close to each other that a fraternal feeling arises in us and hand-in-hand we start climbing toward that peak where the reconciliation of human with God and of human with human starts to become real.[70]

He continues:

> Interfaith dialogue also has some enemies and the chief enemy among these enemies is communalism. Communalism means the misuse of religion for political gains. The second enemy of interfaith dialogue is

'fanaticism' or 'I have the contract on truth, only my religion is true and other faiths are gifts of the devil.' This madness stands on the foundation of spiritual pride. It sows the seeds of disgust and impedes the living together of people of different faiths. The third enemy of interfaith dialogue is our ignorance, i.e., our limited knowledge of each other's religion and [our] misconceptions or unlimited knowledge of [their] so-called faults. As soon as interfaith dialogue starts some ignorant people start describing the faults in the other person's religion and launch such an attack that converts dialogue into argument and argument into fisticuffs. Instead of understanding each other [people] start hating each other. For this reason, interfaith dialogue fails in its goal until one does not have proper knowledge of one's faith and that of another. The fourth main enemy of interfaith dialogue is fundamentalism (Fundamentalism). Hindi, Hindu, Hindustan! Islam is in danger! To exile writers, thinker, and philosophers in the name of religion and *sharia*, to proclaim death *fatwas*, these are examples of religious fanaticism, fundamentalism. Its cries are echoing in the skies on a daily basis. On the other hand, Christianity, Sikhism, Buddhism, Jainism, etc.[71] also are falling victim to fundamentalism. The slogan "proudly declare we are Hindu" is gaining strength in India.[72]

Christianity removed from interfaith dialogue is susceptible to fanaticism. Hence, interfaith dialogue is necessary for religions in India:

This era gravely needs interfaith dialogue. Maybe it is only through these dialogues that we will reclaim our lost unity. Abolish those bad religious practices that have reared their heads. Join together to save those ethical [and] social values that are being lost. Free social life from fear and as a person of faith become able to care for the welfare of another person of faith without any personal benefit.

India is a living example of multiple groups, multiple races, and multiple religions but this plurality's vision of unity in diversity and diversity in unity is starting to appear as a hollow reality in light of rising communalism. Diversity is not taking [us] toward unity but is taking us toward division. Every day we are becoming strangers to one another. Politics has corrupted religion and diverted it from its goal. In light of the current situations prevalent in the nation, interfaith dialogue is needed where, with wide open minds and having adopted a positive attitude toward each other's faith, and having removed enmity and discord from our minds, [we] remove all those misconceptions and accept that the use of religion for political and economic gain is very deserving of scorn. Religion teaches a person to fulfill her duties, especially those duties that bring together a human with God and that fill her spirit with peace and joy and that motivate her to help realize the dream of 'God's kingdom' and 'God's city' in this world.[73]

For Khan, a Christian is called to interfaith dialogue and relations in God's command to love God and neighbor. As discussed earlier, the call to love God and neighbor is itself interpreted in the light of an Indian Christian's particular location as a call to (i) respect people of other faiths, (ii) participate in governance for the sake of welfare in society, (iii) learn about the beliefs and practice of one's neighbors as a means to better love one's neighbors, and importantly, to (iv) care for one's neighbor and fellow citizens without regard for caste, creed, and position in society.

Having examined the way in which Khan's ethics unfolds, it is easier to discern the ways in which he adapts Bonhoeffer's understanding of the relation between Christian ethics and society. Where Bonhoeffer sought a witnessing community that lived in opposition – consider the experiment in communal living that Bonhoeffer led at Zingst and Finkewalde from April 1935[74] – Khan wants Indian Christians to be involved actively and closely in shaping the affairs of the nation. Further, where the rise of *Deutsche Christens* ("German Christians") inspired Bonhoeffer to seek a confessing church independent of state power, Khan asks his readers to embrace politics, participate actively, and imbibe the nation's polity with Christian values. Indian Christians may not constitute a demographic force or dominant democratic power, Khan acknowledges, yet they must bring their values to national governance and in doing so, live actively and fully in the world. In a democratic nation where religion dominates public life, active involvement in building interfaith relations provides Christians with an invaluable basis for public participation. For Christians, interfaith relations not only provide a basis for public participation but they also constitute an effective tool to build public relations.

Public relations: Din Dayal

The corpus of writings by Din Dayal consists of three major publications. The first in 1997, *Uttar Bhārat aur Pākistān meṁ Masīhī Dharm: Pratham Śatābdī se Bīsavīīṁ Śatābdī ke Ārambh Tak* ("The History of Christian Religion in North India and Pakistan: From the First Century to the Beginning of the Twentieth Century"), examined the growth of south Asian Christian communities amidst the political, social, and religious realities of the region. The second major work, *Masīhī Dharm Vijñān kā Paricay* ("An Introduction to Indian Christian Theology") in 2005, provided seminarians, pastors, and lay leaders a primer in Indian Christian theology and encouraged Indian Christians to pay attention to the effects of their theologies on their public relations in India. The third major work, *Vyaktigat Manan-Cintan* ("Personal Reflections") in 2007, invited readers on a journey of daily prayers and reflections. As I will show in his work on theology that is most relevant to this study, Dayal, like Khan, wants Christian theology not only to teach and guide Christian formation but also to facilitate political engagement and public relations in India. Christian words and deeds should attend to their impact on the ways in which people of other faiths may perceive and relate to those words and deeds.

Dayal's biography partly explains his attention to public witness and relations.[75] Dayal was born in the State of Uttar Pradesh in north India on July 20, 1925 in a Christian family. He studied at the Christian High Schools in Etah and Farrukhabad (both in Uttar Pradesh). After working with the Indian Railways for a year after high school, he earned an Intermediate (or pre-University) Certificate from Ewing Christian College (Allahabad) and then a Bachelor of Arts in 1949 from Allahabad University. Involved in church work from an early age, he entered Leonard Theological College (Jabalpur, Madhya Pradesh) in 1949 and earned a Bachelor of Divinity in 1952. From 1952–1953, his church put him in charge of a national project called "The Christian Response to Communism." This was his first 'diplomatic' mission on behalf of north Indian churches: to communicate and explore the Christian response to communism. This project took him all over the country and immersed him for the first time in matters of social policy as a faith leader.

1952–1953 was an important period in the political life of the nation. Independent India had just concluded its first general elections in 1951, which had led to the formation of the first duly elected national government under Jawahar Lal Nehru. The election was held in 26 states and 401 constituencies for 489 seats in the Lok Sabha (the Lower House of the national Parliament). The Indian National Congress won 45 percent of the votes and a majority of the states with 363 seats. The Communist Party of India emerged behind the Indian National Congress with 15 seats in four different regions (seven seats in Madras, one in Orissa, two in Tripura, and five in West Bengal).[76]

Around the nation, other influential developments in polity and governance were also taking place. The Soviet-inspired central Planning Commission, established by the Government of India in March 1950, issued its first five-year plan in 1951 and placed India on the path of socialist development. Further, the Communist Party of India was becoming a political force at the state levels in south, central, and eastern India, challenging the Indian National Congress for dominance in state governance, where a lot of the decisions with the most direct impact on peoples' lives took place. Amidst these developments, Dayal took on the diplomatic challenge to discern the response of north Indian churches to the political, social, and economic trends ascendant in the nation. After completing his research on "The Christian Response to Communism," Dayal was ordained as a pastor in 1953 and served as the chaplain at Allahabad Agricultural Institute from 1953–1955.

The early 1950s saw an ecumenical revival among north Indian churches and, as an expression of this unity, these churches decided to send missionaries to east Africa. Dayal and his wife, Roja, departed for Kenya in 1955 as the first missionaries from the uniting churches in north India to Africa. They served in Kenya from 1955–1964; Dayal built a community center in

Nairobi and they evangelized and shared the fellowship of Indian churches throughout Kenya. This sojourn in Africa was Dayal's second diplomatic mission on behalf of north Indian churches. After Kenya, Dayal and Roja left for his studies in the United States, where he earned a Masters of Theology from Pittsburgh Seminary (1964–1965).

Dayal's life as an ordained minister placed him in public roles. After returning from the United States, Dayal became pastor of a United Church of North India congregation in Allahabad. In a few years he was elected Moderator (or Chairperson) of the North India Synod of the United Church of North India in 1968 and served in that role till 1970. When the United Church of North India merged with other north Indian denominations to form the Church of North India in 1970, Dayal became the Bishop of the Lucknow Diocese of Church of North India. He served as Lucknow's Bishop for 14 years and was elected Deputy Moderator of Church of North India in 1984. In 1987, after 34 years in various roles on behalf of the churches in north India, he was elected the Moderator (or national leader) of one of north India's largest Protestant denominations in 1987. He retired from the Church of North India in 1990.

Leadership roles within the United Church of North India and Church of North India made Dayal a public figure. As the Delhi-based chairperson of Church of North India, Dayal found himself in the political heart of the nation. He represented his denomination in interreligious and ecumenical meetings; engaged with leaders of faiths, politics, business, and society; and kept close attention to the larger life of the church. It is quite appropriate, then, that in his introduction to Dayal's *Uttar Bhārat aur Pākistān meṁ Masīhī Dharm* John Henry Anand felt the need to highlight Dayal's lifelong concern with the "universal life and work of the church" (*kalīsiyā ke sārvalaukik jīvan evam kāry [ke lie]*).[77] While Dayal's biography sheds light on the importance he placed on public relations, such a focus should also be understood in light of the theological arguments he presents in *Masīhī Dharm Vijñān kā Paricay* (2005), his central text on theology, ethics, and public discourse.

Dayal makes a three-pronged theological case for the importance of public relations in *Masīhī Dharm Vijñān kā Paricay* that mostly parallels Khan's proposal. First, Christians are called to live in and shape their societies rather than to create separate, special Christian societies. Second, witnessing in a pluralist context (like India's) invites Christians to understand the impact of their witness on people of other faiths. Third, Christian relationships are the outcome of God's manner of self-revelation. In other words, Dayal's theology of divine self-revelation provides the theological basis for his proposals regarding Christian public relations.

A Christian, for Dayal, is called to public service. The good news of Christ proposes salvation to all. Christ did not come to establish a separate society – see, for instance, Dayal's commentary on the "Kingdom of God," which is discussed in following sections – but rather taught and practiced values on which society and culture at large could be built. Humans, and not God, are the makers (*nirmātā*) of civilization and culture, and Christianity is to culture as salt is to food. In other words, Christianity must flavor culture. To bring about this effect is, Dayal argues, the duty of every Christian. He explains:

> The gospel of Lord Jesus is not in order to establish any special civilization but the gospel is for the salvation of humanity. The creation of civilization and culture is in the hands of humans. Without doubt, Christianity is like salt. For this reason, a Christian's faith must affect culture. It is the duty of Christians that they contribute to the making of culture in the context of their society and nation. Christians do not possess any Christian scheme for culture.[78]

Christians do not possess a plan for culture just as they do not possess a plan to establish Christ's kingdom on earth. They possess, rather, the good news of the Kingdom of God that Jesus shared with them. They are called to preach that good news in the societies and localities in which they live as citizens and members. Is this idea of a Kingdom of God "meaningful in our secular time and in our time of economic and scientific progress?" "Yes," Dayal answers, because "we have always longed for peace"; because "the world is not rid of conflicts and terrible weapons." "Have injustice, poverty, exploitation, and terrible diseases ended?" No. That is why "we have to share the good-news of Christ to the world."[79] Preaching in a pluralist society, however, invites awareness of public relations. Consequently, while Dayal encourages Indian Christians to profess and practice their faith – as is their constitutional right – he also invites them to do so while aware of the relation between what they preach and the beliefs of people of other faiths. He explains:

> Pluralism is a special feature of culture. For this reason, culture is faced with the challenge to accept many beliefs. No society can possess all the virtues even if it likes them all. A society has many beliefs because there are many humans and their goals and needs are many. . . . In a pluralist society, things like the Kingdom of God, Lord Jesus Christ, God the Father and good news are very important beliefs for Christian believers. However, they are important only for Christians.[80]

Christians need not ignore what is important to them. They should, rather, recognize a plurality of beliefs and be able to locate the importance of their beliefs and practices amidst the importance placed by others on other beliefs and practices. Given Dayal's overall thesis, and the fact that he remained committed to ecumenism throughout his ministry, it can be safely argued that 'pluralism-as-the-acceptance-of-many-beliefs' in Dayal's writings may be interpreted as recognition of diversity both among faiths and within them.

Finally, 'pluralism-as-relations-among-people-with-many-beliefs' is a natural outcome of the way in which God self-reveals in the world. Christ's life and actions may be very important to Christians – as noted previously – but God does limit God's self-revelation to the words and deeds of Jesus, Dayal proposes. One cannot "fully understand" another, he explains, until the other reveals or shares about herself. Similarly, people come to understand God because God self-reveals. Further, God self-reveals to all people and all faiths, Dayal explains, but beliefs concerning God differ among people. Different beliefs then represent different understandings of the expressions of God.

Dayal does not clarify whether it is possible to understand God "fully." He implies a "full understanding" of God is possible. But his comments on the different interpretations of God's self-revelation cautions against a robust reading of the "full understanding" clause. Further, Dayal does not make any claims regarding the achievement of full understanding in either type of relations (i.e., divine-human and human-human relations). Full understanding of God and others remains a possibility in *Masīhī Dharm Vijñān* rather than a completed task. As Dayal puts it,

> A person cannot fully understand another person until the other person shares about herself. . . . God self-reveals. He self-reveals his power and nature. It is God who has self-revealed to the entire world and to people of all faiths. For this reason people of all faiths say there is God. It is another matter that there are differences in beliefs regarding God. Most Hindus believe in many goddesses and gods. But their supporters and thoughtful Hindus say that all goddesses and gods are powers of the same Lord. That is why they can worship Lord in any form. In reality very few Hindus worship a formless Brahma. . . . In Islam, there are many beautiful names of Allah that point toward his qualities. Allah is omnipotent and just. Many philosophers say that the supreme spirit is the basis of all life. It is the source of our highest ethical and intellectual desires. It is a living force and directs and attracts all creation.[81]

Dayal's doctrine of self-revelation, which is both a human and a divine act, leads to a few observations. The agency to reveal rests with a God who has self-revealed to all. Consequently, it is difficult to deny the presence of God's self-revelation in other faiths. Human-divine relations are possible because of God's self-revelation. Dayal explains that

> a human's wisdom and judgment contain the likeness of God. If God and human did not share a likeness then a meeting between the two would not have been possible. God would not have self-revealed on a human if a human did not have the ability to understand and meet God.[82]

Each religion has something to contribute to the understanding of God. It follows, then, that a Christian can learn from other religions about God.

The reality of pluralism-as-respect-for-the-value-of-other-beliefs invites Christians to evangelize and attract converts in collegial ways. Dayal lays the groundwork for a particular type of evangelism that is 'gentle,' where one propagates religion but does not force conversion or denigrate other religions. This type of evangelism is the subject of *Parivartan*, a careful work on evangelism by Richard Howell. The timing and context of *Parivartan*'s publication has made it an important contribution to debates on the public posture of evangelical Christianity in contemporary India.

Outlines: Richard Howell

At the time of *Parivartan*'s publication in 2006, Howell was the leader and General Secretary of the Evangelical Fellowship of India.[83] The Evangelical Fellowship of India is a group of more than 250 evangelical, independent, and denominational churches across India. Members of the Fellowship denominations include Pentecostal, Baptist, and Assembly of God, all dedicated to evangelize and plant churches. The Fellowship includes non-denominational ministries like Evangelise India Fellowship, Gospel for India, Hosanna Human Development Society, New Life Ministries, Tribals Transformation India, and the World Cassette Outreach of India. It also includes seminaries across India that train preachers, pastors, and church planters – seminaries like the Pune-based Union Biblical Seminary, which seeks to fulfill the Great Commission in India. Howell's publication carried special weight in evangelical circles due to his national position. And reacting to public perceptions of Indian evangelists as confrontational fundamentalists, Howell made the case for a type of evangelism that is collegial and respectful of people of other faiths. I examined Howell's vocabulary of evangelization earlier. Here I will thicken those comments with an analysis of the larger religious framework within which Howell makes his proposals and locates the task of evangelism.

Howell describes India's pluralist context in the opening chapter of *Parivartan*. The title of the chapter is *Badi Tasvīr ko Dekhnā* ("Seeing the Big Picture"). The Bible narrates the story of God and this is a story of God, God's lost creation, and the re-establishment or reconciling of that creation. "The Bible," Howell writes, "tells us the story of God. It is the story of God, and God's lost creation, and [the story of] its re-establishment."[84] Howell uses an active verb like 'reconciling' rather that a noun like 'reconciliation' to describe the crux of the biblical story because he wants to draw attention to the source and agent of creation and reconciliation. This agency matters to him because his theology is a theology of mutual roles between God and humans, a theological account in which God takes on certain roles and places us in complementary roles within the unfolding of God's reconciling act.

The story of God's reconciling act builds on four motifs. First, God is the source and reconciler of creation that separates itself from God. Second, God creates creatures to be in relationships, with God and with each other (sin ruptures this relationship). Third, God is Lord, Lord of creation, Lord of creatures, and Lord of relationships. In other words, creatures owe certain responsibilities to God. "For this reason," Howell writes, "the Bible begins with this thought that God is in the form of the source, relationships are in the form of a priority, and God is in the form of a Lord."[85] Finally, in light of such an arrangement, God and creatures play certain parts in the biblical accounts. God's parts include God's participation in creation as its creator, sustainer, and guide – Howell uses the word *niyantraṇ*, or "control," to describe God's management but uses it to clarify that while God was the "lord of the bigger picture" ("*is baḍī tasvīr kā mālik vo hī thā*") it is each person's responsibility to control her own actions – law-giver, and its reconciler.

God is the party with authority (the "*adhikārī*," or one possessing authority) in the big-picture divine-human relationship, but in the realm of individual actions, personal responsibility remains paramount. In other words, a Christian cannot lose sight of her responsibilities *qua Christian* even as she recognizes the larger story of divine action within which her story exists. Interpreting Job 38:4, then – where God asks Job, "Where were you when I laid the foundation of the earth?" (New Revised Standard Version) – Howell writes:

> In this big picture our control is limited – rather, speaking truthfully, we never had control. But our control over our behavior is necessary and we certainly should keep our behaviour under control. God's role is in the control of this bigger picture and our role is to be in control of [or, in charge of] ourselves and our responsibilities. This means that we should maintain 'self-control' [under God's overall control].[86]

While recognizing this bigger picture, a Christian has certain responsibilities toward God, and primary among them is the responsibility to be "facilitators" of God's care for God's creation. To those who seek to live responsibly, then, Howell gives the following advice:

> We must gain an understanding of the proper place of our lives in this larger story of the Bible and of what God is doing in this world. We must proceed in our struggle and we must discern our place and role in that great and big plan of God. Beseech God to help you understand and see these things in your life.[87]

Howell, in other words, presents a theology of mutual and corresponding responsibilities. God's role is to be the source; humans are dependents. God is the creator (and creates things to be in relationships); humans are creatures. God controls creation; humans are also responsible for their actions. God judges lives; humans are called not to judge but to live in public discipleship. Howell tabulates these roles as follows:[88]

God	*Human*
God is the source	*We depend on God*
God is the creator	*We are creation and cannot bloom without Him*
God has authority over the world and controls it	*We are self-regulated, i.e., we can control ourselves*
God judges lives	*We experience life*
God created humans and made laws for them	*We follow God's laws in our lives*

In the context of India's pluralist context, these responsibilities take on a different form. Howell (a la Khan and Dayal) argues that it is a Christian's "responsibility" (*kartavy*) to contribute to the religious life of the nation. Howell's call to participate is a call to facilitate healthy relations with others. God orients human toward relationships, Howell explains, and Indian Christians must contribute to India's human needs. Of those needs, he writes,

> Indian democracy is facing new challenges, communal conflicts, the fight against terrorism, and meeting the needs of a young generation. India needs to improve the way it does things. This means the democracy needs people who are decisive, effective, and follow the Constitution, [and it needs the] enjoining of freedom with democracy, the rebuilding of political institutions that are broken and scattered, and above all that government institutions and officials understand and fulfill their duties. They must not only present legal matters but must also present ethical matters before the public and should themselves follow them. Without this democracy will become hollow, not only incompetent but also dangerous, with this freedom will be destroyed, freedom will be used for oppression, and society will be destroyed.[89]

This is especially so because religion is not, Howell argues, a private matter but a public force in India and as such should be approached in a way that recognizes the ways in which religious matters shape public policies. Howell cites the challenge posed to religious freedom by restrictive laws on conversions passed in India. For a Christian to refrain from challenging unjust laws, Howell insists, would be tantamount to accepting injustice. At its core, Indian Christians object to laws that place conditions on the freedom to profess and propagate faith, freedoms enshrined in the Constitution of India. He explains,

> For Christians to abandon the political realm means accepting in a mistaken way the current state of social and political affairs. If certain special policies and injustices are not opposed on religious grounds then

truly we condone them. It is the responsibility of Christians to participate in the political work of the nation, so that they may present their perspectives [on the state of affairs]. Christians in India are constantly having to oppose government schemes. As a small example, [consider] the adoption of religion-related bills in four States. So now what is the path ahead for us, increased participation in politics or a complete separation from politics?

> Christian faith opposes the privatization of faith, [attempts to] limit faith, and to restrict it to the internal realm. Religion cannot be private, religion should be of a person or of a community. Religion always becomes part of many social and interpersonal responsibilities.[90]

Howell's call to challenge conversion-related laws is an appeal to both political freedom and constitutional protections. It is not necessarily an argument claiming that attempts to convert are an indispensable part of Indian Christian identity. In real terms, not all Christians actively seek to convert people of other faiths. Howell is arguing against attempts to understand and present religion as private, internal, and individualistic. Religion can, certainly, be personal, as in being a person's beliefs and practices. Even when of a person, however, religious speech and acts are not limited to that person but as religious speech and acts are always also becoming part of those social and inter-personal relationships in which any person finds herself and for which, theologically speaking for Howell, God has created us. Socio-political witness is not a defining feature of Christian identity in Howell's writings. Nevertheless, Howell describes public witness as a defining element of Christian witness in the context of the rights and responsibilities of a minority religious community that enjoys constitutional rights and privileges. Three arguments are worth noting here.

Christians must avoid two fallacies in their political work. First, they should not use public policies and laws to bring the Kingdom of God on earth. This task is best left to God. A Christian is called to live-out the principles of the Kingdom of God preached by Christ. Second, Christians should not consider it futile to improve social and political policies. They should avoid the temptation to avoid political work in favor of evangelism.

> The reign of God should not be limited to ensuring relationships among humanity, bringing peace, expanding democracy, or to realizing social and occupational freedom. Holy Scripture does not speak of any one particular type of government. All types of politics can be misused. If responsible democracy can protect the decisions of politics, then it can also destroy anarchy. Christians should avoid two fallacies: first, that by changing any plan or system the world can be changed into a new society or the Kingdom of God, and second, that it is not important to improve social-political systems or plans because we are called to preach the good news.[91]

Christians serve the Kingdom of God by serving their neighbor and nation:

> Christian folk, being citizens, serve the Kingdom of God by caring for their neighbor and nation. A mission that brings about conversion truly engages the perspective of Holy Scripture to eradicate social ills and to bring the values of the Kingdom of God to society.[92]

Congregations exist in the world to reveal the reign of God to the world. As Howell puts it, if humans are called to live in mutually-responsible relationships with each other, then they are responsible for the rights and privileges of others. Christians seek to create, or become facilitators of attempts to create communities that meet the type of relationships God desires. He explains,

> When the topic of discussion turns to human responsibility people often become anxious. Holy Scripture says a lot about the struggle for other peoples' rights, but [it] says very little about the struggle for one's rights. On the other hand, when it speaks about us it tells us not about our rights but [about our] responsibilities. We have been told to love God and our neighbor. Holy Scripture emphasizes that it is our responsibility to protect the rights of the other; and to do this we should even be ready to give up our rights.
>
> We [Christians] should accept the fact that the rights of others are our responsibility. The local congregation exists to reveal the Kingdom of God. The congregation should live in the world as a community where human respect and equality are always present, and where people accept their responsibility towards one another, where there is no discrimination [and] favoritism, where [we] struggle on behalf of the poor and weak, and [where] where a human has the right to live as a human, just as God has made them and desires that they should live.[93]

When a Christian community fulfills its roles and responsibilities, it fulfills its calling to be a public sign and symbol to the Kingdom of God. In doing so, it presents to the world a "distinct conduct and character" ("*bhinn caritr va svabhāv*"). It presents to those around it a "distinct culture" ("*bhinn saṃskṛti*") from that in which it finds itself. As a congregation it is responsible for robust involvement in the social and political life of the nation and, when doing so, responsible to "be a sign" and "become a means" and "point toward" the Kingdom of God. Howell explains,

> The distinct conduct and character of the Christian community is reflected in the way those chosen and called by God relate with other people [i.e., those who are not Christians]. The congregation is the people of God; it is the body and bride of Christ and the temple of the Holy Spirit. An awakened congregation is fully a family that is a family of faith. And as we have discussed above, a community of Christ

> should present a distinct culture. The congregation has a responsibility as the people called by God – to be a sign, and to become a means for the Kingdom of God. This means that this community hints towards the coming Kingdom of God. Being a community filled by the Holy Spirit, a congregation should present the Kingdom of God even in its quotidian [literally, "common" or "general"] life. Being a community of Christ, the congregation should manifest that coming kingdom in real terms in the world, because that kingdom empowers the fulfillment of life and justice for society and restoration [literally, "freedom from disease or health"] for the entire creation.[94]

A recognizably Christian public witness is then, in *Parivartan*, an integral part of the Christian story Howell wants to tell in India. Further, as seen in Howell's theology of mutual roles, the preaching of the good news – to which each Christian in India is called and has the constitutional right – must be done in ways that reflect a culture of respect and collegiality toward people of other faiths.

Life in a pluralist society

Khan, Dayal, and Howell call for a robust public witness by Indian Christians. This call is inherent in the ethos of the Hindi Christian view of life. It is noteworthy how these authors – each writing independently, across a span of three decades – use remarkably similar words to describe the role of a Christian in the life of India. For Khan, Dayal, and Howell, a Christian is responsible ("*jimmedār*") for social policy. It is a Christian's duty ("*kartavy*") to seek justice, law, and safety for all. It is necessary ("*āvaśyak*") that a Christian *qua* Christian participate fully in governing the nation and shape the nation's values and ideals. Finally, a Christian must play her part ("*bhūmikā*") as a public communicator of discipleship. Part of this witness is the commitment to impact Christian public relations. Another part is the ability to recognize the impact of Christian words and deeds on public perception and relations. How are Christian actions seen? How are Christians identified in the nation? What is their contribution to public life? How do Christians facilitate relations? These concerns have shaped Hindi Christian works. The recognizable and public witness that Khan, Dayal, and Howell seek has three attributes: political engagement, interfaith relations, and Christian contributions. Khan, Dayal, and Howell propose a particular type of public role for Christians. Christian discipleship, as modeled on Christ's life, must be politically engaged. It must affect the politics and governance of their communities. Being a prophet or naysayer is not enough. The effect on politics must be concrete. Politics in itself is neither good nor evil. A Christian can help good policies prevail.

Public engagement in pluralist India involves a commitment to interfaith relations. As I have discussed previously, Khan's *Saṃvād* marks a culmination of a life-long interest in interfaith relations. Interfaith learning and dialogue seek to improve interfaith relations. Our vocabulary and practices, Howell argues in the context of evangelistic communications, must promote respect for the beliefs and practices of others. Indian Christians have the democratic and constitutional right to propagate their faith; yet the exercise of such a right need not be in ways that, as discussed in the previous chapter, "hurt the feelings of people of other faiths" and in doing so "create trouble for Christians." Howell argues that the practices of foreign missionaries in India also exacerbate the problem of inappropriate or unnecessarily derogatory language. He writes, "We would like to ask the congregations based outside India to be aware that due to the use of inappropriate mission language they not only hurt the feelings of people of other faiths but also create troubles for Christians [literally, 'become an obstacle for Christians']."[95]

Dayal offers a theology of divine self-revelation that makes it difficult for Christians to ignore or denigrate the beliefs and practices of people of other faith and to not learn from them. His theology, as we have seen previously, makes India's pluralism nearly a 'natural outcome' of the way in which God self-reveals to all peoples because, for Dayal, it is God's self-revelation that creates the conditions for knowledge of God among people of different faiths. Dayal, further, is not alone in recognizing the importance of India's pluralist context for Indian Christians. For all three authors, as discussed previously, the context of pluralism within which Christians in India find themselves, necessitates a commitment to interfaith learning and relations. Finally, public participation through political engagements and interfaith relations seeks the propagation and influence of Christian values in polity, politics, and culture. In Khan's political theology, political engagement comes with a larger purpose. Christians are called, he asserts, to 'put the stamp' of Christian values on policies and politics. What are these values? Khan, Dayal, and Howell generally identify them as social welfare, justice, freedom, and safety. These values are, conspicuously, not exclusive to Christian ethical discourses and their presentation in terms that are non-religion-specific makes them accessible and relatable to adherents of other faiths.

Khan identifies the protection of democratic principles as an important goal of Christian public witness. It is the responsibility ("*uttardāyitv*") of Christians, he writes, to "bring political power to the straight path" ("*rājyasattā ko sīdhe mārg par lānā*").[96] He explains, "it is Christianly ethical to oppose a government that neglects the commandments of God, and it is the responsibility of Christians to bring to the straight path politics that is slipping into dictatorship[97] [literally, "politics that is rolling toward a monopoly"]."[98] Similarly, even as Dayal warns his readers (a la Howell) not to equate the Kingdom of God with worldly governance or vice versa, he exhorts Christians to be like "salt to culture" whose duty ("*kartavy*") is to ensure the necessary ("*anivāry*") impact of Christian values on national polity and policies.[99] Finally, Howell's ecclesiology presents churches as the facilitators of God in their particular contexts. Echoing Khan, who adapts Bonhoeffer's ideas on the public role of Christians, Howell calls on Indian churches to imprint the values of the Kingdom of God – justice, peace, fellowship, and freedom – on public policy and governance.[100] Read in light of each other, then, the works of Khan, Dayal, and Howell reveal a consistent and discernible attention to a particular form of Christian public witness in India that is cognizant of the reality of pluralism and of life as a religious minority seeking a healthy public presence in the affairs of the nation.

Notes

1 McGregor, *The Oxford Hindi-English Dictionary*, 606, lists the following as translations of *paricay*: acquaintance (with); knowledge, experience (of); information, data; to introduce (one to); to acquaint (with); to make known (to); or, to demonstrate.

2 Biographical details are from Khan's *Khristīy Nītiśāstr* (1981: viii) and *Bīsavīṃ Śatābdī ke Pramukh Dharmavijñānī* (1990; v–vi).

3 Khan's doctoral dissertation was published in English as *The Concept of Dharma in Valmiki Ramayana* by Munshi Ram Manohar Lal press (Delhi) in 1965.

4 Both *Khristīy Nītiśāstr* (viii) and *Islām: Ek Paricay* ("Islam: An Introduction"; vi) were first and original books in Hindi Christian literature on their subjects. Both books have been quite popular: due to continued demand, *Khristīy Nītiśāstr* was republished in 2009. *Islām* went through a new edition in 1987 and was republished in 2004.

5 Bhajan and Khan, *Islām*, viii.

6 Khan, *Khristīy Nītiśāstr*, v: "*Mere śodh prabandh 'vālmīki rāmāyaṇ meṁ dharm kā svarūp' ke prakāśan uparānt merī yah hārdik abhilāṣā rahī ki maiṁ hindī meṁ khristīy nītiśāstr par bhī pustak likhūṁ aur us samay se hī maiṁ is viṣay kā viśeṣ adhyayan kartā rahā hūṁ.*"

7 Scharf, *Rāmopākhyāna*, 8–15.

8 Scharf, *Rāmopākhyāna*, 429–437.

9 Flood, *Hinduism*, 66.

10 Flood, *Hinduism*, 109.

11 Khan, *Khristīy Nītiśāstr*, vi: "H.T.L.C [*kā*] *āgrah rahā ki sirāmpur kāṁlej kī bī. ṭīec. evam bī. ḍi. parīkṣāoṁ ke chātroṁ ke hitārth tathā unke pāṭhykṛm ke ādhār par khristīy nītiśāstr pustak likhī jāe.*"

12 Bhajan and Khan, *Islām*, vi: "[*Yah*] *pustak sīrāmpur sineṭ ke bī. ṭīec., evam bī. ḍī. ke chātroṁ kī āvaśyakatāoṁ kī pūrti hetu bhī likhī gaī hai.*"

13 Bhajan and Khan, *Islām*, vi: "*Hamārā viśvās hai ki samast hindī bhāṣī pāṭhakoṁ tathā saty ke anveṣakoṁ ke liye hamārā vinamr prayās mūlyavān aur mīlstambh hogā.*"

14 David, in Bhajan and Khan, *Islām*, viii: "*Yah saty ke anveṣakoṁ ko preraṇā pradān karegī, aur paraspar saṃvād evam deś kī ekatā ko baḍhāne meṁ sahāyak hogī.*"

15 Khan, *The Concept of Dharma*, 40.

16 Khan, *The Concept of Dharma*, 135.

17 Khan, *Khristīy Nītiśāstr*, v–vi: "*[K]hristīy dharm evam nītiśāstr, khristīy dharmavijñān evam nītiśāstr aur khristīy viśvās evam nītiśāstr meṁ ek aṭūṭ sambandh hai. . . .*

[Masīhīyatā meṁ] pāpī manuṣy kā parameśvar se mel-milāp pramukh siddhānt hai aur yah khrist ke balidān ko svīkār karne meṁ sambhav hai. Manuṣy kī saccī dhārmiktā uske apne prayās, apnī dhāritā, apne dharmakāry par nirbhar nahīṁ varan

is anubhav par ādhārit hai ki parameśvar se uskā mel-milāp (Reconciliation) huā hai athvā nahīṁ. Manuṣy apnī śakti aur prayās dvārā dhārmik nahīṁ ban saktā. Yah to usmeṁ aham paidā kartā hai. Īśvar ke samakṣ pāpī samarpaṇ kar, īśvar se śakti prāpt kar naitik-kāry kar saktā hai. Isī anubhav se manuṣy ke jīvan, uske kāry aur uske sambandhoṁ meṁ ek nayā moḍ ātā hai aur vah naitik jīvan vyatīt karne lagtā hai. Isīlie khristīy dharm aur khristīy nītiśāstr ek dūsre se pṛthak nahīṁ varan anany hai aur yah bhī saty hai ki khristīy dharm meṁ hum naitik jīvan vyatīt kar īśvar se milāp nahīṁ karte varan īśvar se milāp kar naitik jīvan vyatīt karne kī śakti prāpt karte hai. Isī pūrvdhāraṇā ko samakṣ rakhkar maiṁ khristīy nītiśāstr par ek pustak likhne kā ek choṭā-sā prayās kar rahā hūṁ."

18 Khan, *The Concept of Dharma*, v: "*Vah vṛtti yā ācaraṇ jo lok yā samāj kī sthiti ke lie āvaśyak hai; vah ācār jiske dvārā samāj kī rakṣā tathā sukh-śānti kī vṛddhi ho aur parlok meṁ bhī uttam gati prāpt ho.*"

19 The feminine possessive is my addition; the original possessive (*uskā*) is gender non-specific.

20 Khan, *Khristīy Nītiśāstr*, 18: "*Dharm īśvar ko sat cit ānand kahtā hai. Kucch vidvān satyam-śivam-sundaram kahte haiṁ. Yadi yah paribhāṣā saty hai to nītiśāstr aur dharm meṁ aṭūṭ sambandh pramāṇit hotā hai, kyoṁki jis śubh (śivam, Good) kā naitik śāstr adhyayan kartā hai, vah dharm ke īśvar kā guṇ hai. Fir hum yah bhī jānte haiṁ ki hum naitik praśnoṁ kā us vakt tak koī sahī uttar nahīṁ de sakte jab tak hum is bāt ko niścit na kar leṁ ki manuṣy kī prakṛti kyā hai, brahmāṇḍ meṁ uskā kyā sthān hai, aur brahmāṇḍ kā kyā svarūp hai. Ataḥ hum is niṣkarṣ par pahuṁcte hai ki tārkik evam vyāvahārik rūp se dharm aur nītiśāstr meṁ ghaniṣṭh sambandh hai.*"

21 Khan, *Khristīy Nītiśāstr*, 30: "*Nītiśāstr manuṣy ke vyavahār meṁ śubh aur aśubh ke adhyayan kā sāmāny vijñān hai. Iske adhyayan se hameṁ mānavīy mūlyoṁ kā gyān hotā hai aur hum yah bhī jānte haiṁ ki vyāpār meṁ, cikitsā meṁ, āpsī sambandhoṁ meṁ kaun sā vyavahār ucit hai aur kaunsā anucit hai; kyā śubh aur kyā aśubh hai.*"

22 Bhajan and Khan, *Islām*, v: "*Āj kal masīhiyoṁ meṁ bhī ek nayā āndolan cal rahā hai jis kā lakṣy sansār ke vibhinn dharmoṁ ke mānne vāloṁ ke madhy prem kā sambandh sthāpit karnā hai. Āvaśyakatā is bāt kī hai ki vibhinn dharmoṁ ke mānne vāle āpas meṁ prempūrvak baiṭh kar ek dūsre kī bāt suneṁ aur mil jul kar paramsaty kī khoj kareṁ. Aisā saty jo hṛday meṁ us śānti ko bhar de jis se ek nav-mānav kā uday ho aur jo prem aur āśā se paripūrṇ ho. Is naye āndolan kā nām saṃvād (Dialogue) hai. Is kā matlab yah nahīṁ ki hum ek dūsre par kīcaḍ ucchāleṁ, varan yah hai ki hum premamay vātāvaraṇ meṁ baiṭh kar dhairy aur śānti se ek dūsre kī bāt sahānubhūti se suneṁ aur samjheṁ, ek dūsre se sīkheṁ aur jahāṁ tak ban paḍe jantā kī bhalāī ke liye ek dūsre kī sahāytā kareṁ. Is āndolan ko safal banāne ke liye yah āvaśyak hai ki hum dūsre dharmoṁ ke viśvāsoṁ aur rīti rivājoṁ se bhalī bhāṁti paricay prāpt kareṁ. Is lie aisī pustakeṁ, jo vibhinn dharmoṁ ke viśvāsoṁ, rasmorivājoṁ, naitikatā ādi ko ucit ḍhang se prastut kareṁ, avaśy hī samay kī ek baḍī āvaśyakatā ko pūrā kareṁgī.*"

23 Lossky, *Dictionary of the Ecumenical Movement*, 311–317.

24 Robinson, *Christians Meeting Hindus*, 4–5.

25 Robinson, *Christians Meeting Hindus*, 21.

26 Robinson, *Christians Meeting Hindus*, 32–34.

27 Robinson, *Christians Meeting Hindus*, 60–77.

28 Balagangadhara, *Reconceptualizing India Studies*.

29 Balagangadhara, *Reconceptualizing India Studies*, 159.

30 Balagangadhara, *Reconceptualizing India Studies*, 164.

31 Robinson, *Christians Meeting Hindus*, 77.

32 McGregor, *The Oxford Hindi-English Dictionary*, 913.

33 McGregor, *The Oxford Hindi-English Dictionary*, 967.

34 Bonhoeffer, *Letters and Papers*, 359–360.
35 Bonhoeffer, *Letters and Papers*, 359.
36 Bonhoeffer, *Letters and Papers*, 346.
37 Bonhoeffer, *Letters and Papers*, 326.
38 Bonhoeffer, *Letters and Papers*, 361.
39 Bonhoeffer, *Ethics*, 132 (emphasis added).
40 Bonhoeffer, *Ethics*, 130–132.
41 Metaxas, *Bonhoeffer*, 155.
42 Bonhoeffer, *Ethics*, 193ff.
43 In Bonhoeffer's words: "Ethical thinking in terms of spheres, then, is invalidated by faith in the revelation of the ultimate reality in Jesus Christ, and this means there is no real possibility of being a Christian outside the reality of the world and that there is no real worldly existence outside the reality of Jesus Christ. There is no place to which the Christian can withdraw from the world, whether it be outwardly or in the sphere of the inner life." (Bonhoeffer, *Ethics*, 198)
44 Khan, *Khristīy Nītiśāstr*, 161–162: "*Bāṁnahūfar apnī pustak 'ethiks' meṁ lūthar kī us ālocanā ko jo lūthar ne dvaitavād (Thinking in Terms of Two Spheres) ke viruddh kī thī, svīkār kartā huā manuṣy ke prākṛtik evam aprākṛtik staroṁ kī ghor ālocanā kartā hai. . . . Is dvaitavād ke anusār naitikatā ke bhī do star māne jāne lage . . . niyam, un logoṁ ke lie jo ki prākṛtik star par rahte haiṁ aur ādhyātmik pūrṇatā un logoṁ ke lie jo dharmī haiṁ, jinhoṁne masīhī jīvan vyatīt karne kā niścay kar liyā hai. . . .*

Bāṁnahūfar is dvaitavād ko avāstavik kahtā huā likhtā hai: "Ek masīhī, masīh ko svīkār karne ke paścāt kisī antardvand kā kṣetr nahīṁ ban jātā parantu jis prakār masīh ek hai vah bhī antardvand se mukti pā ek avibhājit ikāī ban jātā hai aur vah do staroṁ par nahīṁ rahtā, sadaiv ek star par rahtā hai." . . . Bāṁnahūfar likhtā hai ki is prākṛtik jīvan ko hum yah na mān baiṭheṁ ki yah masīh ko svīkār karne se pahle kā jīvan hai parantu yah jīvan to vah hai jo masīh yīśu dvārā mānyatā prāpt hai.

Sārāṁś meṁ hum kah sakte haiṁ ki bāṁnahūfar ne upāntim par jor dekar is duniyāvī jīvan ko nayā arth pradān kiyā aur naī mahattvatā dī. Isī prakār do staroṁ athavā dvaitavād ko ḍhah kar yah pramāṇit kiyā ki yah jagat masīh ko is duniyā kā prabhu mānne meṁ avarodh utpann nahīṃ kartā varan sahāyatā detā hai. Ek masīhī ko yah jānnā cāhie ki ek masīhī manuṣy hai aur vahī manuṣy, manuṣy hai jisne ki dehadhārī masīh ko svīkār kiyā hai."
45 McGregor, *The Oxford Hindi-English Dictionary*, 44.
46 Bonhoeffer, *Ethics*, 196.
47 McGregor, *The Oxford Hindi-English Dictionary*, 60; Bulcke, *Aṁgrezī-Hindī Koś;*, 835.
48 Bonhoeffer, *Ethics*, 198.
49 Khan, *Khristīy Nītiśāstr*, 162: "*Masīh mānav jīvan ke lie ek udāharaṇ hai. Usne kyā kiyā, kaise rahā, kyā uskā jīvan thā; vah manuṣyo me rahtā thā, unke sāth khātā-pītā thā, unkī bhāṁti sotā-uṭhtā thā aur unme ek naī mānavatā ko jograt kartā thā. Yahī ek masīhī kā naitik jīvan honā cāhie. Jagat se dūr nahīṁ varan jagat ke madhy aur yahī carc kā kāry bhī honā cāhie.*"
50 Khan, *Khristīy Nītiśāstr*, 162: "*Carc kā is jagat meṁ ek sthān hai. Carc is jagat kā ek ṭukḍā hai. Carc kā is jagat ke prati ek uttardāyitv hai, islie carc ek vah samāj hai jiskā uttardāyitv jagat ke prati hai. Use is sansār meṁ kūd jānā hai, jo īśvar ko nahīṁ māntā. Vah usse dūr rahkar koī kāry nahīṁ kar saktā.*"
51 Bonhoeffer, *Ethics*, 199–200.
52 Bonhoeffer, *Ethics*, 72.
53 Khan, *Bīsavīṃ Śatābdī ke Pramukh Dharmavijñānī*, 146: "*Ādarśoṁ, kāryakrmoṁ, antarātmā, kartavy, uttardāyitv aur sadguṇ dvārā hum sattā kā na to sāmnā kar sakte haiṁ aur na hī us par vijay pā sakte haiṁ. Yah kāry hum īśvar*

se prem ke dvārā, aise prem ke dvārā, jo ek sāmāny pratyay nahīṁ parantu sampūrṇ prem hai, kar sakte haiṁ."

54 Khan, *Bīsavīṃ Śatābdī ke Pramukh Dharmavijñānī*, 146: "*Is prem ko bāṁnahūfar masīh meṁ īśvar se prem kī sagyā detā hai, aur use vah 'īśvar se prem meṁ jīnā' kahtā hai.*"

55 Khan, *Bīsavīṃ Śatābdī ke Pramukh Dharmavijñānī*, 146: "*[Yah prem] manuṣy ko sansār se bhāgne kī preraṇā nahīṁ detā parantu is bāt kī kṣamatā pradān kartā hai ki vah sansā kī sab vipattiyoṃ ko jhele, jaise yīśu-masīh kī deh ne pāp ke krodh ko sahan kiyā. Carc ke liye bhī yah jarūrī hai ki vah sansār ke liye apne āpko jokhim meṁ ḍāle. Ek masīhī, masīh meṁ hotā huā bhī sansār meṁ sthit hai.*"

56 Khan, *Bīsavīṃ Śatābdī ke Pramukh Dharmavijñānī*, 147: "*Bāṁnahūfar . . . hameṁ batātā hai ki hameṁ is sansār ko baḍī sanjīdagī se lenā cāhiye. Ise pyār karnā cāhiye, isī meṁ rahnā cāhiye aur yadi jarūrī ho to iske liye mar miṭnā bhī cāhiye. Hamārā susamācār kisī palāyanvādī dharm kī sthāpanā nahīṁ kartā.*"

57 Khan, *Bīsavīṃ Śatābdī ke Pramukh Dharmavijñānī*, 162: "*[Dharmanirpekṣavādī] dharmavijñān ne carc ko niścit rūp se ek nayā pāṭh paḍhāyā. Vah yah hai ki carc manuṣyoṁ kī sānsārik kaṭhināiyoṁ aur samasyāoṁ meṁ pūrā sakriy yogdān de. Jis prakār purānā niyan kā īśvar isrāel kaum ke ādhyātmik, sāmājik aur bhautik pahaluoṁ ko barābar chūtā hai usī prakār āj aise īśvar kī, jo is sansār meṁ samast mānav-jāti kī ādhyātmik aur bhautik sahāyatā kare, āvaśyakatā hai.*"

58 A 'crore' equals ten million.

59 A 'lakh' equals hundred thousand.

60 Bulcke, *Aṁgrezī-Hindī Koś*, 744.

61 Bhajan and Khan, *Islām*, vii: "***Islām** sansār ke pramukh dharmoṁ meṁ se ek hai. Vartamān bhārat meṁ islām ke anuyāyiyoṁ kī sankhyā bahusankhyak hindū dharmāvalambiyoṁ ke bād hī hai. Inmeṁ se adhikānś hindī bhāṣī kṣetr meṁ rahte haiṁ. 1971 kī janganaṇā ke anusār bhārat meṁ 45.3 karoḍ hindū, 6.1 karoḍ muslim, 1.4 karoḍ khristī, 1 karoḍ sikkh, 38 lākh bauddh aur 20 lākh jain dharmoṁ ke pālan karne vāle haiṁ. Ye ank yahāṁ rāṣṭr kī pṛthakatā ke liye nahīṁ, varan is tathy ke mahatv ko samajhane ke liye die gae haiṁ ki hamāre deś meṁ dharm-viśvāsoṁ evam dharmanītiyoṁ meṁ antar hai aur ki hum ek dūsre ke dharm kā adhyayan kareṁ aur yah jānte hue bhī ki sab dharm samān nahīṁ haiṁ hum ek dūsre kī bhāvanāoṁ kā ādar kareṁ.*

***Islām ek paricay** pustak ke taiyār karne meṁ tīn uddeśy haiṁ jin meṁ se do kā ullekh lekhakoṁ ne apne prākkathan meṁ bhī kiyā hai: pahlā paraspar saṃvād (Dialogue) meṁ sahāyatā prāpt ho; dūsrā sīrāmpur sīneṭ ke bī. ṭiec. aur bī. ḍī. parīkṣāoṁ ke kṣātroṁ kī āvaśyakatāoṁ kī pūrti ho; tīsrā hamāre deś aur viśeṣakar hindī-bhāṣī yah samjheṁ ki dharmoṁ me samāntā na hote hue bhī dharm ke nām par deś meṁ aur viśeṣ kar hindī bhāṣī kṣetr meṁ rāṣṭrīy aur naitik jīvan samṛddh ho. Is ke sāth hī kisī bhī dharm kā samyak gyān apne hī meṁ ek apūrv lābh hotā hai.*"

62 Khan, *Khristīy Nītiśāstr*, 71: "*Masīh ke prem niyam kā dūsrā pakṣ Paṛosī se prem karnā hai. Paṛosī koī amūrt pratyay nahīṁ, varan ek vāstavik sattā hai. Masīh ne yah ādeś nahīṁ diyā ki tū mānavatā athavā manuṣyatā se prem kar. Islie prem kā viṣay Paṛosī hai. Merā Paṛosī kaun hai? Is praśn kā uttar dete huy masīh ne ek sundar dṛṣṭānt prastut kar Paṛosī se prem ke samast tatvoṁ ko pradarśit kiyā hai. Hum aupcārik riśtoṁ kī duniyā meṁ rah rahe haiṁ. Arthārt hum yah jānte haiṁ athavā jānne kī kośiś karte haiṁ ki amuk vyakti kyā hai? Athavā kyā kartā hai? . . . Uske kitne bacce haiṁ? Vah apnā jīvan kis prakār nirvāh kar rahā hai? Vah kitnā sukhī athavā dukhī ādmī hai? Kyā koī uske ghar meṁ bīmār hai? Ityādi. Hamārā paricay ek ūprī paricay rahtā hai, arthāt vah kyā kām kartā hai? Aur is dṛṣṭi se hī hamārā aur uskā sambandh juḍtā hai. Yah*

durbhāgy kī bāt hai ki hum keval uske ek āyām (dimension) ko hī jānne kā prayās karte haiṁ."

63 Khan, *Khristīy Nītiśāstr*, 73–74: "*Kucch logoṁ ko apne gyān, pūṁjī, śārīrik sundartā, varg ādi kā ghamanḍ hotā hai aur yah ghamanḍ mānavīy riśtoṁ meṁ dīvār khaḍī kar detā hai. Ye hameṁ apne Paṛosī kī āvaśyakatāoṁ ko dekhne nahīṁ dete. Bhārat meṁ varṇ-ghamanḍ aur kucch paścimī deśoṁ meṁ rang-garv iske udāharaṇ haiṁ. Khrist ek aur ghamanḍ kī or dhyān ākarṣit karte haiṁ jo us kāl kī naitik evam dhārmik avasthā ko dīmak kī bhāṁti khāe jā rahā thā. Vah thā dhārmik ghamanḍ athavā ādhyātmik hone kā garv . . . [is dhārmik garv] ko bhārī dhakkā lagā, jab unhone yah dekhā ki yīśu to ām logoṁ meṁ uṭhtā-baiṭhtā hai; unke sāth khātā-pītā hai aur unko chūtā bhī hai. . . . Khrist ne 'Paṛosī ke prem' ke ādeś meṁ is sārī vidhivādī naitikatā kā khanḍan kiyā, aur us dīvār ko, jo vidhivādī naitikatā dharmī aur adharmī ke bīc khaḍī kartī hai, garīboṁ aur pāpiyoṁ ke sāth baiṭhkar toḍ diyā.*"

64 Khan, *Khristīy Nītiśāstr*, 214–215: "*Hum masīhī jo bhārat meṁ rahte haiṁ, is bāt ko avaśy dhyān meṁ rakheṁ ki bhāratvarṣ yadyapi dharmanirpekṣ deś hai, tathāpi dharmanirpekṣatā kā arth adharm nahīṁ hai. Pratyek vyakti ko apne-apne dharm ke pālan aur prasār karne kī svatantratā hai aur dūsre ke dharm ke prati ādar kā ādeś hai.*"

65 McGregor, *The Oxford Hindi-English Dictionary*, 25.

66 Khan, *Khristīy Nītiśāstr*, 215: "*Hamāre deś kā pratīk hai 'satyamev jayate' arthāt saty kī hī vijay hai, aur saty kā abhiprāy bhāratīy darśan meṁ īśvar hai . . . Masīhī ke lie masīh saty hai.*"

67 Khan presents a non-exclusive decision involving membership in two distinct realms that, Khan argues, should not be mutually exclusive: *parameśvar kā rājy* and *pṛthvī kā rājy* (literally, "Kingdom of God" and "kingdom of earth").

68 Khan, *Khristīy Nītiśāstr*, 216–217: "*Pahlā, ek masīhī ko yah kahkar ki vah parameśvar ke rājy kā sadasy hai rājanīti se bhāgnā nahīṁ cāhie kyoṁki vah pṛthvī ke rājy kā bhī sadasy hai.*

Dūsrā, masīhī ko nakārātmak rūp se nāgrik hokar deś meṁ nahīṁ rahnā cāhie. Vah keval yahī na kahtā rahe ki deś meṁ bhraṣṭācār hai, nyāy durlabh hai. Vah iskā doṣ dūsroṁ par na lagāe, vah svayam bhī doṣī hai kyoṁki vah masīhī prabhāv ko prabhāvakārī karne meṁ asafal rahā hai.

Tīsrā, use is vicār ko choḍ denā cāhie ki rājanīti meṁ kisī prakār kī svacchatā hotī hai, aur ki rājanīti śaitān kī āṁt hai. Rājanīti svacchatā aur śaitānī kā miśraṇ hai aur masīhī kā yah kartavy hai ki vah rājanīti meṁ sakriy bhāg lekar śubh śakti ko prabal kare.

Cauthā, masīhī kisī pārṭī kā mohrā hī na ban kar rahe parantu ek aisā vyakti bane jo apne adhikār aur mat ko masīh kī śikṣāoṁ ke anusār vyakt kartā hai.

Pāṁcvā, use sadā yah nahīṁ socnā cāhie ki uskā dṛṣṭikoṇ sarvaśreṣṭh hai. Use apnā prabhāv vinamr rūp se ḍālnā cāhie.

Chaṭhvāṁ, masīhī ko yah nahīṁ socnā cāhie ki ek hī samasyā ke hul ho jāne se deś kī pratyek samasyā hul ho jāegī. Udāharaṇ ke lie nasbandī, jūāvarjan ityādi. Use jankalyāṇ, nyāy, svatantratā aur surakṣā kī bhāvanā ko sadṛṛh banāne ke lie sadā prayatnśīl rahnā cāhie."

69 Khan, *Khristīy Nītiśāstr*, 234: "*Rājanīti meṁ bhāg lenā khristīy jīvan kā uttar-dāyitv hai.*"

70 Khan, *Saṃvād*, 1: "*Vartamān sāmpradāyik, asahiṣṇutā, kaṭṭartāvād evam rūḍhivād vibhhin dharmoṁ ke anuyāyiyoṁ meṁ aise bhedabhāv kī bhāvanā ko utpann kar rahā hai jisse ki hamārā āpsī rahan-sahan dūṣit ho gayā hai aur hum ek dūsre ko ghṛṇā aur sanśay kī dṛṣṭi se dekh rahe haiṁ. Isī sthiti meṁ āpsī rahan-sahan hamāre naitik, sāmājik evam ārthik mūlyoṁ par anucit prabhāv ḍāl rahā hai. Kucch log dharm kā durupayog kar apne rājanaitik svārth kī*

pūrti meṁ lage haiṁ. Sāmpradāyik dange, nity-prati jor pakaḍ rahe haiṁ aur alpasankhyak samudāy bhay ke vātāvaraṇ meṁ jī rahe haiṁ. Ek dūsre ke dharm ke prati nity naī galatfahmiyoṁ kā pracār kiyā jā rahā hai. Naitik mūly, viśeṣ kar nyāy durlabh haiṁ. Kucch dharm kurītiyāṁ bhī punaḥ apnā sir uṭhā rahī haiṁ. In hālāt meṁ 'antardhārmik saṃvād' ek āvaśyakatā bantā jā rahā hai. Is antardhārmik saṃvād dvārā hum mil julkar naitik patan aur girte hue dhārmik mūlyoṁ ko sambhālne ke lie sāmūhik prayās kar sakte haiṁ. Antardhārmik saṃvād keval pūrvāgrhoṁ kā hī unmūlan nahīṁ parantu vah vibhinn dharmoṁ ke anuyāyiyoṁ meṁ mil-jul kar rahne kī samajh ko baḍhāvā detā hai. Jaisā hum pīche likh āye haiṁ antardhārmik saṃvād ek aisī prakriyā hai jiske dvārā hum dūsre dharm kī rītiyoṁ, mūlyoṁ evam dhārmik anubhavoṁ ko samajhne kā prayās karte haiṁ. Yadi iske pīcche ek saccī bhāvanā hai to samast dūriyoṁ kā vilop ho jātā hai aur hum ek dūsre ke itne nikaṭ ā jāte haiṁ ki hummeṁ dabī huī bhrātṛ bhāvanā punaḥ jāg jātī hai aur hum ek dūsre ke hāth meṁ hāth ḍāl dharm ke us śikhar kī or baḍhne lagte haiṁ jahāṁ par manuṣy aur parameśvar kā milan evam manuṣy aur manuṣy kā milan vāstavikatā meṁ badal jātā hai."

71 i.e., minority religious communities.

72 Khan, *Saṃvād*, 1–2: "*Antardhārmik saṃvād ke kucch śatru bhī haiṁ aur in śatruoṁ meṁ pramukh śatru sāmpradāyikatāvād hai. Sāmpradāyikatāvād kā arth hai rājanaitik lābh ke lie dharm kā durupayog. Antardhārmik saṃvād kā dūsrā śatru 'kaṭṭartāvād' hai arthārt 'mere pās hī saty kā ṭhekā hai, merā hī dharm saccā hai aur any dharm śaitān den hai.' Yah unmād ādhyātmik ahankār kī nīṁv par khaḍā hai. Yah ghṛṇā ke bīj botā hai aur vibhinn dharmoṁ ke anuyāyiyoṁ ke mil julkar rahne meṁ bādhā utpann kartā hai. Antardhārmik saṃvād kā tīsrā śatru hamārā agyān hai arthāt ek dūsre ke dharm ke prati hamārā sankucit gyān aur galatfahmiyoṁ athavā tathākathit burāiyoṁ kī apār jānkārī. Jaise hī antardhārmik saṃvād śurū hotā hai kucch agyānī dusroṁ ke dharm kī burāiyoṁ kā vyākhyān kar ek aisā prahār śurū kar dete haiṁ jo saṃvād ko vād-vivād meṁ aur vād-vivād ko māradhāḍ meṁ badal detā hai. Ek dūsre ko samajhane ke sthān par ek dūsre se ghṛṇā karne lagte haiṁ. Islie jab tak apne dharm aur dūsre ke dharm kā sahī-sahī gyān na ho, saṃvād apne uddeśy meṁ vifal ho jātā hai. Antardhārmik saṃvād kā cauthā mukhy śatru rūḍhivād (Fundamentalism) hai. Hindī, hindū, hindustān! Islām khatre meṁ hai! Lekhakoṁ, cintakoṁ, dārśnikoṁ ko dharm, śarīyat ke nām par deś-nikālā denā, maut kā fatvā jārī karnā, yah dhārmik kaṭṭarvād, rūḍhivād kā udāharaṇ hai. Inke nāre din pratidin vāyumaṇḍal ko garmā rahe haiṁ. Udhar masīhī dharm, sikkhdharm, buddh dharm, jain dharm ityādi bhī rūḍhivād ke śikār hote jā rahe haiṁ. Bhāratvarṣ meṁ 'garv se kaho hum hindū hai' kā nārā buland ho rahā hai.*"

73 Khan, *Saṃvād*, 2: "*Is yug meṁ antardhārmik saṃvād kī atyant āvaśyakatā hai. Śāyad in saṃvādoṁ ke dvārā hī hum vah ekatā jo hum kho cuke haiṁ vāpas pā leṁ. Dhārmik kurītiyāṁ jo apnā sir uṭhā rahī haiṁ unkā unmūlan kar sakeṁ. Mil-julkar girte hue naitik, sāmājik mūlyoṁ kā bacāv kar sakeṁ. Sāmājik jīvan bhay se mukt kar sakeṁ aur ek dharm viśvāsī, dūsre dharm viśvāsī kī nissvārth kalyāṇ kī kāmnā kar sakeṁ.*

Bhārat varṣ bahu samudāy, bahu jāti evam bahudharmoṁ kā ek jītā jāgtā udāharaṇ hai kintu yah bahuvād anekatā meṁ ekatā aur ekatā meṁ anekatā kā darśan ubharte hue sāmpradāyikatāvād meṁ ek thothā sā niyam pratīt hone lagā hai. Anekatā, ekatā kī or to nahīṁ le jā rahī varan vah hameṁ vibhājan kī or le jā rahī hai. Prati din hum ek dūsre ke lie ajnabī bante jā rahe haiṁ. Rājanīti ne dharm ko dūṣit kar use apne lakṣy se bhaṭkā diyā hai. Deś meṁ ghaṭṭī huī in vartamān paristhitiyoṁ ko dekhkar antardhārmik saṃvād kī āvaśyakatā hai jahāṁ hum baḍe khule dimāg se aur ek dūsre ke dharm ke prati sakārātmak ravaiyā apnāte hue aur kaṭutā aur viṣamatā ko man se dūr karte hue, un samast galatfahmiyoṁ ko dūr kareṁ aur yah svīkār kareṁ ki rājanaitik evam ārthik lābhoṁ ke lie dharm kā upayog ati nindanīya hai. Dharm manuṣy ko apne kartavyoṁ kā pālan sikhātā hai, viśeṣakar ve kartavy jo manuṣy ko īśvar se joḍte haiṁ aur uskī ātmā meṁ śānti aur ānand ko bhar dete haiṁ aur manuṣy is sansār meṁ 'īśvar rājy' athavā 'īśvar nagarī' kā svapn sākār karne meṁ agrasar ho jātā hai."

74 Which he described in *Life Together* (orig. German 1938). For an introduction to the experiment, see Bonhoeffer, *Life Together*, 10–11 and Metaxas, *Bonhoeffer*, 262–277.

75 Biography from Dayal, *Uttar Bhārat*, iv–v and Dayal, *Masīhī Dharm Vijñān*, iv–v.

76 1951 election results at www.elections.in/parliamentary-constituencies/1951-election-results.html (accessed 24 July 2015).

77 Anand's "brief introduction of the author," in Dayal, *Uttar Bhārat*, iv.

78 Dayal, *Masīhī Dharm Vijñān*, 29–30: "*Prabhu yeśu kā śubh samācār kisī viśeṣ sabhyatā ko sthāpit karne ke lie nahīṁ hai balki śubh samācār manuṣy ke uddhār ke lie hai. Sabhyatā aur sanskṛti kā nirmāṇ manuṣy ke hāth meṁ hai. Nissandeh masīhīyat namak ke samān hai. Islie masīhī jan ke viśvās kā prabhāv sanskṛti par paḍhnā anivāry hai. Masīhīyoṁ kā kartavy hai ki ve apne samāj aur rāṣṭr ke sandarbh meṁ sanskṛti ke nirmāṇ meṁ yogdān deṃ. Masīhīyoṁ ke pās sanskṛti ke lie koī masīhī yojanā nahīṁ hai.*"

79 Dayal, *Masīhī Dharm Vijñān*, 187: "*Praśn hai ki kyā parameśvar ke rājy kā hamāre dharm nirpekṣ evam ārthik aur vaigyānik unnati ke kāl meṁ mahatv rah gayā hai? Uttar hai, hāṁ. Śānti kī lālsā hameśā se rahī hai. . . . Sansār meṁ laḍāiyoṁ aur bhayaṅkar hathiyāroṁ kā ant nahīṁ huā hai. Kyā anyāy, garībī, śoṣaṇ, bhayaṅkar bīmāriyāṁ khatm ho gaī haiṁ? . . . Khrist ke śubhsandeś ko hameṁ vartamān sansār ko sunānā hai.*"

80 Dayal, *Masīhī Dharm Vijñān*, 28–29: "*Anekavād (Pluralism) sanskṛti kī mahatvapūrṇ viśiṣṭatā hai. Islie sanskṛti ke sāmne bahut sī mānyatāoṁ ko svīkār karne kī cunautī rahtī hai. Koī bhī samāj sāre guṇoṁ ko cāhne ke bāvajūd unheṁ prāpt nahīṁ kar saktā. Samāj kī mānyatāeṁ anek haiṁ, kyoṅki manuṣy anek haiṁ aur unke uddeśy aur āvaśyakatāeṁ anek haiṁ. . . . Anekavādī samāj meṁ parameśvar kā rājy, prabhu yeśu masīh, pitā parameśvar aur śubhasamācār ye bāteṁ masīhī viśvāsiyoṁ ke lie bahut hī mahatvapūrṇ mānyatāeṁ haiṁ. Kintu ye keval masīhīyoṁ ke lie mahatvapūrṇ haiṁ.*"

81 Dayal, *Masīhī Dharm Vijñān*, 22: "*Ek vyakti dūsre vyakti ko pūrṇ rūp se jān [nahīṁ] saktā hai jab tak dūsrā vyakti svayam apne bāre meṁ na batāe. . . . Parameśvar svayam apne ko prakaṭ kartā hai. Vah apnī sāmarthy aur svabhāv ko prakaṭ kartā hai. Parameśvar hī sāre jagat aur sāre dharmoṁ ke logoṁ par svayam prakaṭ huā hai. Isīlie sabhī dharmoṁ ke anuyāyī kahte haiṁ ki parameśvar hai. Yah bāt alag hai ki parameśvar ke viṣay meṁ viśvāsoṁ meṁ bhinnatā hai. Adhiktar hindū anek devī-devatāoṁ ko mānte haiṁ. Kintu inke samarthak vicāraśīl hindū kahte haiṁ ki sāre devī-devatā ek hī īśvar kī śakti haiṁ. Islie ve kisī bhī rūp meṁ īśvar kī bhakti kar sakte haiṁ. Vāstav meṁ bahut kam hindū nirguṇ brahm kī Ārādhǎnā karte haiṁ. . . . Islām meṁ allāh ke anek sundar nām haiṁ jinse uske guṇoṁ kā sanket hotā hai. Allāh sarvaśaktimān aur nyāyapūrṇ hai. Anek dārśanik kahte haiṁ ki param tatv samast prāṇiyoṁ kā mūl ādhār haiṁ. Vah hamāre sarvocc naitik aur bauddhik ākāṅkṣāoṁ kā strot hai. Vah sajīv śakti hai jo samast sṛṣṭi ko sancālit aur ākarṣit kartī hai.*"

82 Dayal, *Masīhī Dharm Vijñān*, 127: "[*Manuṣy ke*] *buddhi aur vivek meṁ parameśvar kā svarūp hai. Yadi parameśvar aur manuṣy meṁ samāntā nahīṁ hotī to donoṁ meṁ sangati sambhav nahīṁ hotī. Parameśvar svayam ko manuṣy par prakaṭ nahīṁ kartā yadi manuṣy meṁ parameṣvar ko samajhane aur usse saṅgati karne kī kṣamatā na hotī.*"

83 Howell was ordained by the Evangelical Church of India. From 1990–1996 he served as the Principal of Allahabad Bible Seminary and from 1996–1997 as the Associate General Secretary of E.F.I. He was elected General Secretary of E.F.I.

in May 1997. He has also served as the Secretary of the Evangelical Fellowship of Asia, Member of the Continuation Committee of the Global Christian Forum, and Vice-Chairperson of the International Council of the World Evangelical Alliance. Howell's works include *Free to Choose* and *Transformation at Work* (both in English) and *Mission* (in Hindi). He also serves as the chief editor of *Aim*, the monthly newsletter of E.F.I. (Biographic details from Howell, *Parivartan*)

84 Howell, *Parivartan*, 7: "*Bāibal hamem̐ parameśvar kī kahānī batātī hai. Ye parameśvar kī aur uski khoī huī sr̥ṣṭi evam use punaḥsthāpit karne kī kahānī hai.*"

85 Howell, *Parivartan*, 10: "*Islie bāibal kā ārambh isī vicār ke sāth hotā hai ki parameśvar ek srot ke rūp mem̐, sambandh ek prāthamikatā ke rūp mem̐ aur parameśvar ek adhikārī ke rūp mem̐ hai.*"

86 Howell, *Parivartan*, 11–12: "*Is baḍī tasvīr mem̐ hamārā niyantraṇ sīmit hai – balki sac kahem̐ to hamārā niyantraṇ thā hī nahīm̐. Parantu apne vyavahār par hamārā niyantraṇ avaśy hai aur hamem̐ apne vyavahār par niyantraṇ rakhnā bhī cāhie. Parameśvar kī bhūmikā us baḍī tasvīr ko niyantraṇ mem̐ hai aur hamārī bhūmikā svayam ko aur apnī jimmedāriyom̐ ko niyantraṇ mem̐ rakhnā hai. Kahne kā tātpary yah hai hamem̐ 'ātm-niyantraṇ' banāe rakhnā hai.*"

87 Howell, *Parivartan*, 18: "*Bāibil kī is pūrī kahānī mem̐ hamāre jīvan kā ucit sthān kyā hai, aur parameśvar is saṃsār mem̐ kyā kucch kar rahā hai is bāt kā hamem̐ jñān prāpt karnā hai. Hamem̐ apne sangharṣom̐ se āge baṛhnā hai aur parameśvar ke us vr̥had aur baḍī yojanā mem̐ hamārā sthān evam bhūmikā kyā hai isko jānnā hai. Parameśvar se kahie ki ve āpko jīvan ke in viṣayom̐ ko jānne aur dekhne mem̐ āpkī madad karem̐.*"

88 Howell, *Parivartan*, 15:

Parameśvar	*Manuṣy*
Parameśvar srot hai	*Hum parameśvar par nirbhar haim̐*
Parameśvar racayitā hai	*Hum racnā hai aur uske binā vidvān nahīm̐ rah sakte*
Parameśvar ke pās saṃsār kā adhikār hai aur vah us par niyantraṇ kartā hai	*Hum svayam-kendrit hai arthāt apne ko niyantrit kar sakte haim̐*
Parameśvar jindagiyom̐ kā nyāy karne vālā hai	*Hum jīvan kā anubhav karte haim̐*
Parameśvar ne manuṣy kī racnā kī aur uske lie niyam banāem̐	*Hum parameśvar dvārā batāe niyamom̐ kā apnī jindagiyom̐ mem̐ pālan karte haim̐.*

89 Howell, *Parivartan*, 252: "*Bhāratīy prajātantr naī cunautiyom̐ kā, sāmudāyik sangharṣ, ātankvād se laṛnā, yuvā samāj kī vicārdhārāom̐ ke sāth calnā, in sabkā sāmnā kartā hai. Bhārat ko apnī paddhatī ko behtar banāne kī āvaśyakatā hai. Iskā arth prajātantr ko nirṇay lenevālā, prabhāvī, saṃvidhānātmak, svatantratāvād ko prajātantr ke vyavahār mem̐ jorṇā, ṭūṭī aur bikharī huyī rājanītik saṃsthāom̐ kā purṇnirmāṇ karnā aur sabse baḍhkar sarkārī saṃsthāom̐ tathā sattādhāriyom̐ ko apnī jimmevārī samajhnā aur use nibhānā atyant āvaśyak hai. Unhem̐ keval kānūnī nahīm̐ parantu naitik bātom̐ kā udāharaṇ logom̐ ke sāmne rakhnā cāhie aur uskā svayam pālan karnā cāhie. Iske bagair prajātantr khokhlā ban jāegā, keval akṣam hī nahīm̐ parantu khatarnāk bhī, iske sāth svatantratāvād naṣṭ ho jāegā, svatantratā kā upayog atyācār ke lie kiyā jāegā aur sāmāny jan jīvan naṣṭ ho jāegā.*"

90 Howell, *Parivartan*, 252–253: "*Masīhiyom̐ kā rājanīti ke kṣetr se haṭ jāne kā arth hai ki galat rīti se vartamān mem̐ sthit sāmājik-rājanītik dr̥ṣṭikoṇ ko svīkār karnā. Kucch viśiṣṭ yojanāom̐ aur anyāy ke viruddh yadi dhārmik pratirodh*

nahīṁ kiyā gayā to vāstav meṁ hum unko sahmatī dete haiṁ. Deś ke rājanītik kāryoṁ meṁ sahbhāg denā yah masīhiyoṁ kā kartavy hai, tāki ve apne dṛṣṭikoṇ ko sāmne rakh sakeṁ. Bhārat meṁ masīhiyoṁ ko sarkārī yojanāoṁ se lagātār ṭakkar lenī paḍ rahī hai. Iskā ek choṭā udāharaṇ hai, cār rājyoṁ meṁ dharm sambandhi bil kī manjūrī pradān karnā. To fir ab hamāre sāmne kyā mārg hai, rājanīti meṁ masīhiyoṁ kā adhik sahyog yā fir rājanīti se pūrṇ rūp se dūr rahnā?

Masīhī viśvās – dharm ke nijīkaraṇ ke, dharm ko sīmit karne, aur use keval jīvan ke āntarik kṣetr tak hī rakhne, kā virodh kartā hai. Dharm nijī nahīṁ ho saktā, dharm kisī ek vyakti kā yā samudāy kā honā cāhie. Dharm sadaiv anek sāmājik tathā āpsī sambandho kī jimmedārī meṁ śāmil hotā jātā hai."

91 Howell, *Parivartan*, 253: "*Parameśvar ke rājy ko mānavatā meṁ mel-milāp karnā, śānti lānā prajātantr kā vistār karnā yā sāmājik tathā vyāvasāyik svatantratā lāne tak sīmit nahīṁ karnā cāhie. Pavitr śāstr kisī ek viśiṣṭ prakār kī sarkār kī bāt nahīṁ kartā hai. Rājanīti ke sabhī prakāroṁ kā durupayog kiyā jā saktā hai. Agar jimmedār prajātantr rājanīti ke apne nirṇayoṁ kī rakṣā kar saktā hai, to vah arājakatā ko naṣṭ bhī kar saktā hai. Masīhiyoṁ ko do gambhīr galtiyoṁ se backar rahnā cāhie: pahlī bāt yah kī yojanā yā paddhatī ke badalne se saṃsār nae samāj yā parameśvar ke rājy meṁ badlā jā saktā hai aur dūsrī yah kī sāmājik-rājanītik paddhati yā yojanāeṁ vikasit karnā mahattvapūrṇ nahīṁ hai kyoṁki hameṁ susamācār pracār karne ke lie bulāyā gayā hai.*"

92 Howell, *Parivartan*, 254: "*Masīhī log, nāgarik hone ke nāte apne Paṛosī kī tathā rāṣṭr kī cintā karne ke dvārā parameśvar ke rājy kī sevā karte haiṁ. Parivartan lāne vālā miśan vāstav meṁ sāmājik burāī haṭāne tathā samāj meṁ parameśvar ke rājy ke mūlyoṁ ko lāne ke lie pavitr śāstr ke dṛṣṭikoṇ kā upayog kartā hai.*"

93 Howell, *Parivartan*, 271: "*Jab carcā kā viṣay mānavīy jimmedārī kī or jātā hai tab log aksar becain ho jāte hai. Pavitr śāstr dūsroṁ ke adhikāroṁ ke lie sangharṣ karne ke viṣay meṁ bahut kucch kahtā hai, parantu apne adhikāroṁ ke lie sangharṣ karne ke viṣay meṁ bahut thoḍā batāyā gayā hai. Dūsrī or jab vah hamāre viṣay meṁ kahtā hai to hameṁ apne adhikāroṁ ke viṣay meṁ nahīṁ parantu jimmedāriyoṁ ke viṣay meṁ batātā hai. Hameṁ parameśvar tathā apne Paṛosī se prem karne ke lie kahā gayā hai. Pavitr śāstr is bāt par jor detā hai ki dūsre vyakti ke adhikāroṁ kī rakṣā karnā hamārī jimmedārī hai; aur aisā karne ke lie hameṁ adhikār bhī choṛne ke lie taiyār rahnā cāhie.*

Hameṁ is bāt ko svīkār karnā cāhie ki dūsre logoṁ ke adhikār hamārī jimmedārī hai. Sthānīy kalīsiyā kā jīvan parameśvar ke rājy ko pragaṭ karne ke lie hai. Kalīsiyā ko saṃsār meṁ ek samudāy ke rūp meṁ rahnā cāhie jahāṁ mānav sammān aur samānatā ko sadaiv sthān diyā jātā hai, aur logoṁ kī ek dūsre ke prati jimmedārī ko svīkār kiyā jātā hai jismeṁ koī bhedbhāv nahīṁ, pakṣpāt nahīṁ, jahāṁ garīb aur kamjoroṁ ke lie sangharṣ kiyā jātā hai aur mānav ko mānav bankar rahne kā adhikār hai, ṭhīk usī prakār jis prakār parameśvar ne unheṁ banāyā aur cāhā ki ve usī prakār raheṁ."

94 Howell, *Parivartan*, 272: "*Parameśvar ne jin logoṁ ko cunā aur bulāyā hai unke any logoṁ ke sāth sambandh meṁ masīh samudāy kā bhinn caritr va svabhāv dikhāī detā hai. Kalīsiyā parameśvar ke log haiṁ, yah masīh kā śarīr aur dulhan hai aur pavitr ātmā kā mandir hai. Jāgarūk kalīsiyā sampūrṇ rīti se ek parivār hai jo viśvās kā parivār hai. Aur jaise humne pahle hī carcā kī hai masīh ke samudāy ko bhinn saṃskṛti ko pragaṭ karnā cāhie. Parameśvar ke bulāe hue log hone ke nāte kalīsiyā kī ek jimmedārī hai – cinh honā, aur parameśvar ke rājy kā sādhan bannā. Iskā arth yah huā ki yah samudāy parameśvar ke āne vāle rājy kī or iśārā kartā hai. Pavitr ātmā se paripūrṇ samudāy hone ke nāte, kalīsiyā ko apne sāmāny jīvan ke dvārā bhī parameśvar ke āne vāle rājy ko pragaṭ karnā cāhie. Masīh kā samudāy hone ke nāte kalīsiyā ko us āne vāle rājy ko saṃsār meṁ vāstavik rūp meṁ pradarśit karnā cāhie, kyoṁki vah rājy vyakti jīvan kī pūrṇatā aur samāj ke lie nyāy aur sampūrṇ sṛṣṭi ke lie ārogyatā pradān kartā hai.*"

95 Howell, *Parivartan*, 171. "*Hum bhārat ke bāhar sthit kalīsiyāoṁ se kahnā cāhte haiṁ ki ve is bāt ke viṣay meṁ sacet raheṁ ki miśan kī ayogy bhāṣā ke prayog ke kāraṇ ve yahāṁ any viśvās ke logoṁ kī bhāvanāoṁ ko hī keval thes nahīṁ pahuṁcāte parantu masīhiyoṁ ke lie bhī bādhā kā kāraṇ ban jāte haiṁ.*"
96 Khan, *Khristīy Nītiśāstr*, 214.
97 Or, the rule of one party, person, or institution. See Bahri, *Rājpāl Hindī Śabdakoś*, 128.
98 Khan, *Khristīy Nītiśāstr*, 214: "*Vah rājy jo parameśvar kī ājñāoṁ kī avahelanā kare, uskā virodh karnā masīhī naitikatā hai, aur jo rājanīti ekādhikār kī or ludhak rahī ho usko sīdhe mārg par lānā masīhiyoṁ kā uttardāyitv haiṁ.*"
99 Dayal, *Masīhī Dharm Vijñān*, 30.
100 Howell, *Parivartan*, 271.

References

Bahri, Hardev. *Rājpāl Hindī Śabdakoś* [Rajpal Hindi Dictionary]. Delhi: Rajpal & Sons, 2010.

Balagangadhara, S.N. *Reconceptualizing India Studies*. New Delhi: Oxford University Press, 2012.

Bhajan, Sam V. and Benjamin Khan. *Islām: Ek Paricay* [Islam: An Introduction]. Jabalpur: Hindi Theological Literature Committee, 2004 [1974].

Bonhoeffer, Dietrich. *Life Together: The Classic Exploration of Christian Community*. New York: HarperOne, 1954 [1938].

Bonhoeffer, Dietrich. *Ethics*. New York: Touchstone, 1995 [1949].

Bonhoeffer, Dietrich. *Letters and Papers from Prison*. New York: Touchstone, 1997 [1951].

Bulcke, Camille. *Aṁgrezī-Hindī Koś, An English-Hindi Dictionary*. Ranchi: Catholic Press, 2007 [1968].

Dayal, Din. *Uttar Bhārat aur Pākistān meṁ Masīhī Dharm: Pratham Śatābdī se Bīsvīṁ Śatābdī ke Ārambh Tak* [The History of Christian Religion in North India and Pakistan: From the First Century to the Beginning of the Twentieth Century]. Jabalpur: Hindi Theological Literature Committee, 1997.

Engineer, Asghar Ali, ed. *Babri-Masjid Ramjanambhoomi Controversy*. Delhi: Ajanta Publications (India), 1990.

Flood, Gavin. *An Introduction to Hinduism*. Cambridge: University of Cambridge Press, 1996.

Howell, Richard. *Parivartan: Masīh se Milāp* [Conversion: A Meeting with Christ]. New Delhi: Evangelical Fellowship of India, 2006.

Khan, Benjamin. *The Concept of Dharma in Valmiki Ramayana*. Delhi: Munshi Ram Manohar Lal, 1965.

Khan, Benjamin. *Khristīy Nītiśāstr* [Christian Ethics]. Jabalpur: Hindi Theological Literature Committee, 2009 [1981].

Khan, Benjamin. *Bīsvīṁ Śatābdī ke Pramukh Dharmavijñānī* [Major Christian Theologians of the Twentieth Century]. Jabalpur: Hindi Theological Literature Committee, 1990.

Khan, Benjamin. *Saṃvād: Kyoṁ aur Kaise, Masīhī Driṣṭikoṇ Se* [Dialogue: Why and How, from a Christian Perspective]. Jabalpur: Hindi Theological Literature Committee, 1994.

Lossky, Nicholas, José Míguez Bonino, John Pobee, Tom F. Stransky, Geoffrey Wainwright, and Pauline Webb, eds. *Dictionary of the Ecumenical Movement*. Geneva: World Council of Churches Publications, 2002.

McGregor, Ronald S., ed. *The Oxford Hindi-English Dictionary*. New Delhi: Oxford University Press, 1993.

Metaxas, Eric. *Bonhoeffer: Pastor, Martyr, Prophet, Spy, A Righteous Gentile vs. the Third Reich*. Nashville: Thomas Nelson, 2010.

Robinson, Bob. *Christians Meeting Hindus: An Analysis and Theological Critique of the Hindu-Christian Encounter in India*. Milton Keynes: Regnum Books International, 2004.

Scharf, Peter. *Rāmopākhyāna – the Story of Rāma in the Mahābhārata, And Independent-Study Reader in Sanskrit*. New York: RoutledgeCurzon, 2003.

6 Message matters

The form and content of Hindi Christian texts have been shaped by a particular set of forces. As examined in the first three chapters, three forces in particular – mission history, Indian Christianity in the nineteenth and twentieth centuries, and India's cultural milieu at large – have played a crucial role in their development and continue to shape Hindi Christian literature in India. But how did these forces shape this literature? First, Western Christian missions in central and north India helped plant the seeds for many of the denominations and publishing houses that now constitute the bulk of the sources of production of Hindi-language Protestant Christian materials. From the Methodist Publishing House in Lucknow to the Hindi Theological Literature Committee in Jabalpur, missionary agencies and Hindi-focused missionaries provided the early impetus to and supported the development of Christian congregations and literature in the Hindi-speaking regions of India. The Baptist Missionary Society in Serampore and Fort William College in Calcutta produced materials in Hindi and provided instructions in reading and writing Hindi. Anglicans, and Methodist missionaries like C.W. David, started the Hindi Theological Literature Committee in 1956. Translations of the Hindi Bible by the Bible Society of India and other missionary agencies helped spread the gospel in Hindi. A majority of the publishing houses that produce Hindi Christian texts today are continuations or extensions of these denominational publishing houses. The spirit of ecumenism that captivated global Christianity in the twentieth century also affected the production and distribution of Hindi Christian texts by bringing denominational bodies together in common institutions with shared goals and joint projects concerning Hindi materials. Such efforts included institutions like the Hindi Theological Literature Committee, Leonard Theological College, and the Indian Society for the Promotion of Christian Knowledge, which were created to prepare pastors, educators, and leaders for Hindi-speaking churches, and joint projects like the popular hymn-book *Ārādhănā ke Gīt*, *The Oxford Hindi Dictionary of the Christian Church*, and an ongoing multi-volume *Pulpit Bible Series*.

Second, the mission field in which early Christians found themselves affected not just the choice of the language(s) used for evangelization and congregational life but also the type of messages that most resonated with the new congregations. A few aspects of this larger context within which Hindi Christianity has taken shape are particularly noteworthy for the way they shaped the development of Hindi congregations and theology and continue to shape them today. For instance, much Christian work in India took place among people who belonged to backward or marginal socio-economic and political backgrounds. In the Indian context and especially in its official vocabulary, "backward" is a specific, legal, and measurable category. It marks a group's comparative performance against national and state standards of educational, social, and economic development. For instance, according to the 1979 *B.P. Mandal Commission on Backwardness*, a caste or class of people is *educationally backward* if the number of children five-to-fifteen years old who never attended school is at least 25 percent above the state average, or it is *economically backward* if the source of drinking water is beyond half a kilometer for more than 50 percent of the households. Eleven such makers were used by the Mandal Commission and have since been used by successive Indian governments. Backward groups are generally classified under three broad categories: Scheduled Caste, Scheduled Tribe, and Other Backward Class. India's constitution provides that the State bear the burden to address backwardness caused by generations of caste-based discrimination. To meet this obligation, Articles 15 and 16 the Constitution of India permit positive discrimination by the State in favor of those disadvantaged groups officially classified as "backward." Such positive discrimination is usually achieved by reserving a certain number of government jobs and admissions in public institutions of education for members of backward groups. This system is colloquially known as 'reservations' (or, Ārakṣaṇ) in India. In order to identify and designate the backward groups that can benefit from such reservations, successive central and state governments have appointed special commissions under Article 340 of the Constitution. Along with various State Commissions, all-India Commissions include the Kalelkar Commission (1953–1955), the first of its kind, the B.P. Mandal Commission (1979–1980), and the Mishra Commission on Religious and Linguistic Minorities (2004–2007), which is the latest pan-India effort to identify and designate Scheduled Castes, Scheduled Tribes, and Other Backward Classes.

Most Christians in India have come from Dalit or 'backward' backgrounds, and conversion to Christianity itself has not meant the eradication of backwardness. Neither has conversion meant, particularly in India, an erasure of boundaries between old and new faiths or an inevitable transition from oppressive socio-religious (casteist) realities to healthier ones – as works by Gauri Viswanathan and Sebastian Kim have shown. Being a Christian and being marginal are not mutually exclusive. To the works of Selva Raj and Corinne Dempsey among others on these topics, we can also add the voices of Ruth Manorama,[1] Monica J. Melanchthon,[2] Godwin Shiri,[3] and Mohan Larbeer,[4] among many others. The demographic make-up of congregations has impacted their theology and practices in the form of a noticeable rejection of Brahmanic ideas and concepts in Hindi Christian speech and acts. Unlike many early Christian theologians writing in English, who sought to find common ground between their own pre-Christian high-caste backgrounds and elite Hindu interlocutors, Hindi Christian authors rejected Brahmanical forms of Christianity in favor of speech and vocabulary that created conceptual distance from those forms of Christianity. Similarly, vernaculars like Hindi started to occupy a larger role as the language of communication because vernaculars – rather than English or Latin or Syriac – were the languages of choice for a growing number of Christian converts.

Third, recognition of their status as minority Christians in a multifaith context has led to particular forms of discourse and values. In one instance, Hindi Christians have sought to use Hindi in ways that help them identify themselves as both Hindi and Christian. As a result, they have mostly rejected *avătār* in favor of *dehadhāraṇ*, yet have readily deployed polytraditional ideas like *mandir* (a concept shared with Hindus), *khudā* and *īmān* (concepts shared with Muslims), and honorific language for their Lord (a cultural practice shared with both Hindus and Muslims). In another way, they have opposed attempts to identify Christianity with English by insisting that Christians must recognize that they are called to serve in Hindi, criticizing portrayals of Christians in mass media as Westerners, and questioning the association of Christianity with Urdu-inflected Hindi in *Bāibal kī Kahāniyāṁ* (more on these arguments later). In a further sign of the weight given to the recognition that Hindi Christians witness as minority citizens of a multifaith nation, Hindi Christian texts have emphasized the importance of respectful evangelism, pluralistic attitudes, Christian contribution to public life, and the need to seek and build interfaith relations intentionally.

Though committed to the self-government and self-expression of Indian churches, some prominent Indian Christians, like Bishop Victor Azariah, were reluctant supporters of India's Independence movement due to their preference to be governed by British co-religionists rather than come under Hindu or Brahmin rule.[5] Hindi Christian authors, however, do not display any reluctance toward sharing governance with India's Hindus (and for that matter, its other citizens). Azariah's context was of course quite different from that in which Hindi Christians find themselves: independence was still on the horizon, the shape of Indian democracy was unclear, there was no guarantee that India would adopt a secular constitution, nor could Azariah have envisioned the role interfaith relations would play in the public life of post-independence India.

Hindi Christians are trying to be Hindi, Indian, and Christian. This desire has manifested itself in a variety of attempts to curate a Christian voice that is an active participant in Hindi symbols and India's governance. I explored these attempts through five case studies in the previous chapters. The first study covered debates on the use of *avătār* among Indian Christians and the development of a neologism to distinguish an important Christian expression in Hindi from Hindu motifs. The second case concerned the construction of discipleship in Hindi Christian works. In the next case, I shed light on the ways in which Christian ethics are interpreted in terms of national needs. The fourth case examined public portrayals of Christianity in mass media through Hindi Christian commentary on the Hindi-ness of *Bāibal kī Kahāniyāṁ*. Finally, the fifth study looked at the ways in which certain public goals have shaped conceptions of ethics in Hindi Christian works. Attempts to promote Hindi as the language of expression and attempts to foster public works as the mode of discipleship represent complementary ways to Indianize Christianity in the imagination of Hindi Christian authors.

Sharing codes

Insights from the relationship of Hindi Christian literature to other Indian Christian writing and bhakti motifs are telling regarding the complex relationship between Hindi Christianity and its religious and cultural contexts. And the type of engagement between Hindi Christians and their religious and linguistic milieu that emerges in Hindi Christian literature demonstrates a search for Christian credibility. The assessment of Robin Boyd's history of Indian Christian theology in Hindi Christian circles, which was discussed previously, is a case in point. The translation of Boyd's study into Hindi was popular – it has already run in two editions and multiple prints, with the most recent print in 2004 producing 1100 copies (a considerable number for a Hindi Christian book) – and helped a generation of Hindi-language seminarians and Christians learn about the growth and development of Christian theology in India. Yet embedded within C.W. David's Hindi translation of Boyd's work are clear hints at the unease of the Hindi Theological Literature Committee in producing a book on Indian Christian theology that seemed to tie the Indian-ness of Christian theology in India too closely to Hindu worldviews in India – as if Christian theologizing in India was theology done primarily under the umbrella of Hindu worldviews.

Hindi Christian authors found problematic the readiness with which, in their estimation, many early Christian thinkers in India borrowed heavily from Hindu views of the world and tried to bridge the gap between the two faiths. Ideas like *sat*, *chit*, *ānand* (using the triune form of Brahma as an analogy for the Triune nature of God), the synonymity of the Hindu term *avătār* and the Christian notion of the incarnation of the Word, and an advaitic understanding of God's relationship with the world (which led to a theology of svamārg, i.e., a believer was on a personal journey to find oneness with God) were popular and – maybe even dominant – among Christian theologizing in India. Boyd's *Indian Christian Theology* (1976) and Khan's *Major Christian Theologians of the Twentieth Century* (1990) were, after all, compilations in which examples of attempts by Indian Christian thinkers to bridge the distance between Western Christian thinkers and relatable Hindu concepts were prevalent. Hindi Christian leaders in India resisted this choice to place Christian concepts in Hindu terms when they chose *dehadhāraṇ* over *avătār* to communicate one of the most-important and defining claims of Christianity.

Yet such distinctions between Hindu concepts were not clear cut and the complexity of the relationship of Christian claims to Hindu expressions could be understood in multiple ways. It could, for instance, be understood in terms of the fluidity of ideas across religious boundaries in Christian communities – e.g., polytraditional words existed along with exclusively Christian terms. It could be understood also in terms of the weight given to the concept being communicated – e.g., it was important to distinguish between Jesus and other incarnations because of what was at stake: the exclusive claim of Jesus on salvation. The use of a Hindu word like *mandir* in the Hindi Bible, however, was not a matter of great concern because not much was at stake when referring to the physical structure in which God was said to reside and be worshipped. Finally, it could be viewed in light of the value placed on recognizable boundaries in 'formal' venues like Hindi translations of the Bible (where *dehadhāraṇ* has been consistently used) and 'informal' venues like popular hymns (where we find *avătār* and polytraditional terms) and self-published works (like Arya's poems on the Gospel of Mark) where the authors and the users of their works were open to placing Christian and Hindu claims in synonymity with each other. The use of *dehadhāraṇ* in conjunction with polytraditional words like *mandir* points to another aspect of Hindi Christian claims: the insistence that Christianity in India be Christianity in Hindi. Hindi authorship by Christians in India emerged not only from missionary-era objectives but also from the desire of an increasingly Indianizing church to speak and use the language used by the vast majority of its members. To be a Christian did not mean to abandon or set aside one's cultural history and heritage. Hindi was a big part of this story. As a result, in the works of Hindi Christian writers we find a call for Christians in the region to use Hindi in their religious lives and worship.

Like the attempts in Hindi Christian texts to secure a Christian witness that is credible as both linguistically Hindi and theo-ethically Christian, the search for recognition as Christian by their neighbors of other faiths has also played out in a few noticeable ways. On one hand, words like *dehadhāraṇ* allowed Hindi Christians to communicate a vocabulary that was distinguishable from their Hindu neighbors and from other forms of Indian Christianity that in certain (Brahmanical) versions readily adopted Sanskritic terms and the philosophical worldviews of Hindu schools of thought to communicate Christian claims. This form of Christianity in India itself acquired its Brahmanical flavor as the result of primarily two complementary movements: the conversion of upper-caste elites in urban settings, many of whom were invested in a renaissance within Hinduism (like the Bengali Brahmin convert Brahmabandhab Upadhyay [1861–1907]); and, the adoption of inculturation into Hindu ways of life, like ashrams and the philosophy of Vedanta, as expressed in the life and ministry of Catholic missionaries like de Nobili; Jules Monchanin and Henri Le Saux (who took the name Abhishiktananda), founders of the Saccidananda Ashram in 1950; the English Benedictine priest, Bede Griffiths (1906–1993); and, Sara Grant, who led the Christa Prema Seva Ashram in Pune in the 1970s and onwards.[6]

A 'Hindu-ized' or 'Indianized' or 'swadeshi' (or, native) Christianity, however, was not uncontested within Indian Christianity.[7] Hindi Christian arguments against *avătār* turned on the concept's inability to properly mark-out the unique salvific person and work of Jesus Christ as compared to that of other *avătārs*. In the context of a Hindu worldview and Brahmanical Christian claims, Hindi Christians adopted *dehadhāraṇ* as a way to stand apart within that context. In other words, a term like *dehadhāraṇ* served to distinguish Hindi Christian vocabulary from (Hindu) *avătār* and from certain (Brahminical) forms of Indian Christianity. Hindi Christians, however, were not alone in doing so. The turn to *bhakti* and social concerns, and the turn away from Sanskritic thought, in Indian Christian circles, as exemplified in Dalit theology and bhakti theology, complemented the attitude of Hindi Christians. As Ganeri writes of Catholic Christianity in India, "The Indian identity of the Catholic community is . . . neither solely that of Dalit culture nor Brahmanical Hindu culture."[8] This observation would also hold true for Protestant Christian thoughts in India.

Yet it is important to recall that Hindi Christians writers sought recognition not only in their standing apart but also in their comfort with using religious terms in Hindi that were readily available to Christians and non-Christians alike, and in their attention to the cultural practices of their religious neighbors. In this vein, terms like *mandir* and other similar polytraditional words allowed Hindi Christianity to remain connected with its surrounding religious milieu and vocabulary. Along with serving as connective tissues, polytraditional concepts in Hindi Christian literature should also be seen as reflective of a desire to be grounded in Hindi. This desire is most visible in two ways. Hindi Christian guidebooks on communication, as we saw in the examples from Anand's and Lall's works, insisted that Christians communicate in Hindi and communicate in ways that accommodate the (equally real) claims of peoples of other faiths. Similarly, Hindi Christian authors sought to safeguard the association of Hindi with Christianity, and to project Christianity as a Hindi faith. It is in the context of this interest – that has played out against the backdrop of Hindu nationalists who want to preserve 'India's language,' Hindi, exclusively for Hindus and who want to link India, Hindi, and Hindu seamlessly together (an area for further research discussed later) – that our understanding of Anand's diagnosis of the failure of *Bāibal kī Kahāniyāṁ* acquires more depth.

The commentary among Hindi Christians regarding the failure of *Bāibal kī Kahānīyāṁ* suggests that blame for its demise can be assigned to the decision of the writers of *Bāibal kī Kahānīyāṁ* to dilute the Hindi-content of the serial. A fall in ratings and bureaucratic controversies partly explain the demise of *Bāibal kī Kahānīyāṁ*. Nevertheless, in the estimation of Hindi Christians the serial lost a large portion of its Christian audience – and consequently its run on Doordarshan – because Christians in India could not recognize the heavily Urdu-inflected language of *Bāibal kī Kahānīyāṁ*. As noted earlier, Mankekar's work questions such interpretations of the affair. Hindi Christian assessments, however, make sense in light of the attempts by Hindi Christians to make their faith recognizable as a faith grounded in Hindi. As expressed in Anand's arguments, Christians must fight attempts to portray Christianity as a religion of the English language or of Urdu and should claim for themselves an identity as members of a 'Hindi religion.' In summary, then, a study of the role of *dehadhāraṇ*, the deployment of polytraditional words, and Hindi Christian assessments of the failure of *Bāibal kī Kahānīyāṁ* helps us recognize that Hindi Christians have used the importance of using Hindi as a means to stake their Christian witness as one that is credibly and recognizably Christian and Hindi.

Many widely-read Hindi Christian authors argue that virtuous lives serve an intentional and particular type of public purpose. The Christian witness proposed in Hindi Christian texts comes in the form of a witness that is both necessary and necessarily public in nature. As discussed in chapter 5, Hindi Christian authors have routinely employed terms like *kartavy* (duty),[9] *dāyitv* or *uttardāyitv* (obligation or liability),[10] *jimmedāri* (responsibility),[11] *bhūmikā* (role),[12] and *āvaśyak* (necessary)[13] to communicate a robust sense of responsibility to witness in public that is incumbent on those who follow Christ. It is no accident, then, that this necessary, public aspect of Christian witness is prominent in texts on ethics that seek to explain and provide practical guidelines for a virtuous life in the wider religious and social environments in which Christians in central and northern India find themselves. In Hindi Christian texts, Christian discipleship is a necessary feature of accepting Christ; this argument is rather commonplace in Christian literature, both within and outside India. Hindi Christian texts, however, claim a further role that is incumbent on Christian communities that exist and preach in a language that is shared by the vast majority of their non-Christian neighbors. In addition to being a Christian disciple, one should also be a disciple in public ways. For many Hindi Christian scholars, an attention to Christian discipleship is accompanied by an insistence that such discipleship face outward toward people of other faiths.

Three general reasons explain the demand for public witness in Hindi Christian sources. First, calls for the public nature of Hindi Christian witness reflect the fact that Hindi Christians are called to use Hindi, a language they share with neighbors of other faiths. Second, commentaries on public engagement reflect the social and religious location of (Hindi) Christians in India as Christians in a pluralist context dominated by non-Christian neighbors. From this perspective, interfaith relations and dialogue matter even as Christians continue to evangelize and preach the gospel through their witness. Third, the desire for Christian participation in democracy and public governance has inspired a lot of Hindi Christians discourse on the public nature of Christian witness in India. But how have these objectives inspired and shaped the call for public witness in Hindi Christian texts? The commitment to use Hindi impacted and shaped Hindi Christian arguments in certain ways. This is especially so when Hindi Christian writers argued why Indian Christians should focus on Hindi as their language rather than use other languages. Such arguments were not, as the evidence from Hindi Christian commentary on the *Bāibal kī Kahāniyāṁ* suggests, nationalistic in nature. After all, Hindi Christian authors did not argue that Christians throughout the nation should use Hindi. Such broad claims are noticeably absent in Hindi Christian literature. Rather, authors like John Anand were wary of the neglect of Hindi and of attempts to separate it from Christianity. As Anand cautioned, when Christians in India use 'non-Indian' components of cultures (for instance, a language like English) they place themselves in Trishanku's position – neither here nor there.

The image of a cassock-wearing Catholic priest did not appropriately represent Indian Christianity. Anand's caricature of Indian Catholics as culturally foreign is demonstrably weak. Catholics in India, like their Syrian Orthodox co-religionists in southern India, have had a longer history of assimilative thoughts and practices than their Protestant kin. Further, Indian Catholics have proposed ideas and concepts, like *param-prasād*, that are mobile across religious borders. At the same time, Catholic institutions in India, including Catholic seminaries, research centers, and the Catholic Bishops' Conference of India, have regularly supported creative developments in interfaith relations, theologies, and practices in India. Further, the vocabularies, practices, and vestments of mainline Protestant liturgy have also drawn inspiration from and followed the traditions of Christian liturgical practices outside India. In light of these facts, it is appropriate to seriously question Anand's negative portrayal of Catholic Christianity in India. Yet it is also important to note that Anand's comment was not so much a denial of the Indianness of Catholics in India but more a comment on Christian portrayals in forums of mass media like films. Indian Catholics, of course, do not control how Bollywood has portrayed them. They have been mostly on the sidelines when Bollywood has chosen Indian Catholics to stand in for Indian Christians at large. For Anand, the same could be said of a form of Hindi heavily inflected with Urdu vocabulary. In Anand's metaphor, then, being stuck in the middle of "here" (i.e., Hindi and Indian culture) and "there" (English and Western garb) was not good and, implicit in the metaphor, Hindi Christians were asked to remain "here" (the preferred option) or "there" rather than remain stuck in the middle.

Hindi-language commercial films do not portray Indian Christians in nuanced and balanced ways. The portrayal is rather monochromatic and ignores the range of Christian varieties found in India. Anand's critique of images of cassock-wearing priests in Hindi films should be understood in the context of mass media portrayals of Christianity in India. His comments on Catholic priests (or, more to Anand's point, Roman Catholic priests) are not a critique of Catholic Christianity in India per se but of the predominant way in which Indian Christians have been portrayed in Hindi films. Pankaj Jain has studied the portrayal of Christians in Indian films. Jain concludes his somewhat brief study with a rather positive observation that in Indian films, "Christians are rarely, if at all, singled out for criticism."[14] Jain's work is revelatory in another way: the vast majority of Christian characters found in Hindi films are Roman Catholic characters.

Second, using Hindi meant recognizing both the mutual intelligibility afforded by the strategy and the gaps it revealed. Mutual intelligibility as a tactic emerged in the ready adoption of and comfort with polytraditional words in Hindi Christian texts like the Hindi Bible, hymns, songs, poetry, and sermons, to name a few forms of Christian discourse. Polytraditional words were not the only expression of the search for mutual intelligibility. The transition in Hindi Bible translations from non-honorific to honorific addresses for Jesus Christ stemmed from a similar desire to acquire cultural parity with Hindu expressions in other faiths. As John Anand explains,

> We want to make a personal request of you that when [old editions of] these books were published, in those days the editor of the *Ādhyātmik Śikṣā Mālā* [the Spiritual Instruction Series] and Christian authors had not paid attention to important issues like language and culture and for the founder of the Christian faith Lord Jesus, and [for] Christian religious teachers, prophets, apostles and the like, they did not use honorific pronouns appropriate for Indian culture, due to which even today in church uncultured [or crude or impolite[15]] forms of address like 'Jesus calls,' 'Jesus says' [the original Hindi is non-honorific] are in use.[16]

A few things are noteworthy about Anand's request. First, as editor-in-chief of the Hindi Theological Literature Committee over the last two decades, Anand has attached this request to many Hindi Christian works published by the Committee. One can find this request as a preface to many new editions of pre-1980s texts. Most texts after the 1980s lack such a note. While I have not traced in detail the timeline of the shift to honorific texts, it seems clear that Hindi Christian publications over the last three decades have paid persistent attention to ways in which Hindi Christian works can (or cannot) be recognized as (culturally) Indian – by which I mean a degree of cultural parity between Hindi Christian and other (in this case, mostly Hindu) forms of religious speech. Presumably, editors and writers, in contrast to their predecessors, have caught on to the importance of cultural parity.

Further, it seems to be the case that cultural sensitivity has found a place in texts and literature more than it has in quotidian Christian speech and church practices. Hence, in 2009 Anand could bemoan the continued use of non-honorific speech in churches. There is, Anand's note suggests, a lag between adoptions of honorific speech in Christian literature and in church practices. This lag is especially conspicuous in light of the fact that, as demonstrated previously, the Hindi Bible of 1988–1989 had already adopted honorific language. At least since 1989, then, Christians have used a Hindi Bible with honorific religious speech. Yet, 20 years later, that speech pattern has, at least according to the Hindi Theological Literature Committee, failed to eradicate "uncultured" or crude forms of address for Jesus in church life.

Mutual intelligibility was not the only outcome of writing in Hindi. Using Hindi also led Hindi Christians to face the limits of mutual intelligibility. They found that gaps may arise when trying to use a language that is deeply part of other faith traditions. One such gap emerged around the use of *avătār* to speak of the Christian notion of God's incarnation. Even though Hindu religious literature in the region, and nineteenth- and twentieth-century Indian Christian discourses, were replete with the idea and its use, Hindi Christian authors rejected *avătār* and (nearly exclusively) adopted *dehadhāraṇ* to communicate the Christian idea of God's incarnation. Unlike English Christian Indian authors who found similarities between Christ and Buddha[17] or Christ and Krishna (Mohammed), Hindi Christian authors insisted that Christ is unique and not like those saviors. In doing so, Hindi Christian theologians followed in the footsteps of those missionaries and scholars and teachers who cautioned against conflating other saviors (like Krishna and Buddha) with Christ.

Linguistic code-sharing with Hindu and Muslim neighbors was not the only impetus among Hindi Christians to recognize their relations with people of other faiths. They were also motivated by the recognition of their particular location as Christians in a secular and pluralist democracy. In other words, interfaith relations mattered. A commitment to being Christian in ways that are recognizably Christian to people of other faiths went hand-in-hand with the acknowledgement that Christian witness should not undermine interfaith relations. So, for instance, Dayal attended to the public posture of Christianity and the impact of Christian speech and acts on public relations. Similarly, Howell (like Lall) asked Indian Christians to evangelize in ways that built relations and did not denigrate the beliefs of people of other faiths. Linguistic code-sharing, in an interesting way, attuned Christians to interfaith relations. An interest in how Christians communicated and what they communicated was accompanied by an interest in what that communication bore and how a Christian could communicate in relational ways. Howell's emphasis on a relational form of evangelism symbolized the impact of the concern for interfaith relations on the form and content of Hindi Christian texts.

Other prominent works discussed previously that draw our attention to the role of interfaith relations have been Khan's *Khristīy Nītiśāstr* and Dayal's *Masīhī Dharm Vijñān kā Paricay*. In Khan's ethics, as in his subsequent works, interfaith dialogue acquired prime place as an expression of Christian service. More importantly, Christian witness acquired its public profile because, for Khan, interfaith dialogue was the necessary precursor to interfaith relations, which were the special goal of Christian theo-ethics in India. Dayal echoed this theme and argued for the public nature of Christian witness on the ground that interfaith relations were a necessary outcome of Christian theology for three reasons: Christ calls his disciples to shape the societies in which they find themselves rather than to seclude themselves from public affairs; God's placement of Christians in India is a call to engage people of other faiths; and, finally, God's way of self-revelation, which includes God's self-revelation to people of other faiths, makes interfaith engagements by Christians (theologically) inevitable.

Finally, the commitment to use Hindi and to strengthen interfaith relations was accompanied by a commitment to public service and participation in public affairs. In light of the previous two commitments, it is not hard to see why Hindi Christian scholars have favored influential roles in public affairs. Social management is not the sole purview of the secular. How can this be so, in a context infused with religion anyway? As Khan has argued, India is not an a-religious nation. Indian Christians are, as a result, called to be citizens and participants and shapers of politics in the context of public spaces that are infused with the values and claims of many religious communities. As Khan reminds his readers, for Christians to abdicate their civil duties would be to have "failed to make Christian values influential [in public life]."[18]

In line with Khan's and Dayal's commentary on public service, the guidebooks of James, Paul, Anand, and Lall also present Christian discipleship in ways that press it into the service of larger social goals. As discussed in chapter 4, Hindi Christian guidebooks are replete with insights on proper discipleship and tie that discipleship inseparably to the responsibility to be disciples in public ways and shape public life. As James puts it, a Christian "is responsible to her family, her society, [and] to her nation."[19] While Anand and Lall invite their readers to build relations between Christians and non-Christians, and Lall and Howell propose strategies for relational evangelism, the works of James, Paul, and Khan invite their readers to attend to their role as Indians in the management of public affairs and social development. It is, then, clear from the evidence that the claim that Christian witness should be necessarily public arose from a combination of factors. The use of Hindi allowed code-sharing with people of other faiths. Such code-sharing complemented context-inspired ethics and theologies that demonstrated a necessary Christian commitment to interfaith relations. And, the relationship between language, ethics, and context ensured that Christian speech was not separated from Christian acts, whether at the individual, communal, or political levels.

Paving the way

By their very nature, early works on new topics invite scholars to engage in further research, take the research in new directions, test claims, and explore the ways in which such studies can relate to larger conversations. Original works, in other words, are both fecund and inviting. Benjamin Khan is instructive in this regard. In the foreword to his pioneering work on twentieth-century Christian theologians – the first of its kind in Hindi – he writes,

> In first attempts, there always remain some deficits and defects. [It is my hope that] readers and critics will look beyond these deficits and defects and will benefit from the materials that are the warp and woof of this book. It is also incumbent on critics and readers to convey the deficits and defects of the book to the author so that the author may correct them in the second edition.[20]

Khan used his preface to open a conversation on Christian theologies in India. I have found his comments helpful because they can also serve as an invitation to open a conversation on Hindi Christian literature in India. I am particularly attracted to his recognition of the communal and continuing nature of scholarship because there are many historical and contemporary topics that scholars can explore with the help of Hindi Christian texts. Borne out of my interests and ongoing research, I have identified a selection of those topics in following sections. It is apropos of Khan's observation to take some time to turn our gaze outward and to look beyond the scope of this book. A hitherto unengaged family of texts like Hindi Christian literature offers scholars of Christianity in India a rich source of data to study a range of issues. I highlight five such topics.

The first topic concerns the way in which debates in Hindi Christian literature challenge attempts by Hindu nationalists to hoard Hindi for Hindus. King traces the origin of the Hindi movement of the nineteenth century to the early 1860s as a movement that sought to express a form of Hindu nationalism "whose essence lay in the denial of existing assimilation to cultural traditions associated with Muslim rule and the affirmation of potential differentiation from these traditions."[21] Denying assimilations and affirming differences between Hindi and Urdu were central to a strategy that aimed to mark-out Hindi as the language distinctively of the Hindus and Urdu as distinctively that of the Muslims. Urdu-loving Hindus and Hindi-loving Muslims – not to mention the general ease with which these languages co-existed in central and northern India, and especially in Uttar Pradesh (the research field for King's study) – were ignored, marginalized, and opposed on grounds that such attitudes displayed divided loyalties. Cultural and emotional attitudes within the Hindi movement "led to its anti-Muslim aspects" and to look to the glory of Hindi literature was to look to those periods of Hindu rule in which "Muslims acted as invaders and villains."[22] In other words, King writes, "to revive Hindi literature meant to revive the communal rivalries expressed therein,"[23] rivalries that could be mapped on to languages only when Hindi and Urdu could be marked-out, respectively and exclusively, for Hindus and Muslims.

In the construction of Hindi-Urdu relations, nuance was expelled and assimilation was opposed. Early nineteenth-century literature in "Hindee" (Hindi) and "Hindoostanee" (Urdu) presented itself as two forms of Khaṛī Bolī – the former form inflected with Sanskrit words and the latter form with Persian and Arabic word – whose informal forms "approach[ed] complete mutual intelligibility"[24] when spoken. By the latter half of the nineteenth century, however, the division between Urdu and Hindi literature had blossomed into debates on mutual exclusivity and on whether Urdu and Hindi, rather than Urdu-Hindi, should be accorded status as the language of government and public affairs. Hindi's advocates attacked Urdu as "foreign," its script "illegible and ambiguous." Urdu's advocates attacked Hindi as "unstandardized and poor in technical and scientific vocabulary," its Nagari script "slow and clumsy."[25]

When written, Hindi and Urdu use different scripts. The Urdu script is a modified version of the Persian script, which is itself a modified version of the Arabic script. It is written from right to left with curves, loops, dotted accents, and in long connecting lines. The Hindi script is a Nagari or Devanagari script written from left to right, in blocks of characters hanging below blocks of separate lines that string the character into words, with looping, dotted, and curved accents both above the lines and below them. These different scripts reflect connections to languages of different religions. As King notes, "the Sanskrit texts of Hinduism appear in Nagari, while most versions of the Koran use the Arabic script." This relation of script to religion further reinforces the relation of language to religion.[26] The general, mutual intelligibility of Hindi and Urdu in speech and unintelligibility in script is apparent to any speaker of Hindi who cannot read the Urdu script. Beyond these 'technical' claims based on script and precision, however, an emotional and nativist claim dominated and "reappeared ad nauseam: the good of the Hindu majority required the introduction of Hindi [for official purposes in the North West Provinces, modern-day Uttar Pradesh] even if the Muslim minority should suffer from the change."[27] Proponents of Hindi won their battle with the introduction in 1900 of Hindi as a language on par with Urdu by the government of the North Western Provinces and Oudh[28] and further prevailed when Uttar Pradesh adopted Hindi as its official language in 1947. Two forces combined to accomplish this state of affairs.

On one hand, the incompatibility of the Hindi and Urdu script became a potent vehicle to ignore and sideline the compatibility of their vocabularies. While writers could use Persian, Arabic, and Sanskrit words – as we saw in the case of *Bāibal kī Kahānīyāṁ* – and speakers of the languages could be, to a considerable extent, mutually intelligible, a writer could not write in mixed Urdu and Nagari scripts. The fusing of "language, script, and religion," in other words, made it easier to differentiate Hindi from Urdu and align Hindi distinctively with the interests of Hindus and Urdu with the interests of Muslims. On the other hand, the separation between Hindi and Urdu took on a nationalist flavor. Not only were these languages practically incompatible and represented the interests of different religious groups, they also connoted different types of relationship with the nation writ large. Earlier where Hindi = Hindu + Muslim, for Hindu nationalists their Aryan culture was at stake and tied to the fate of Hindi.[29] In 1868, for instance, Babu Shiva Prasad, a prominent official in the government of the North Western Provinces and Oudh, wrote a memorandum in favor of making Hindi the official language in which he explained the threat of Urdu to Hindu culture:

> The Persian [in this context, including Urdu or 'semi-Persian'] of our day is half Arabic; and I cannot see the wisdom of the policy which thrusts a Semitic element into the bosoms of Hindus and alienates them from their Aryan speech [i.e., Hindi]; not only speech, but all that is Aryan; because through speech ideas are formed, and through ideas the manners and customs. *To read Persian is to become Persianized, all our ideas become corrupt and our nationality is lost. Cursed be the day which saw the Muhammadans cross the Indus; all the evils which we find amongst us we are indebted for to our 'beloved brethren' the Muhammadans.*[30]

Prasad strongly blamed the British for forcing a foreign language on the Hindu masses. Many arguments were put forward in this regard by different organizations out to promote and 'protect' Hindi: Hindi was not only a vernacular, but apart from Sanskrit, the only medium through which people at large – read, the (Hindu) majority in India – could be instructed in their social and religious duties (so claimed the Satya Dharmavolambini Sabha, or the Society for Supporting the True Religion, founded in 1878 in Aligarh);[31] Hindi had a positive moral influence on people, while Urdu enticed people to dissolute and immoral lives (Hardoi Union Club, in Allahabad);[32] to continue to use Urdu as the court's language was to perpetuate Muslim tyranny in India (Babu Bireshwar Mittra, in a petition to the High Court of the North Western Provinces);[33] and, Nagari or Hindu was virtuous and moral but Urdu was immoral and a source of vice for the masses.[34]

The religious and nationalistic allegiance to Hindi promoted by the Hindi movement of the nineteenth century is aptly captured in the views ascribed by King to Shyam Sunder Das, based on the latter's biography.[35] Das was the most influential of the three founders of the 'Nagari Pracharini Sabha' (the Society for the Promulgation of Nagari), the preeminent organization promoting Hindi over Urdu in the nineteenth century and rightly credited as one of the most influential organizations in the Hindi movement. Founded in Banaras in1893, the Sabha used its strategic location to champion links between Hindi, Hinduism, and the nation. Banaras, long renowned for its Sanskrit heritage, was also a center for Hindi literature by the nineteenth century. It was also one of the holiest sites in Hinduism, attracting thousands of Hindus every year from all over the nation to banks of the Ganges and to its thousands of temples. These pilgrims spoke different languages – Bengali,

Tamil, Gujarati, Nepali, Punjabi, among others – and found themselves in contact with the varied Hindi dialects in the city. The Sabha capitalized substantially and strategically on these interactions and on the flow of people through Banaras to spread the gospel of Hindi and Hindu throughout the region and the nation.

For Das, King writes, "Hindustani could never embody the common religious and cultural heritage of the Hindus of India [and as the Hindus were the majority in India, Hindu values were India's values], because this style replaced Sanskrit words with Urdu words, striking a mortal blow at the very root of Hindi."[36] Put differently, advocates of Hindi sought not only to distinguish their language from Urdu but further to purify or cleanse their language of Urdu and Perso-Arabic content.[37] This process led to certain linguistic transformations. First, Hindi and Urdu were split into branches from the "common trunk"[38] of Khaṛī Bolī. Then, proponents of each language sought to further purify their branch. From Hindi, *śuddh* or highly Sanskritized Hindi emerged. From Urdu, Persianized Urdu emerged. This process culminated in "slogans such as "Hindi, Hindu, Hindustan," whose creators saw no room for non-Hindi speakers and non-Hindus in Hindustan."[39] The process had reached its goal: what King called, the "Sanskritization of Khaṛī Bolī."[40] And, as noted previously, 'Sanskritization' to a large extent was a form of Hinduization.[41] It is against this backdrop of attempts at differentiation and purification in Hindi-Urdu debates that a study of Hindi Christian literature can make valuable interventions.

King is right to demonstrate that the alignments Hindi = Hindu and Urdu = Muslims are rather recent and have religious, political, and nationalist antecedents. Such alignments, however, were not isolated to those between Hindi and Urdu and between Hindus and Muslims. To the best of my knowledge, no studies exist that examine the attempts by twentieth-century Hindu nationalists to create English = Christian, though it is clear from the works of Hindi Christian scholars like John Anand and Benjamin Khan that their use of Hindi was, in considerable part, a response to notions that Indian Christians are 'foreign' and not 'Indian.' As discussed before, Lall writes that Christianity was accused of being "destructive of culture," where 'culture' denotes the dominant Hindu culture. In response, Anand invites his readers to promote Hindi Christian literature and become proficient in Hindi as the language of Christianity. Similarly, Khan has asked his readers to use Hindi as "our" language.

For Hindi advocates of the nineteenth and twentieth centuries, Urdu was "foreign" and synonymous with Muslim. For Hindu nationalists in India, English is foreign and synonymous with Christian. Hindu nationalism in India has been vigorous and potent in trying to align the loyalties and cultures of Indian Christians with foreign nations and cultures (whether Roman (Catholic), Syrian (Orthodox) or Western (Protestant)). Some studies – like Chad Bauman's discussed next – have explained the fusing of Pentecostal-Evangelical Christians in India with foreign interests. But his work does not address the claims of Hindu nationalists regarding Protestant Christians. Further, no studies, including Bauman's, address the linguistic alignment in Hindu nationalist discourse of Christians in India with English, which is perceived as the foreign language of the colonizers and of the West.

A study of Hindi Christian sources draws attention to the response of Indian Christians to Hindu attempts at such linguistic alignments. They offer insights into the responses by Indian Christians in Hindi to public portrayals of Christians as "foreign." While Bauman has studied the relation of violence to such portrayals, his work does not pay sufficient attention to the response offered by Indian Christians to such portrayals. A study of Christian writings in Hindi, compared to studying those in English, offers a unique perspective into the relationships of language, script, and religion that go beyond studies of theology, ritual, and culture. Rather than focusing on assimilations and differentiations in matters of theology and culture – e.g., by asking whether Indian Christianity is 'incultured' or whether its inculturation is 'Brahmanical' or 'plebian' in nature – Hindi Christian writings allow us to get at the issue of language itself in debates on the 'nativeness of Indian Christianity.' As we have discussed earlier, Hindi Christian authors have championed Hindi not simply as a convenient vernacular but as the language of their (cultural) identity and (recognizable) rootedness in India. They have championed Hindi as a language of Christianity in India.

The second topic concerns the relationship of Hindi Christian literature to Indian Christian literature at large. This is relevant in two ways. First, there is the matter of the ways in which Hindi Christianity can be compared to other forms of Indian Christianity like those found in Indian Roman Catholic, Orthodox, Evangelical, Pentecostal, and independent church communities. Second, there is the matter of the ways in which the Protestant writings in Hindi I have studied compare to and relate with other Christian literature in Hindi. As mentioned in chapter 1, I have identified "Hindi Christian" in terms primarily of mainline, Protestant church bodies in India. But many other traditions of Christianity exist and produce scholarship in the Hindi-speaking regions of India.

One could, for instance, study the relationship between Hindi Christian texts and Roman Catholic works. In this area, two topics of study are most conspicuous in the context of the subjects I have covered in this book. First, there is, quite understandably, substantial work in Catholic circles on the benefits and limits of *avătār* in Christian theology. These include not only the works of Catholic missionaries and scholars in India – like Roberto de Nobili, Michael Amaladoss, and Francis X. D'Sa[42] – but also those of a wide range of scholars of Hinduism from a Catholic perspective – like Raimundo Panikker[43] and Francis X. Clooney[44] – and of scholars writing on the relationship between *avătār* and incarnation from other Christian perspectives – like Steven Tsoukalas in *Kṛṣṇa and Christ* (2006). We could also study the ways in which Hindi Protestant Christians and Hindi Catholic Christians have made different translation choices. One such difference was highlighted earlier in translations of the 'Eucharist' or 'Last Supper' into Hindi. As explored in chapter 2, Protestants have used *prabhu-bhoj* while *param-prasād* is common in Catholic circles. Which claims are being made with these translations? What are the theological, cultural, and communicative antecedents that have shaped these choices? Are there different theologies of religions at play? Such questions offer exciting areas for further research.

The third issue relates to the reception of the Hindi Christian witness in India. In other words, has the attention to a distinct, credible, and public witness that I have identified in Hindi Christian literature borne fruit? While this book has examined the form of Christian witness prevalent in Hindi Christian literature, it has not examined the ways in which this witness has succeeded or failed in being credible, recognizable, and public in India. There are many ways in which this topic can be explored. From one perspective, we could analyze the impact this witness has had in promoting interfaith relations. From the perspective of insiders and outsiders, is Christian speech in Hindi recognizably Christian? For instance, does the word *dehadhāraṇ* evoke 'Christian' in non-Christian contexts? Further, from these etic and emic perspectives, has the use of Hindi led to better interfaith relations in identifiable communities or contexts – which is one of the stated goals in such literature?

Chad Bauman's study of anti-Christian violence against Pentecostals in India suggests Hindu-Christian relations are, at least in the case of Pentecostals in India, strained. He acknowledges that, comparatively speaking, less violence is directed at mainline Protestants. Based on my field research among Hindi Christian communities, I find this observation partly accurate. Many Hindi Christian communities face little persistent violence and when violence flares it is usually on complex grounds – localized conflicts, caste-based hostilities, or against overtly evangelical pastors who aggressively seek converts. At the same time, Hindi Christian mainline communities in central and north India, along with Catholic ones, have faced enormous pressure and targeted violence from local Hindu forces. My conversations with Hindi Christians have regularly led to observations by my interlocutors that localized restrictions on Christian activities and hostilities against Christians – both overtly violent and subtler – have been regularly instigated, carried out, and promoted by local Hindu groups and governments associated with the Bharatiya Janata Party, Rashtriya Swayamsevak Sangh, and the Vishva Hindu Parishad. An evangelical zeal is, Bauman rightly suggests, not the sole province of Pentecostals or Evangelical churches in India. Many independent mission agencies – like *Gospel for Asia* in India – are also interested in expanding their reach and many mainline churches – like the Evangelical Lutheran Church in Madhya Pradesh and the Church of North India – are also engaged in planting new churches. The extent then, to which Hindi Christians have been able to improve their public profile and interfaith relationships – whether reflected in improved relations or in the degree of hostilities directed at them – has not been examined in my study of Hindi Christianity in India.

Bauman's study of Pentecostals is also a reminder of a fourth way in which further research can strengthen our understanding of Hindi Christian literature in India. This book has limited itself to the literature of mainline Protestant churches and has not engaged the vast range of materials in Hindi produced by 'newer' Christian communities like charismatic churches and the numerous interdenominational and independent mission agencies active in the region. Bauman reports, for instance, that of the 800 American Protestant mission agencies surveyed in 2008 by the *Mission Handbook*, 185 reported operations in India (second only to Mexico by a very small margin).[45] India also has the third-largest number of domestic and foreign missionaries in the world according to *Operation World*, a document that tracks missionary deployment. Of the 82,950 missionaries in India in 2010, most are deployed domestically within India.[46] Then there are the missionaries from Korea who have started to make their place in India. Many of these churches, missionaries, and mission agencies are active in Hindi-speaking regions and are responsible for a variety of materials like tracts, books, sermons, hymns, audio CDs, Christian videos, MP3s, and Christian broadcasts.[47] In other words, a substantial amount of 'non-mainline' Christian materials in Hindi exists that has not been addressed in this book.

A fifth issue concerns the extent to which a focus on texts and literature can adequately claim to capture the views of the communities from which such materials have emerged. I have limited this book to a study of claims in literature and have kept to a minimum the results of my fieldwork in the form of observations and interviews. This is partly because as I delved more into the works of Hindi Christian authors, I realized the scope of the work at hand. Consequently, the many ways in which the gap between what Hindi Christian authors have expressed and what Hindi-speaking Christians have done has been unexamined so far. Put differently, have the authors and their readers 'walked the talk'? Have Hindi Christian communities adopted intentional public profiles? Have they engaged in internal debates on the merits or demerits of polytraditional words or the fusion of Hindi with Christianity? Have they done so in communities of worship and practice, or have such debates been limited to academic books and scholarly fora?

Hindi Christian scholarship is deeply rooted in communities of Indian Christians. The need to use *dehadhāraṇ*, for instance, is evident in the context of the desire within Christian communities to say something unique about the incarnation of God. Or, as Anand writes, the need to transition from non-honorific to honorific references in the Hindi Bible was born of the desire among Christians to accord their Lord, Jesus, the same dignity and respect that their Hindu neighbors accorded their gods and lords. Yet it is also the case – and this is especially so in the case of Hindi ethical guidebooks – that the impact of Hindi Christian texts on its readers is yet unexplored. Such a study of the impact of texts is further complicated by the social context in which such texts have emerged and continue to function. While I have tried to use both academic texts – like the textbooks of Khan and Dayal – and popular works of 'lived religion' – like the poetry of Arya and widely-used hymnbooks – a focus on texts, by its very nature, limits this study to the views of literate Hindi Christians. However, in light of the fact that a large proportion of Hindi Christians come from marginalized backgrounds, examinations of the effects of texts on such communities will need to be grounded in an understanding of the literacy levels in such communities. The matter of access to such texts necessitates another layer of analysis. Textbooks, after all, are not commonly available and are more likely to be found in church offices, scholarly collections, and seminary libraries. I have tried to mitigate the detrimental effects of low literacy rates and limited access by including in my analysis accessible works and materials like self-published poems, popular hymns, and sermons and short stories that are sung and heard rather than necessarily read and studied.

Raindrops and elephant trunks

Only English can express Christian ideas. Christianity is English, and English is the ideal language to convey Christianity. Ancient Hebrew and Greek have their place in Christian history. They were used by God in their time and place. In the modern world, however, God speaks in English. English, not Sanskrit, is the true language of God in the world of men. It is, after all, the ideal language of the One True God. English is more than an ideal choice to express Christianity. Only the use of English to spread Christianity will banish the specter of idolatry and heathens. Non-English languages cannot convey Christian ideas, at least not in the best way. Vernaculars may shine a dim light on Christianity, but Christian ideas and motifs are most radiant when expressed in English. Translating Christian scriptures in vernaculars is, for the most part, a fool's errand. The best way to deal with vernaculars is, rather, to transliterate them in English and give them structure. The production of structure, anchored in dictionaries that tried to create linguistic standards, was central to the English-ization of Christianity in India.

The evidence is compelling. Missionaries in eighteenth-century India did not mince their words. On one side were the Serampore Trio, trying to translate and use vernaculars to spread the good news. On the other side were the Anglophiles, adamant that only English would do to civilize and save India. And lest one forgets: to civilize India was to save India, and to save India was to Christianize it, and to Christianize India was to Anglicize it. Duff is quite clear about the stakes. Which should be the "*language of learning* in India?" Should it be Sanskrit or should it be English? In balance hangs the fate of all India, not just its worldly fate but its spiritual fate too. "The determination of this choice," Duff explains, is a "decision of one of the momentous practical questions *connected with the ultimate evangelization of India*."[48]

State-sponsored and missionary-supported English language instruction for Indians was a way to promote Christianity.[49] Other missionaries were no less implicit about the relation between politics, language, and religion in British India. While the East India Company may have been hesitant about mixing religion with politics because it could be bad for business, agents of the British raj had considerably fewer qualms about the enterprise. Duff was not alone in his perspective. William Ward, a counterparty to Duff on many issues, agreed with him on the politics of language and religion. Robert Yelle sheds light on the "causal connection" between monotheism and colonization in Ward's words: "I fear more for the continuance of the British power in India, from the encouragement which Englishmen have given to the idolatry of the Hindoos, than from any other quarter whatever."[50]

Partiality to Hindu ideas was a risk not only to British power in India but also to the evangelical enterprise. Ward takes to task "professed Christians" who amaze at the "antiquity of the Hindoo writings" beyond the Christian scriptures, treat the content of Hindu writings with "great reverence," and claim that "the primitive religion of the Hindoos" has "revealed the most sublime doctrines, and inculcated a pure morality."[51] The risk to Christian claims is the most threatening aspect of respect of an idolatrous religion. Ward was more sympathetic to vernaculars and cultural inculturation than Duff was to either approach among missionaries. Nevertheless, Ward's sympathy, like Duff's, did not extend to non-European Christianity in India or India's other historic religions. On one hand, European missionaries in India had very little to say, negative or otherwise, about the Christianity that existed in India before they arrived. On the other hand, they had a lot to say, and quite confidently so, about non-Christian religions that existed in India before they arrived. Given the place of Hinduism in the religious landscape of upper India, Indian missionaries did not mince words. Caustic portrayals of non-Christian religions proliferated in the eighteenth and nineteenth centuries. And such portrayals were not limited to the European imagination. American representations of India were no less sparing.[52] But returning to India's colonial discourse, here is the English Baptist Ward on Hinduism:

> The *sum* of the Hindoo doctrine, then, is this: spirit dwelling in bodies, and partaking of the passions incident to residence in matter, is purified by austerities and numerous transmigrations, and at length re-obtains absorption into the divine nature. Religious practice leads to better destiny, and divine destiny draws the person to abstraction and religious austerities. Such is the Hindoo religion.[53]

Further, Hindus are lost to idolatry, and as such just lost:

> It cannot be doubted, that in every case in which either a person, or a nation, begins to think favorably of idolatry, it is a mark of departure in heart and practice from the living God: it was always so considered

> among the Jews. There is scarcely any thing in Hindooism, when truly known, in which a learned man can delight, or of which a benevolent man can approve; and I am fully persuaded, that there will soon be but one opinion on the subject, and that this opinion will be, that the Hindoo system is less ancient than the Egyptian, and that it is the most PURRILE, IMPURE, AND BLOODY OF ANY SYSTEM OF IDOLATRY THAT WAS EVER ESTABLISHED ON EARTH.[54]

Ward's reference to Jews and Egyptians is not accidental. In the early nineteenth century, comparisons between Hindus and Jews in order to denigrate them before Christianity were strategic rhetorical tools. The antiquity of Hindus was imprinted on the development of Judaism in efforts to define them both as hopelessly stuck in rituals and laws when compared to the liberating spirit of Christianity. Duff explains:

> Unlike Christianity, which is all *spirit* and *life*, Hinduism is all *letter* and *death*. The Indian codes of divine law deal comparatively little in general principles; they at once extend to all the *accessories* and *circumstantials* of conduct, with *a tenfold greater minuteness than Judaism ever knew* – descend into the most insignificant 'trivials and quadrivials' of life, – anticipate every varying event and circumstance, – and prescribe with rigid precision the correspondent varying form of ritual duty, whether personal or domestic, social or economical.[55]

It is well acknowledged (and not surprising) that European colonizers and missionaries colluded to promote Christianity, especially after the rule of the East India Company had given way to the rule of the British Crown in India. It is, however, a less well-known fact that the promotion of Christianity took a very particular form in colonial India: the propagation of Christianity *in English through the Roman alphabet*. The religious work of colonialism in India had a specific, linguistic goal: the establishment of English as the universal language of India with Christianity in its wake.

English in the Roman alphabet served a triple purpose. It could transmit the culture and output of Europe to India. It could, as noted before, also transmit Christianity to India better than India's vernaculars. Finally, it could help unite the administration of the British empire, from north to south and east to west. "No one can dispute," Monier Williams argued in 1859, "the desirableness of one common medium of expression for the Babel of languages current in our Indian empire." English was this ideal medium: "and no one, I presume," he continued, "will call in question the comparative simplicity of the Roman alphabet, and the superior facility it affords for cheap and easy printing."[56] India had an alphabet problem. There were at least five, each with loyal users and a congeries of history, pride, and culture. There were two distinct alphabets in the north (Devanagari or Nagarai and Arabic) and three in the south (Telegu, Tamil, and Malayalam). Indians across the empire, and especially Hindus across the empire, were using these alphabets and rightly so. However, Williams asks, how can we best transmit our culture and religion? The Hindu has a right to his own religion, science, and arts, Williams writes, but does anyone rightly object that this is reason enough "why we should not give him the advantage of our superiority in all these respects by any means in our power?" If we do not share our superior wisdom, William asks, is not our mission in India "anything but a mockery?"[57]

What did this superiority look like? What were its implications? Let me illustrate via two stories, one regarding religion, one regarding science, both regarding the self-satisfaction of missionary knowledge. The first story comes from 1817. The head-teacher of Sanskrit at the College of Fort William was discussing the nature of God with William Ward and others at the College. The teacher was well-versed "in his own shastrās" and started sharing a parable about God. There existed a village of blind men, who had heard of an amazing animal called an elephant but had never seen it. One day an elephant stopped outside the village. Villagers gathered around the animal and started touching it to "see." One of them grabbed its trunk, another its ear, another its tail, and another one of its legs.

After the elephant left, the men gathered and started talking about the shape of the animal. The one who had grabbed the elephant's trunk said the elephant must look like a plantain tree. The one who grabbed the ear said the animal must be like a winnowing fan. The man by the tail thought an elephant must resemble a rope. Finally, the man who had caught the elephant's leg declared that the animal must look like a pillar. Another man of "some wisdom" was hearing these descriptions. There was no agreement on what the elephant looked like. After some time, the wise man said, 'you all are right, because you all have touched the elephant. Putting your views together, it then seems like the part of the elephant that resembled a plantain tree must be its trunk, what you thought was a fan must be its ear, what you thought was a rope must be its tail, and what you thought was a pillar must be its leg. When you out these conjectures and reasoning together, we can make out something of the shape of an elephant.' Having narrated the parable, the Sanskrit teacher then explained. Regarding knowledge of God, we are all blind and have experienced different aspects of God. However, putting the collective knowledge of humankind regarding God together, we can start to say something about the nature of God. In response to the parable, Ward writes, "It is an irresistible argument in favour of the majesty, simplicity, and truth of the Holy Scriptures, that nothing of this uncertainty has been left on the mind of the most illiterate Christian."[58] In Christian countries, he continues, we never hear the question – What is God? Here is the superiority of Christianity to Hinduism, of the Christian Bible to the Hindu scriptures (*Śāstras*), the certainty of Christianity against the openness of Hinduism. And underlying this claim the implied claim that certainty is superior to caution concerning claims about the nature of the divine Being.

The second parable is from 1859 and involves another elephant and its trunk.[59] This time the topic was "rain," and unbeknownst to the missionaries, in discussing the origins of rain an idea would emerge that would thoroughly demolish Hinduism, that "most ancient system of error now on the face of the earth."[60] The setting was Calcutta. While having a conversation with a group of Hindus, the topic of rain came up and the missionaries asked, 'where does rain come from?' The Hindus were eager to reply: But of course, from the trunk of Airāvata, Indra's elephant. Airāvata lives in the clouds and from there the rain comes down. How do we know this, the Hindus continue? Because our *Śāstras* say so. And while we have not read the scriptures, our Guru, who knows the scriptures, has said so. And what the *Śāstras* say must be true. Duff's response is diplomatic. "True to our original . . . design," he writes, "we did not choose *directly* to contradict the Shastra, by casting ridicule on the alleged theory, as palpably absurd; or branding it as absolutely false."[61] Rather, Duff and his friends decide to counter the theory by presenting their version of events.

Duff explains: according to our Guru in Scotland, rain is the result of condensation, and nothing else. It is the same process in play when you boil rice. Observe, that water gathers under a dry lid when rice is boiled. Boiling water evaporates and rises as vapor into the air. The rising vapors is trapped by the lid and gathers under it. When the lid cools down, that vapor condenses and falls down as waterdrops. This is what happens at a much larger scale when rain falls down. When the ground is wet and the sun is strong, you can see vapors rising from the ground. These rising vapors are trapped in clouds. When the clouds condense, the water in vaporized form returns to earth as rain. "Such . . . is the simple theory of the origin of rain," Duff writes with evident self-satisfaction, "which we once learn from our Guru in Scotland."[62] As Duff reports, the vapor theory landed with force and its impact was immediate. It led to a scramble and a reorientation of truth. Here is Duff's recollection of the Hindus' response:

> Ah! What have I been thinking? *If your account be the true one, what becomes of our Shastra? – what becomes of our Shastra? If your account be true, then must our Shastra be false. Our Shastra must either not be from God, or God must have written lies. But that is impossible; the Shastra is true, Brahma is true; – so your Guru's account must be false: – and yet it looks so like the truth!*[63]

Duff's interest in teaching science was tangential at best. Rather, the encounter mattered to Duff for other important reasons. The story captured the deployment of secular knowledge in the service of evangelization. Duff has stumbled upon a new tool to tear down error. Preaching the gospel and refuting Shastras by using the Bible was one way to supplant Hinduism with Christianity. But here was another way. Scientific explanations that challenged religious explanations and in doing so undermined the source of those religious explanations. After all, the truth of science cannot be denied ("and yet it looks so like the truth!"), even in the face of belief ("the Shastra is true"). Science, for Duff, had unexpectedly become a gateway to the gospel. It is, therefore, with surprise and glee that Duff compares his takedown of Hinduism via the simple theory of rain to Newton's discovery of gravity via the fall of a little apple![64] Duff had no problems taking his own scriptures at face value: that "God" has revealed "Himself" to be "one almighty, omniscient, omnipresent Mediator and Advocate" who, "as an almighty Saviour," has "offered himself, in the stead of sinners, as a complete oblation and satisfaction to divine justice."[65] To Duff and his compatriots, though, the comparison was illogical. One set of scriptures was true, the other was false. Hence, how could they even be compared? 'Christian philanthropists,' Duff's derisive nickname for missionaries who wanted to educate Christians before (or worse, instead of) converting them, were guilty of softening the opposition of Christian truth to non-Christian error. The "conversion of lost souls to God" was the "grand end towards which all our labors must ever be directed." All education plans by missionaries should be subservient to that goal. Only with the grand end in mind could Christians summon the vigor to "root out the monstrous errors of Hinduism" and substitute for them true science and true doctrine.[66]

Having established the need to share superior European wisdom with Indians, the question remained: which is the best medium to transmit such wisdom? English cannot supplant India's languages, William explains, but to "advance the cause of Christianity and civilisation" everything must be done to promote "English type throughout the length and breadth of the land."[67] He elaborates:

> Let us gradually, and in a Christian spirit of conciliation, induce our fellow-subjects to adopt our views of religion and science, to study our languages and literature, to benefit by our mechanical knowledge and our various appliances for economising time, labour, and money. . . . As surely as railroads, electric telegraphs, steam-printing, penny postage, and every other European improvement, must in due time find their way into the remotest corners of our Eastern empire, so surely must the simple Roman alphabet, with Christian instructions in its train, take the place of the complicated symbols which now obstruct the path of knowledge and enlightenment.[68]

Studies on missionary translations in vernaculars tend to highlight the promotion of vernaculars by such endeavors.[69] They address the role of dictionaries in the development of languages. They examine the standardization of vernaculars. Most of these studies, however, ignore the fusion of language and religion in the political promotion of scripts and languages. The works of Rasiah Sugirtharajah and Robert Yelle are exceptions to this trend.[70] Nevertheless, the impact of missionary attitudes toward translation on contemporary perceptions of the relationship between languages and religion cannot be ignored. If English has been considered the language of Christians in India, and as such is a mark of their foreignness, Hindu antagonists are not the only ones to make this claim. The perception that Christianity is foreign to modern India due to the religion's association with English is a legacy of the religio-linguistic, Christo-English policies of European settlers in colonial India.

The joint promotion of Christianity-English in the eighteenth and nineteenth centuries found a counterpart in the joint promotion of Hinduism-Hindi in the late-nineteenth and early- twentieth centuries in the wake of Hindu-Muslim relations in northern India. The Nagari Pracharini Sabha was founded in Banaras in 1893. Its purpose was to promote Hindi. By design and actions, however, the Sabha did not promote Hindi *per se* but only one form of Hindi: Nagari Hindi. In the 1900s, 'Hindi' still meant a combination of Hindi-Urdu vocabulary and script. In accordance with British policy, Urdu dominated as the language of official business in the North-Western Provinces and Oudh during the Raj. The North-Western Provinces and Oudh were merged in 1877 and renamed the United Provinces. Most of the North-Western Provinces were amalgamated as Uttar Pradesh after independence.[71] The Sabha achieved a milestone when in 1900 the provincial government of the North-Western Provinces and Oudh declared the Nagari script on par with the Urdu script in matters of official business.[72] Forty-seven years later, the Sabha would achieve its dream of making Nagari Hindi the sole official language of the region. The Sabha would achieve more success through the Hindi Sahitya Sammelan (Society for Hindi Literature), which the Sabha helped found in 1910 to promote Hindi and Nagari at the national level.[73]

The Sabha did not intend to promote Hindi-Urdu. On the contrary, by design the Sabha sought to promote Hindi in opposition to Urdu. It is not an accident that the Sabha was named a society to promote Nagari, a script, rather than Hindi, a language.[74] This design was not merely linguistic in origin. It was fostered also by communal rivalries concerning state power. The official government was dominated by Urdu, and supporters of Urdu, who were mostly Muslims and the Kayasths, enjoyed access to state power and state patronage. Non-Kayasth Hindus started agitating for state power in the 1860s. By 1873, supporters of Hindi and Nagari had petitioned the provincial government to elevate Nagari Hindi on par with Urdu. The petition asked for the "restoration of Hindi or Nagari characters" in all courts and offices where Persian Urdu was used.[75] The Sabha succeeded in its efforts when the newly-formed state of Uttar Pradesh declared Hindi in Devanagari as its official language in 1947.

The promotion of Nagari meant the promotion of Hindi as a language of official use and the simultaneous promotion of Nagari-scripted Hindi as the language of the Hindus. Supporters of Nagari Hindi insisted on the nexus of language and religion in India. The British were particularly upbraided for ignoring this nexus and trying to circumvent it. To support Nagari Hindi further meant opposing Urdu. A duality of forces – support of Hindu Hindi, denigration of Muslim Urdu – characterized the Hindi language movement in the late-nineteenth and early-twentieth centuries. The Muslim was always the "other" of Hindu nationalists in India;[76] here, the Muslim was the "other" of Hindi nationalists as well. Here is Babu Shiva Prasad, a prominent supporter of Hindi, in his 1868 memorandum to the provincial government:

> The Persian of our day is half Arabic; and I cannot see the wisdom of the policy which thrusts a Semitic element [Urdu] into the bosoms of Hindus and alienates them from their Aryan speech [Hindi]; not only speech, but all that is Aryan; because through speech ideas are formed, and through ideas the manners and customs. To read Persian is to become Persianized, all our ideas become corrupt and our nationality is lost. Cursed be the day which saw the Muhammadans cross the Indus; all the evils which we find amongst us are indebted to our 'beloved brethren' the Muhammadans. . . . I again say I do not see the wisdom of the policy which is now trying to turn all the Hindus into semi-Muhammadans and destroy our Hindu nationality.[77]

Consistently, and over many decades leading up to and including India's drive for independence, the Sabha and complementary groups did not promote Hindi in Nagari in order to foster Nagari Hindi across India for use by Hindu, Muslims, Christians, and Indians alike regardless of religious affiliation. The promotion of Nagari Hindi was a religious affair yoked with and presented as a line of defense of the Hindu majority. The promotion of Nagari Hindi was presented as a necessary task for the protection of the Hindu majority against the effects of Urdu and Islam. Nagari Hindi was Hindu Hindi and as such necessary to promote in a majority Hindu nation. On the other hand, Urdu was Muslim and as such a threat to both Hindus and Hindi. Literature and art reflected the opposition of Hindi and Urdu on religious terms. For instance, plays by Hindi-lovers contrasted the "virtue and morality of Nagari or Hindi with the vice and immorality of Urdu."[78] The membership of groups promoting Hindi reflected the opposition of Hindi and Urdu on religious terms. For the first four years of its existence, the Nagari Pracharini Sabha did not include a single Muslim member. In 1897, a single Muslim had joined. By 1899, there were two more Muslims. Brahmans, Rajputs, and Vaishyas accounted for most of the Sabha's membership. Brahmans alone accounted for more than 40 percent of members.[79]

The fusion of language and religion has been a recurring feature of Indian polity. The nexus of language and religion has been an important part of India's history. While the British did not care much for languages in the administration of their affairs, vernaculars played an important role in their plans to share power with Indians in running India.[80] The debate over India's national languages played out against the backdrop of Hindu-Muslim relations. The movement to promote Nagari Hindi was a political movement to make Hindi the national language of the Hindus.[81] Indian nationalists produced slogans like 'Hindi, Hindu, Hindustan' ("Hindi, Hindu, India").[82] Leaders of the independence movement like Gandhi and Nehru sought to promote Hindustani as the national language as a way to politically unite different religious communities Hindu and Muslims. The constitution of independent India affirmed Hindi as the national language but quickly faced resistance from regional languages. As King notes, many of the movements for the linguistic reorganization of independent India drew upon caste and communal loyalties.[83] These loyalties stretch far back in time on the subcontinent. Contemporary attempts to claim or assign languages to one's own or another religion reflect the long tradition of religio-linguistic politics in India.

Underlining the treatment of Christians in India is the perception that one cannot be both a loyal Christian and an Indian. A Hindu is original to India and India is Hindu. A Christian is a foreign and not an Indian. Allegiance to one group (India) cannot overlap with allegiance to another (Christianity). Aligning with both is bad. It can only divide loyalty. Nineteenth-century Hindu advocates for the national primacy of Hindi made similar claims regarding the foreignness of Urdu and Muslims in India. It is in light of the public attitudes toward Christians in India – as aggressive evangelists, followers of a foreign faith, and culturally not Indian – that the attempts of Hindi Christian scholars to portray their faith as linguistically Hindi, culturally Indian, and theo-ethically Christian is best understood. Metaphors like 'Trishanku' challenge Indian Christians. Hindi Christian bards, poets, preachers and authors are inviting their listeners and readers to claim Hindi. The proposals by Hindi Christians authors that have been studied in this book insist on a form of religion that is Hindi, Indian, and Christian in form and content. In doing so, Hindi Christian works reconfigure the politics of language and religion in India.

Notes

1 Manorama, "Dalit Women: The Thrice Alienated." Manorama has studied the exceptional impact of discrimination on the women of backward communities and has described such women as the "Dalits among the Dalits."

2 Melanchthon, "A Dalit Reading of Genesis 10–11:9." Melanchthon is currently an associate professor of Old Testament at the University of Divinity in Australia. She formerly taught at Gurukul Lutheran Theological College and Research Institute, Chennai, and was a member of the Senate of Serampore College, Serampore. She has written extensively on the intersection of Dalit studies, gender, and biblical interpretation.

3 Shiri, *The Plight of Christian Dalits*. Shiri's work has drawn attention to the reality of caste-discrimination *within* churches in India by shedding light on caste relations within Indian churches.

4 Larbeer, "The Story of the Dalits of India." Larbeer's work has reminded us of the continuing mistreatment of backward Christians as people who are still socially ostracized, subjected to violence, deprived of their rights, exploited for cheap labor, and denied justice and denied the equal protection of the State.
5 Harper, *In the Shadow of the Mahatma*, 355–357.
6 On 'vedantic' Christianity, see Ganeri, "Catholic Encounter with Hindus," 415–418.
7 Tharamangalam, "Whose Swadeshi?" 232–246.
8 Ganeri, "Catholic Encounter with Hindus," 426–427.
9 In the works of Dayal, James, Khan, and Howell discussed earlier.
10 In the works of Jonathan and Khan discussed earlier.
11 In the works of James and Howell discussed earlier.
12 In the work of Howell discussed earlier.
13 In the works of Anand, Dayal, Howell, James, Khan, Lall, and Paul discussed earlier.
14 Jain, "From *Kil-Arni* to *Anthony*," 17.
15 McGregor, *The Oxford Hindi-English Dictionary*, 66.
16 Anand, in a "Personal Request to Readers" (dated 2009) in Khan, *Khristīy Nītiśāstr*, iv: "*Ham āpse nijī nivedan karnā cāhte haiṁ ki jab ye pustakeṁ prakāśit huī thī, un dinoṁ ādhyātmik śikṣā mālā ke sampādak tathā masīhī lekhakoṁ kā dhyān bhāṣā aur saṃskṛti jaise mahatvapūrṇ praśn kī or nahīṁ gayā thā, aur unhoṁne masīhī dharm ke saṃsthāpak prabhu yeśu, evam masīhī dharmguruoṁ, nabiyoṁ, preritoṁ ādi ke lie bhāratīy saṃskṛti ke anukūl, ādarsūcak sarvanām kā prayog nahīṁ kiyā thā, jiske kāraṇ carc meṁ āj bhī 'yeśu bulātā hai', 'yeśu kahtā hai' jaise aśiṣṭ sambodhan prayukt kie jāte haiṁ.*"
17 Yagi, "Christ and Buddha"; Pieris, "The Buddha and the Christ."
18 Khan, *Khristīy Nītiśāstr*, 216–217.
19 James, *Mahilā Dharmavijñān*, 108.
20 Khan, *Bīsvīṁ Śatābdī ke Pramukh Dharmavijñānī*, xi: "*Pratham prayās meṁ sadaiv kuch kamiyāṁ, aur trutiyāṁ rah jātī haiṁ. Pāṭhak evam ālocak in kamiyoṁ aur truṭiyoṁ ko najarandāj karte huye us sāmagrī se lābh uṭhāyenge jo is pustak kā tānā bānā hai. Ālocakoṁ aur pāṭhakoṁ kā yah bhī kartavy hotā hai ki pustak kī kamiyoṁ aur truṭiyoṁ ko lekhak tak pahuṁcāyeṁ tāki vah dvitīy saṃskaraṇ meṁ in ko dūr kar sake.*" McGregor suggests "warp and woof" to translate '*tānā bānā*.' McGregor, *The Oxford Hindi-English Dictionary*, 448. "Warp and woof" captures the intent of the phrase, which is to point the reader to the 'heart of the matter.'
21 King, *One Language, Two Scripts*, 15.
22 King, *One Language, Two Scripts*, 16.
23 King, *One Language, Two Scripts*, 17.
24 King, *One Language, Two Scripts*, 8.
25 King, *One Language, Two Scripts*, 129.
26 King, *One Language, Two Scripts*, 9.
27 King, *One Language, Two Scripts*, 129.
28 King, *One Language, Two Scripts*, 153.
29 King, *One Language, Two Scripts*, 29.
30 King, *One Language, Two Scripts*, 131; original emphasis.
31 King, *One Language, Two Scripts*, 134.
32 King, *One Language, Two Scripts*, 134.
33 King, *One Language, Two Scripts*, 134.
34 King, *One Language, Two Scripts*, 137.
35 King, *One Language, Two Scripts*, 139–142.
36 King, *One Language, Two Scripts*, 148.
37 King, *One Language, Two Scripts*, 175.
38 King, *One Language, Two Scripts*, 177.

39 King, *One Language, Two Scripts*, 177.
40 King, *One Language, Two Scripts*, 177.
41 Van der Veer, *Religious Nationalism*, 166.
42 D'Sa, "Christian Incarnation and Hindu Avatara."
43 Panikker, *The Unknown Christ of Hinduism.*
44 Clooney, *Hindu God, Christian God.*
45 Bauman, *Pentecostals*, 140.
46 Bauman, *Pentecostals*, 135.
47 Bauman, *Pentecostals*, 37.
48 Duff, *India, and India Missions*, 517. Emphasis added.
49 Yelle, *The Language of Disenchantment*, 85.
50 Ward, *A View of the History*, ciii; cited in Yelle, *The Language of Disenchantment*, 101.
51 Ward, *A View of the History*, xcvii–xcix.
52 Altman, *Heathen, Hindoo, Hindu.*
53 Ward, *A View of the History*, lxxx. Emphasis added.
54 Ward, *A View of the History*, ciii.
55 Duff, *India, and India Missions*, 129; see also Yelle, *The Language of Disenchantment*, 148–149.
56 Williams, *Original Papers*, 254–255.
57 Williams, *Original Papers*, 257.
58 Ward, *A View of the History*, lxxxvii–lxxxviii.
59 Duff, *India, and India Missions*, 556–559.
60 Duff, *India, and India Missions*, 556.
61 Duff, *India, and India Missions*, 558.
62 Duff, *India, and India Missions*, 559.
63 Duff, *India, and India Missions*, 560.
64 Duff, *India, and India Missions*, 557.
65 Duff, *India, and India Missions*, 274–276.
66 Duff, *India, and India Missions*, 596.
67 Williams, *Original Papers*, 269.
68 Williams, *Original Papers*, 264–265.
69 Lalhmangaiha, *Holistic Mission*, 88–94, 132–135.
70 Sugirtharajah, *The Bible and the Third World*; Yelle, *The Language of Disenchantment.*
71 King, *One Language, Two Scripts*, 199.
72 King, *One Language, Two Scripts*, 123.
73 King, *One Language, Two Scripts*, 127.
74 Mankekar, "Epic Contests."
75 King, *One Language, Two Scripts*, 131.
76 Van der Veer, *Religious Nationalism*, 10.
77 Prasad, quoted from King, *One Language, Two Scripts*, 131.
78 King, *One Language, Two Scripts*, 137.
79 King, *One Language, Two Scripts*, 144–145.
80 King, *Nehru and the Language Politics of India*, 55–57, 60.
81 Dalmia, *The Nationalization of Hindu Traditions*, 146–221.
82 Pandey, *The Construction of Communalism*, 216.
83 King, *Nehru and the Language Politics of India*, 70–73.

References

Altman, Michael J. *Heathen, Hindoo, Hindu: American Representations of India, 1721–1893*. New York: Oxford University Press, 2017.

Bauman, Chad M. *Pentecostals, Proselytization, and Anti-Christian Violence in Contemporary India*. New York: Oxford University Press, 2015.

Clooney, Francis X. *Hindu God, Christian God: How Reason Helps Break Down the Boundaries Between Religions*. New York: Oxford University Press, 2001.
Dalmia, Vasudha. *The Nationalization of Hindu Traditions: Bhāratendu Hariśchandra and Nineteenth-Century Banaras*. Ranikhet: Permanent Black, 2010 [1997].
D'Sa, Francis X. "Christian Incarnation and Hindu Avatara." *Concilium* 2 (1993): 77–85.
Duff, Alexander. *India and India Missions: Including Sketches of the Gigantic System of Hinduism, both in Theory and Practice; also, Notices of Some of the Principal Agencies Employed in Conducting the Process of Indian Evangelization*. Edinburgh: John Johnstone, 1839.
Ganeri, Martin. "Catholic Encounter with Hindus in the Twentieth Century: In Search of an Indian Christianity." *New Blackfriars* 88, no. 1016 (2007): 410–432.
Harper, Susan Billington. *In the Shadow of the Mahatma: Bishop V. S. Azariah and the Travails of Christianity in British India*. Grand Rapids: William B. Eerdmans, 2000.
Jain, Pankaj. "From *Kil-Arni* to *Anthony*: The Portrayal of Christians in Indian Films." *Visual Anthropology* 23, no. 1(2009): 13–19.
James, Elizabeth E., et al. *Mahilā Dharmavijñān Pāthya-Pustak* [Women's Theological Text Book]. Jabalpur: Hindi Theological Literature Committee, 2010 [1978].
Khan, Benjamin. *Khristīy Nītiśāstr* [Christian Ethics]. Jabalpur: Hindi Theological Literature Committee, 2009 [1981].
Khan, Benjamin. *Bīsvīṁ Śatābdī ke Pramukh Dharmavijñānī* [Major Christian Theologians of the Twentieth Century]. Jabalpur: Hindi Theological Literature Committee, 1990.
King, Christopher R. *One Language, Two Scripts: The Hindi Movement in Nineteenth Century North India*. Delhi: Oxford University Press, 1994.
King, Robert D. *Nehru and the Language Politics of India*. Delhi: Oxford University Press, 1998.
Lalhmangaiha, Andrew. *Holistic Mission and the Serampore Trio*. Delhi: Indian Society for Promoting Christian Knowledge, 2010.
Larbeer, Mohan. "The Story of the Dalits of India." In *God, Christ & God's People in Asia*, edited by Dhyanchand Carr. Hong Kong: Christian Conference of Asia, 1995.
Mankekar, Purnima. "Epic Contests: Television and Religious Identity in India." In *Media Worlds: Anthropology on New Terrain*, edited by Faye D. Ginsburg, Lila Abu-Lughod, and Brian Larkin. Berkeley: University of California Press, 2002.
Manorama, Ruth. "Dalit Women: The Thrice Alienated." In *Asian Expressions of Christian Commitment: A Reader in Asian Theology*, edited by T. Dayanandan Francis and F.J. Balasundaram. Madras: The Christian Literature Society, 1992.
McGregor, Ronald S., ed. *The Oxford Hindi-English Dictionary*. New Delhi: Oxford University Press, 1993.
Melanchthon, Monica Jyotsna. "A Dalit Reading of Genesis 10–11:9." In *Scripture, Community, and Mission: Essays in Honor of D. Preman Niles*, edited by Philip L. Wickeri. Hong Kong: Christian Conference of Asia, 2003.
Pandey, Gyanendra. *The Construction of Communalism in Colonial North India*, third edition. New Delhi: Oxford University Press, 2006 [1990].
Panikkar, Raimundo. *The Unknown Christ of Hinduism: Towards an Ecumenical Christophany*. Maryknoll: Orbis Books, 1981 [1964].
Pieris, Aloysius. "The Buddha and the Christ: Mediators of Liberation." In *Asian Faces of Jesus*, edited by R.S. Sugirtharajah. Maryknoll: Orbis Books, 1993.
Shiri, Godwin. *The Plight of Christian Dalits – A South Indian Case Study*. Bangalore: Asian Trading Corporation, 1997.

Sugirtharajah, Rasiah S. *The Bible and the Third World: Precolonial, Colonial and Postcolonial Encounters*. Cambridge: Cambridge University Press, 2001.

Van der Veer, Peter. *Religious Nationalism: Hindus and Muslims in India*. Berkeley: University of California Press, 1994.

Ward, William. *A View of the History, Literature, and Religion of the Hindoos: Including a Minute Description of their Manners and Customs, and Translation from their Principal Works*. Volume 1, third edition. London: Black, Parbury, and Allen, 1817.

Williams, Monier, ed. *Original Papers Illustrating the History of the Application of the Roman Alphabet to the Languages of India*. London: Longman, Brown, Green, Longmans, and Roberts, 1859.

Yagi, Seiichi. "Christ and Buddha." In *Asian Faces of Jesus*, edited by R.S. Sugirtharajah. Maryknoll: Orbis Books, 1993.

Yelle, Robert A. *The Language of Disenchantment: Protestant Literalism and Colonial Discourse in British India*. New York: Oxford University Press, 2013.

Index

Note: Page numbers in **bold** indicate a table on the corresponding page.

Cost of Discipleship, The (Bonhoeffer) 107–108
cross-faith learning 153
cultural adaptations 19
cultural values 127–128

Dās, Bhayaharn 14
Das, Shyam Sunder 203–204
David, C.W. 16–17, 34–35, 161–162, 193
Dayal, Din 54–55, 120–121, 147, 167–172, 199–200
Deccan North Indian Muslims 9–10
dehadhāraṇ(en-fleshing) 92–97, 192, 194–196, 199, 206–207
Delhi language 10
democracy, Indian 174
Devanagari script 4, 10, 11, 48–49
Devanandan, Paul 154
dharma 149–152
dharm jāgāraṇ (spiritual awakening) 123
discipleship 106–119, 161
divine self-revelation 178
D'Mello, Edward 62–64, 66, 71
doctrinal works 54–59
Doordarshan broadcasting 123–125, 127–128, 135
Dravidian group of languages 8–9
Duff, Alexander 85, 154, 208–216

economically backward 191
educationally backward 191
education books 151
elephant trunk parable 208–216
English as a foreign language 4
English language 208–216
ethics and theology 65, 149–159
Evangelical Fellowship of India 172
Evangelical Lutheran Church 61
evangelical zeal 206–207
evangelism/evangelization: interfaith relationships 122–123, 178; relationship-building through 199; shaping identity 105, 113; women in 117–119

faithful living advice 65
fanaticism 165–166
form criticism 59
Frei, Hans W. 59–60

Gandhi, Indira 124, 132
Gandhi, Rajiv 49–50, 123, 129–132
'gender-shared' Christianity 119
Gilchrist, John B. 7, 48–49, 81
Gill, S.S. 125–129
God: creation *vs.* in Christianity 23; devotee of 20; Jesus's relationship with 66–67; multiple paths to 19; song narratives of 60–61; speech-acts of God in Christ 66; story of God 172–177, **174**
good works 120–123
Gospel accounts of Jesus 60–68
Grierson, George Abraham 24
guidebooks in Hindi 112–113, 116, 123
guru traditions 95

Hindi: Christian uses of 82–88; defined 11–13; guidebooks in 112–113, 116, 123; as national language 216; politics of 47–53; religious meaning of 33–34
Hindi Bible 118, 137, 190, 199
Hindi Christian education 147
Hindi Christian message: code sharing 193–200; early works 200–208; English language 208–216; introduction to 190–193
Hindi Christian politics: demographics of 33; description of 6–16; doctrinal works 54–59; general body of works 51–53; holiness *vs.* presence in 68–71; introduction to 1–6; language and religion 16–20; milieu of 20–36; narrative works 59–68; readership growth 109–111; types of works 53–68
Hindi imperialism 79
Hindi nationalism 3–4
Hindi Theological Literature Committee 13–14, 17–18, 34, 51–52, 109, 137, 190, 193
Hindi-Urdu 201–202, 214
Hindu-Muslim relations 49
Hindu nationalism (Hindutva) 3–5, 12, 125, 128–130, 204–205
Hindustani 7, 11, 49–50, 81
HIV/AIDS crisis 58
Holy Scriptures 211
honorific language 87–88
Howell, Richard 147–148, 172–177, **174**
human-divine relations 171

identity shaping: discipleship 106–119; good works/social ethics 120–123; introduction to 105–108; mass religion 123–138

incarnation, defined 89–90
Indian Christians: appropriate representations of 197; caste-based discrimination 57–58; defined 16; Hindi Christians and 32–33; introduction to 5–6
Indian Christian Theology (Boyd) 193–194
Indian democracy 174
Indian National Congress 49, 129, 168
Indian theology 35–36
indigenization 86
Indo-Aryan and Hindi (Chatterji) 8
Indo-Aryan language 7–8
Indus Valley Civilization 47
interfaith relations 105, 113–114, 148–167
Islam 161–162

James, Elizabeth 117
Jesus Christ: acceptance of 68–71; as *avătār* 88–97; behavior of 122; birth story in Hindi 81; Christian ethics and 159–160; debate over how to address 87–88; Gospel accounts of 60–68; Kingdom of God and 170, 175–176; Krishna *vs.* 90–91; as mediator 107–108; Mohammed *vs.* 1–2; political discernment and 164–165; relationship with God 66–67
Jews 209–210
John the Baptist 63
Jonathan, Franklin 2–3
Jones, Arun 24–25

Kaise Pāyā Muktidātā, arthāt Bhayaharṇadās kā Itihās (Dās) 14
Kalelkar Commission 191
Kalīsiyā (Mahendra) 56–57
Kant, Krishan 2–3
karma-yoga (proper actions) 21
Khan, Benjamin 35, 62–64, 67, 148–167, 199–201
Kharī Bolī 10–11, 48, 204
Khrist Bhaktas (San Chirico) 18
Khristīy Nītiśāstr (Khan) 149–158, 162, 199–200
Kingdom of God 170, 175–176
Krishna-*bhakti* 24

Leonard Theological College 17–18, 190
linguistic/language politics: *avătār*, defined 88–97; Christian uses of Hindi 82–88; code sharing 190; introduction to 5, 79–82; religion and 16–20, 215–216
lived ethics 157

Madhya Pradesh Christian Council 17
Mahendra, Shivraj Kumar 55–58
Mahilā Dharmavijñān Pāthya-Pustak (James) 117
Major Christian Theologians of the Twentieth Century (Khan) 193–194
Malinar, Angelika 19
mandir (temple, body) 96–97, 194
Mankekar, Purnima 196
Māno Yā Na Māno (Khan) 62–63
Masih, Komal 59, 60
*Masīhī Ācaraṇ*112, 122
Masīhī Dalit: Ik Itihāsik Parīkshā (Massey) 16
Masīhī Dharm Vijñān kā Paricay (Dayal) 54–55, 147, 167, 171, 199–200
Masīh Merī Manzil (Mahendra) 55–56
Massey, James 16
mass religion 123–138
Mataji, Vandana 16
media representations of Indian Christians 6
Methodist Church in India 17
Middle Indo-Aryan language 7
Mirabai (*bhakti* saint) 22–23
Mishra Commission on Religious and Linguistic Minorities 191
missionaries (Christian): goals of 57, 80; Hindu use by 85–86; operations in India 207; promotion of vernaculars 213–214; reaction to interfaith needs 114–115
modern, standard Hindi 7, 49
Mohammed *vs.* Jesus 1–2
Mosse, David 19
Muslim League 129
Muslims 48, 203

Nagarai Hindi 10, 214–215
Nagari Pracharini Sabha 214, 215
Nagpur Congress 49
Narayanan, Vasudha 18
narrative works 59–68
National Council of Churches 154
natural law 156
Nehru, Jawaharlal 49–51, 79, 131
Neill, Stephen 112, 122
Nestorian Christianity 24

New Indo-Aryan language 8
Nirguna bhakti 30
non-honorific language 87–88, 207

Official Languages Act (1965) 50

pāp (sin, evil) 29
Paramahamsa, Ramakrishna 88–89
param-prasād (The Eucharist) 70–71, 197, 206
Parī Bolī 10
Parivartan: Masīh se Milāp (Howell) 147–148, 172
Pāstarī Viddhyā (Patlia) 121
Paul, Winifred 112, 119, 146
Pentecostals 207
Persianized Hindi (Urdu) 10
Persian language 48, 215
Perso-Arabic Urdu 11
Peter, Christopher 59, 60
pluralism 170–171, 174, 177–179
polytraditional words 96, 192, 198
polyvalent Christology 62
Prākrit (spoken Aryan India dialect) 9–10, 47–48
Prasad, S.W. 62, 203
prasād (blessed food) 20
pre-Zoroastrian Iranians 8
Protestant Christianity 71, 147, 205, 207
public witness 196–197
pūjā (worship) 20

Quranic language 137
Quran *vs.* Bible 1–2

raindrops parable 208–216
Rajagopal, Arvind 124–125, 129, 132–133
Ramayan 123–129, 132–133
Ram-*bhakti* 24
Ram Janambhoomi-Babri Masjid issue 129–130
Ram temple movement 133–134
Rashtriya Swayamsevak Sangh 206
readership growth 109–111
realization of the self *(svayaṁ ka anubhav)* 93
redaction criticism 59
religion overview 16–20
Religions in Practice (Bowen) 20
religious communication 115–116
Rig Veda 8, 47
Roman Catholics 13, 18

Śabd, Śaktī, Sangam (Mataji) 16
saṁvād (speech together) 156, 165, 177–178
San Chirico, Kerry P.C. 18
Sanskrit 8–12, 14–15, 28, 32–33, 85–87, 90, 148
Sanskritized Hindi 11, 15, 49, 125, 132–133, 136
Santal Catholics 18
Schultze, Benjamin 15
Scott, David 23
secularism 121, 125–132, 151–152, 156–157, 161–163, 192, 200, 212
'seven sayings' of Jesus 61–62
social ethics 120–123
Society for Supporting the True Religion 203
speech-acts of God in Christ 66
Spirit of God 2
śraddhā (veneration) 20
Standard Hindi 11–12
States Reorganisation Act (1956) 79
story of God 172–177, **174**
Summa Doctrinae Christianae (Schultze) 15
supernatural, defined 158–159
Syrian Catholics 13

Tabaqāt-i-Akbarī (1022) 9
Tamil Catholicism 19–20
Thiemann, Ronald F. 59–60
Tilak, Viman 16
Tiwari, Narayan 7
Trishanku story 115–116, 197, 216

Urdu language 9–10, 48, 135–136, 201–204
Usne Kahā Thā (Mahendra) 56

Varshney, Ashutosh 80, 130–134
Vedic Indians 8
vernacular language use 86
vernaculars 213–214
Vishva Hindu Parishad 206
Vivekananda, Swami 88–89
Vyaktigat Manan-Cintan (Dayal) 120–121, 167

Ward, William 209, 211
Western Apabhraṁśa 9
Wiros 8
women in evangelism 117–119
World Council of Churches 154

Printed in the United States
By Bookmasters